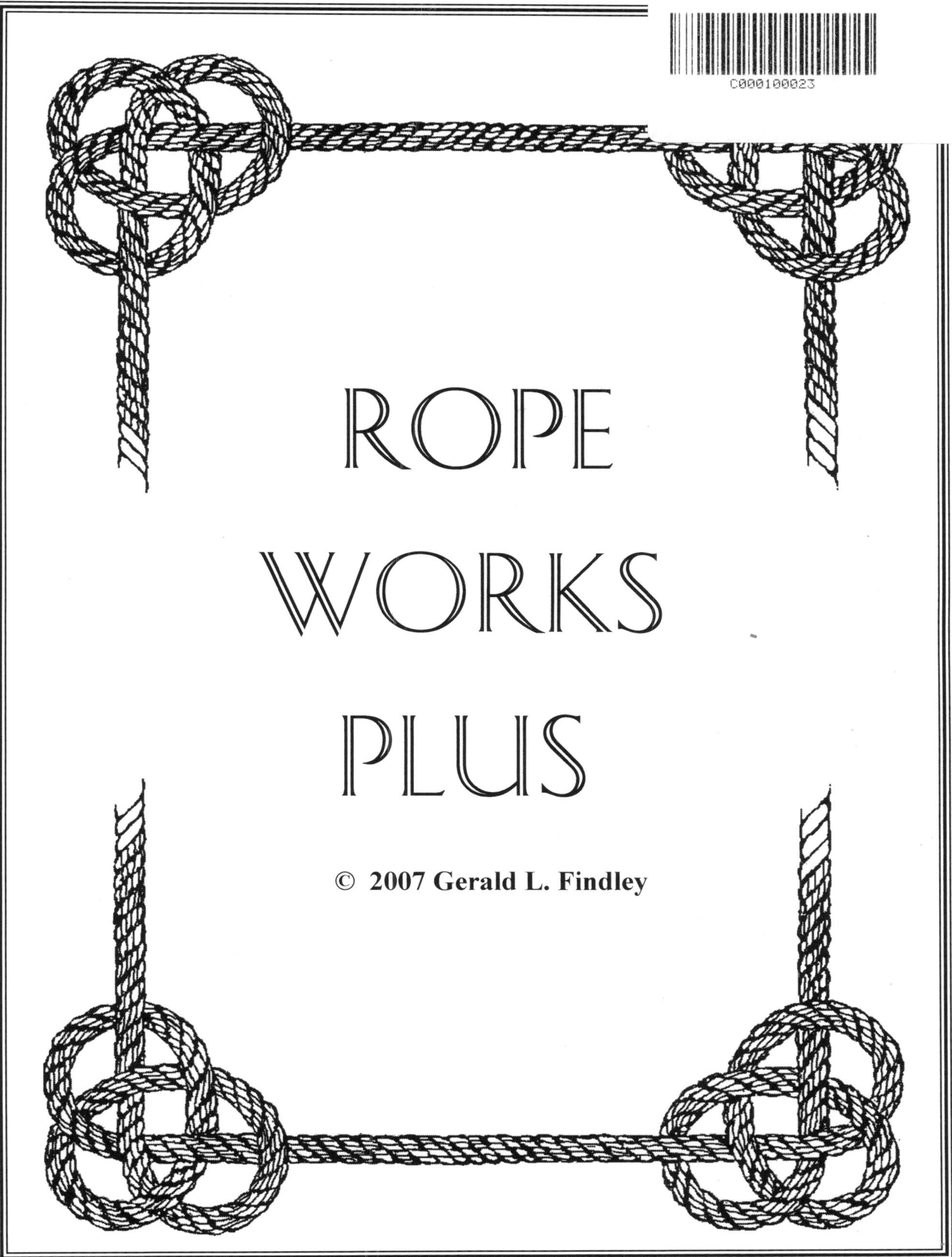

ROPE WORKS PLUS

ISBN: 1-4196-6656-8

Library of Congress
Control number: 2007903025

To order additional copies, please contact us.
www.booksurge.com
1-866-308-6235
order@booksurge.com

CONTENTS

KNOTS AND HITCHES ---------- 1
KNOT SAFETY: ---------- 2
PARTS OF A ROPE: ---------- 3
FUSING: ---------- 5
WHIPPING: ---------- 6
SERVICE: ---------- 12
GRAPEVINE SERVICE: ---------- 13
RINGBOLT HITCHING: ---------- 15
SEIZING: ---------- 17
SEIZING: WITH RACKING TURNS ---------- 19
STOPPER KNOT: ---------- 21
STEVEDORE KNOT: ---------- 23
FIGURE-EIGHT KNOT: ---------- 25
FIGURE-EIGHT ON A BIGHT: ---------- 26
WATER KNOT: ---------- 27
SQUARE KNOT: ---------- 30
SHEET BEND: ---------- 33
WEAVER'S KNOT: ---------- 34
BECKET HITCH: ---------- 36
DOUBLE SHEET BEND: ---------- 36
SHEET BEND ON A SHORT END: ---------- 37
BOWLINE: ---------- 39
BOWLINE ON A BIGHT: ---------- 42
FRENCH BOWLINE: ---------- 44
LINEMAN'S LOOP: ---------- 46
SHEEPSHANK: ---------- 48
TRUMPET KNOT: ---------- 49
SHEEPSHANK: QUICK ---------- 51
CLOVE HITCH: ---------- 53
CONSTRICTOR KNOT: ---------- 55

TRANSOM KNOT: ---------- 59
TWO HALF HITCHES: ---------- 61
PIPE HITCH: ---------- 62
LARK'S HEAD: ---------- 63
GIRTH HITCH: ---------- 65
TAUT-LINE HITCH: ---------- 66
MIDSHIPMAN'S HITCH: ---------- 68
ANCHOR HITCH: ---------- 69
TIMBER HITCH: ---------- 71
MARLIN SPIKE HITCH: ---------- 73
SLIP NOOSE: ---------- 74
SLIP KNOT: ---------- 74
MOORING HITCH: ---------- 75
TURK'S HEAD: ---------- 77
MONKEY'S PAW: ---------- 79
BOATSWAIN'S WHISTLE KNOT: ---------- 82
JUG KNOT: ---------- 85
BELAYING TO A CLEAT: ---------- 87
MASTHEAD KNOT: ---------- 89

SPLICING ---------- 93

CROWN KNOT: ---------- 95
BACK SPLICE: ---------- 97
EYE SPLICE: ---------- 99
SHORT SPLICE: ---------- 101
ADDING ROUND OF TUCKS: ---------- 103
SLIDING EYE SPLICE: ---------- 105
ENDING A SPLICE: ---------- 106
GROMMET: ---------- 108

LASHINGS ---------- 111

SQUARE LASHING: ---------- 113
JAPANESE SQUARE LASHING: ---------- 116
MODIFIED SQUARE LASHING: ---------- 119
HALF KNOT SQUARE LASHING: ---------- 121

DIAGONAL LASHING: ---------- 125
FILIPINO DIAGONAL LASHING: ---------- 127
SHEAR LASHING: ---------- 129
QUICK SHEAR LASHING: ---------- 132
TRIPOD LASHING: ---------- 134
QUICK TRIPOD LASHING: ---------- 139
ROUND LASHING: ---------- 140
WEST COUNTRY ROUND LASHING: ---------- 142
HALF HITCH ROUND LASHING: ---------- 143
FLOOR LASHING: ---------- 145
LADDER LASHING: ---------- 147

NETTING ---------- 149
NETTING: ---------- 150
NET MESH BAG: ---------- 157
HAMMOCK: ---------- 160

ROPE MAKING ---------- 163

GEARED ROPE MACHINE ---------- 169

TOOLS AND MORE ---------- 177
ROPE WRENCH: ---------- 178
FIDS: ---------- 179
MAULS: ---------- 182
CAMP SAW: ---------- 186
SPANISH WINDLASS: ---------- 193
ANCHOR POINT: ---------- 195
TARP/DINING FLY: ---------- 198
FLAG LANYARD: ---------- 200
MODELS: ---------- 203
CAMP STOOL: ---------- 207
LIFE BASKET: ---------- 210

GLOSSARY ---------- 213

INDEX ---------- 217

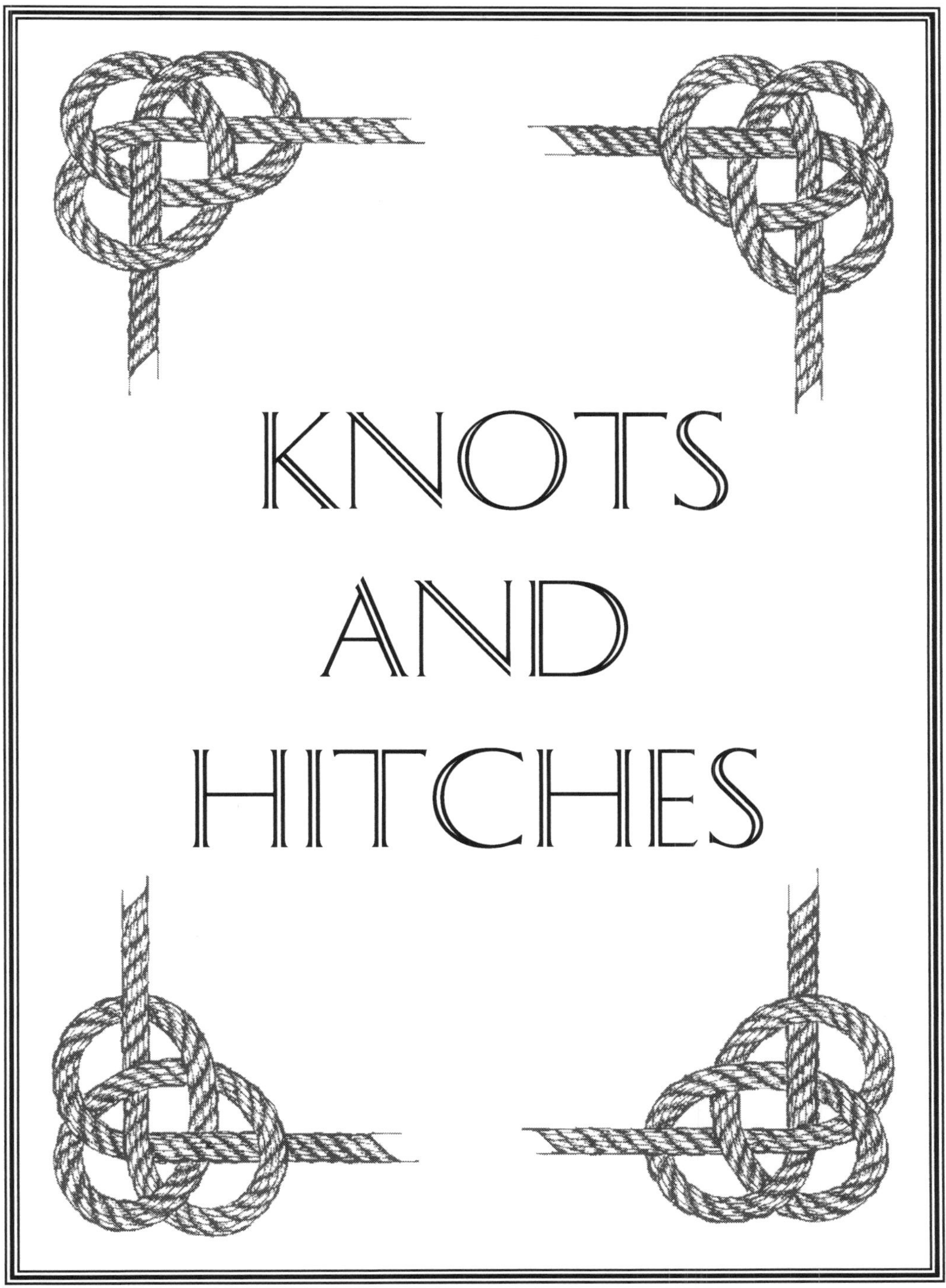
KNOTS
AND
HITCHES

INTRODUCTION: KNOTBOARD

There are two types of knotboards: display and instructional. Display knotboards that only show finished knots can be frustrating to the user. On the other hand, instructional knotboards, knotboards that show step by step how to tie knots, can be used for self instruction of the beginner and reinforcement and extension of the knowledge of the experienced.

The instructional knotboards contained in this book are accompanied by text that describes the knot, its use, and how to tie it.

The sequence in which the knots are presented is based on the structure of the knot. Thus knots, hitches, and bends that have similar structure are grouped together.

KNOT SAFETY:

If a knot is improperly tied or a wrong knot is used, an unsafe condition is created. Therefore, it is not just enough for the teacher to teach someone how to tie a knot correctly, but it is also necessary to teach them how to use the knot correctly. Likewise, it is the student's responsibility to learn how to correctly tie and use the knot. If either the teacher or the student does not accept their responsibility, they are endangering themselves and others.

The most commonly used rope is right-hand-lay rope; that is, as you are looking at the rope, it appears to twist to the right and away from you. Because of the right-hand lay of most rope, the majority of knots hold best when tied in a right-hand manner. If the knot is tied in a left-hand manner, or the mirror image of its usual form, the knot may fail because the right-hand twist of the rope may cause the knot to loosen or spill more easily. This is especially true if the tension on the rope is repeatedly changed.

PARTS OF A ROPE:

Comments ---- Knowing the name to apply to the different parts of a rope and the different structures within a knot will help you to remember the structure of the knot and the sequence of steps required to tie it.

The following knotboard is made up of three sections: PARTS OF A ROPE, LOOPS, and OVERHAND KNOT. These three sections are presented to illustrate the use of their names in describing how to tie a knot.

Narration ---- (For PARTS OF A ROPE) The standing part of the rope is the part of the rope that does not move while a knot is being tied. The running part of the rope is the part of the rope that is moved while tying a knot. A bight is a fold in the rope.

[NOTE] The standing part is usually held in the left hand and the right hand is used to move the running part while the knot is being tied.

Narration ---- (For LOOPS) There are two main types of loops; the overhand loop and the underhand loop. An overhand loop is formed by passing the running part over the standing part. An underhand loop is formed by passing the running part under the standing part. The space enclosed by the loop is called an eye.

PARTS OF A ROPE

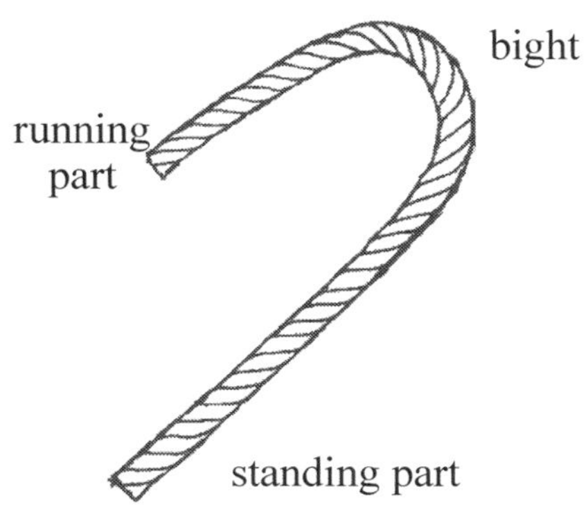

LOOPS

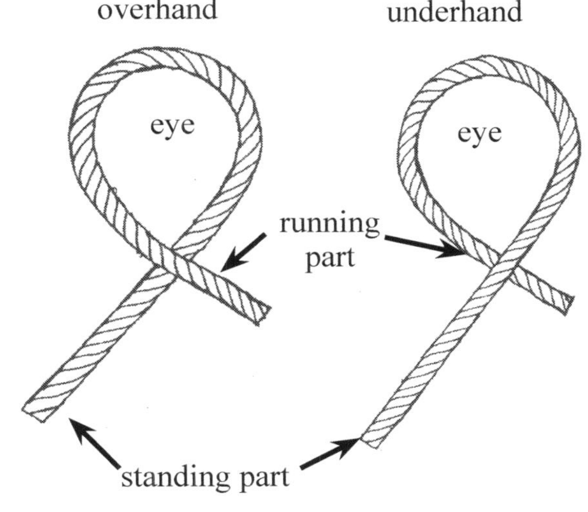

OVERHAND KNOT

1.

overhand loop

eye

standing part

running part

2.

3.

eye

turn

4.

5.

Narration ---- (For OVERHAND KNOT) **(1)** Hold the standing part of the rope in your left hand. Form an overhand loop by grasping the running part with you right hand and passing the running part over the standing part. **(2)** While holding the overhand loop in your left hand, take a bight with the running part around the standing part toward the eye of the overhand loop. **(3)** Bring the running part through the eye of the overhand loop so that you have taken a turn around the standing part. **(4 and 5)** Tighten the knot by pulling the standing part and the running part in opposite directions.

[NOTE] As an illustration of the importance of tying knots in a right hand manner, tie an Overhand Knot as described in the directions. Then tie an Overhand Knot starting with an underhand loop. The first thing you should notice is that the Overhand Knot tied by beginning with an overhand loop is easier to tighten than the Overhand Knot that began with the underhand loop. The reason the Overhand Knot that began with the overhand loop tightens easier is that the turn around the standing part is with the lay of the rope (in the same direction as) and the Overhand Knot that begins with the underhand loop is against the lay of the rope (in the opposite direction of).

FUSING:

The ends of a synthetic rope can be fused to prevent the rope from fraying. This is done by heating the end of the rope so that the ends of the rope fibers melt together.

The fusing can be done by holding the end of the rope to the side of a candle or other small flame. If the end of the rope is placed in the flame or held too close to the flame, the plastic will ignite causing the end of the rope to turn black. Burning plastic can also give off toxic fumes. If the end of the rope is held above the flame, unburned carbon particles will be deposited on the melted plastic causing it to turn black. A candle flame will generate enough heat to fuse the end of a rope up to about one inch in diameter. If the rope is larger than one inch, a propane torch will work better.

[WARNING] Do not use a butane cigarette lighter to fuse rope. A butane lighter can explode if it is permitted to burn too long.

[NOTE] If the rope is cut to length with a soldering iron or other hot cutting tool, the ends of the rope will be fused as the rope is being cut to length.

[NOTE] A small lamp such as an alcohol lamp or a small oil lamp works very well for fusing rope.

WHIPPING:

Description ---- Twine wrapped and secured to the end of a rope.

Use ---- To prevent the fraying of the end of a rope.

Comments ---- Even though Whipping is done in several different ways, the finished Whippings have a similar appearance: the ends are secured under the turns, the length of the Whipping should be equal to the diameter of the rope, and all turns are parallel.

Synthetic rope, rope made of plastic, should be whipped and fused to prevent the rope from fraying. Fusing helps to hold the Whipping in place and the Whipping helps to prevent the fused rope strands from breaking apart.

Other Names ---- Serving: When a rope is wrapped with twine to prevent chafing or wearing; the wrapping is done using the similar methods to Whipping. ---- Seizing: When twine is wrapped around two or more strands of rope to hold the rope in place; the wrapping is done using methods similar to Shear Lashing.

Materials ---- The twine that is used for Whipping should be tightly spun or braided twine that is less then 1/8 the size of the rope to be whipped. Twine made of synthetic material should be used to whip synthetic rope. If natural fiber twine is used, the capillary action along the fibers of the rope draw water under the Whipping causing the Whipping to remain damp so that rot quickly sets in. Likewise, natural fiber twine should be used to whip natural fiber rope. The poor wicking action of synthetic fibers allows the Whipping to trap moisture in the natural fiber rope causing the rope to rot.

WHIPPING: METHOD 1

Narration ---- (For knotboard) **(1)** Form a loop in a 12 inch piece of twine so that the ends of the twine are parallel and in opposite directions. Lay the loop on the end of the rope so that the ends of the twine and the rope are all parallel and one end of the twine is extending beyond the end of the rope. **(2)** While holding the twine in place between the thumb and forefinger, pass the loop of twine around the end of the rope so that the wrap is with the lay of the rope. **(3)** To finish the wrapping, pull the twine under the thumb so that the twine is wrapped toward the standing part of the rope; pull the twine tight. **(4)** Hold the last wrapping in place between the thumb and forefinger; add additional wraps by passing the loop of twine around the end of the rope and pulling the wrap tight under the thumb for each wrap. **(5)** Continue to add wraps until the length of the whipping is equal to the diameter of the rope. **(6)** While still holding the last wrap tightly between the thumb and forefinger, pull the loop closed by pulling on the end of the twine that is sticking out past the end of the rope. **(7)** Tighten the Whipping by pulling on both ends of the twine. **(8)** Finish the Whipping by cutting off the ends of the twine.

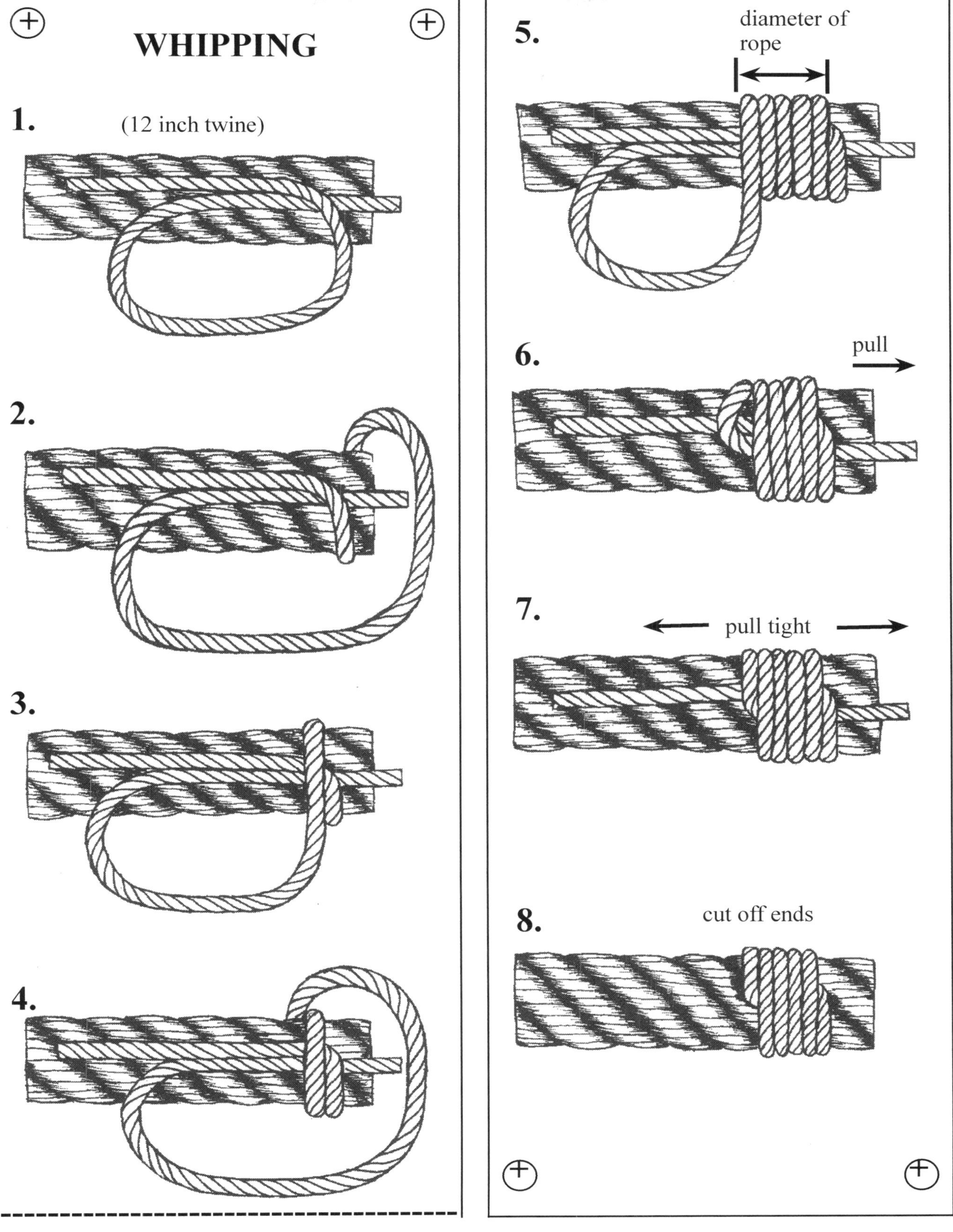
WHIPPING
1.
(12 inch twine)
2.
3.
4.
5.
diameter of
rope
6.
pull
7.
pull tight
8.
cut off ends

WHIPPING: METHOD 2

Narration ---- (For knotboard) **(1)** Form a bight in the end of a 24 inch piece of twine and lay it parallel to the end of the rope so that part of the short side of the bight is extending beyond the end of the rope. **(2)** Take a wrap around the end of the rope; hold the bight and the wrapping in place with the thumb and forefinger; pull wrapping tight. **(3)** When the length of the Whipping is equal to the diameter of the rope, reeve the end of the twine through the eye of the bight. **(4)** Pull wrappings tight. **(5)** Pull on the end of the twine that is extending beyond the end of the rope until a bight of the free end of the twine is pulled under and to the midpoint of the wrappings. **(6)** Finish the Whipping by cutting off the ends of the twine.

[NOTES]

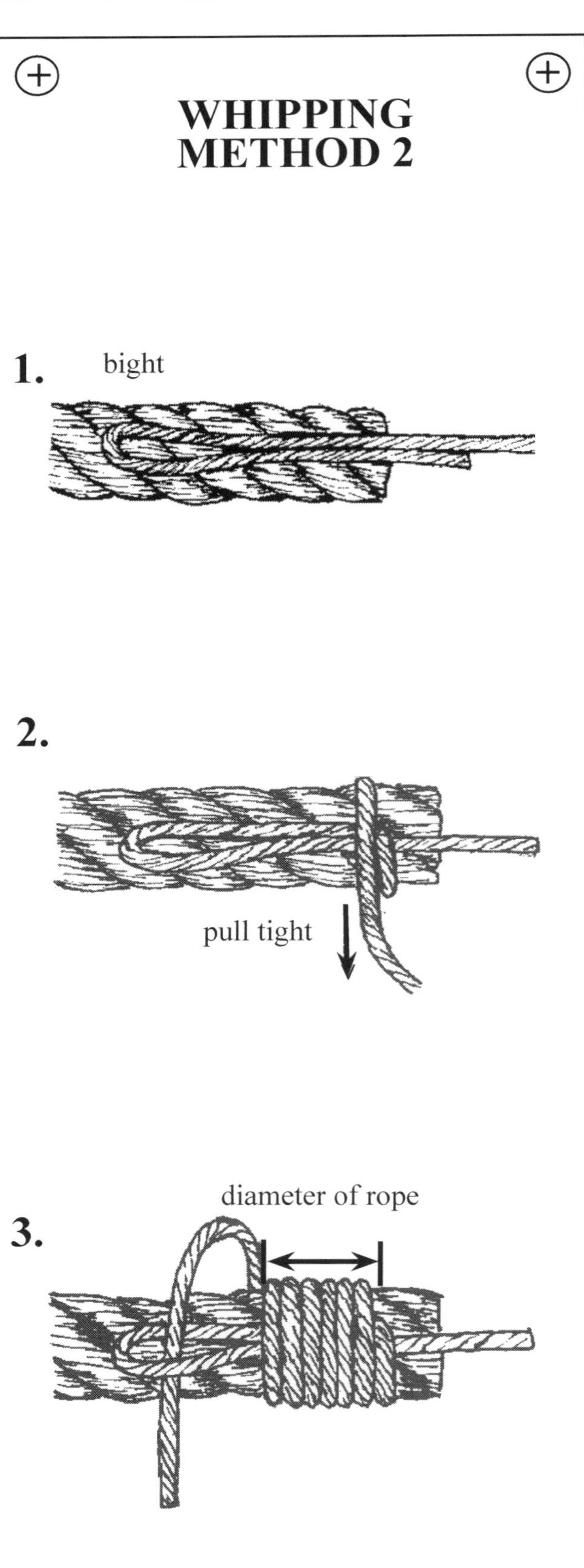

4.

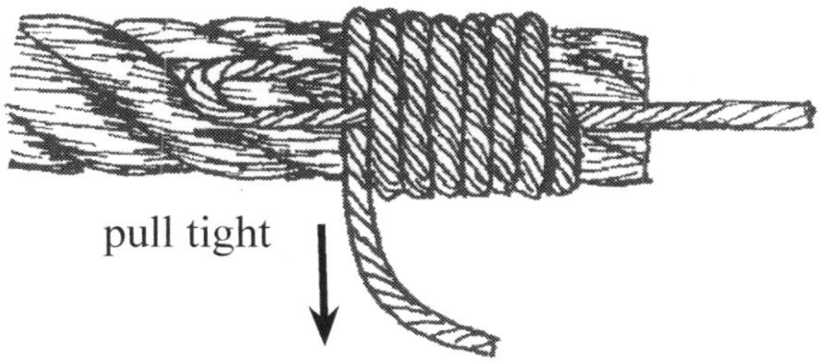

pull tight

5.

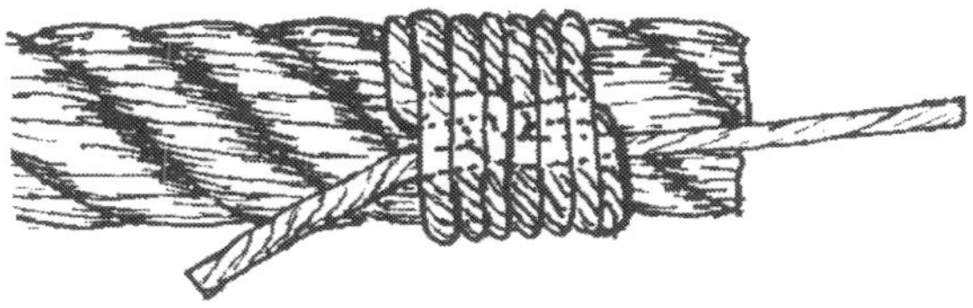

pull to center

6.

cut off ends

WHIPPING METHOD 3

1.

short bight

2.

12 inch twine

3.

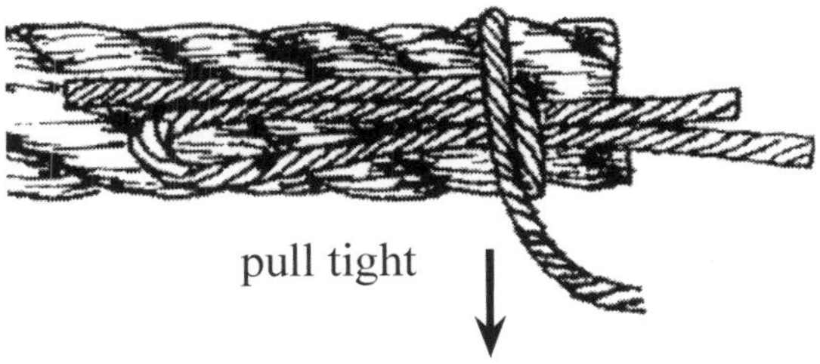

pull tight

4.

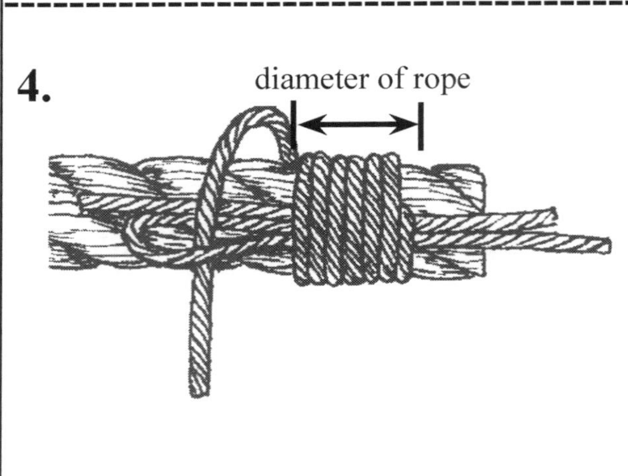

5.

6.

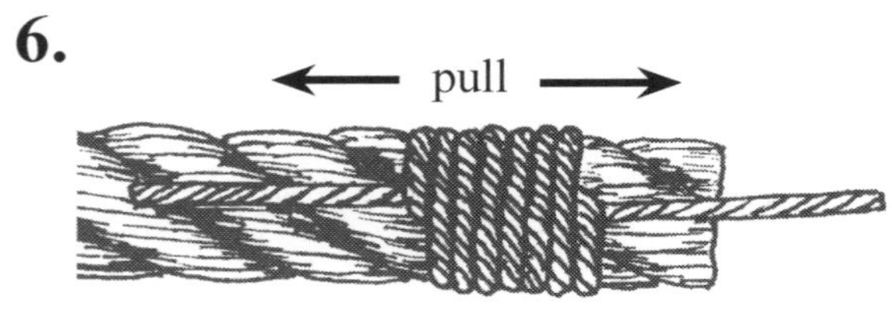

7.

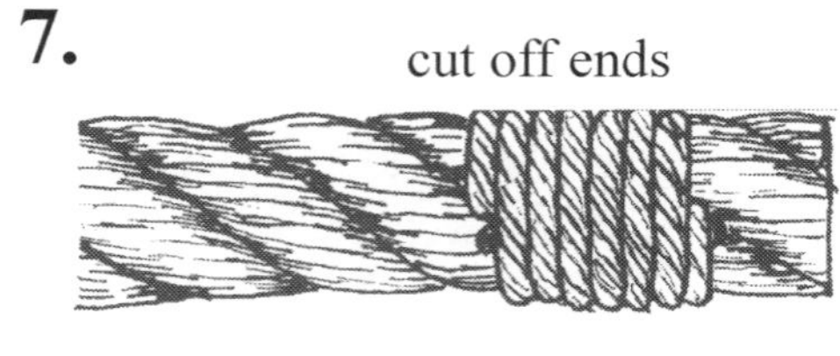

WHIPPING: METHOD 3

Narration ---- (For knotboard) **(1)** Form a bight in a 6 inch piece of twine; lay the bight parallel to the end of the rope with the ends of the twine extending past the end of the rope. **(2)** Lay the end of a 12 inch piece of twine next to the loop with the long end extending past the end of the rope. **(3)** Take a wrap around the end of the rope; hold the bight and the wrapping in place with the thumb and forefinger; pull wrapping tight. **(4)** When the length of the Whipping is equal to the diameter of the rope, reeve the end of the twine through the eye of the bight. **(5)** Use the bight to pull the free end of the twine under the wrappings. **(6)** Tighten the Whipping by pulling on the ends of the twine. **(7)** Finish the Whipping by cutting off the end of the twine.

BOUND WHIPPING:

Description ---- A Whipping with strands across the wraps.

Use ---- As a secure permanent Whipping.

Comments ---- Bound Whipping secures the wrapping turns by adding frapping turns to a standard Whipping.

Other Names ---- Sailmaker's Whipping (usually done with a needle).

Tying a Bound Whipping:

STEP 1: Lay a loop formed from a 24 inch piece of twine in one of the grooves between the strands of the rope. The end of the twine toward the standing part of the rope should be about 3 inches long.

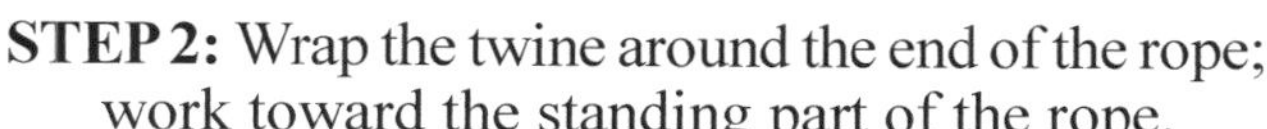

STEP 2: Wrap the twine around the end of the rope; work toward the standing part of the rope.

STEP 3: When the length of the Whipping is equal to the diameter of the rope, close the loop by pulling on the end of the twine that extends beyond the end of the rope.

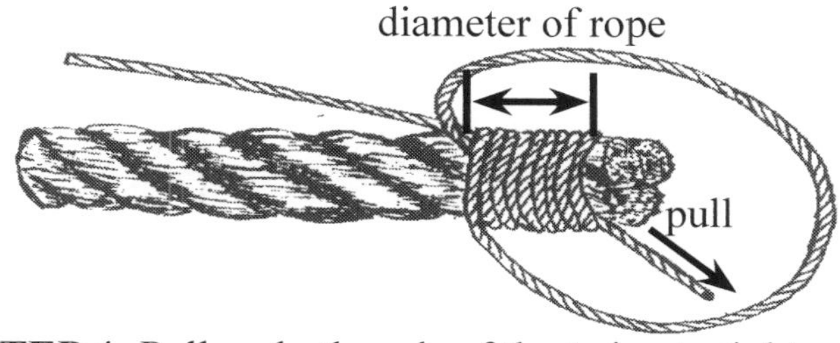

STEP 4: Pull on both ends of the twine to tighten the Whipping around the rope.

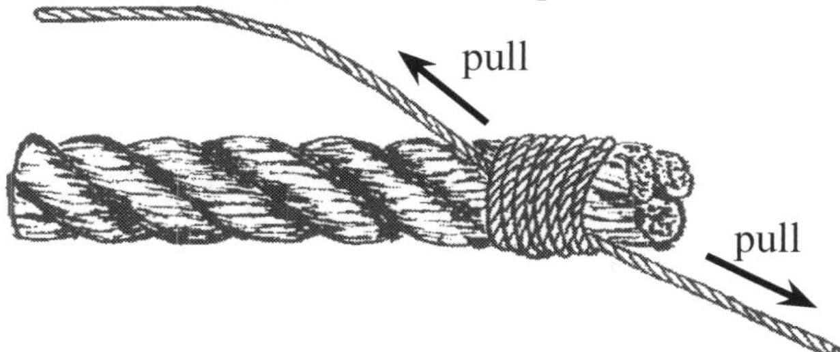

STEP 5: Separate the ends of the rope strands; pull the twine between the strand to the right of the groove that the twine was originally laid in and the other two strands.

STEP 6: Use a fid to lift the strand of the rope as shown in the diagram (this is the same strand that the twine went around at the end of the rope) reeve the twine under the strand; pull twine tight.

STEP 7: Lay the twine over the original groove and then pull the twine between the ends of the rope strands so that the twine is around the rope strand to the left of the original groove; pull twine tight.

STEP 8: Use a fid to lift the rope strand as shown in the diagram (this is the same strand that the twine went around at the end of the rope) reeve the ends of the twine through the opening and tie a Half Knot as shown in the diagram; pull twine tight.

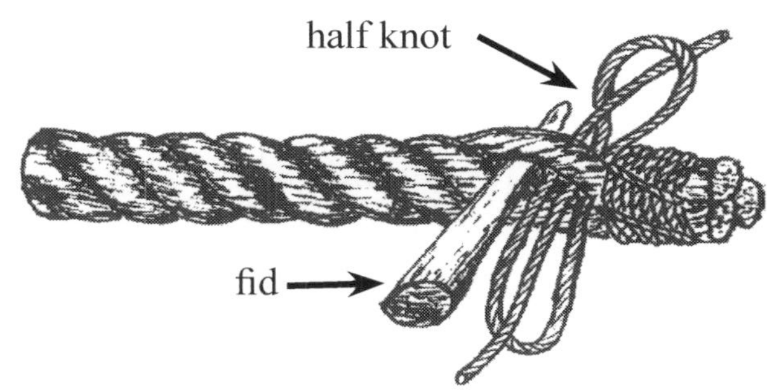

STEP 9: Reeve the ends of the twine through the opening again; tie a second Half Knot in the opposite direction as shown in the diagram; pull twine tight to form a Square Knot.

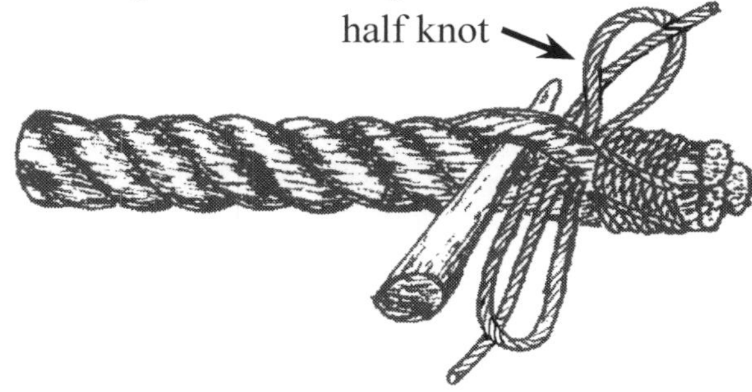

STEP 10: Remove the fid and trim the ends of the twine close to the surface of the rope.

[NOTE] If synthetic rope and twine were used, the ends of the rope and the twine may be fused.

SERVICE:

Description ---- Looks like extended Whipping.

Use ---- To protect a rope from chafing.

Comments ---- In the past, a rope was parceled and served to protect the rope from the weather and chafing. This was done by covering the rope with tarred canvas (parceling) and then wrapping the rope with twine to hold the parceling in place (serving). Because of synthetic ropes, the need to protect rope from moisture no longer exists, but the need to protect rope from the damage caused by chafing is more important than ever. Friction not only wears away the surface of a synthetic rope, but also generates heat which can damage the rope fiber beneath the surface. In the past, entire lengths of rope were served, especially standing rigging of ships. With synthetic rope it is only necessary to service those parts of a rope that are subjected to repeated rubbing such as the eye of an eye splice.

Because of nylon's wear resistant properties, nylon twine is perhaps one of the best synthetic materials to use when serving a rope. Nylon mason's twine or braided nylon fishing line works very well.

Narration ---- (For knotboard) **(1)** Lay one end of the twine on and parallel to the rope. **(2)** Secure the end of the twine by wrapping the twine over top of it. **(3)** Continue to wrap the twine around the rope; be sure to pull each wrap tight until only 5 or 6 more wraps are needed to finish the Service. **(4)** Form a bight in a short piece of twine; lay the bight on the rope so that the ends of the twine are over the part of the rope that has already been served and the eye of the bight is toward the unfinished part of the rope. **(5)** Continue wrapping the twine around the rope. **(6)** When the service is long enough, reeve the end of the twine through the eye of the bight. **(7)** Use the bight to pull the end of the twine under the wrapping. **(8)** Work the wrappings tight by pulling on the end of the twine. **(9)** Cut off the end of the twine.

[NOTE] If synthetic twine is used, fusing the ends of the twine will help hold it in place.

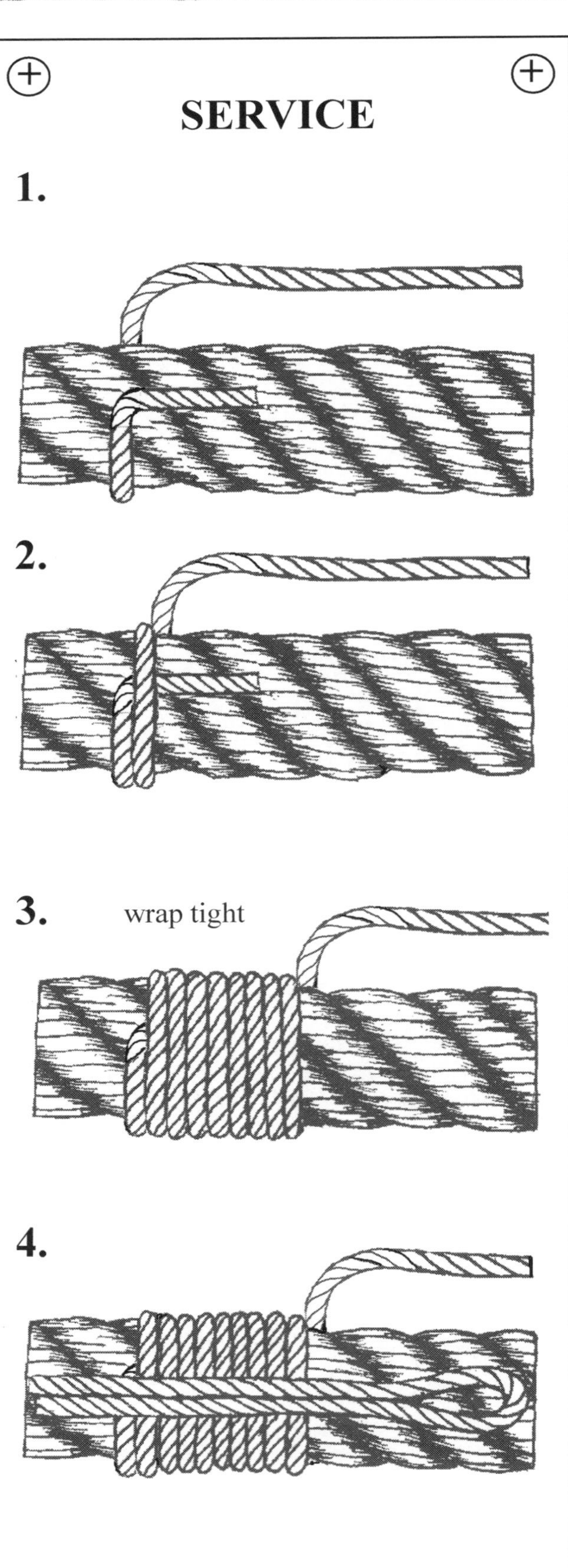

5.

6.

7.

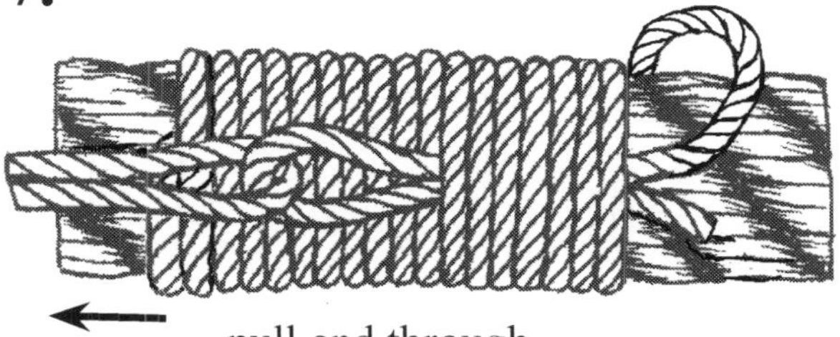

pull end through

8.

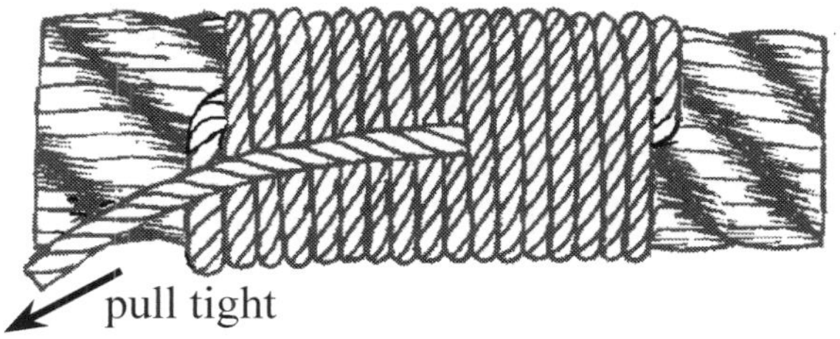

pull tight

9.

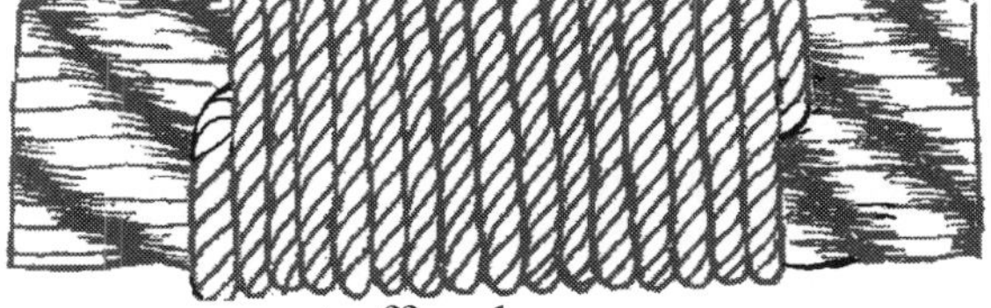

cut off end

GRAPEVINE SERVICE:

Description ---- A series of Running Half Hitches that forms a spiraling ridge around the rope.

Use ---- To protect rope from chafing, to add texture to the surface of a rope or other hand hold so that it easier to grasp, or as a decoration.

Comments ---- Grapevine Service is made up of a series of Half Hitches. Because of this it is easy to keep the twine tight as the rope is being served. As each Half Hitch is made it is pulled tight with a marlin spike or fid to lock it against the one before it.

When used on a hand rail or hand hold, the Grapevine Serving not only adds a decorative effect but also adds texture to the rail. This makes it easier to grip and to protect the rail and its finish from being worn down. In cold weather, Grapevine Servicing around a metal rail protects a bare hand or wet glove from freezing fast to the rail.

Other Names ---- Running Half Hitches; French Whipping.

Narration ---- (For knotboard) **(1)** Start by tying one end of the twine to the rope with a Half Knot so that the standing part is pointing in the direction of the work. **(2)** Add a Half Hitch in the running part. **(3)** Work the Half Hitch tight. **(4)** Add another Half Hitch. **(5)** Work the Half Hitch tight. **(6)** Continue adding Half Hitches until the work will need only 6 to 10 more Half Hitches to complete the work; pull each Half Hitch tight as it is tied. **(7)** Form a bight in a short piece of twine and lay it under the running part so that the eye of the bight is pointed toward the unfinished end. **(8)** Secure the bight in place with a Half Hitch. **(9)** Work the Half Hitch tight. **(10)** Complete the work; reeve the running part through the eye of the bight. **(11)** Pull the running part under the Half Hitches. **(12)** Work the Half Hitches tight. **(13)** Cut off the end.

GRAPEVINE SERVICE

1. half knot

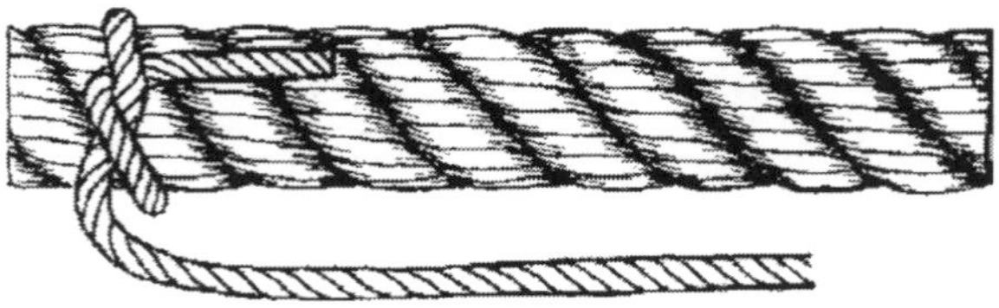

2. half hitch

3. 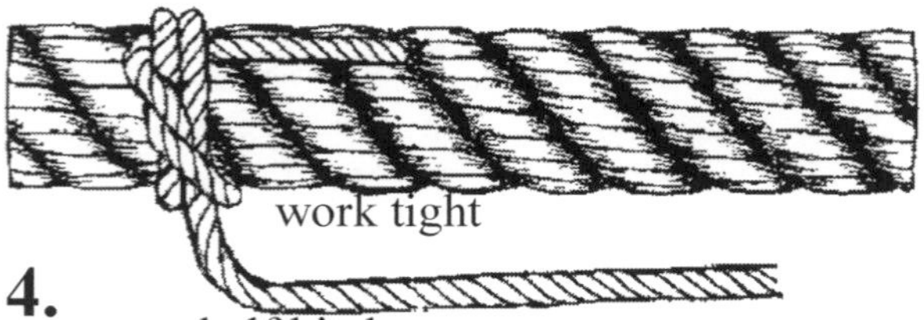 work tight

4. half hitch

5. 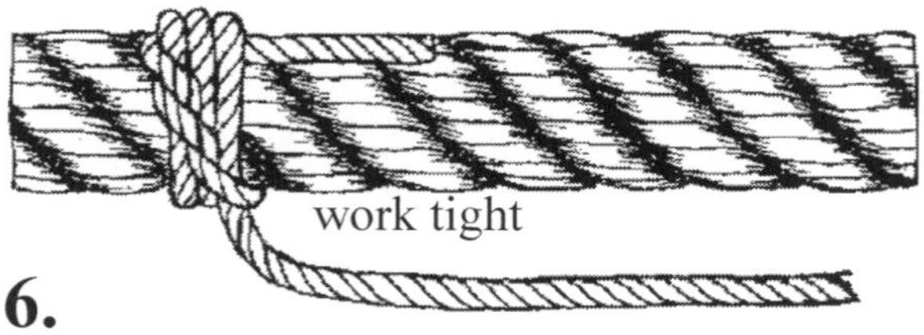 work tight

6. add half hitch

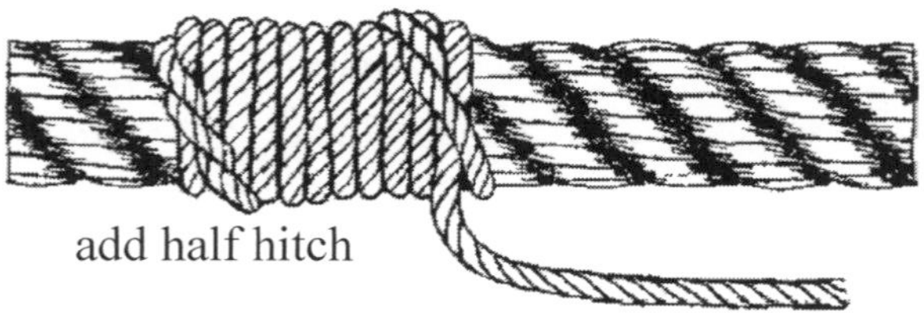

7.

8.

9. half hitch

work tight

10.

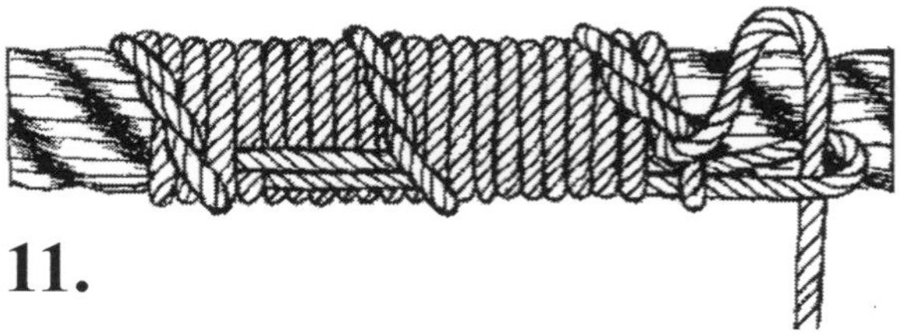

11.

pull through

12.

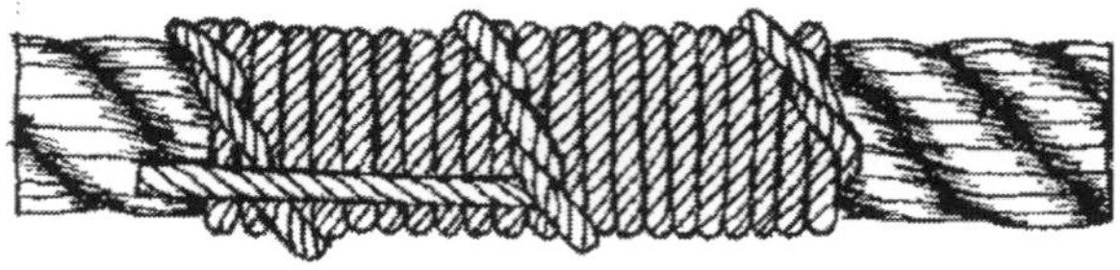

13. cut off end

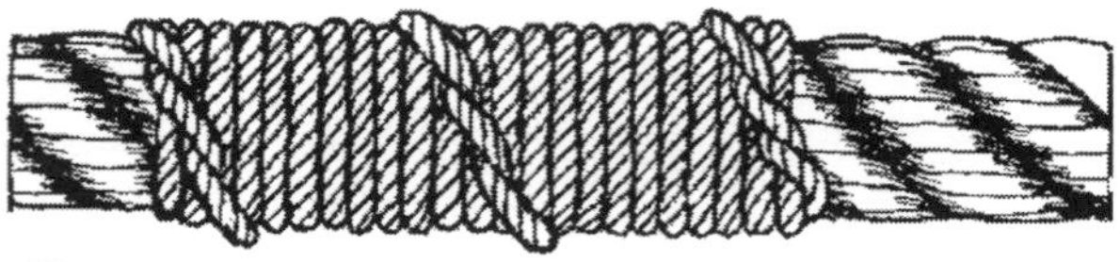

RINGBOLT HITCHING:

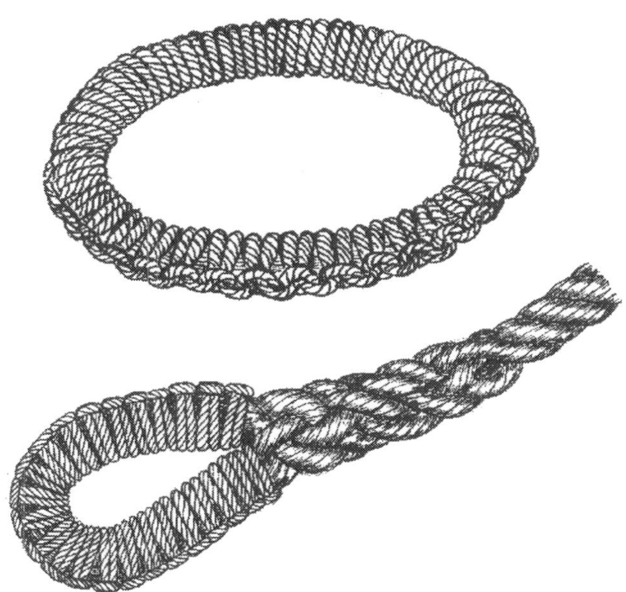

Description ---- A series of interlocking Lark's Head Knots that form a ridge around the outside of a ring or loop.

Use ---- To prevent chafing; as a decoration.

Comments ---- There are many forms of Ringbolt Hitching. The form shown here is one of the simplest and does not require the use of a needle as many other forms do. Ringbolt Hitching was used to prevent the chafing of ropes that were reeved through hand forged iron rings and to keep them from clanging against objects around them. In the present, the use of Ringbolt Hitching can be used to protect synthetic ropes that are easily chafed by applying a layer of material that is not easily chafed.

Other Names ---- Platted Ring; Hog Backing; Cockscombing.

Narration ---- (For knotboard.) **(1)** Start the Ringbolt Hitching by tying a Half Knot around the object. **(2)** Tie a Half Hitch around the object so that the standing end is trapped under the Half Hitch. **(3)** Pull the Half Hitch tight. **(4)** Tie the next Half Hitch in the opposite direction around the object. **(5)** Pull the Half Hitch tight. **(6)** Tie another Half Hitch around the object in the opposite direction; the same direction as the

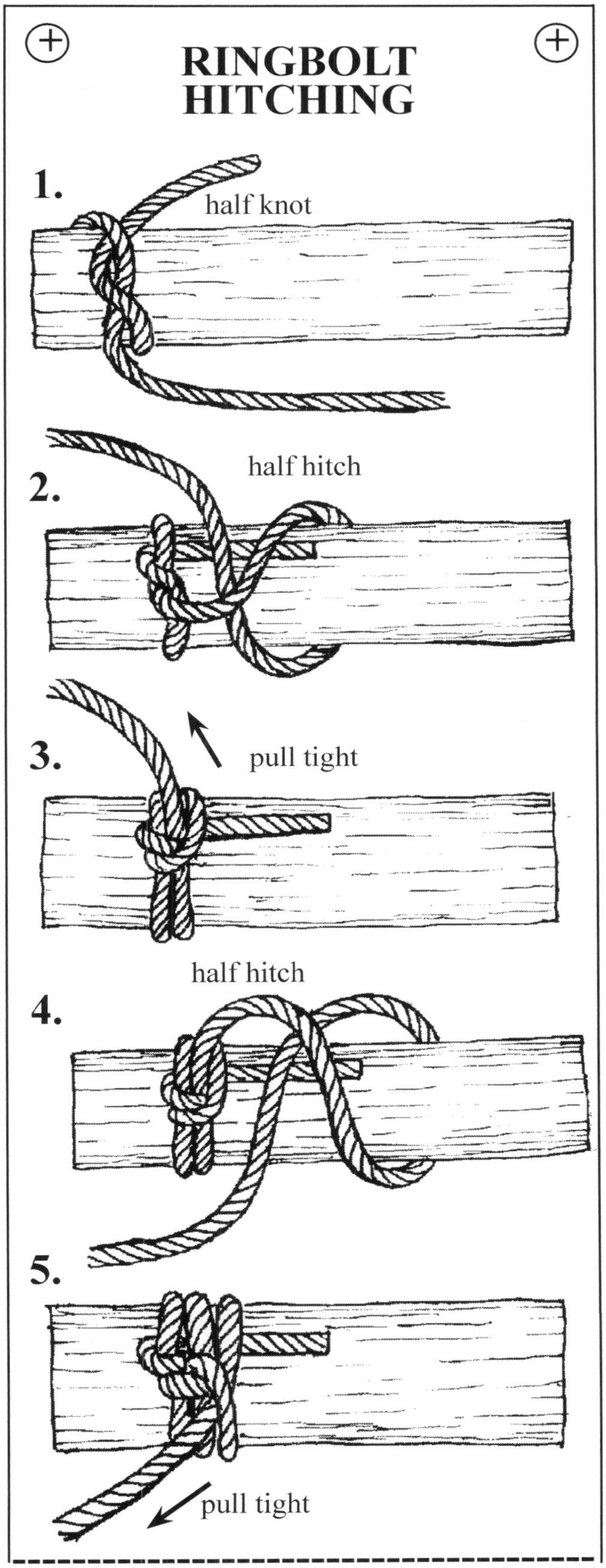

RINGBOLT HITCHING

1. half knot

2. half hitch

3. pull tight

4. half hitch

5. pull tight

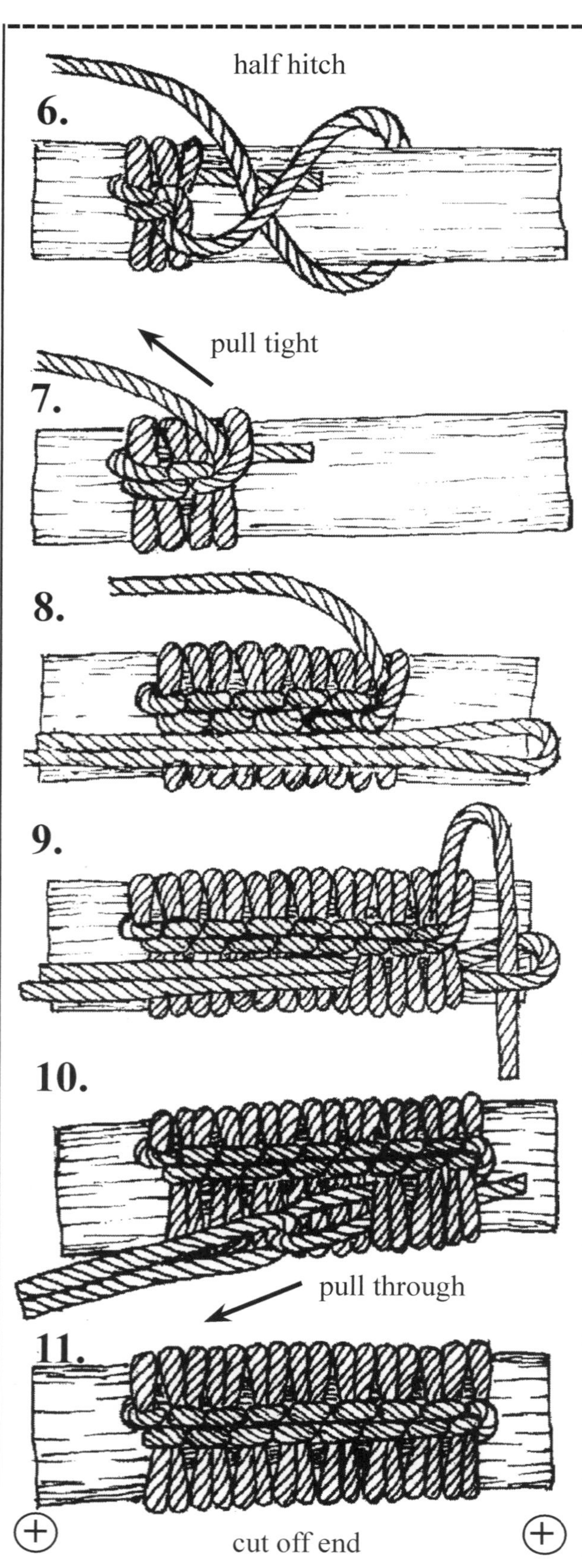

first Half Hitch. **(7)** Pull the Half Hitch tight. **(8)** When the length of the Ringbolt Hitching is within 5 or 6 Half Hitches of being long enough, form a bight in a short piece of twine so that the eye of the bight is toward the end of the work. **(9)** Continue to add Half Hitches until the Ringbolt Hitching is completed; reeve the running end through the eye of the bight. **(10)** Use the short piece of twine to pull the running end under the Half Hitches. **(11)** Cut off the end of the twine.

[NOTES]

SEIZING:

Use ---- To bind ropes together or to bind a rope to an object. Sometimes used to bind the running end of a rope to the standing end of the rope to prevent a knot from spilling.

Comments ---- Seizings do not use as much material and are not as bulky as a knot or a splice; nor does the seizing damage the fiber of the rope. The fibers of a rope do not need to be bent or separated to be seized as they do when a knot is being tied or a splice worked. If the seizing is no longer needed, the seizing can be cut away and the rope is undamaged.

The Seizings shown here can be worked without the use of a needle. However there are some forms of seizing that require the use of a needle to apply them to a rope.

To form an eye, 3 to 4 Seizings should be used. This ensures that the eye will safely remain in place even if one of the seizings is damaged.

If there is additional strain on the ropes such as at the first Seizing of an eye, racked turns should be used.

Materials ---- The diameter of the twine that is being used to do the seizing should be 1/8 to 1/12 the diameter of the rope being seized. The length of the twine should be about 3 feet for each 1 inch of diameter of the rope.

Narration ---- (For knotboard) **(1)** Fold a piece of twine in half over one strand of the rope. **(2)** Start the first layer of wrapping turns by laying the end of the twine that is between the ropes over the other end. **(3)** Wrap the outside strand around the ropes so that the wrapping turns are parallel to each other; pull each wrapping turn tight. **(4)** When the width of the wrappings are equal to the diameter of the rope, end the first layer of wrapping turns by reeving the twine between the ropes; pull tight. **(5)** Add a layer of riding turns; the riding turns are laid in the groove between the wrapping turns and pulled tight but not so tight as to separate the wrapping turns of the first layer. **(6)** When the riding turns have been completed, end the riding turns by reeving the end of the twine between the ropes so that it is in the opposite direction to the other end of the twine. **(7)** Add 2 frapping turns; reeve the end of the twine between the ropes at the other end of the wrappings; pull tight. **(8)** Use a Square Knot to end the frapping turns; reeve the ends of the twine between the ropes again; tie a Half Knot; pull the Half Knot and the frapping turns tight. **(9)** Reeve the ends of the twine between the ropes again; tie the second Half Knot of the Square Knot. **(10)** Pull the second Half Knot tight so that the Square Knot is between the strands of the rope. Cut off the ends of the twine.

SEIZING

1. center of twine

2.

3.

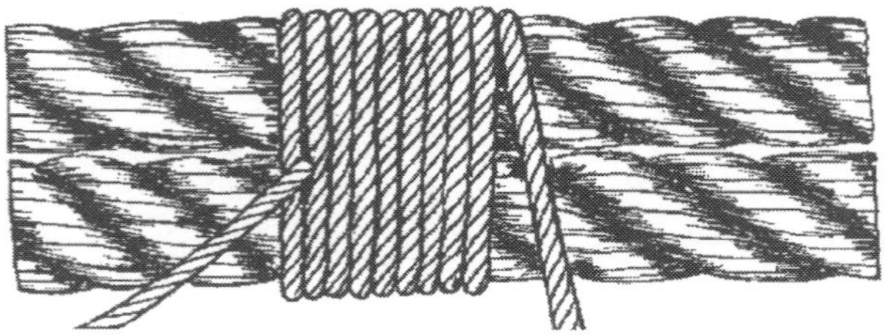

4.

5. add riding turns

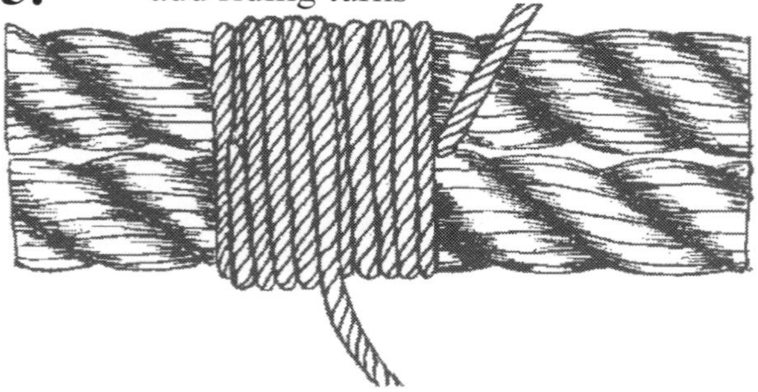

6.

7. add frapping

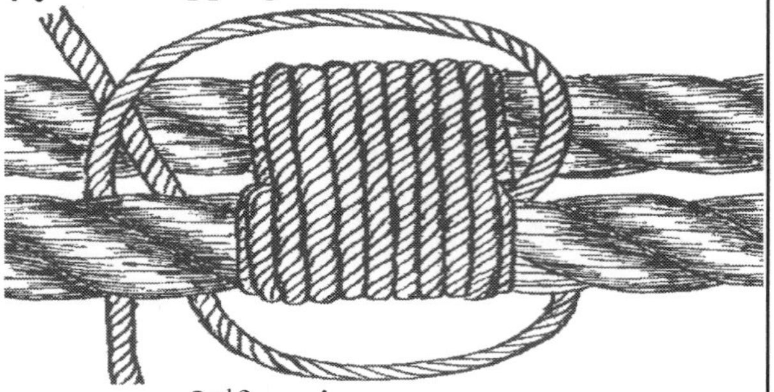

8. 2nd frapping; half knot

2nd half knot

9.

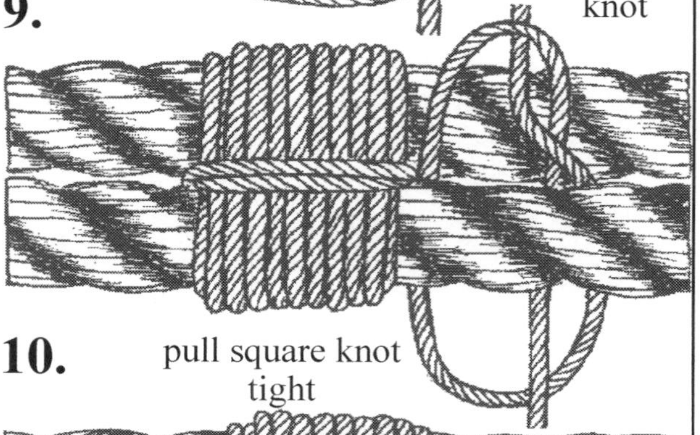

10. pull square knot tight

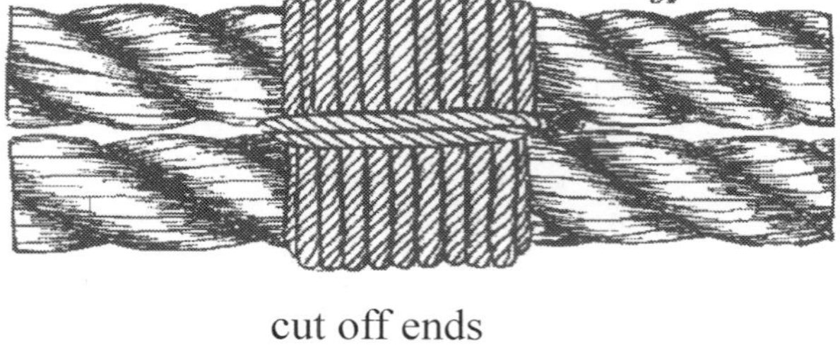

cut off ends

SEIZING: WITH RACKING TURNS

Narration ---- (For knotboard) **(1)** Use a Half Knot to tie the center of a piece of twine around one strand of the rope so that the Half Knot is between the ropes. **(2)** Take racking turns with the twine by taking a bight around the second rope and reeving the twine between the ropes. **(3)** Then take a bight around the first rope and reeve the twine between the ropes again. (each racking turn forms a figure "8" around the ropes) **(4)** When the length of the layer of racking turns is equal to the diameter of the rope, end the layer of racking turns with a Half Hitch around the second rope. **(5)** Work Half Hitch tight. **(6)** Add a layer of riding turns; the riding turns are laid in the groove between the wrapping turns and pulled tight but not so tight as to separate the wrapping turns of the first layer. **(7)** Add 2 frapping turns; reeve the end of the twine between the ropes at the other end of the wrappings; pull tight. **(8)** Use a Square Knot to end the frapping turns. Reeve the ends of the twine between the ropes again; tie first Half Knot of the Square Knot; pull the Half Knot and the frapping turns tight. **(9)** Reeve the ends of the twine between the ropes again; tie the second Half Knot of the Square Knot. **(10)** Pull the second Half Knot tight so that the Square Knot is between the strands of the rope. Cut off the ends of the twine.

SEIZING WITH RACKING TURNS

1. half knot

2. bight

3. bight

4. half hitch

5. pull tight

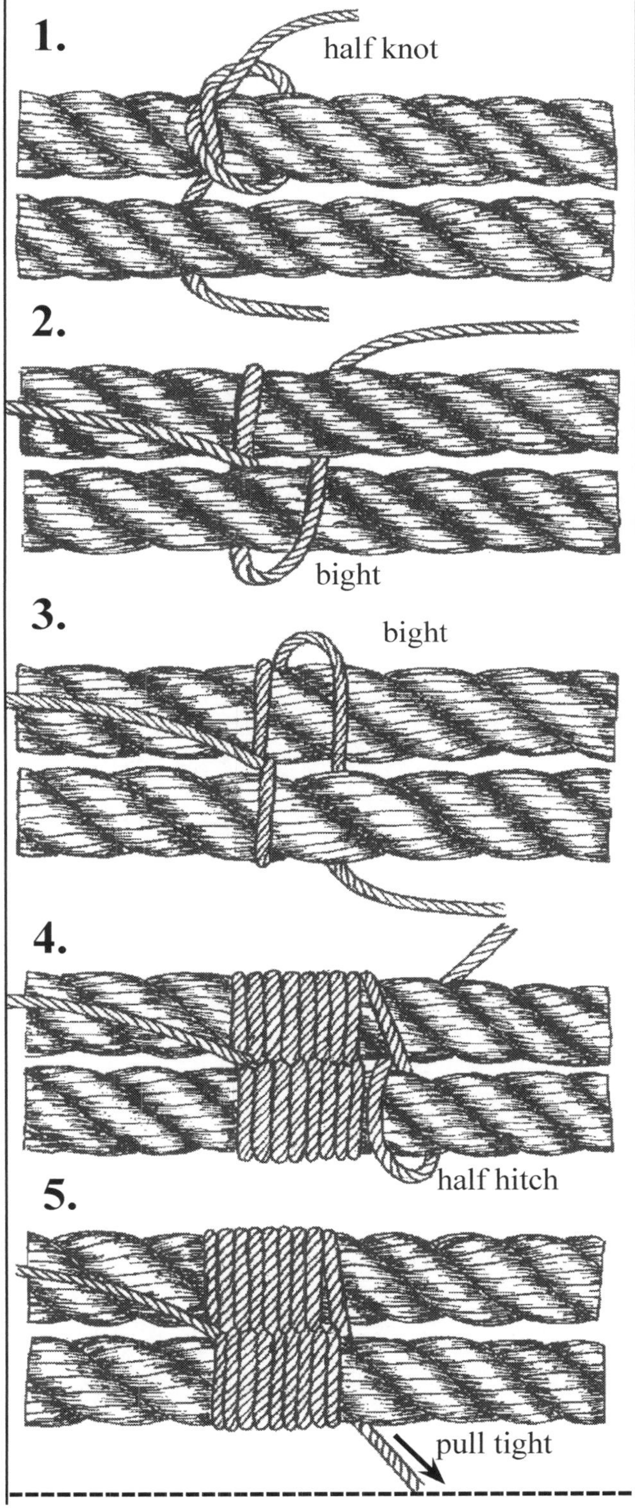

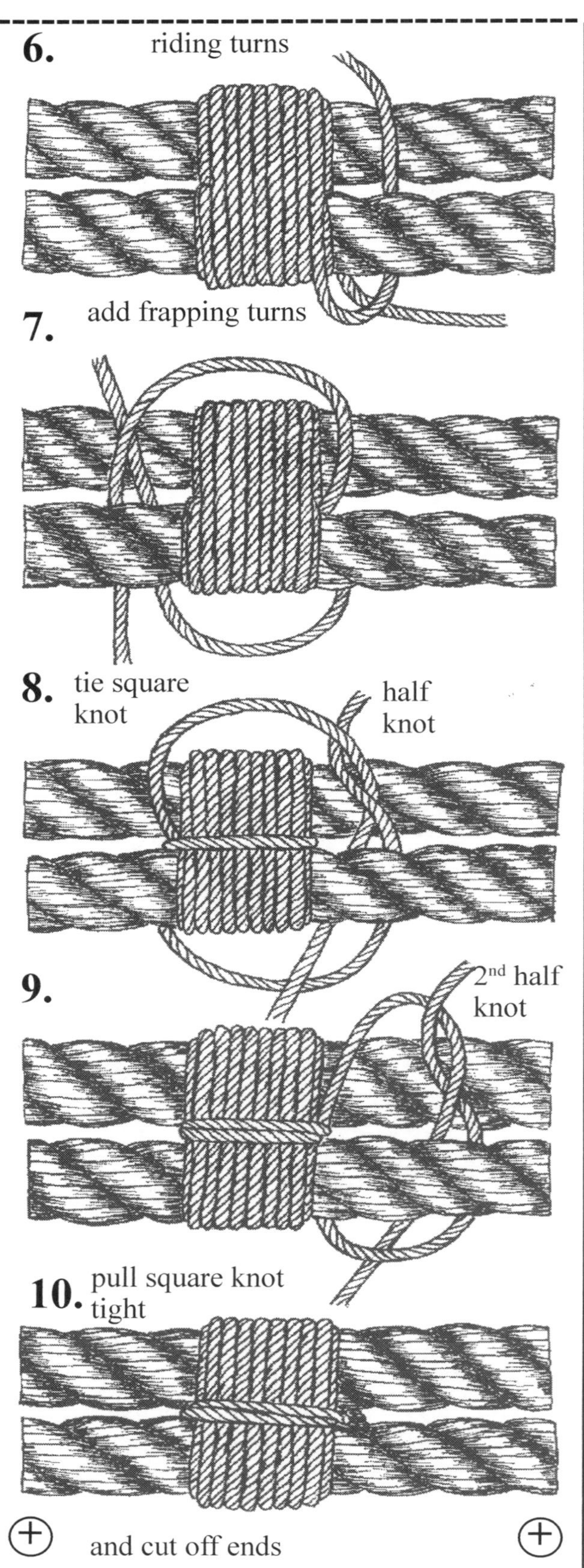
6.
riding turns
7.
add frapping turns
8.
tie square knot
half knot
9.
2nd half knot
10.
pull square knot tight
and cut off ends

[NOTES]

STOPPER KNOT:

Description ---- An Overhand Knot with extra turns.

Use ---- As a Stopper Knot to prevent unreeving or unlaying of a rope. As a decorative knot.

Comments ---- A more secure knot, easier to untie, less damaging to the rope fiber than the Overhand Knot. When used as a decorative knot additional turns can be made, but the extra turns must be worked in place as the knot is tightened.

Other Names ---- Twofold Overhand Knot or Threefold Overhand Knot depending on the number of extra turns. ---- Stopper Knot is also the name given to any one of a group of knots that is used to prevent a rope from unreeving or unlaying.

Narration ---- (For knotboard) **(1)** Form an overhand loop in the running part. **(2)** Take a bight around the standing part to the inside of the eye of the loop. **(3)** Reeve the running part through the eye of the loop to form a loose overhand knot. **(4)** Take a second turn around the standing part to the inside of the loop. **(5A)** Pull tight to form a Twofold Stopper Knot. **(5B)** Take a third turn around the standing part to the inside of the loop. **(6)** Pull and work tight to form a Threefold Stopper Knot.

STOPPER KNOT

1.

overhand loop

2.

bight

3.

overhand knot

4.

2nd turn

5A.

work tight

5B.

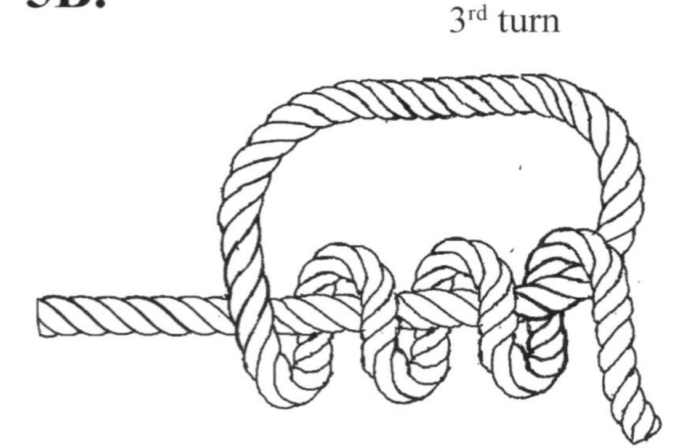

6.

work tight

[NOTES]

STEVEDORE KNOT:

Description ---- AFigure-Eight Knot with an extra turn around the standing part.

Use ---- As a Stopper Knot to prevent a rope from unreeving through a pulley block or other similar setup.

Comments ---- Easier to untie and does not damage the fiber of the rope like an Overhand Knot. The Stevedore Knot has a greater bulk than an Overhand Knot or a Figure-Eight Knot, therefore it was the preferred Stopper Knot used on cargo tackle. This preference was due to the larger sized pulley blocks used by dock workers (stevedores).

Narration ---- (For knotboard) **(1)** Form a bight **(2)** into an overhand loop. **(3)** Take a bight around the standing part. **(4)** Next take a complete turn around the standing part. **(5)** Bring the running part over the top edge of the overhand loop. **(6 and 7)** Reeve the running part through the eye of the overhand loop. **(8 and 9)** Complete the knot by working it tight.

STEVEDORE KNOT

1.

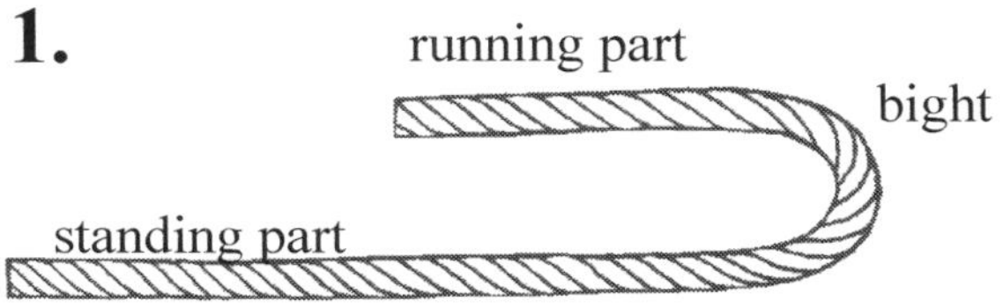

2.

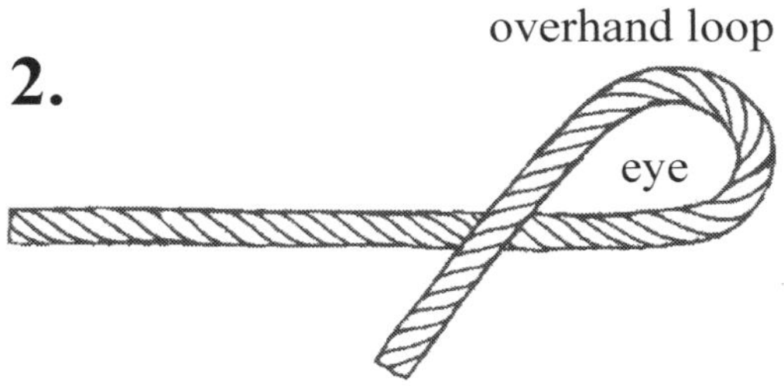

3.

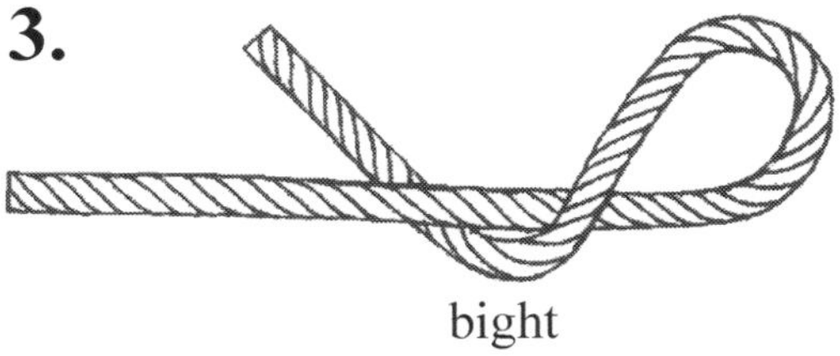

4.

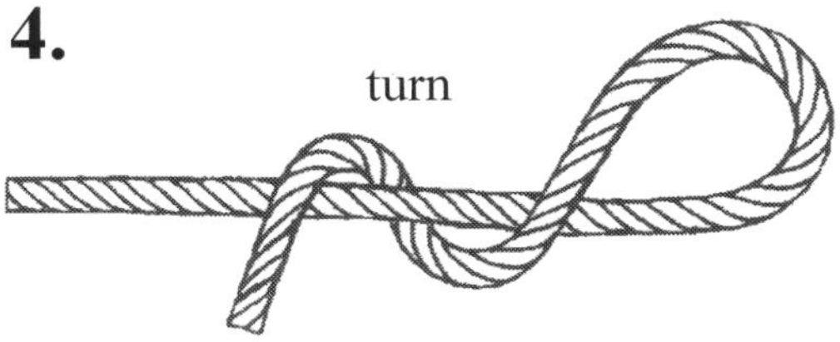

5.

6.

7.

8.

9.

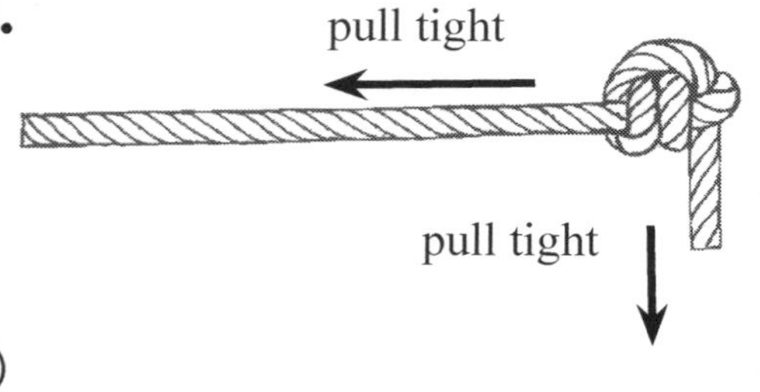

[NOTES]

FIGURE-EIGHT KNOT:

Description ---- Interlocking overhand loops; the running part goes through the eye of one loop and the standing part goes through the eye of the other loop.

Use ---- (1) As a Stopper Knot; to keep a rope from unreeving from a pulley block; to prevent a rope from unlaying. **(2)** When tied on a bight, it makes a reliable loop for rescue work and mountaineering.

Comments ---- Easier to tie and untie than an Overhand Knot; does not damage the rope fiber or jam like an Overhand Knot.

Narration ---- (For knotboard) **(1)** Form an overhand loop. **(2)** Take a bight around the standing part. **(3)** Form the second overhand loop by passing the running part over the top edge of the first overhand loop. **(4)** Complete the knot by reeving the running part through the eye of the first overhand loop **(5)** and pull tight.

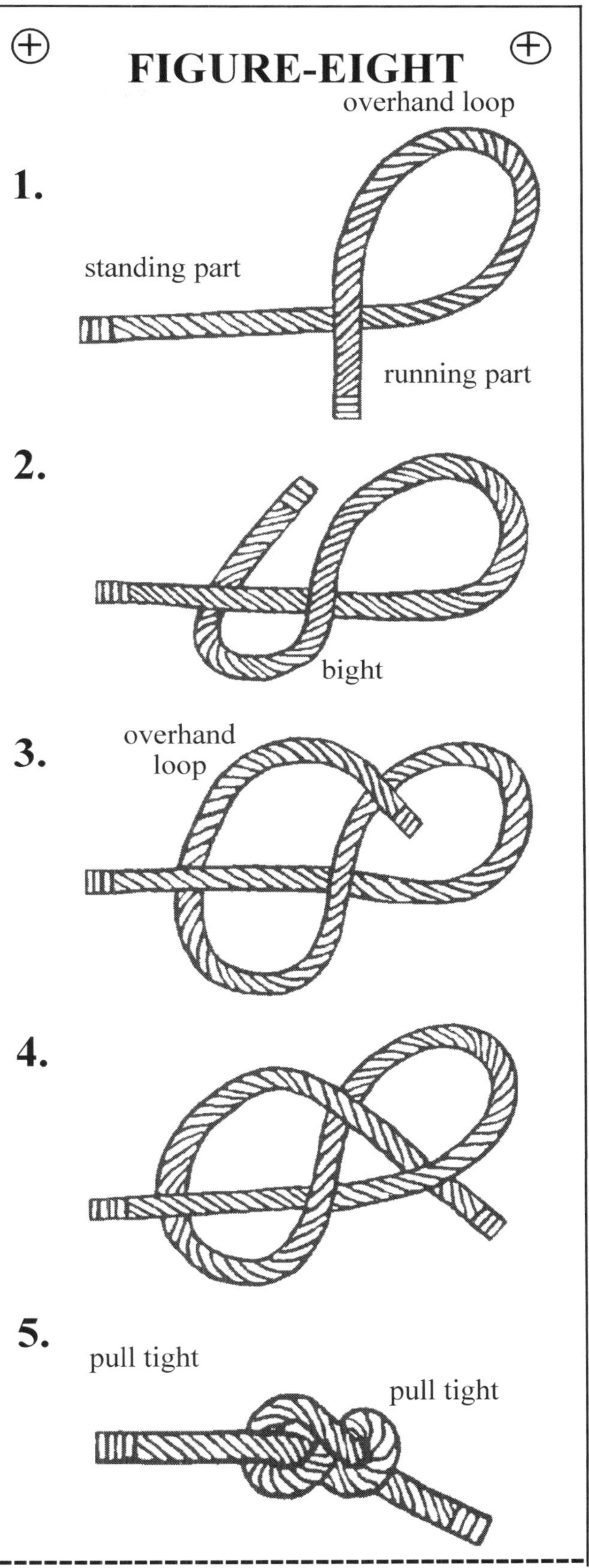

FIGURE-EIGHT ON A BIGHT

1. bight

2. overhand loop

3. bight

4. 2nd overhand loop

5.

6. pull tight pull tight

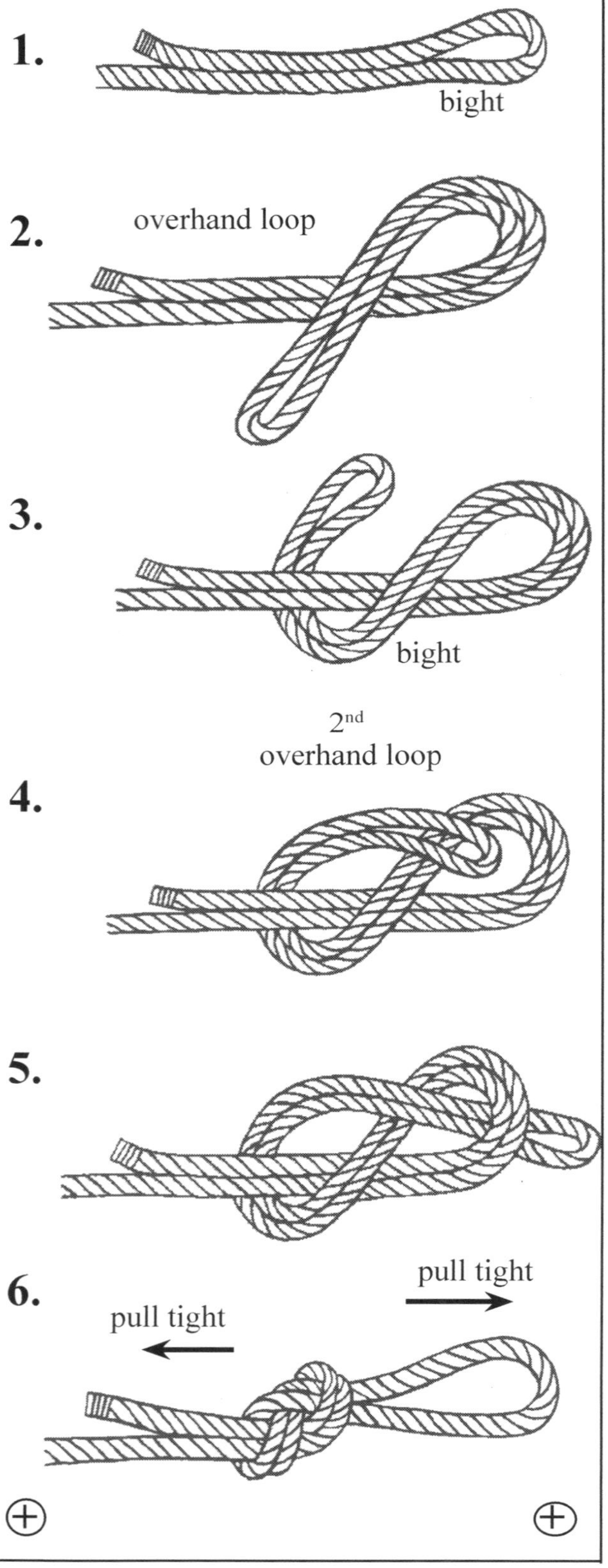

FIGURE-EIGHT ON A BIGHT:

Description ---- Interlocking overhand loops tied on a bight in the running part (the bight is used as the running part); the running part goes through the eye of one loop and the standing part goes through the eye of the other loop.

Use ---- **(1)** Makes a reliable loop for rescue work and mountaineering. **(2)** As a Stopper Knot; to keep a rope from unreeving from a pulley block; to prevent a rope from unlaying.

Comments ---- Easier to tie and untie than an Overhand Knot; does not damage the rope fiber or jam like an Overhand Knot on a bight.

Narration ---- (For knotboard) **(1)** Form a bight in the rope. **[NOTE]** Treat the two strands of the bight as a single strand as the rest of the knot is tied. **(2)** Form an overhand loop. **(3)** Take a bight around the standing part. **(4)** Form the second overhand loop by passing the running part over the top edge of the first overhand loop. **(5)** Complete the knot by reeving the running part through the eye of the first overhand loop. **(6)** Pull tight.

[NOTES]

WATER KNOT:

Description ---- An Overhand Knot that is doubled by "chasing" or following the rope strand of the first Overhand Knot.

Use ---- A permanent knot to join smooth twine or rope; to join straps.

Comments ---- Difficult to untie; a secure knot for monofilament line; recommended for joining twine when knitting a net; a secure knot for joining straps, especially woven synthetic straps.

Other Names ---- Ring Knot.

Narration ---- (For knotboard #1) **(1)** Tie an Overhand Knot in the end of one rope. **(2)** Lay the running end of the second rope next to the running end of the first rope, but in the opposite direction. **(3 and 4)** Chase (follow) the strand through the Overhand Knot until **(5)** the running part of the second rope is lying parallel to the standing part of the first rope. **(6)** Pull tight.

[NOTES]

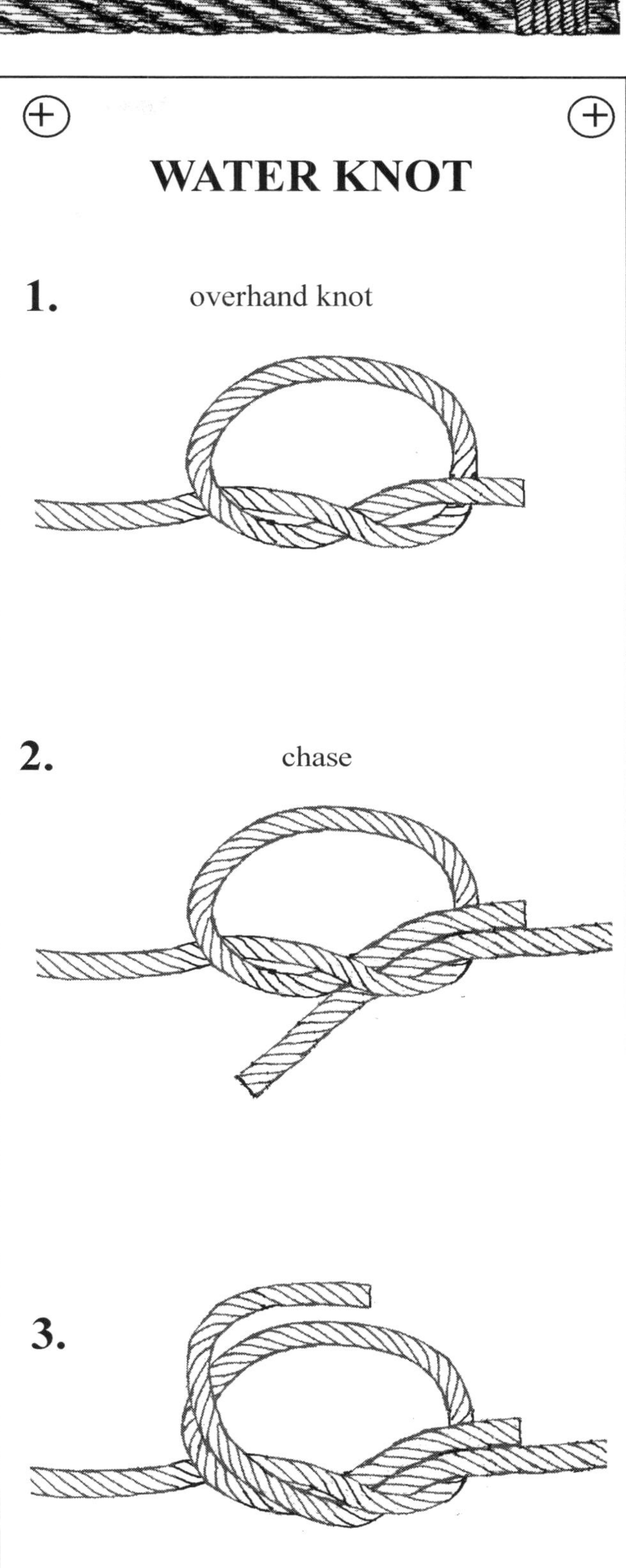

4.

5.

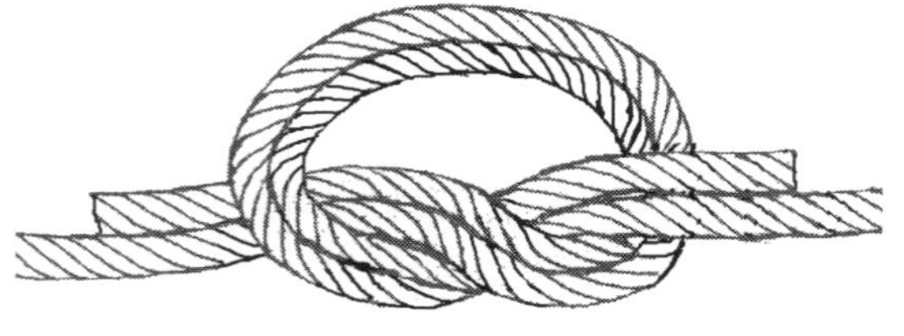

6.

← pull tight

pull tight →

WATER KNOT: METHOD 2

Narration ---- (For knotboard #2) **(1)** Tie a Half Knot by taking the running part of the left rope over the running part of the right rope. **(2)** Cross the right running part over the left running part. **(3)** Lay the running part of the left rope next to the standing part of the right rope. **(4)** Chase the standing part of the right rope back through the knot with the running part of the left rope. **(5)** Lay the running part of the right rope next to the standing part of the left rope. **(6)** Chase the standing part of the left rope back through the knot with the running part of the right rope. **(7)** Grasp the running part and the standing part that extend from each side of the knot and pull the knot tight.

[NOTES]

WATER KNOT METHOD 2

1.

half knot

2.

left

right

3.

4.

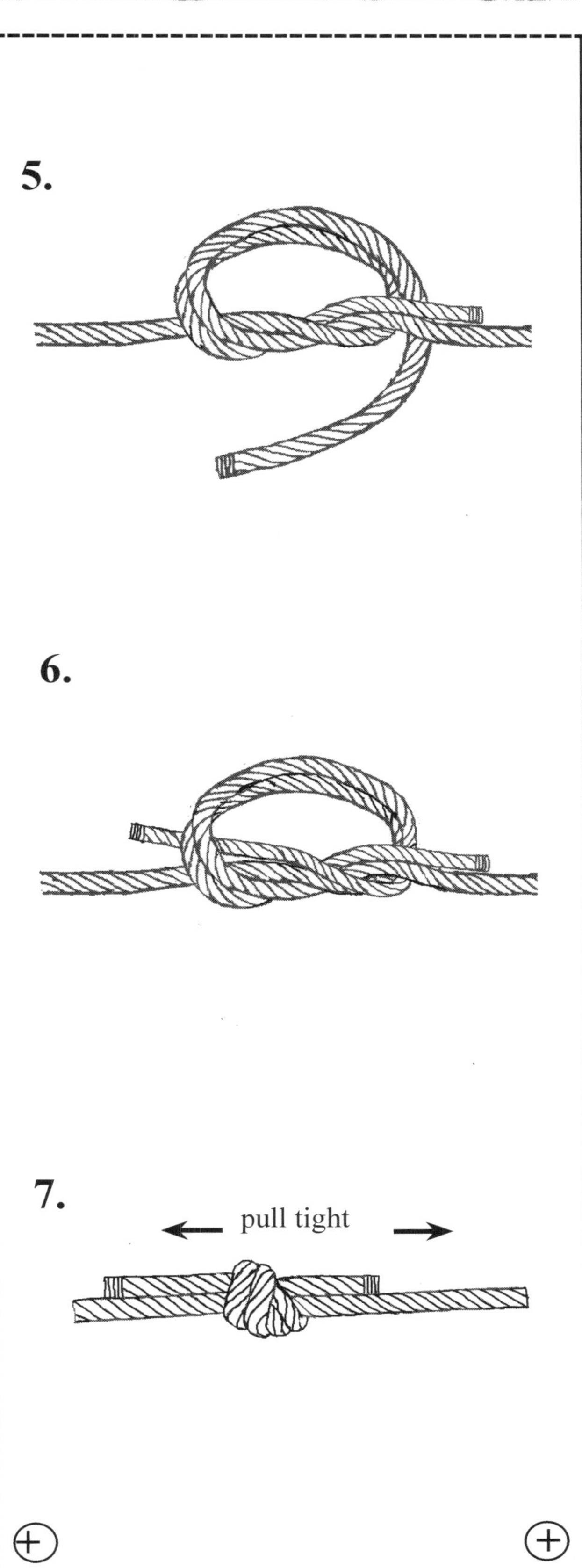

SQUARE KNOT:

Description ---- (1) Two Half Knots, one tied in one direction and the second tied in the other direction. **(2)** Two interlocking bights.

Use ---- Use only as a binding knot; to tie bandages for first aid, tent flaps and packages.

Other Names ---- Reef Knot; this name comes from its use to reef or tie up sails.

Comments ---- The Square Knot, improperly used, is a dangerous knot. It can be easily upset into a Lark's Head Knot and then spill allowing the two ends of the rope to separate. Because of the ease with which a Square Knot can be upset it should never be used to join ropes that will be relied on to support a person or a load that can be accidently released. However, this same feature makes the Square Knot useful for tying bandages, tent flaps, bundles, or anything else that needs to be held securely but also needs to be untied easily and quickly.

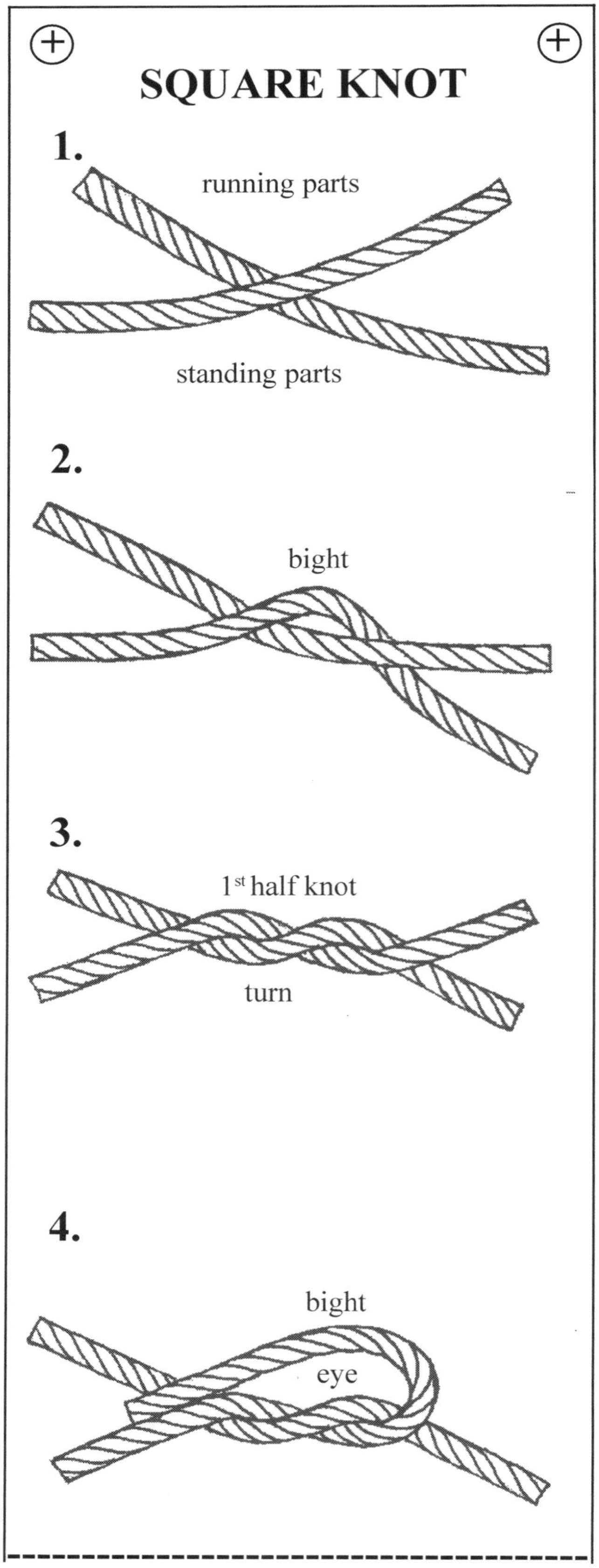

SQUARE KNOT

1.

running parts

standing parts

2.

bight

3.

1st half knot

turn

4.

bight

eye

5. bight

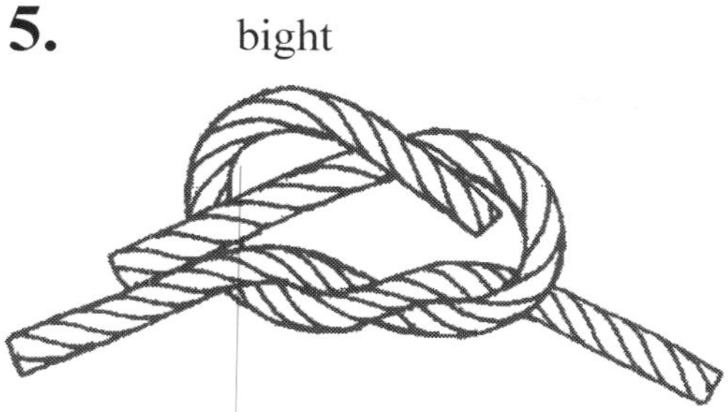

6. 2nd half knot

7. pull tight

Narration ---- (For knotboard) **(1)** Start to form the first Half Knot by crossing the running parts of the two ropes. **(2)** Then take a bight around one rope with the other rope. **(3)** Complete the first Half Knot by bringing the end of the rope around so that the ropes make a complete turn around each other. **(4)** Form a bight in one running end by laying it back along its own standing part. **(5)** Form the second bight by folding the other running part back along its standing part. **(6)** Reeve the running part of the second bight through the eye of the first bight. **(7)** Pull tight.

UPSETTING A SQUARE KNOT:

[W**ARNING]** Because the Square Knot can be upset easily by pulling on the running part and the standing part of one of its ropes, it should not be used to join ropes that will be supporting a load that can be accidently released if the knot is upset.

(1)

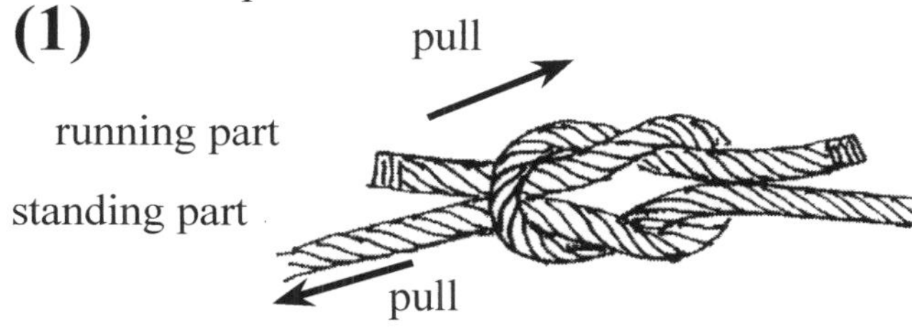

(2)

(3)

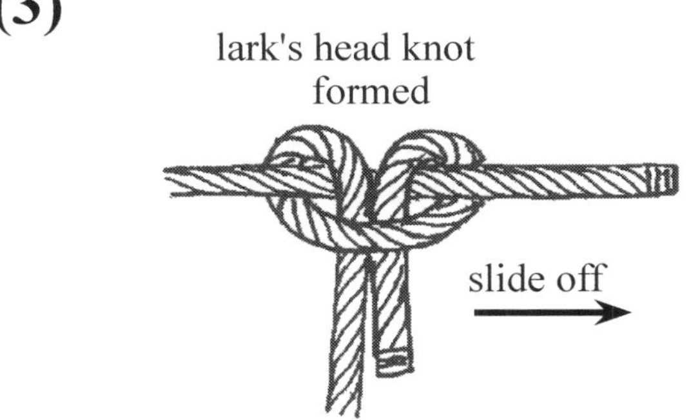

STOPPED SQUARE KNOT:

Comments ---- A Square Knot can be stopped to prevent it from being upset. This is done by taking a Half Hitch around the standing part of each rope.

Pull the Half Hitches up snug against the Square Knot, but not so tight as to distort the Square Knot.

SLIPPED SQUARE KNOT:

Description ---- A Square Knot with a bight pulled through one side.

Use ---- The same as a Square Knot.

Comments ---- Can be spilled quickly by pulling the running end of the bight so as to pull the bight back through the knot.

Other Names ---- Slipped Reef Knot; Half Bowknot; Single Bowknot.

SHOESTRING KNOT:

Description ---- A Square Knot where the second Half Knot is tied with a bight in each running end.

Use ---- As a binding knot; to tie shoeslaces or drawstrings in pieces on clothing or storage bags; to tie bundles.

Comments ---- Can be untied easily by pulling on either running part.

Other Names ----Double Bowknot; Double Slipped Reef Knot.

Narration ---- (For Shoestring Knot) **(1)** Tie a Half Knot in the two running parts. **(2)** Fold the running parts over to form a bight in each end. **(3)** Form a second Half Knot with the bights. **(4)** Pull tight.

(1 and 2)

(3 and 4)

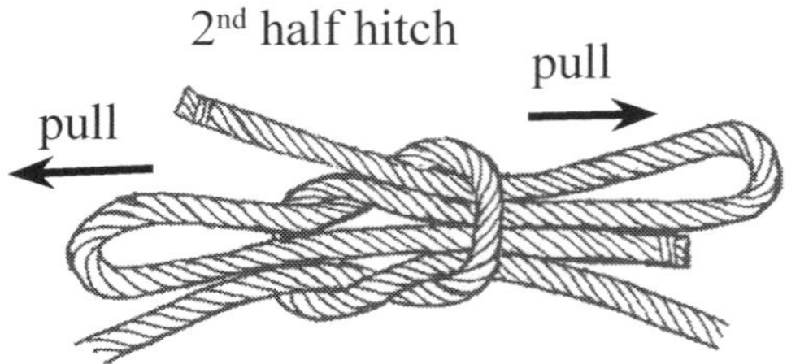

SHEET BEND:

Description ---- An interlocked Half Hitch and bight.

Use ---- To temporarily join two ropes, especially if the ropes are of different sizes.

Comments ---- The Sheet Bend is a secure but easily untied knot. ---- When tying the Sheet Bend, the running parts should be left long because there is some initial slip in the knot when the knot is first brought under tension. ---- The proper and more secure way to tie the Sheet Bend is so that the running parts of the finished knot are on the same side of the knot. ---- Repeated loading can cause the Sheet Bend to slip enough to come apart. This slipping can be prevented by tying a Half Hitch with each running part around its own standing part.

Other Names ---- Weaver's Knot.

Related Knots ---- Bowline; Becket Hitch; these knots share the same form but are tied in a different way or have a different use.

Narration ---- (For knotboard) **(1)** Form a bight in the running part of the left-hand rope. **(2)** Reeve the running part of the right-hand rope through the eye of the bight in the left-hand rope. **(3)** With the right-hand running part take a bight around the running part and the standing part of the left-hand rope. **(4)** Pass the right-hand running part over the left-hand standing part, **(5)** under the right-hand rope, and **(6)** over the running part of the left-hand rope. **(7)** Pull tight.

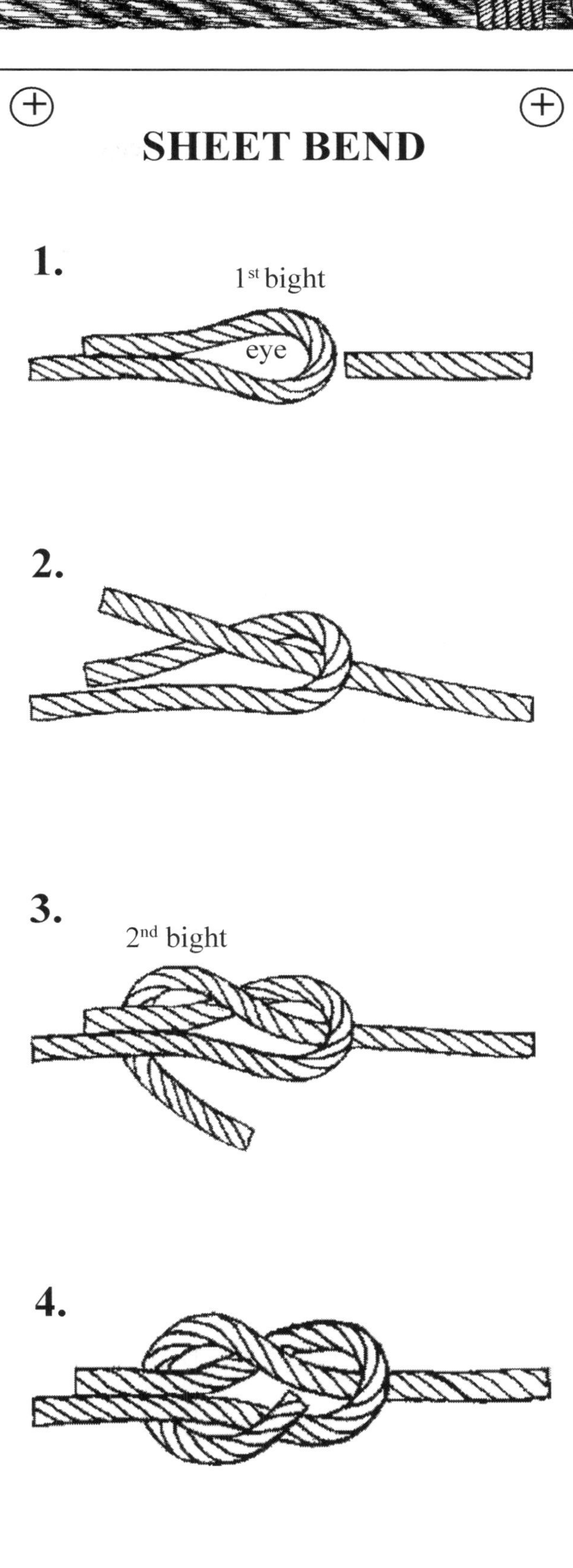

5.

6.

7.

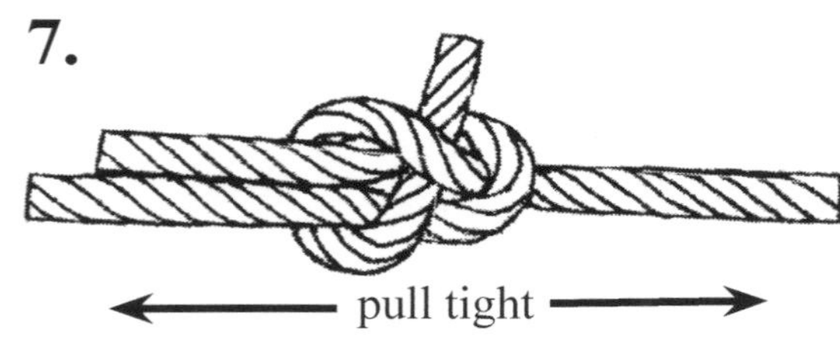

(back)

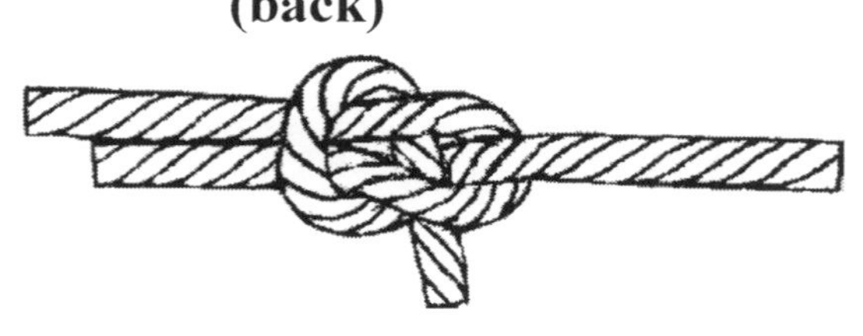

WEAVER'S KNOT:

Description ---- A different method of tying a Sheet Bend.

Use ---- For joining light twine and yarn together, used especially by weavers.

Comments ---- This method of tying the Sheet Bend is faster than the usual method.

Narration ---- (For knotboard) **(1)** Cross the left-hand running part over the right-hand running part. Hold this cross point together between the thumb and first finger of the left hand. **(2)** With the right hand, grasp the right-hand standing part and make a loop over the thumb and **(3)** between the standing parts so as to form a Half Hitch around the left-hand rope. **(4)** Fold the running part of the left-hand rope back along itself to form a bight around the standing part of the right-hand rope. **(5)** Reeve the running part of the left-hand rope through the eye of the Half Hitch and **(6)** pull tight to complete the knot.

[NOTES]

WEAVER'S KNOT:

1.

2.

3.  half hitch

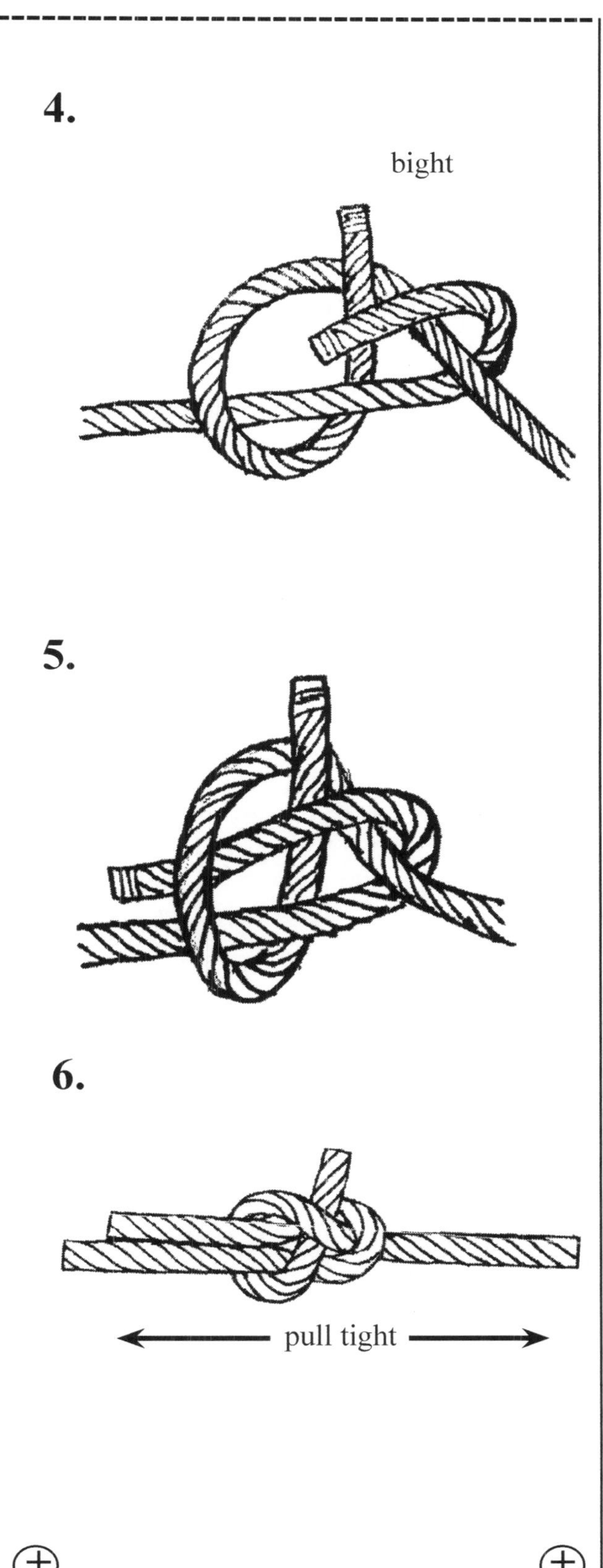

BECKET HITCH:

Description ---- A Half Hitch tied around a permanent eye, such as the eye of an Eye Splice or a hook.

Use ---- To tie a rope to an Eye Splice, a hook or a ring.

Comments ---- The Becket Hitch has the same form as the Sheet Bend but is used to tie a rope to an eye or hook, whereas the Sheet Bend is used to join two ropes.

DOUBLE SHEET BEND:

Comments ---- This method of tying the Sheet Bend is the most secure form of the Sheet Bend and should be used if there is a significant difference in the size of the two ropes that are being used.

Narration ---- (For knotboard) **(1)** Form a bight in the larger of the two ropes. **(2)** Reeve the smaller rope through the eye of the bight. **(3)** Then take a bight around the parts of the larger rope; be sure to take the bight from the standing part side to the running part side. **(4)** Bring the running part of the smaller rope over the larger rope and **(5)** under the smaller rope to form a half hitch around the two parts of the bight in the larger rope. This forms the first turn. **(6)** Take a second bight around the larger rope. **(7)** Again bring the smaller rope over the larger rope and under the smaller rope to complete the second turn. **(8)** Pull tight.

[NOTE] If the difference in the sizes of the ropes is significant or the ropes are very smooth, additional turns of the smaller rope will help to prevent the ropes from slipping.

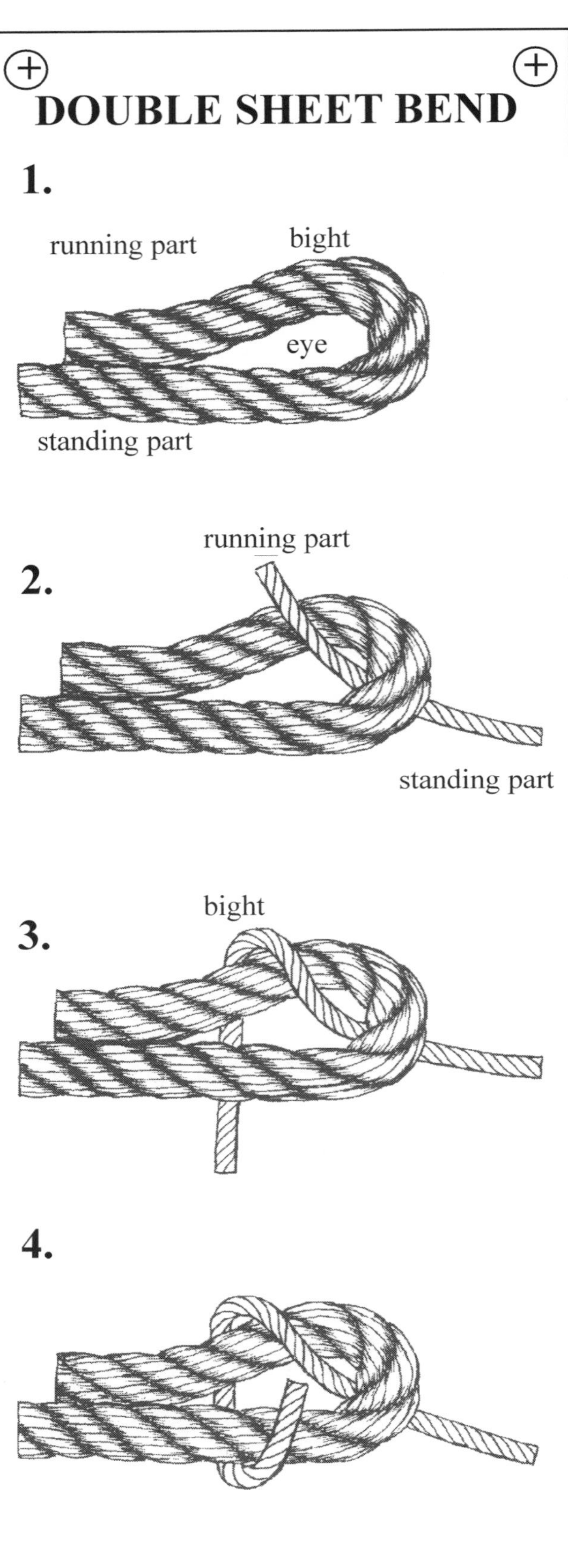

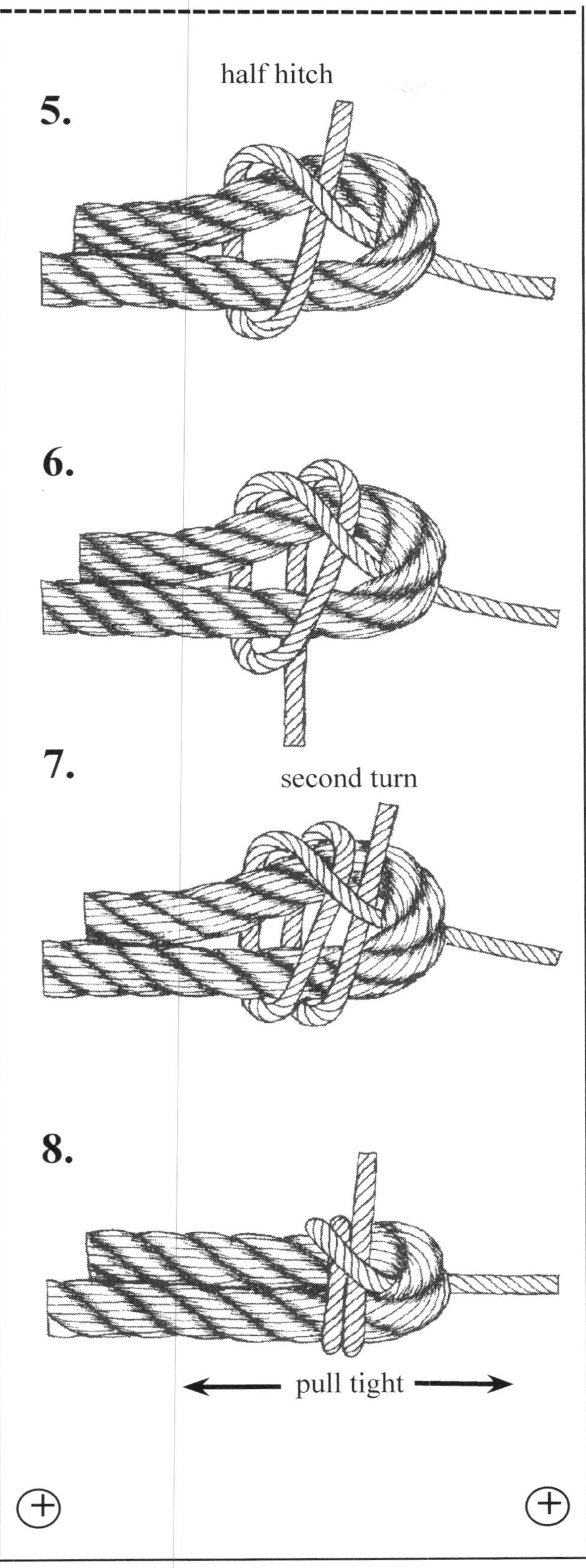

SHEET BEND ON A SHORT END:

Use ---- For joining light rope, twine, thread, and yarn.

Comments ---- This method of tying the Sheet Bend is useful for tying a piece of rope onto another rope when the end of the rope is very short.

Narration ---- (For knotboard) **(1)** Form an overhand loop. **(2)** Fold the loop over onto its standing part. **(3)** Pull a bight of the standing part through the loop to form an Overhand Knot in the running part. **(4)** Pull on the standing part and the running part of the Overhand Knot to close the eye around the standing part to form a Slip Noose. **(5)** Place the eye of the Slip Noose over the running part of the second rope. **(6)** Pull on the running part of the first rope and push on the Overhand Knot to upset the Slip Noose so that a bight of the second rope is pulled through the overhand loop to form the Sheet Bend. **(7)** Pull on the standing parts of each rope to tighten the Sheet Bend.

[NOTES]

SHEET BEND SHORT END

1.

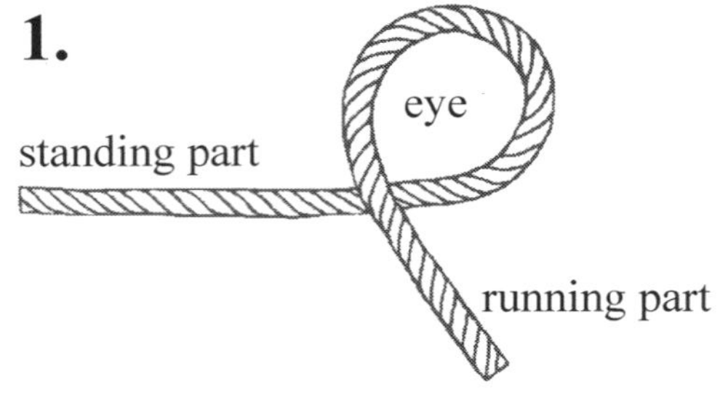

2.

fold over

3.

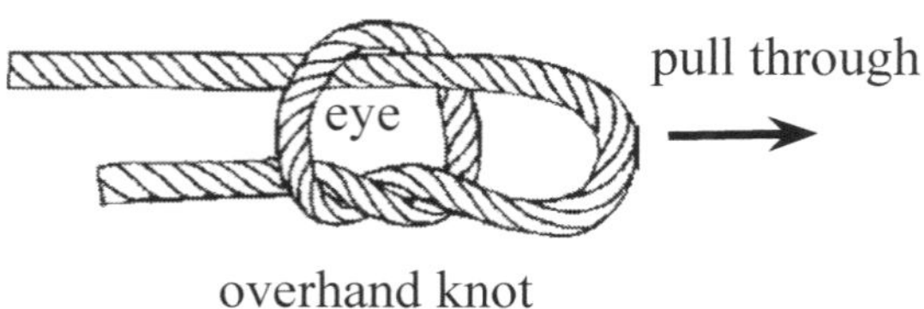

4.

slip noose

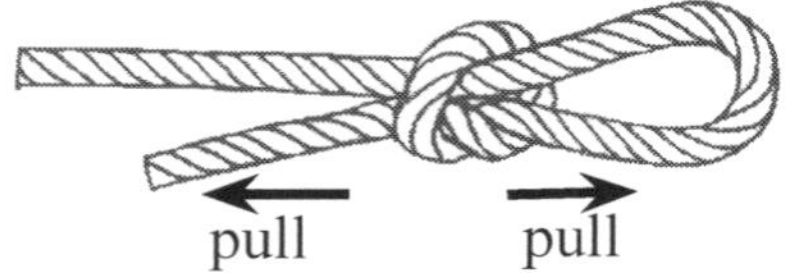

5.

6.

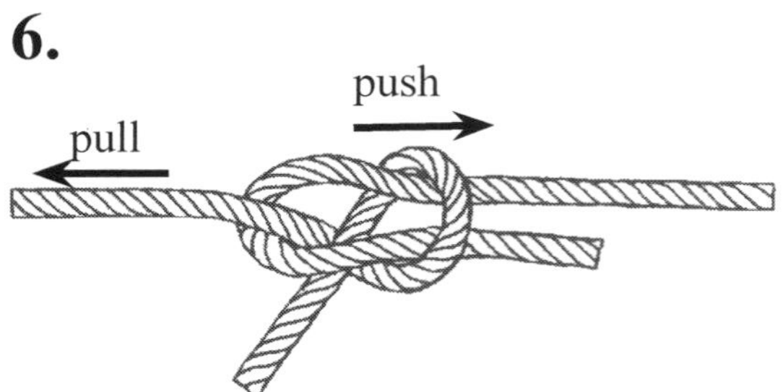

7.

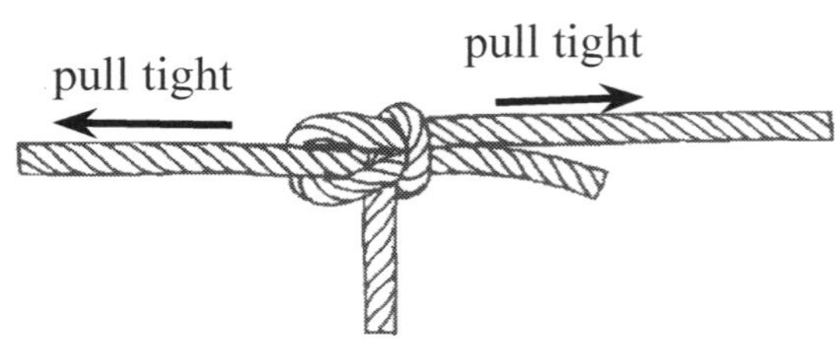

(back)

BOWLINE:

Description ---- A loop formed by an interlocking Half Hitch and a bight.

Use ---- As a nonslip loop; especially useful in rescue work.

Comments ---- The Bowline is related to and has the same form as the Sheet Bend. ---- The Bowline is one of the most reliable loop knots; it is easy to tie and untie. ---- When doing mountaineering or rescue work, if the rope is very smooth and slippery, tie a Half Hitch or two around the standing part.

Narration ---- (For knotboard) **(1)** Form an overhand loop. **(2)** Form the eye of the Bowline by forming a bight with its running part under the overhand loop. **(3)** Reeve the running part up through the eye of the overhand loop. **(4)** Pass the running part behind the standing part. **(5)** Complete the bight around the standing part. **(6)** Reeve the running part back through the eye of the overhand loop so that it lies parallel to itself. **(7)** Grasp the parallel strands of the running part bight in one hand and the standing part in the other hand; pull tight. **(8)** Back view. **[NOTE]** In steps 2 through 4, the strands of the rope appear to be woven in an over and under manner.

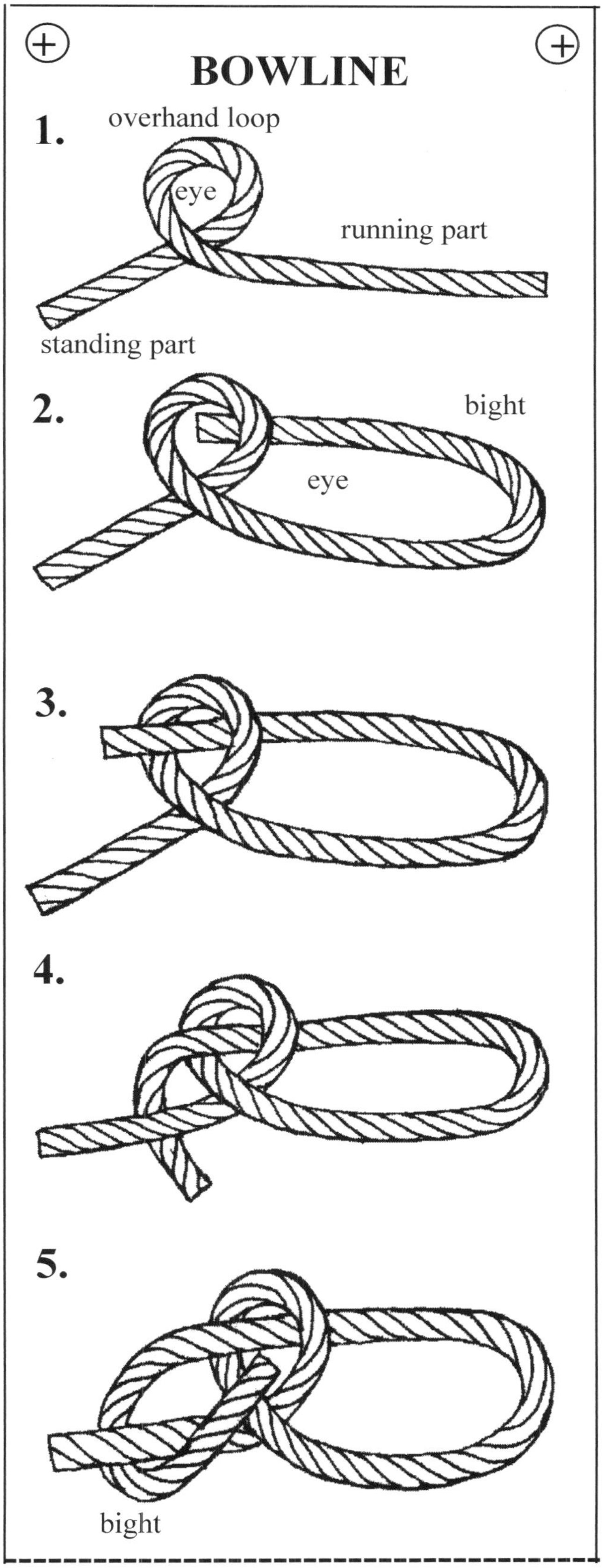

BOWLINE

1. overhand loop

eye

running part

standing part

2. bight

eye

3.

4.

5.

bight

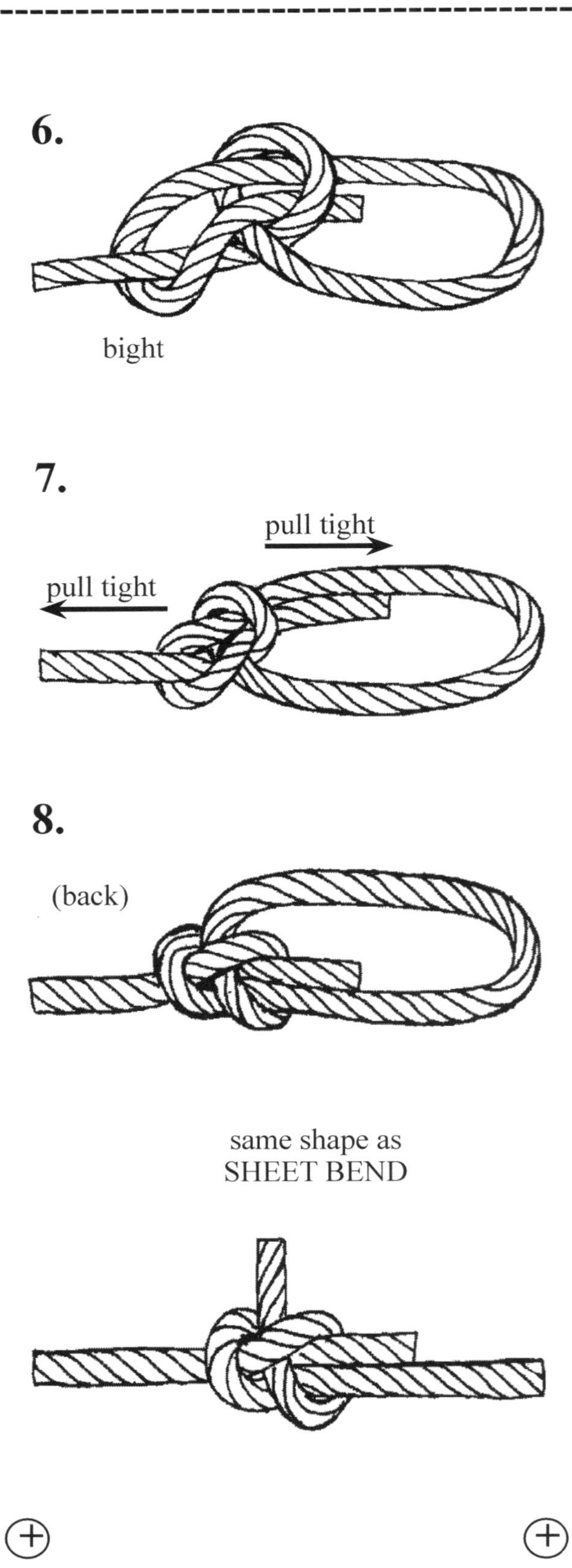

BOWLINE: ALTERNATE METHOD

Comments ---- This method of tying the Bowline works well when using light or flexible rope and for twine or thread.

Narration ---- (For knotboard) **(1)** Form an overhand loop in the running part. **(2)** Fold the eye of the running part back over the standing part. **(3)** Start at the running part side of the overhand loop, weave the running part over the top part of the loop, **(4)** under the standing part and **(5)** then over the standing part of the overhand loop. **(6)** Fold the running part back on itself so that a bight is formed around the standing part. **(7)** Allow the overhand loop to flip over to its original position. **(8)** Grasp the parallel strands of the running part bight in one hand and the standing part in the other hand; pull tight.

Untying the Bowline ---- **(1)** Hold the Bowline so that you are looking at the back side of the knot. **(2)** Fold the standing part down so that it is parallel to the running part. **(3)** This will enable you to fold the bight of the running part toward the standing part. **(4)** Pull the standing part back through the bight of the running part; this will loosen the knot so that it can be easily untied.

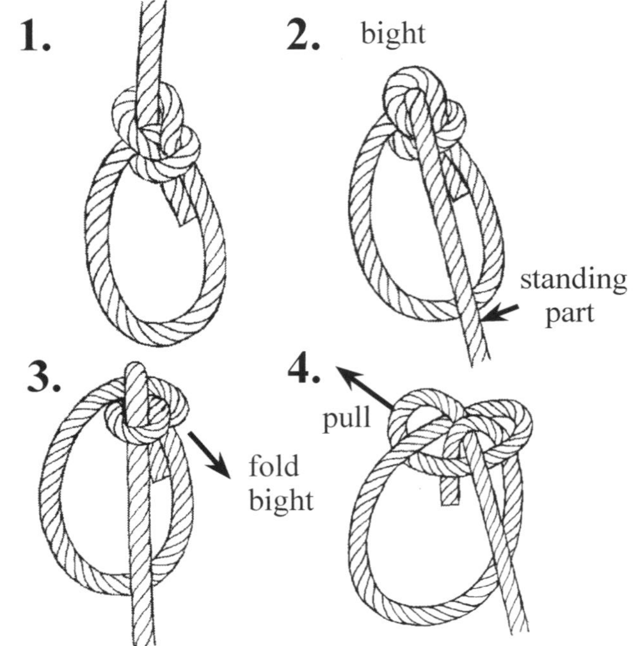

BOWLINE ALTERNATE METHOD

overhand loop

1.

eye

standing part

running part

2.

fold

3.

bight

eye

4.

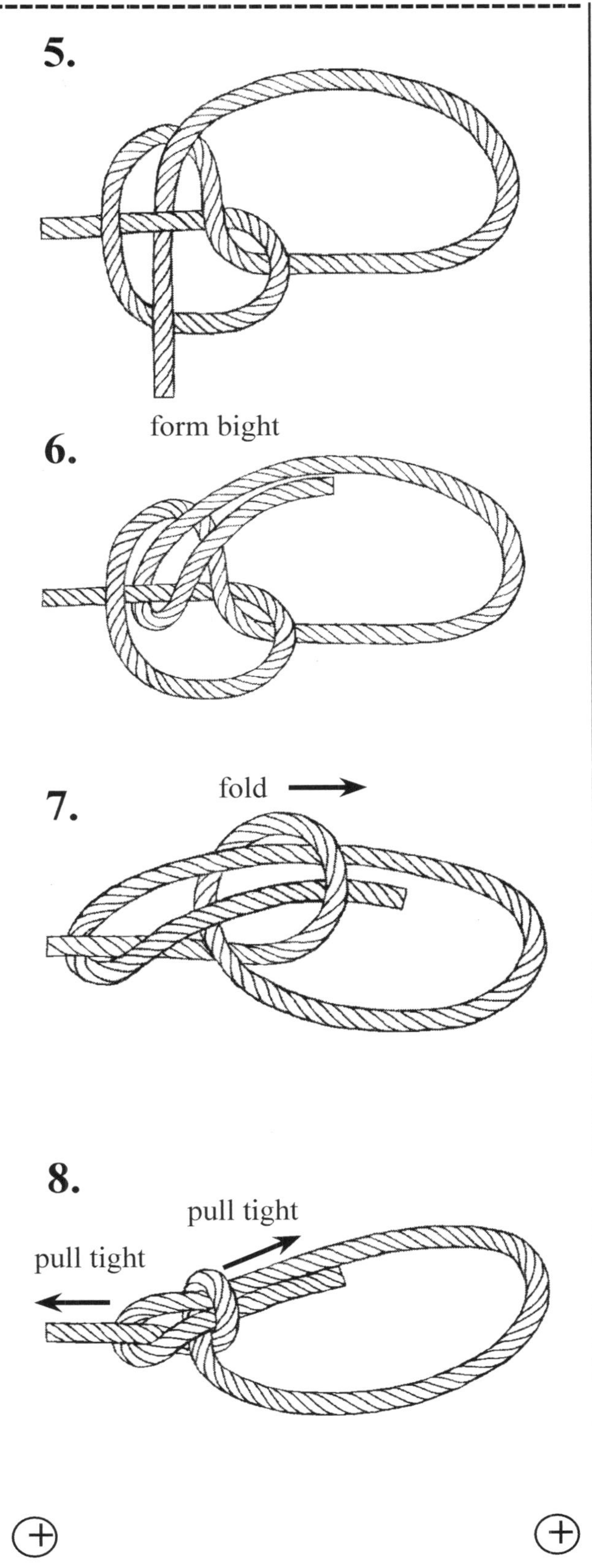

BOWLINE ON A BIGHT:

Description ---- A double loop Bowline tied by interlocking a doubled Half Hitch and a bight.

Use ---- As a nonslip double loop; as a loop any where along the length of a rope; as a secure loop for rescue work; as the start of a Life Basket Harness; as an emergency Boatswain Chair.

Comments ---- The Bowline On a Bight is a secure double loop that can be tied anywhere along the length of a rope. Can be used as a "dead eye" for tightening a rope when securing a load or guy line.

Narration ---- (For knotboard) **(1)** Take a bight in the rope. **(2)** Using the bight as the running part, make a double strand overhand loop. **(3)** Take the running part under the overhand loop. This forms a double strand loop that will become the eye of the knot. **(4)** Reeve the running part through the eye of the overhand loop. **(5)** Spread the eye of the running part (bight). **(6)** Pull the running part (bight) through the overhand loop until you can enlarge it enough **(7)** to pass it over the double strand bight. **(8)** When the eye of the running part (bight) is around the standing part, **(9)** grasp the double loop (bight) and the standing part and pull the knot tight.

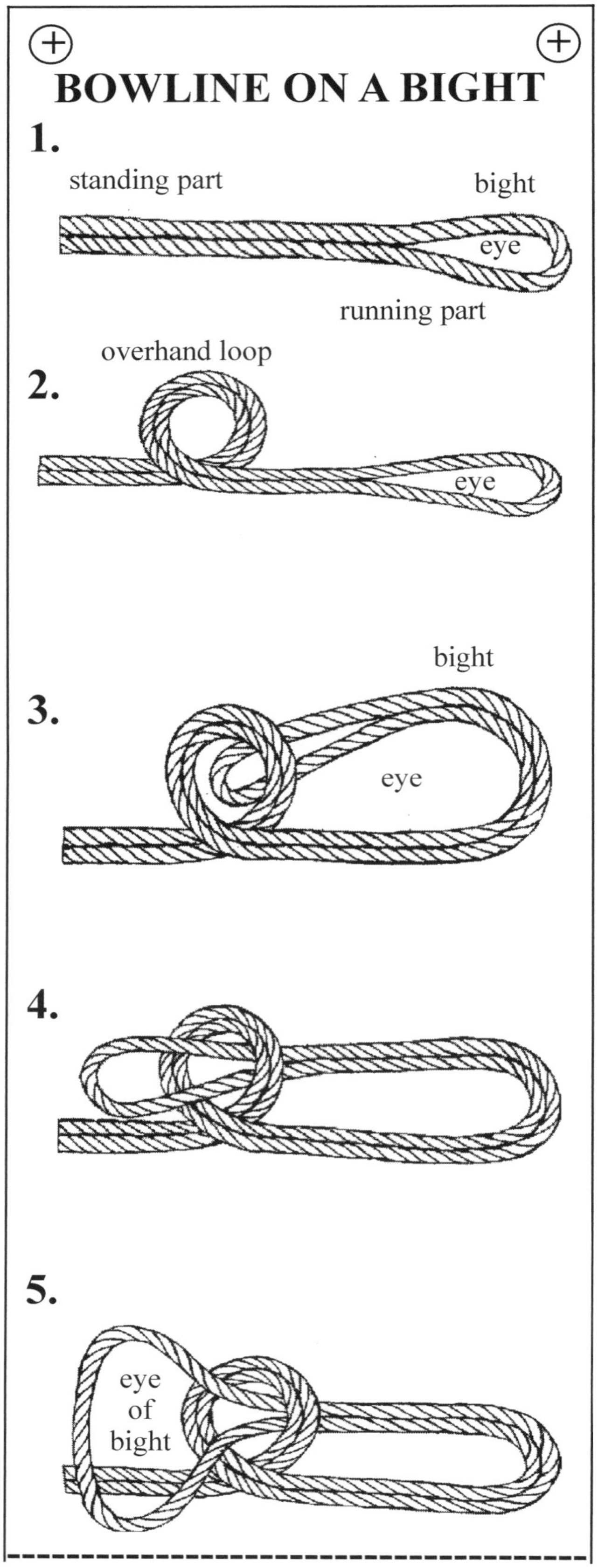

BOWLINE ON A BIGHT

1.

standing part

bight

eye

running part

2.

overhand loop

eye

3.

bight

eye

4.

5.

eye
of
bight

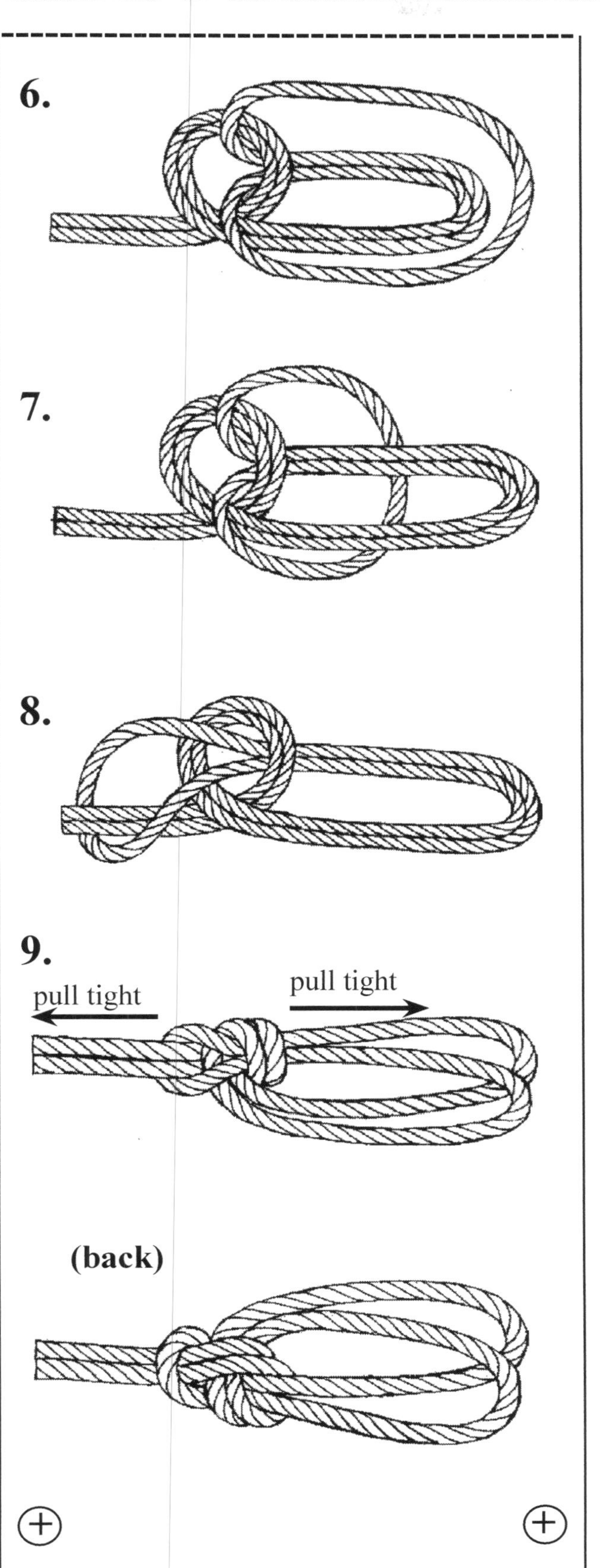

[NOTES]

FRENCH BOWLINE:

Description ---- A Bowline tied with a double strand eye.

Use ---- As a secure loop for rescue work; as the part of a Life Basket Harness; as an emergency Boatswain Chair.

Comments ---- The French Bowline is a secure double loop knot that can be tied in the end of a rope. The size of the loops can be adjusted by pulling on one loop or the other.

Other Name ---- Portuguese Bowline.

Narration ---- (For knotboard) **(1)** Form an overhand loop. **(2)** Form the first eye by taking a bight in the running part. **(3)** Pass the running part under the overhand loop and **(4)** reeve it through the eye of the overhand loop. **(5)** Form the second eye by forming a second bight parallel to the first bight. **(6)** Again, pass the running part under the overhand loop and **(7)** reeve it through the overhand loop a second time. **(8)** Pass the running part behind the standing part. **(9)** Reeve the running part back through the overhand loop and **(10)** pull tight.

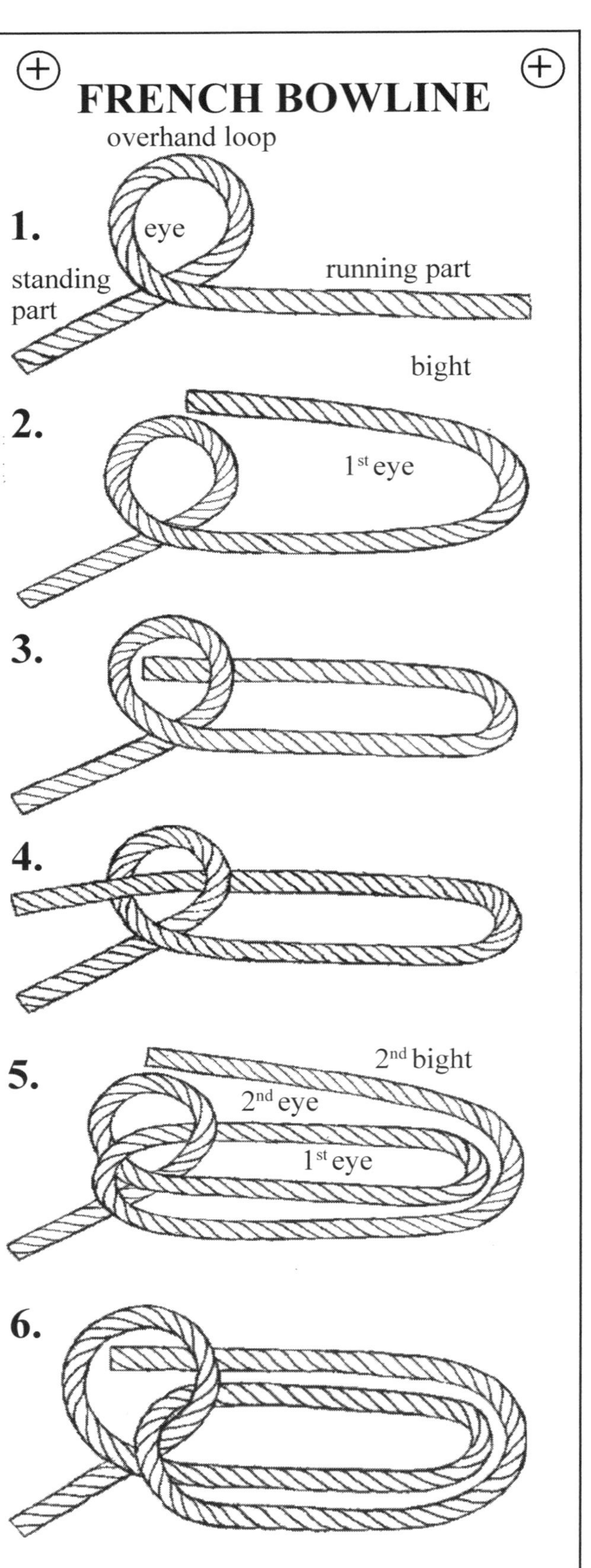

7.

8.

9.

10.

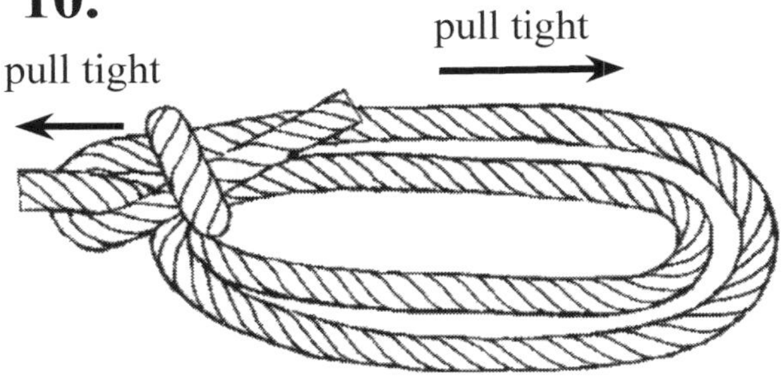

pull tight

pull tight

(back)

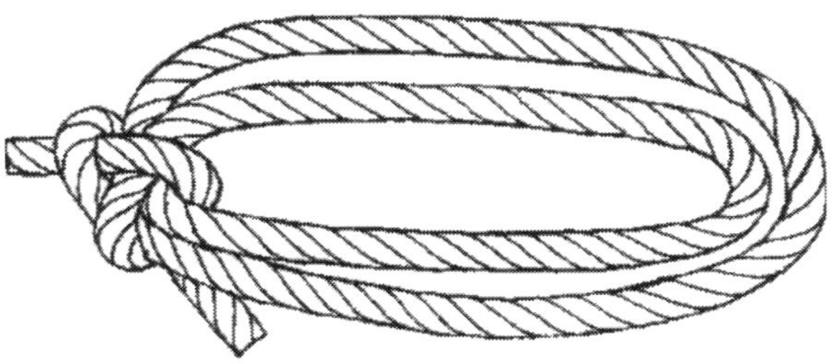

[NOTES]

LINEMAN'S LOOP:

Description ---- A single loop on a bight that resembles two Bowlines meshed together.

Use ---- As a secure loop for rescue work and mountaineering; as a loop to be used as a "man harness".

Comments ---- The Lineman's Loop is a secure single loop knot that can be tied on a bight anywhere along the length of a rope. The Lineman's Loop has many similarities in its structure to the Bowline. Because of the mirror image structure of the Lineman's Loop, it can be loaded along either side of the loop and it will not jam or spill. The fact that it will not jam or distort makes the Lineman's Loop one of the best single loop knots that can be tied on a bight. In addition, it is easily untied in the same way that a Bowline can be untied.

Other Names ---- Alpine Butterfly Knot; Butterfly Knot.

Narration ---- (For knotboard) **(1)** Form a bight in the rope. **(2)** Grasp the bight, give it a half twist; check to see that the twist is with the lay of the rope. **(3)** If the twist is with the lay of the rope, give the bight a second half twist. **(4)** Enlarge the eye of the bight and fold it back

LINEMAN'S LOOP

1. bight

2. 1/2 twist

3. full twist

4.

5. eye

6.

7.

8.

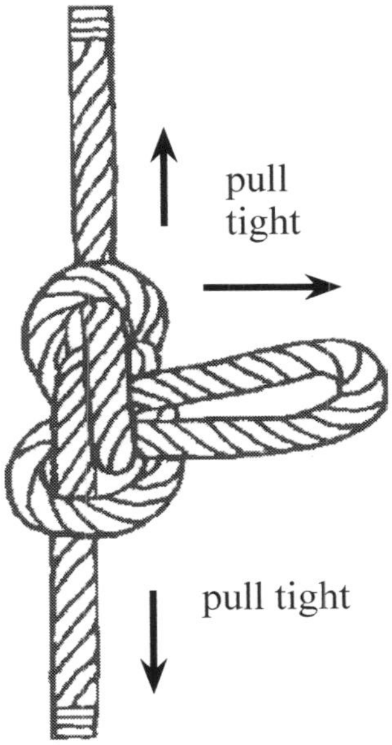

over the twist. **(5)** Enlarge the eye between the two cross-points of the twists. **(6)** Pull the bight under the first cross-point of the twists. **(7)** Then, reeve the bight through the eye between the twists and over the second cross-point. **(8)** Pull tight by pulling on the loop formed by the bight and the two standing parts.

[NOTES]

SHEEPSHANK:

Description ---- Two bights, in opposite directions, held in place with a Half Hitch around each bight.

Use ---- To shorten a rope; to isolate a damaged length of a rope.

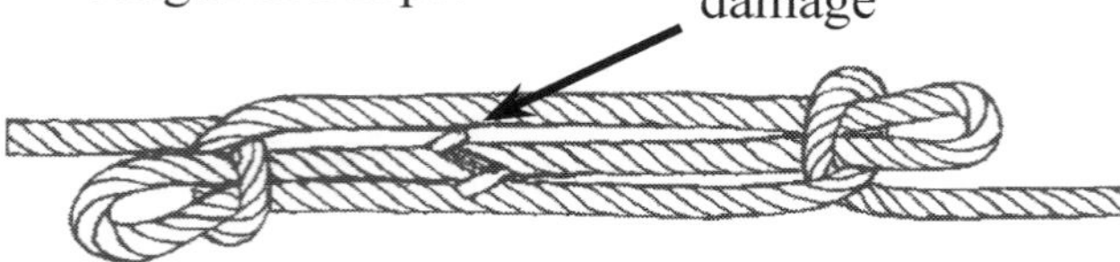

Comments ---- The Sheepshank is a secure knot that is easy to tie and untie. The rope is shortened by about twice the length of the Sheepshank.

If a heavy load is going to be placed on the rope, the Sheepshank can be made even more secure by adding additional Half Hitches to each end of the knot.

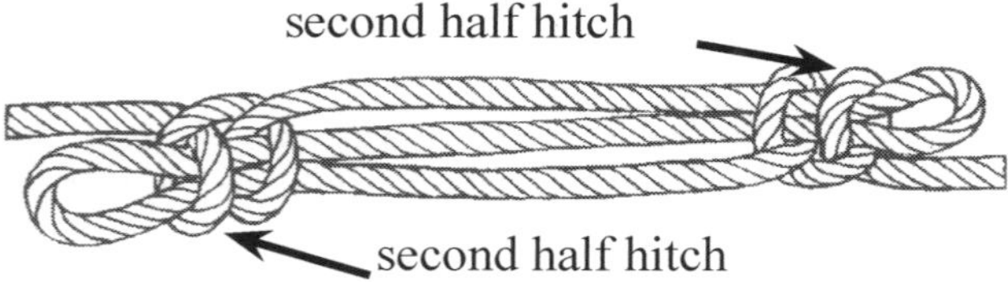

When a Sheepshank is to be left in a rope for a long time and you wish to ensure that the knot will remain secure and will not be accidently spilled, the bight at each end can be toggled or seized to the standing part.

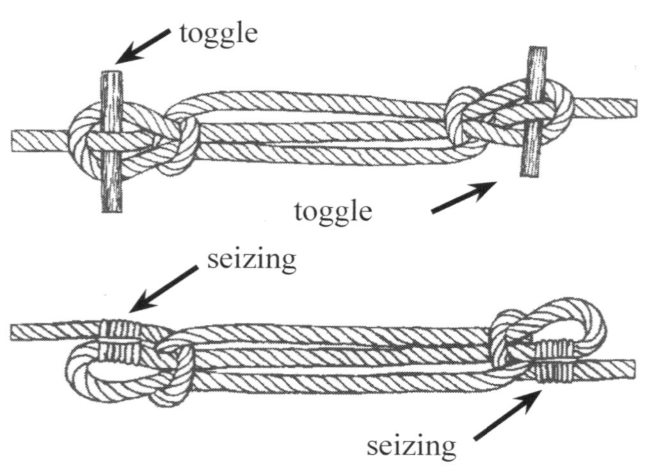

SHEEPSHANK

1.

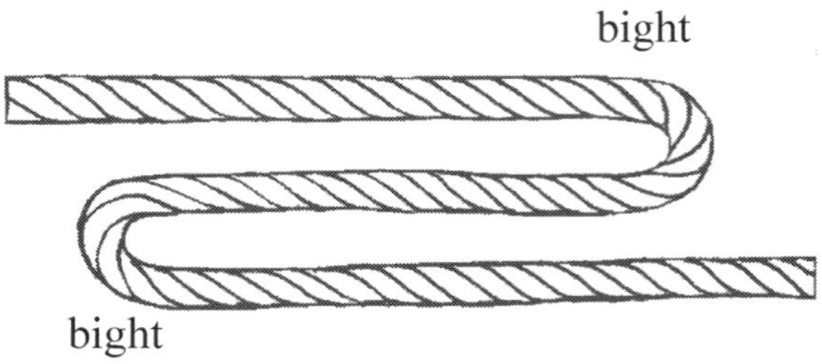

bight

bight

2.

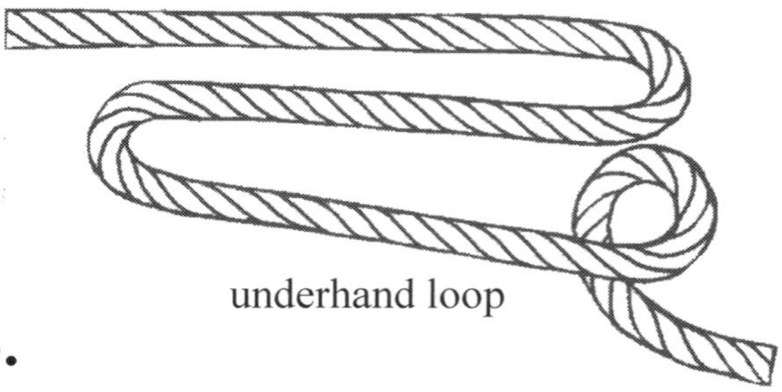

underhand loop

3.

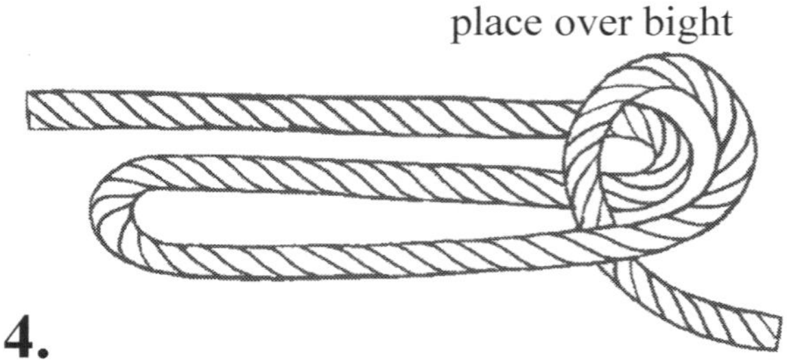

place over bight

4.

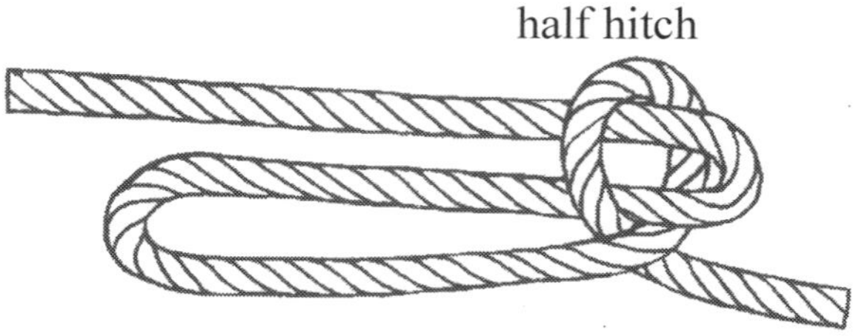

half hitch

5. 2nd underhand loop

6. place over bight

7. 2nd half hitch

8. pull tight ←

→ pull tight

SHEEPSHANK:

Comments ---- This method of tying the Sheepshank allows you to tie it at any length. Also, when heavy rope is being used, this method allows you to lay the knot out on the ground as you tie it.

Narration ---- (For knotboard) **(1)** Fold the rope over on itself so that you have a bight in each direction. **(2)** Make an underhand loop at one end. **(3)** Place the underhand loop over the bight. **(4)** Reeve the bight through the underhand loop to form a Half Hitch around the bight. **(5)** Make a second underhand loop at the other end. **(6)** Place the second underhand loop over the bight at that end. **(7)** Reeve the bight through the second underhand loop to form a Half Hitch around the bight. **(8)** Pull tight.

TRUMPET KNOT:

Description ---- A Sheepshank with two of the strands between the Half Hitches crossed.

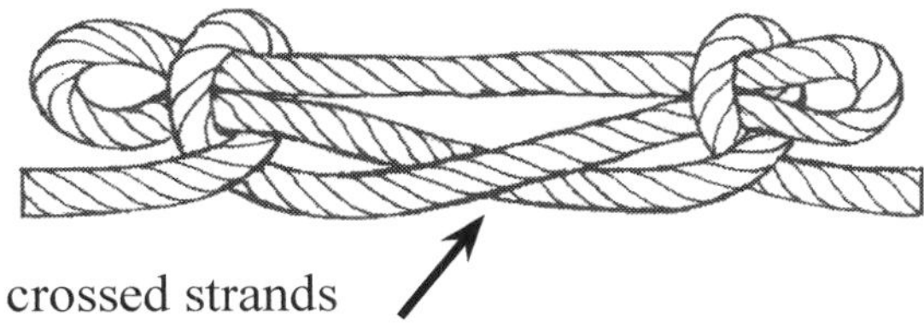

crossed strands ↗

Comments ---- The Trumpet Knot is a variation of the Sheepshank and can be used for the same purposes as the Sheepshank.

Narration ---- (For knotboard) **(1)** Form an underhand loop. **(2)** Form a second underhand loop and **(3)** place the edge of the second underhand loop over the edge of the first underhand loop. **(4)** Form a third underhand loop and **(5)** place the edge of the third underhand loop over the edge of the second underhand loop. **(6)** Reeve the edge of the second underhand loop through the eye of the third underhand loop so that the third underhand loop becomes a Half Hitch. **(7)** Reeve the other edge of the second underhand loop through the eye of the first underhand loop to form a second Half Hitch. **(8)** Pull the Half Hitches tight.

TRUMPET KNOT

1.

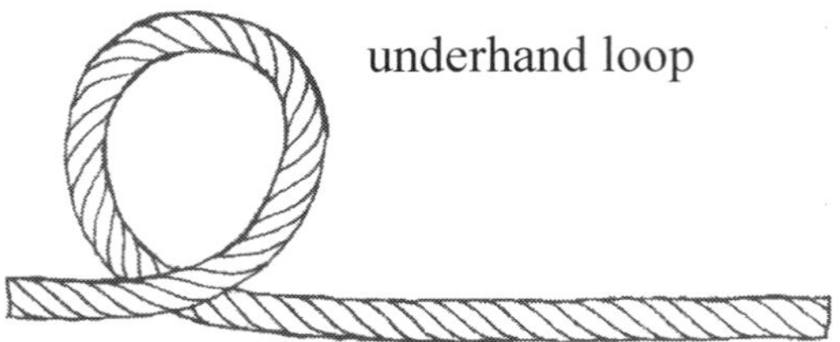

2.

3.

4.

5.

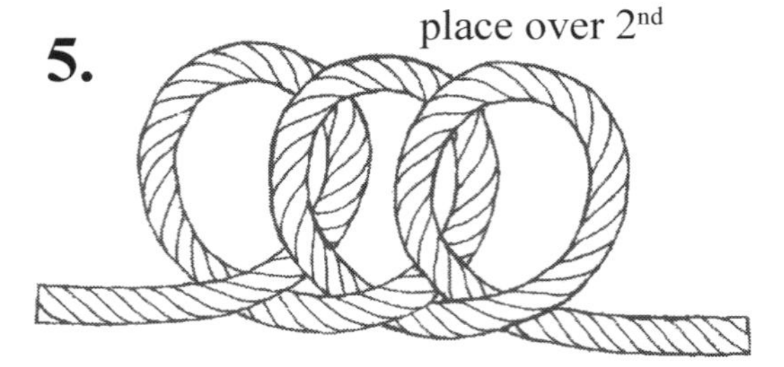

6.

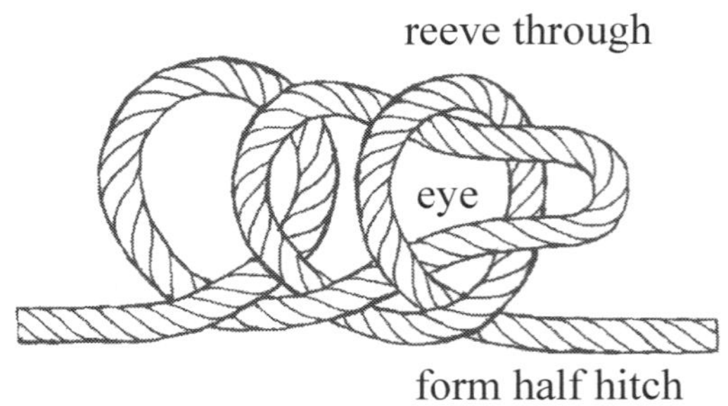

7.

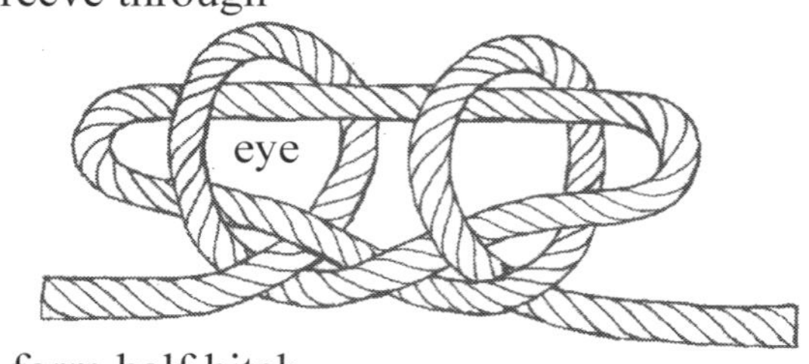

8.

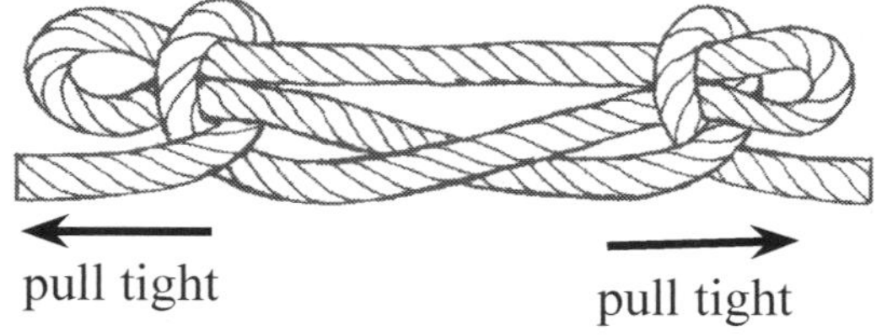

SHEEPSHANK: QUICK

Description ---- A Sheepshank that looks similar to the Trumpet Knot, but the ends can be rotated to remove the cross strands.

Trumpet Knot

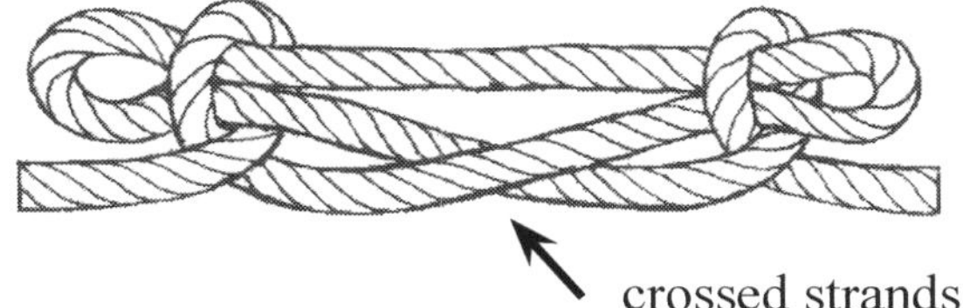

Sheepshank

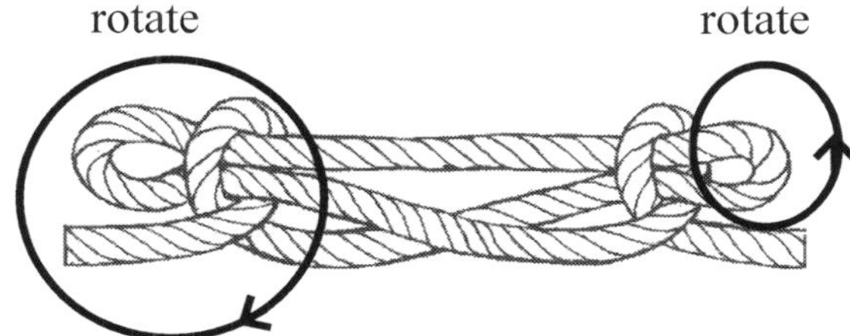

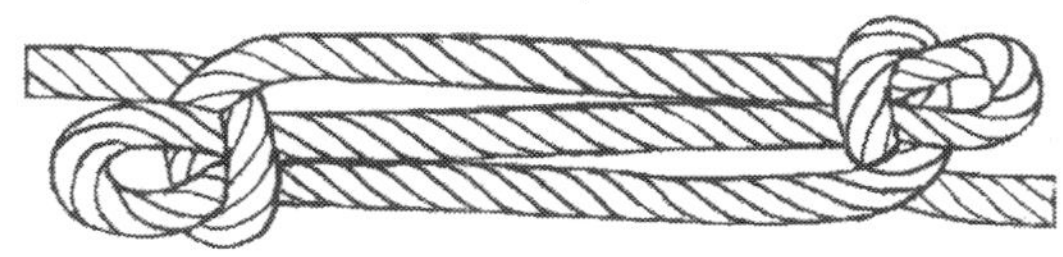

Comments ---- A Sheepshank that can be tied quickly but the resulting knot is usually short in length.

Narration ---- (For knotboard) **(1)** Form an underhand loop. **(2)** Next form an overhand loop and **(3)** place the edge of the overhand loop over the edge of the underhand loop. **(4)** Form a second underhand loop and **(5)** place the edge of the second underhand loop over the edge of the overhand loop. **(6)** Reeve the edge of the overhand loop through the eye of the second underhand loop so that the second underhand loop becomes a Half Hitch. **(7)** Reeve the other edge of the overhand loop through the eye of the first underhand loop to form a second Half Hitch. **(8)** Pull the Half Hitches tight.

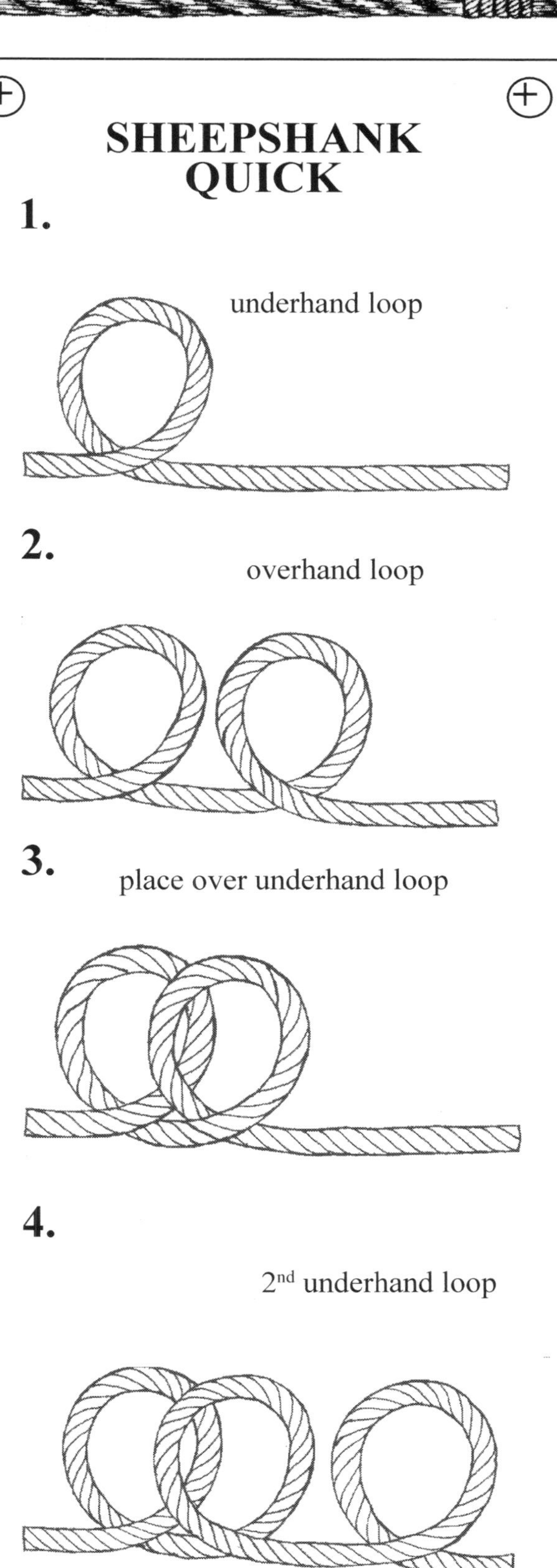

5. place over overhand loop

6.

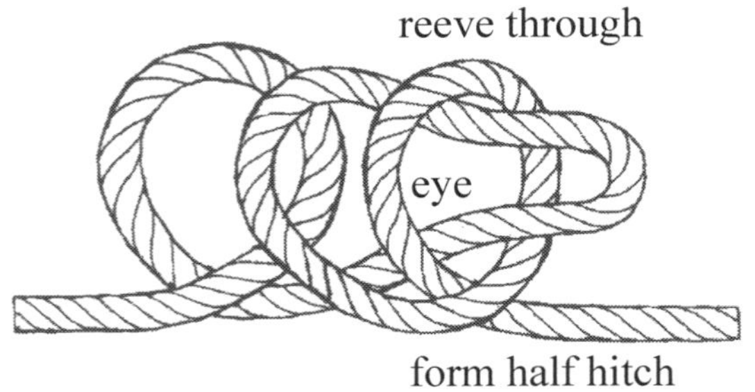

7.

reeve through

form half hitch

8. pull half hitches tight

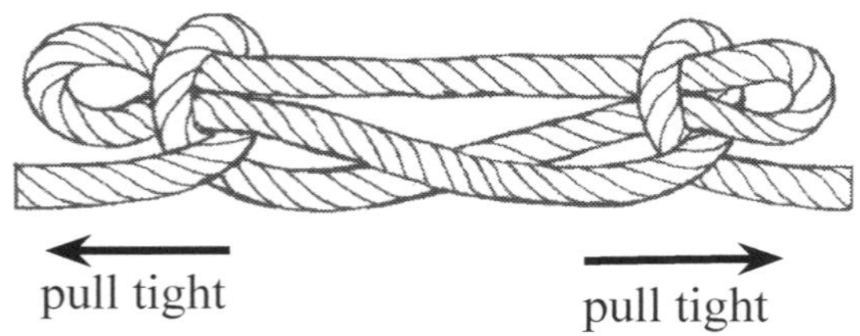

[NOTES]

CLOVE HITCH:

Description ---- Two Single Hitches (Half Hitches) tied in the same direction around an object.

Uses ---- To secure a line to a post or pole; to start and end most lashings.

Comments ---- Can be untied (spilled) by pulling on the standing part so that it rotates the cross-point in the knot until the cross-point goes over the end of the rope.

The length of the standing part can be adjusted by rotating the loops of the knot around the pole. To shorten the standing part, pull on the running end so that it rotates the cross-point toward the standing end. To lengthen the standing part, pull on the standing part so that the cross-point is rotated toward the running part.

Because the Clove Hitch can be spilled by rotating the standing part against the cross-point, the Clove Hitch will spill itself if it is tied so that the standing part moves back and forth in such a way that it causes the loops of the knot to slide around the pole. To prevent the Clove Hitch from spilling, 'stop' it by tying two Half Hitches around the standing part.

Narration ---- (For knotboard) **(1)** Start the Clove Hitch by taking a bight around an object with the running part. **(2)** Cross the running part over the standing part to form a Half Hitch. **(3)** Start the second Half Hitch by continuing to wrap the standing part around the object in the same direction as the first Half Hitch. **(4)** Form a second bight around the object. **(5)** Finish the second Half Hitch. **(6 and 7)** Grasp the standing part and the running part; pull the Clove Hitch tight.

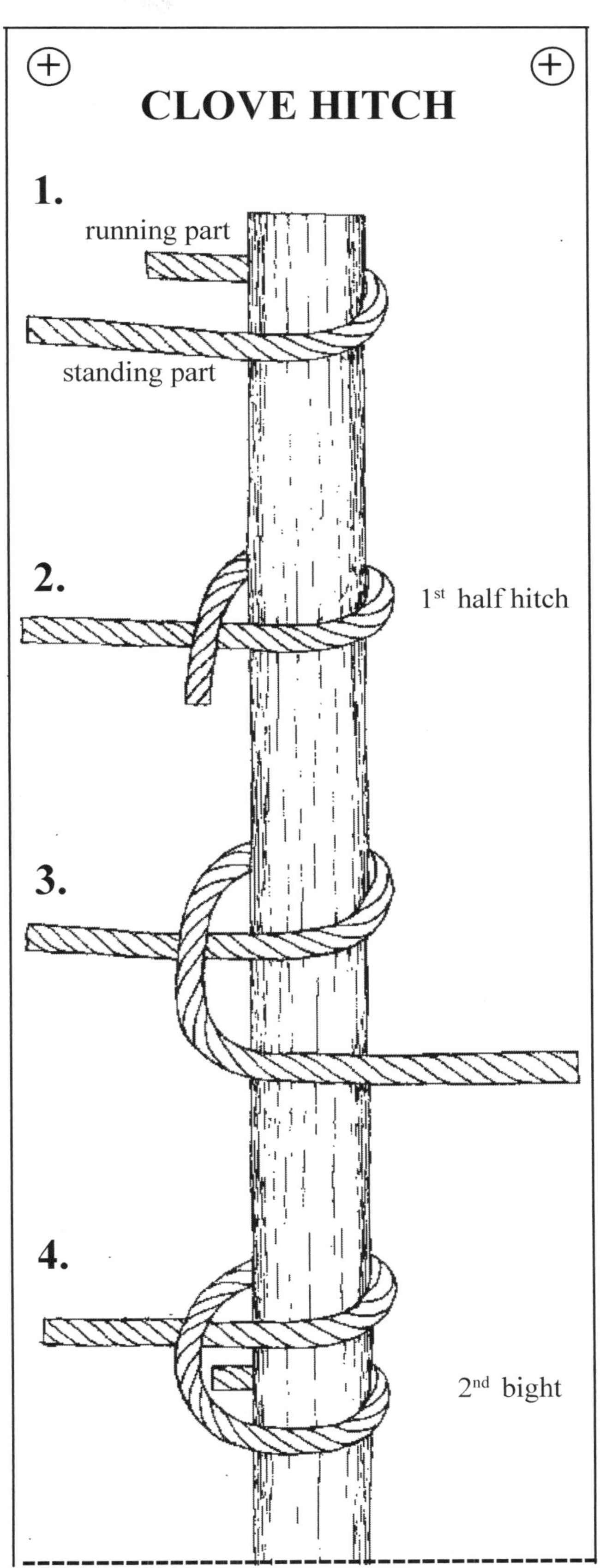

5.

2nd half hitch

6.

standing part

running part

7. (front)

pull tight

pull tight

(back)

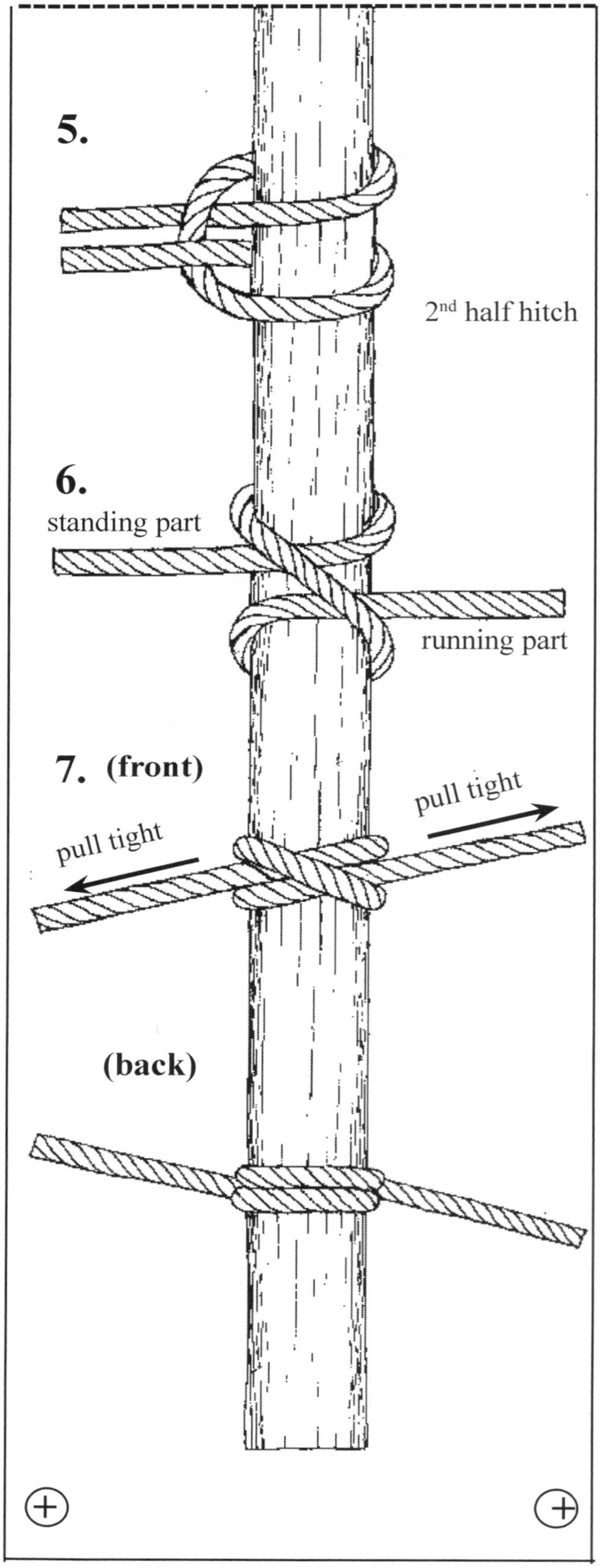

STOPPED CLOVE HITCH:

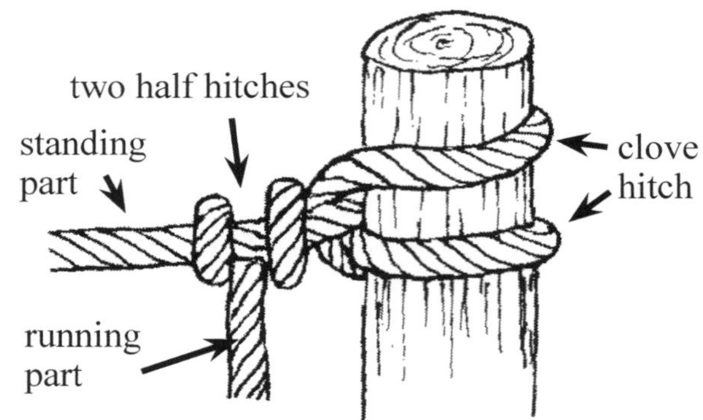

[NOTE] When under constant tension, the Clove Hitch has little tendency to slide along the length of the pole even if the tension is nearly parallel to the pole.

CLOVE HITCH: OVER AN END

A Clove Hitch can be tied over the end of a pole or stake by using this method.

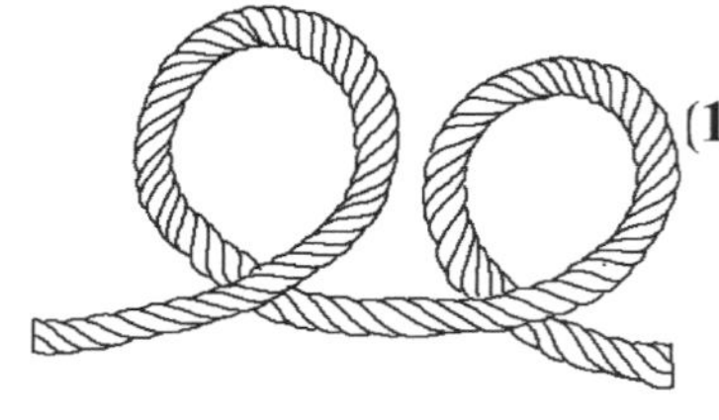

(1) Form two underhand loops in the running part of the rope.

(2) Place the right underhand loop on top of the left underhand loop.

(3) Drop the loops over the end of the pole.

(4) Pull tight.

CONSTRICTOR KNOT:

Description ---- A Clove Hitch with a Half Knot under the cross-point.

Use ---- To tie a smaller rope to a larger one, or to tie a rope to a stake or pole; a substitute for Whipping; as a lashing for light construction; as a hose clamp.

Comments ---- A secure nonslip knot; difficult to untie without cutting.

METHODS OF TYING:

Method # 1:

[NOTE] Use this method of tying the Constrictor Knot on either side of where you intend to cut a rope. This is a fast and easy way to prevent a rope from unlaying when it is cut.

Narration ---- (For knotboard) **(1)** Take a bight around a pole. **(2)** Continue wrapping the running part around the pole so that the running part crosses over the standing part. **(3)** Complete the turn around the pole. **(4)** Cross the running part over the standing part so that **(5)** a bight is formed around the standing part. **(6)** Reeve the running part under the cross part of the loop in the standing part to form a Half Knot under the cross-point. **(7)** Pull the standing part tight. **(8)** Lock the knot tight by pulling hard on both the standing part and the running part.

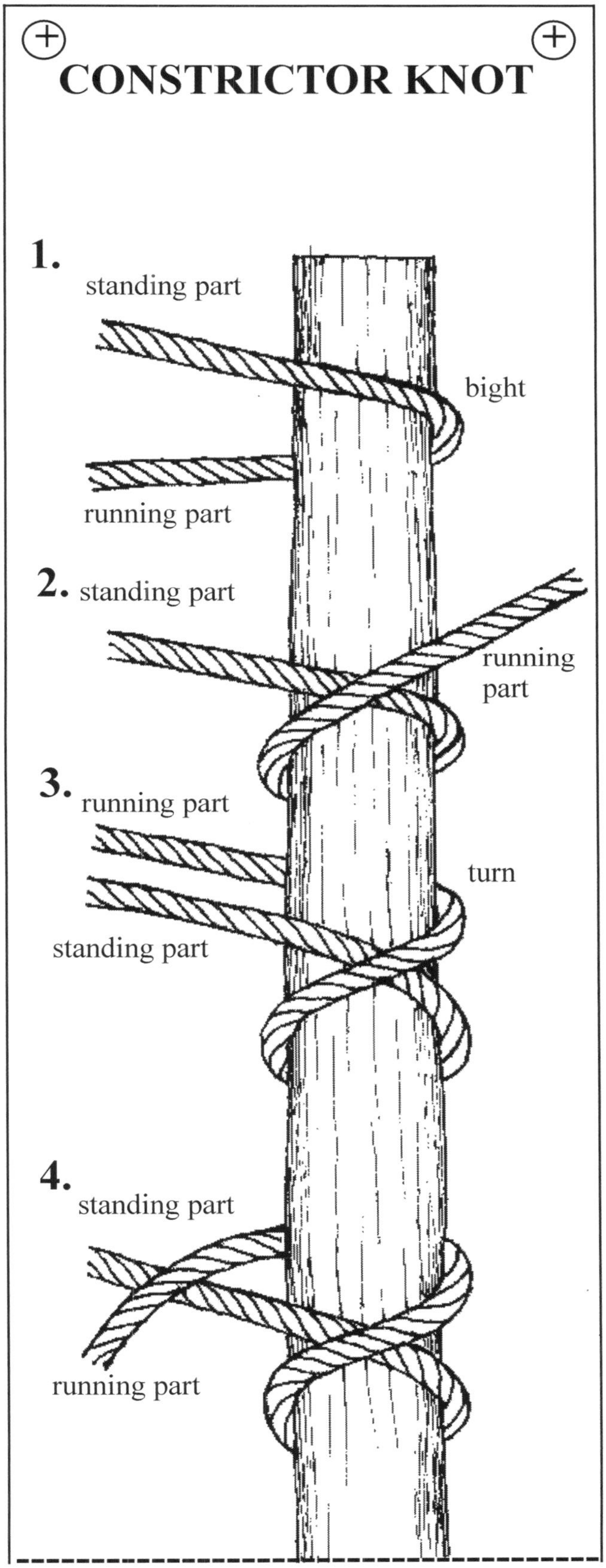

CONSTRICTOR KNOT

1. standing part

bight

running part

2. standing part

running part

3. running part

turn

standing part

4. standing part

running part

5.
standing part
bight
running part
6.
standing part
cross-point
running part
7.
half knot
pull
8.
pull hard
pull hard

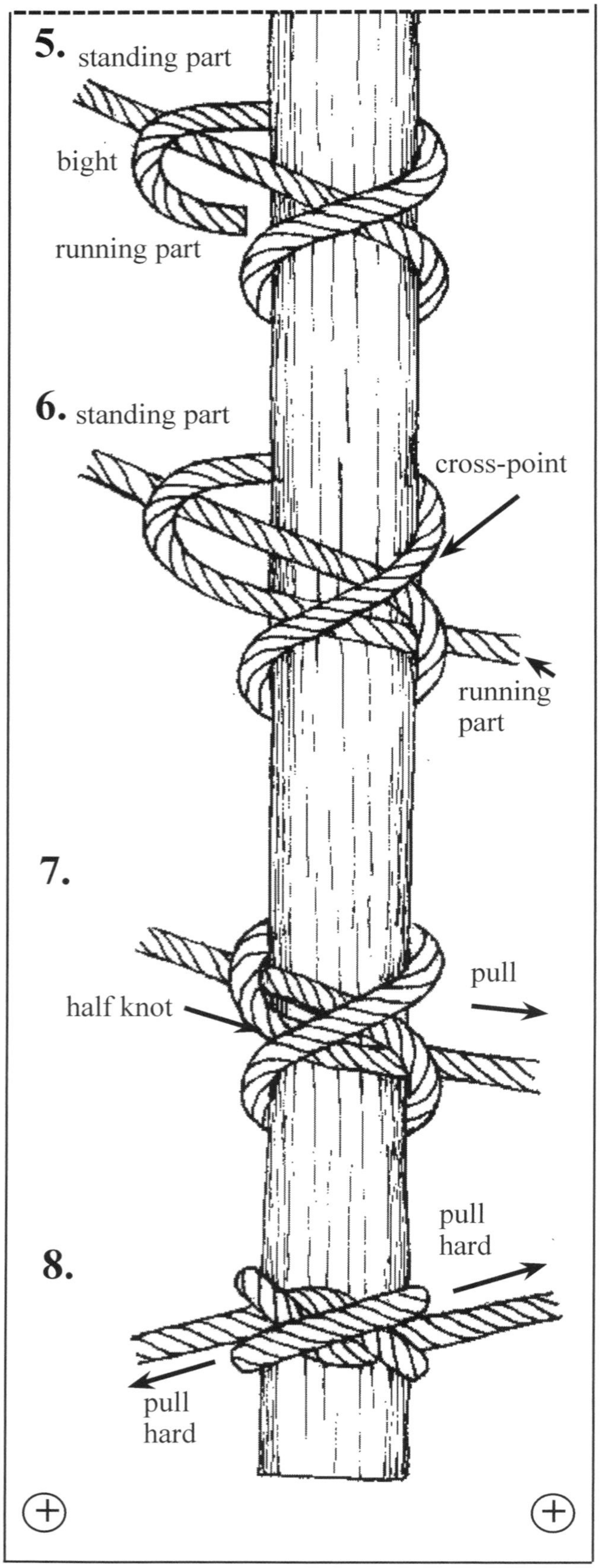

Method # 2:
Over the end of a pole or rope.

[1] Start with an underhand loop laid on the pole.

underhand loop

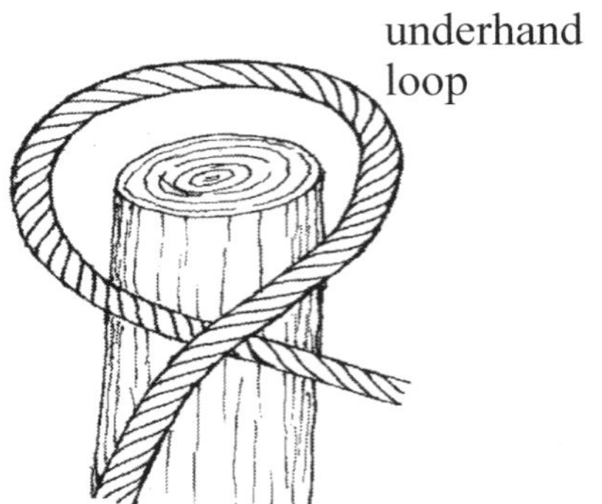

[2] Place the loop over the end of the pole.

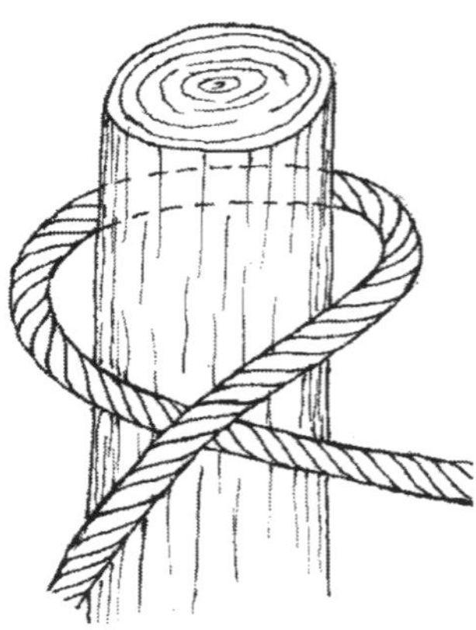

[3] Pull the back side of the loop down and under the cross-point of the underhand loop.

cross-point
down & under

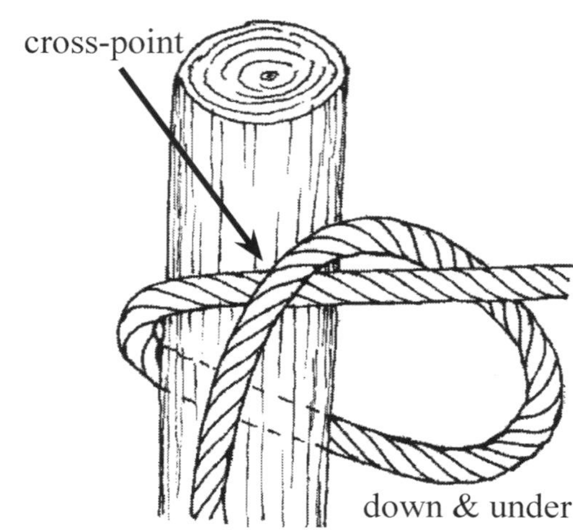

[**4**] Then pull it up and over the end of the pole **.....**

[**5**] **.....** to form a second loop around the pole and a Half Knot under the cross point of the knot.

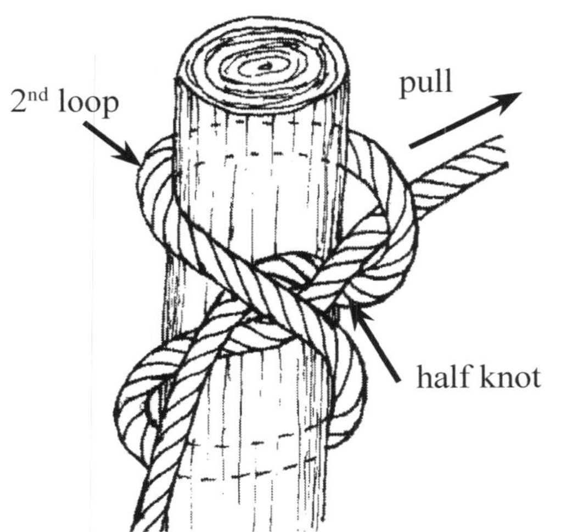

[**6**] Pull the two ends tight. The harder you pull, the tighter the knot.

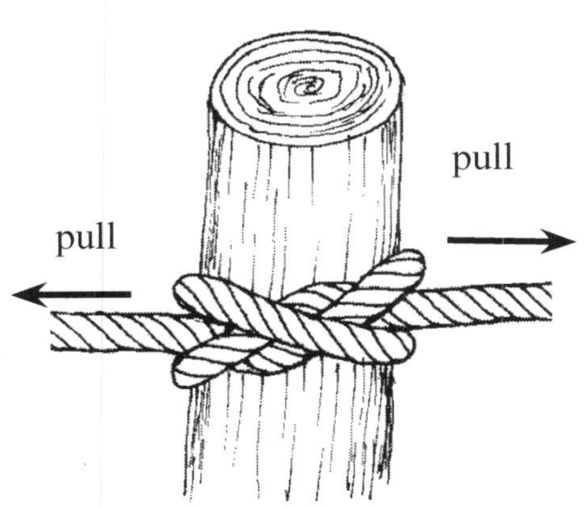

Slippery Constrictor Knot:

[NOTE] This method of tying the Constrictor Knot allows it to be untied quickly and easily.

Narration ---- (1) Tie the Slippery Constrictor Knot the same way as a regular Constrictor Knot but **(2)** form a bight in the running end before it is **(3)** reeved under the cross part of the loop in the standing part. Pull the standing part tight. **(4)** Lock the Half Knot tight by pulling hard on both the standing part and the running part.

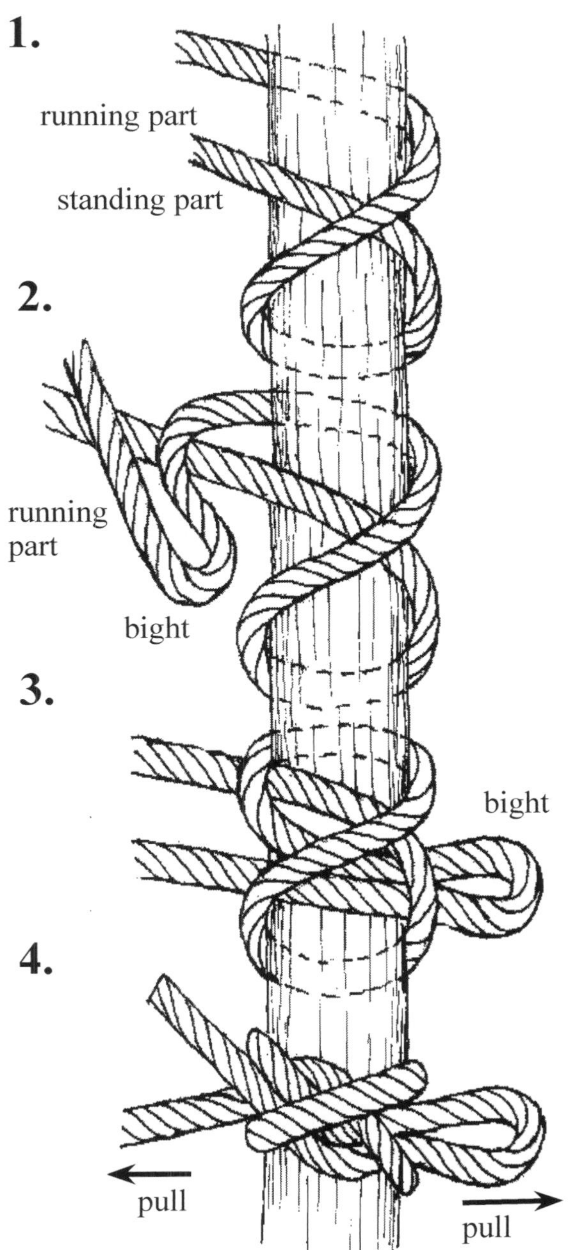

As a Lashing:

SUGGESTED USES:

whipping

spaced rungs

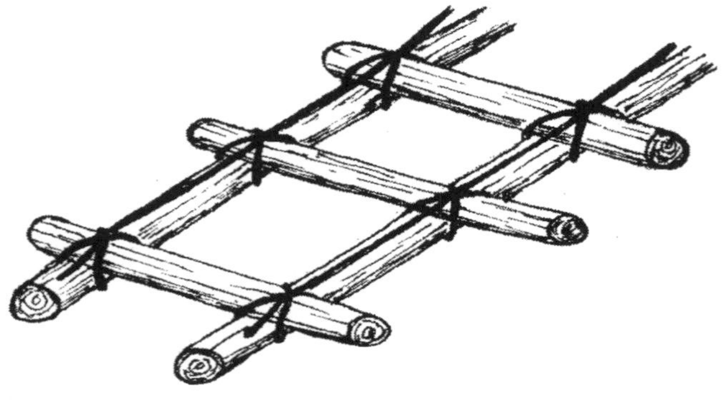

tying to a stake or pole

round lashing

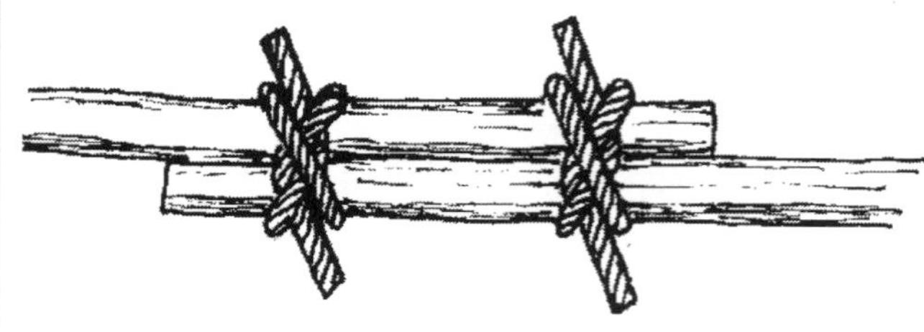

[NOTES]

TRANSOM KNOT:

Description ---- Similar to the Constrictor Knot but the ends of the rope go through the loops of the knot.

Use ---- To tie a smaller rope to a larger one, or to tie a rope to a stake or pole; a substitute for Whipping; as a lashing for light construction.

Comments ---- A secure nonslip knot; difficult to untie without cutting. The Transom Knot and the Constrictor Knot are closely related and can be used for many of the same things. The difference is in the tying of the Half Knot under the cross-point. In the Constrictor Knot the ends of the rope are between the loops of the knot. In the Transom Knot the ends of the rope go through the loops of the knot.

Narration ---- (For knotboard) **(1)** Take a bight around the pole. **(2)** Continue to wrap the rope around the pole so that the running part crosses the standing part. **(3)** Complete the turn around the pole. **(4)** Wrap the running part over the standing part a second time. **(5)** Form a bight in the running part so that the running part is parallel to the pole. **(6)** Reeve the running part under the cross-point of the loop in the standing part to form a Half Knot under the cross-point. **(7)** Lock the knot tight by pulling hard on both the standing part and the running part.

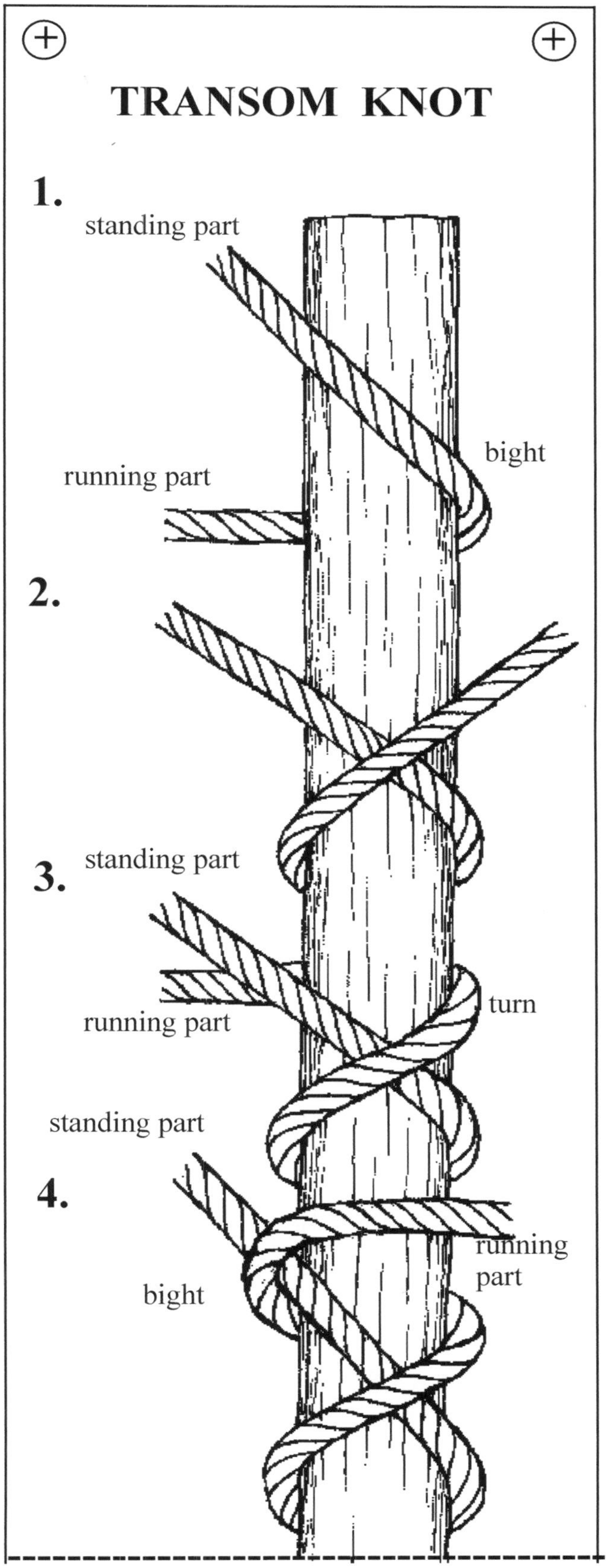

TRANSOM KNOT

1\.
standing part
bight
running part

2\.

3\.
standing part
turn
running part

standing part

4\.
running part
bight

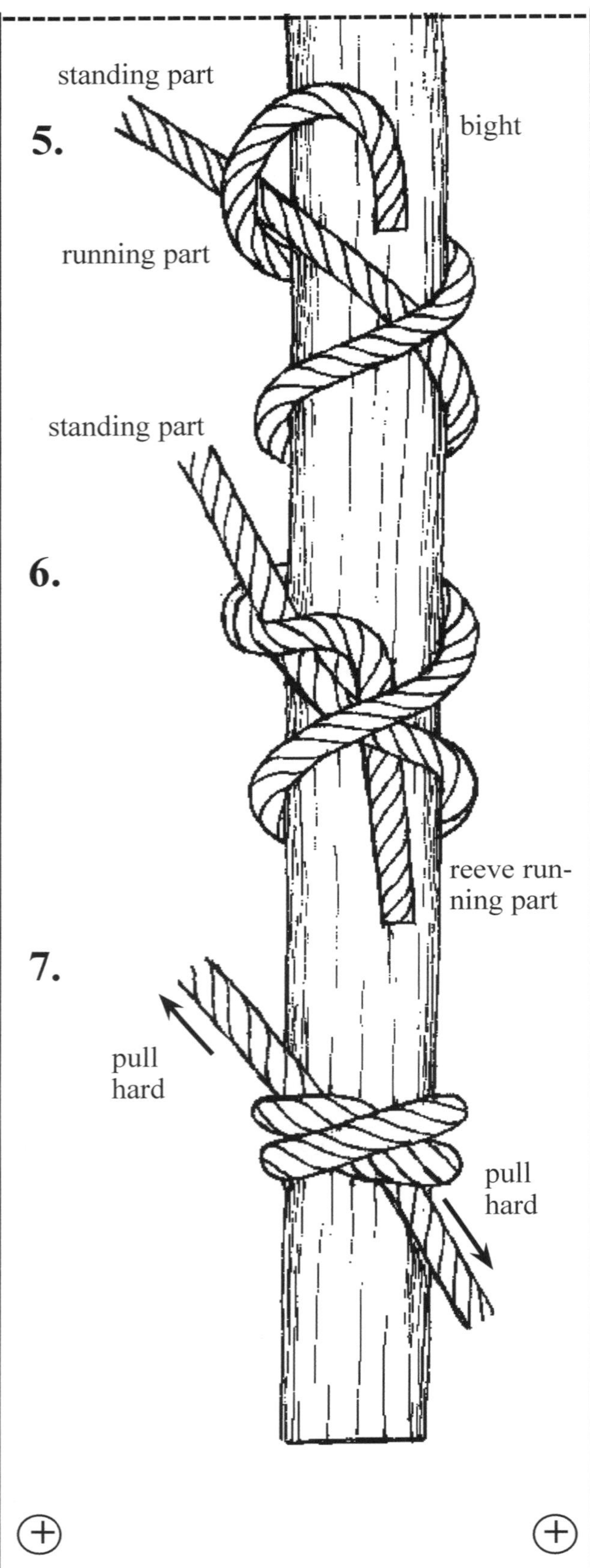
standing part
5.
bight
running part
standing part
6.
reeve running part
7.
pull hard
pull hard

[NOTES]

TWO HALF HITCHES:

Description ---- (1) Two Single Hitches tied around the standing part after taking a bight around an object. **(2)** A Clove Hitch tied around its own standing part.

Use ---- To secure a rope to a pole or other object.

Comments ---- Forms a loop that will close; a secure hitch if the force is directly away from the object that it is tied to, but tends to slip along the length of the object if the force is applied at an angle that is other than perpendicular to the object.

Narration ---- (For knotboard) **(1)** Take a bight around the pole. **(2)** Form the eye of the hitch by crossing the running part over the standing part. **(3)** Take a bight around the standing part. **(4)** Pass the running part through the eye of the hitch; this forms the first Half Hitch. **(5)** Pull the Half Hitch tight around the standing part. **(6)** Start the second Half Hitch by passing the running part over the standing part in the same direction as the first Half Hitch. **(7)** Take a second bight around the standing part. **(8)** Pass the running part between the bight and the first Half Hitch; this forms the second Half Hitch. **(9)** Pull the second Half Hitch tight around the standing part. **(10)** Finish the hitch by sliding it tight against the object.

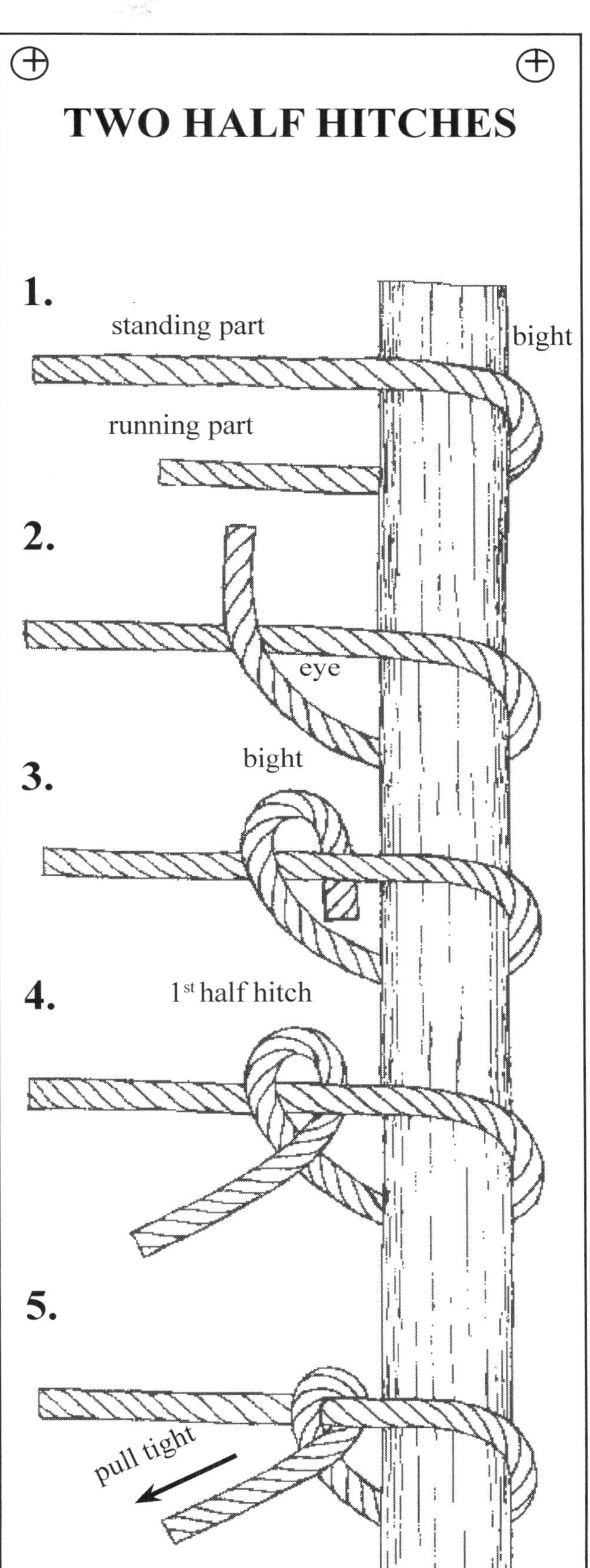

6.

7. bight

8. 2nd half hitch

9. pull tight

10. pull tight slide

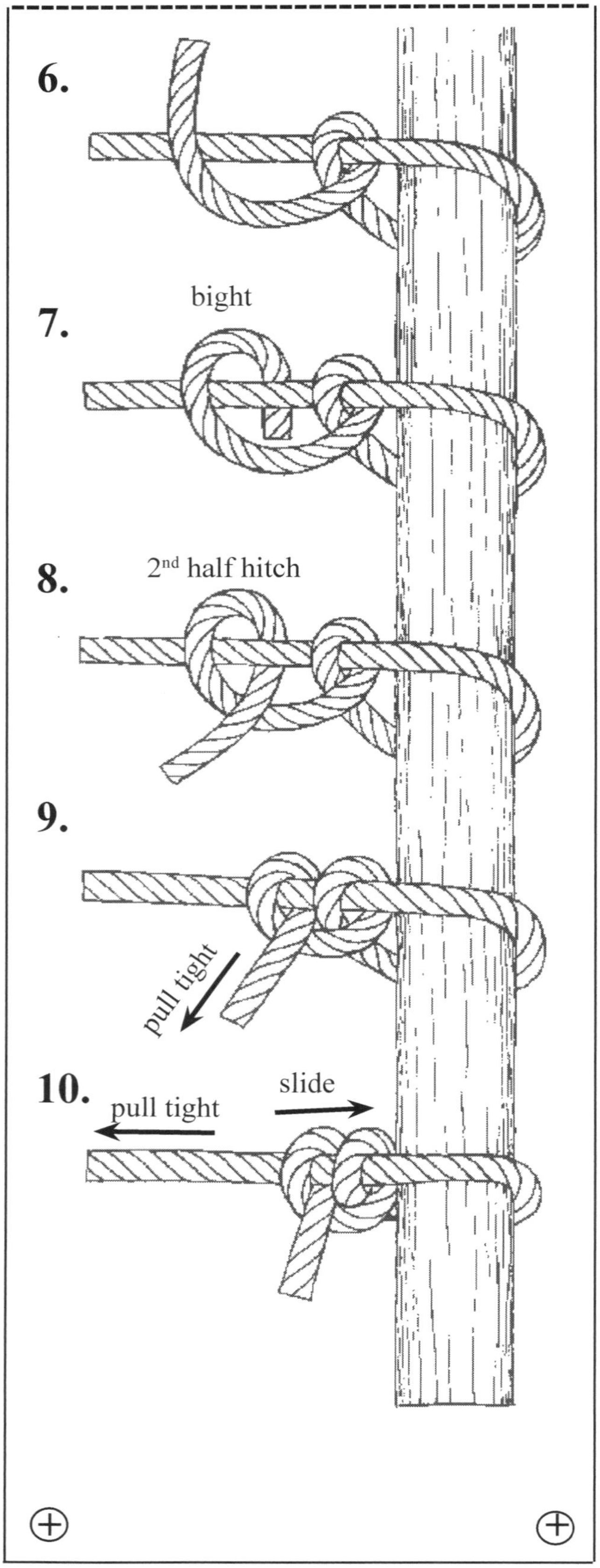

TWO HALF HITCHES: WITH ROUND TURN

Description ---- Same as Two Half Hitches, but with 1 complete turn around the object.

Use ---- To secure a rope to an object so that the rope does not slip along the length of the object.

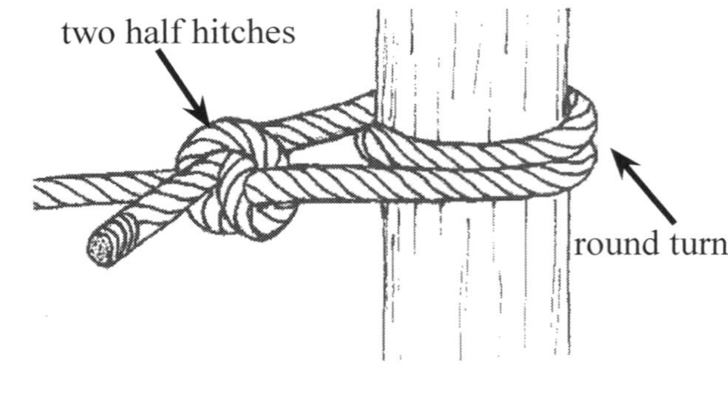

PIPE HITCH:

Description ---- Same as Two Half Hitches, but has 3 or 4 turns around the object.

Use ---- To secure a rope to a smooth object, such as a pipe or varnished pole, so that the rope does not slip along the length of the object.

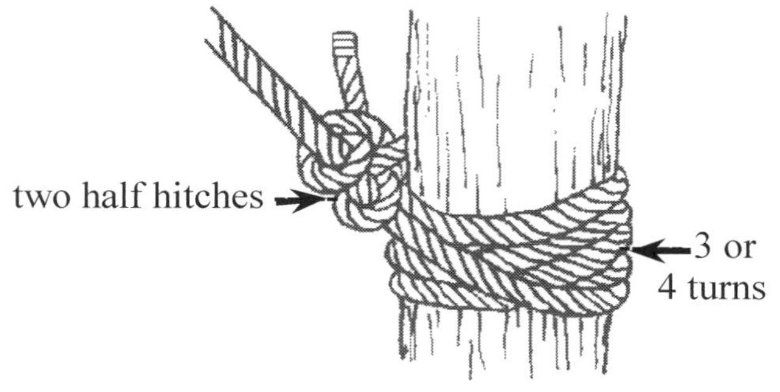

LARK'S HEAD:

Description ---- Two Single Hitches; one tied one way around an object and one tied in the opposite direction.

Use ---- To attach a rope or strap to a post, ring, or hook.

Comments ---- Easy to tie and untie; does not jam. Can be used in place of Clove Hitch but has a tendency to slip along the length or around the object it is tied to. The Lark's Head does not tighten around the object it is tied to like a Clove Hitch does, nor will it untie itself when rotated around a pole.

Other Names ---- Cow Hitch; Ring Hitch; when tied in a strap, Girth Hitch.

LARK'S HEAD: AROUND A POLE

Narration ---- (For knotboard) **(1)** Take a bight around the pole. **(2)** Form a Half Hitch by taking a bight around the standing part with the running part. **(3)** Take a second bight around the pole in the opposite direction to the first bight. **(4)** Reeve the running part through the bight that is around the standing part to form the second Half Hitch. **(5)** Pull tight to complete the knot.

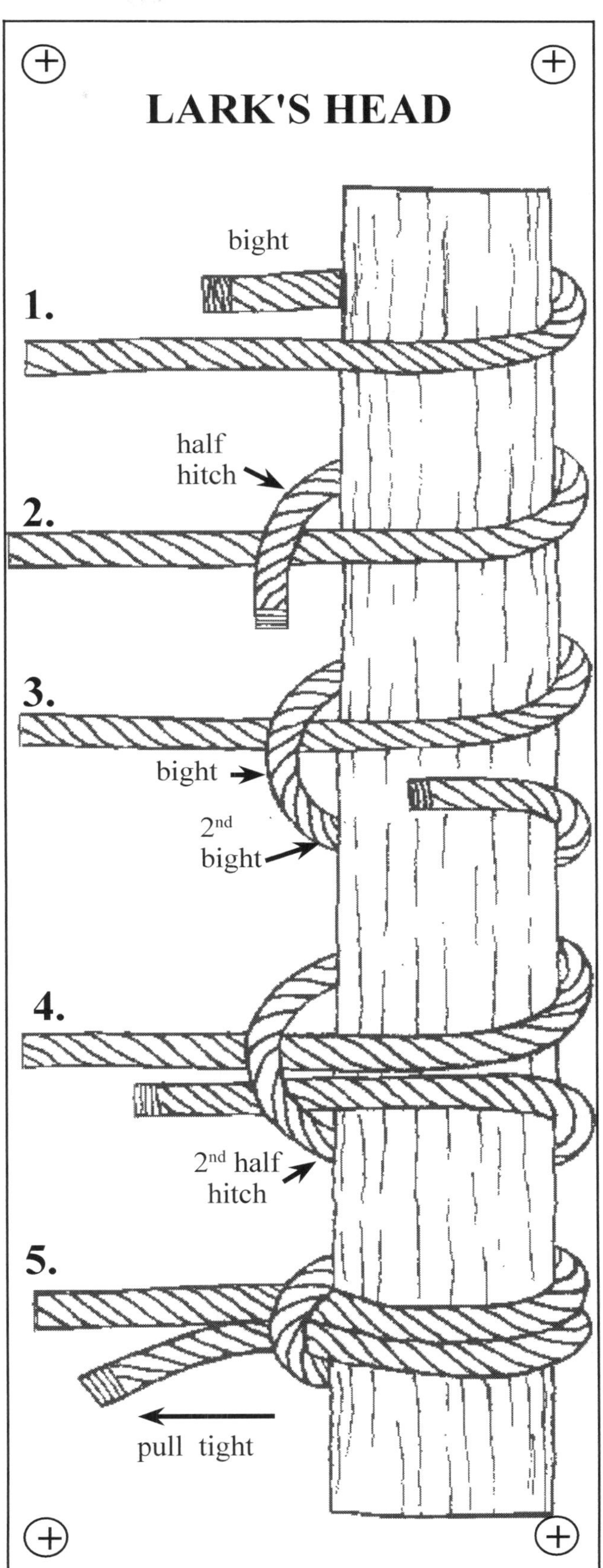

LARK'S HEAD: OVER AN END

(STEP 1) Form an underhand loop and an overhand loop in the rope.

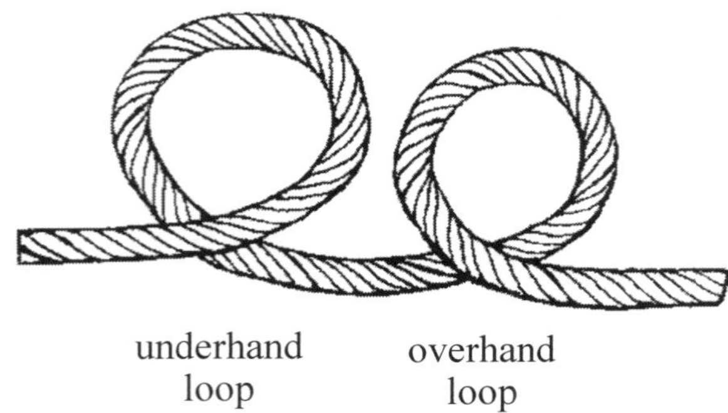

(STEP 2) Fold the loops together so that the rope between the loops forms a bight around both the standing part and the running part.

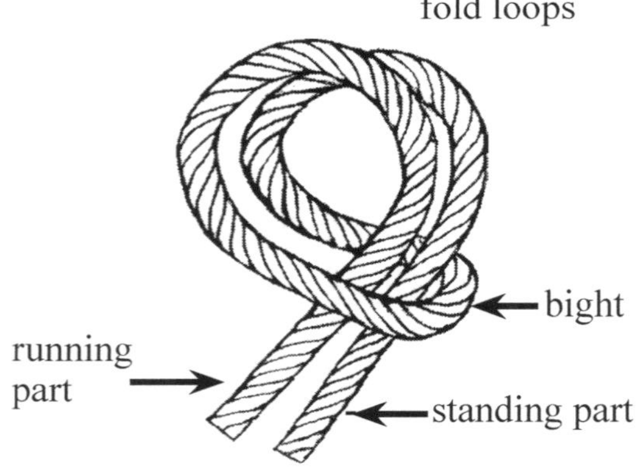

(STEP 3) Place the loops over the end of a pole and pull tight to complete the knot.

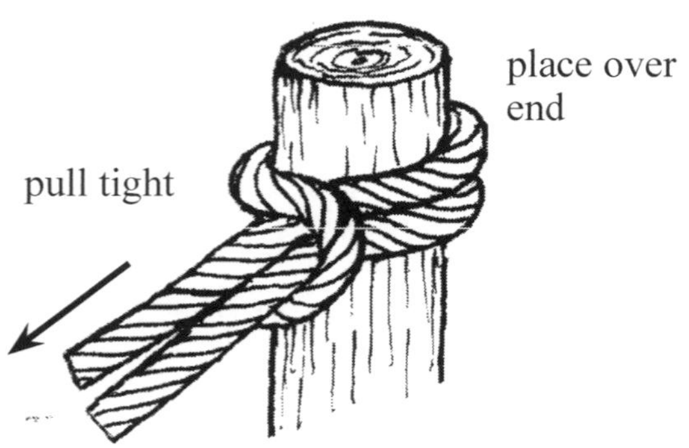

LARK'S HEAD: THROUGH A RING

(STEP 1) Form a bight in the rope and reeve it through the ring.

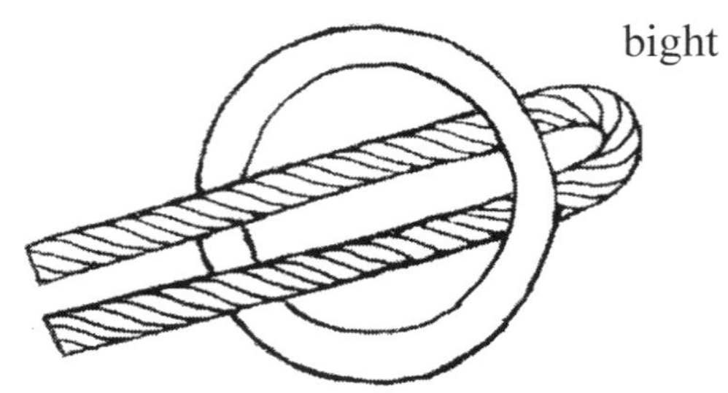

(STEP 2) Enlarge the loop formed by the bight.

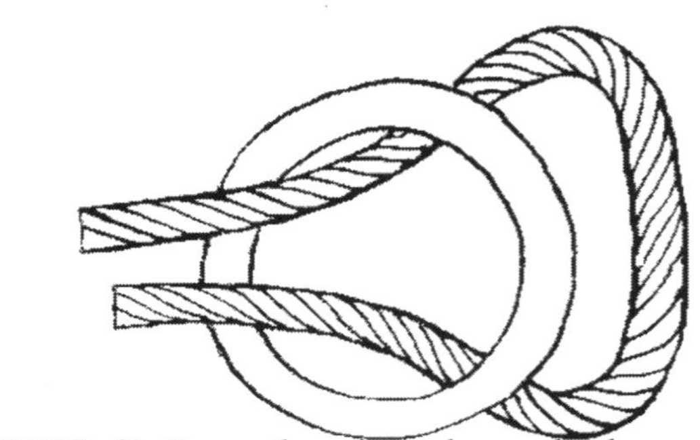

(STEP 3) Pass the ring through the enlarged loop.

(STEP 4) Pull tight.

GIRTH HITCH:

(STEP 1) Reeve the strap through the ring.

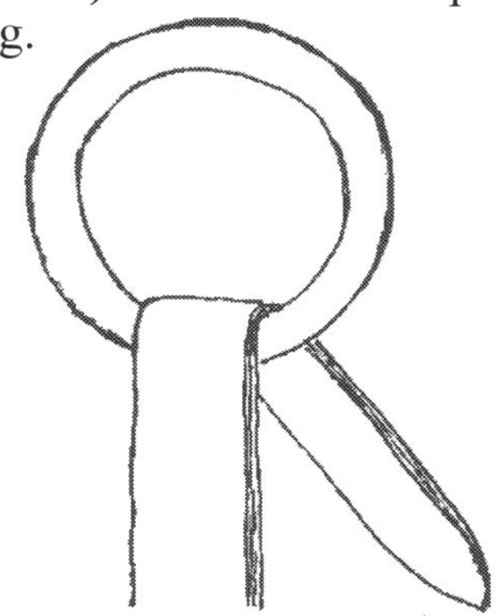

(STEP 2) Then take a bight around the standing part.

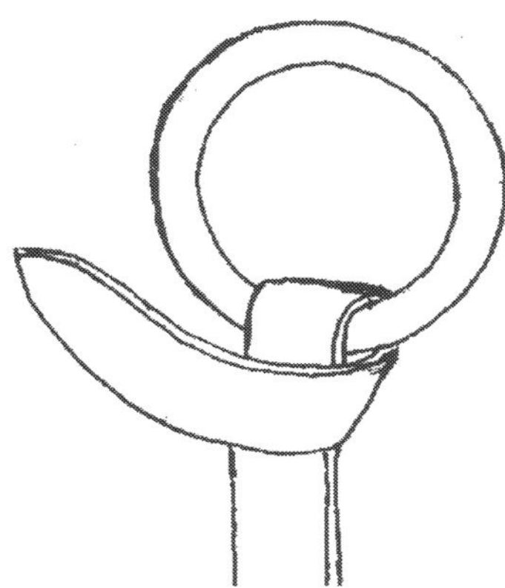

(STEP 3) Reeve the strap through the ring in the opposite direction.

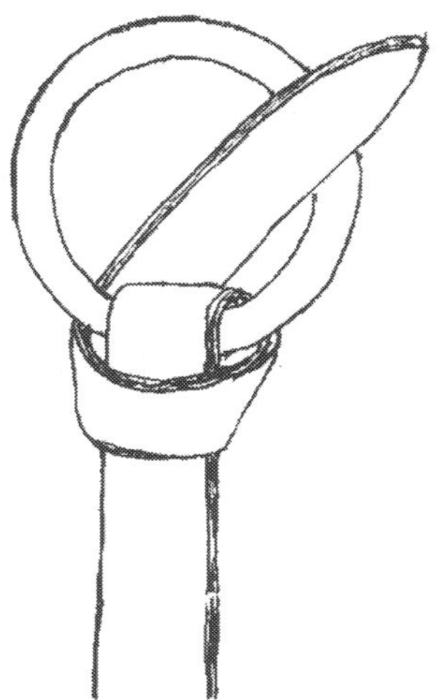

(STEP 4) Reeve the strap through the bight that is around the standing part and pull tight to complete the knot.

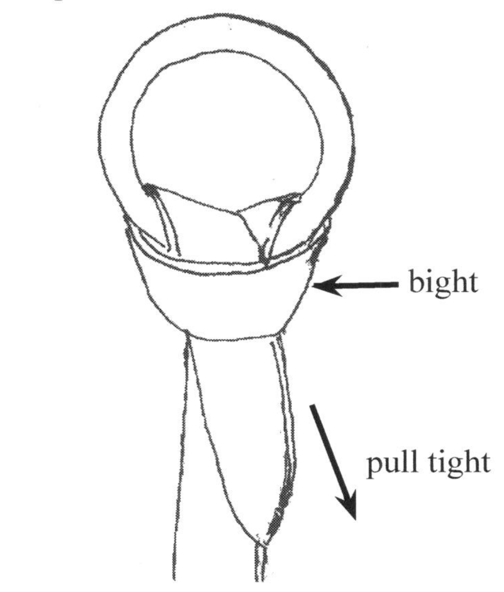

[NOTES]

TAUT-LINE HITCH:

Description ---- Two Half Hitches with an extra turn.

Use ---- To adjust the tension on a guy line.

Comments ---- The tension is adjusted by sliding the knot along the standing part of the rope.

To increase the tension on a guy line, grasp the standing part inside the loop, then slide the knot away from your hand.

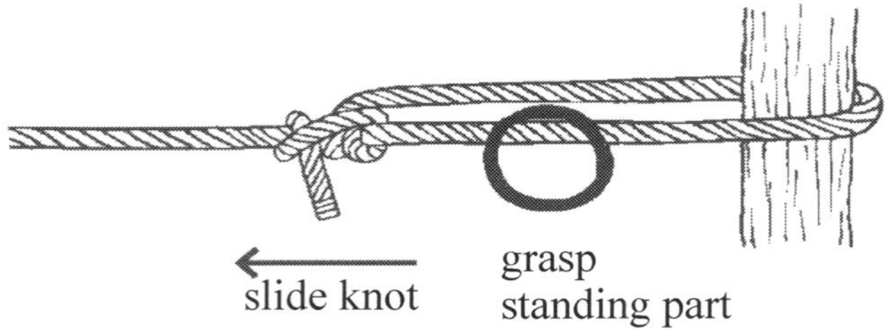

To decrease the tension on a guy line, grasp the standing part just outside the loop, then slide the knot away from your hand.

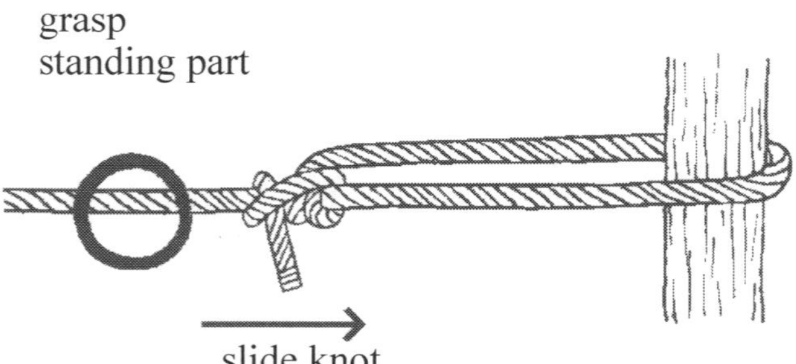

Other Names ---- There are several other names that are used interchangeably for the Taut-Line Hitch and several related knots. Rolling Hitch, Magnus Hitch, Midshipman's Hitch, and Adjustable Jam Hitch. The following seems to be the most common usage of these names:

(1) Taut-Line Hitch:

When tied around its own standing part.

(2) Rolling Hitch / Magnus Hitch:

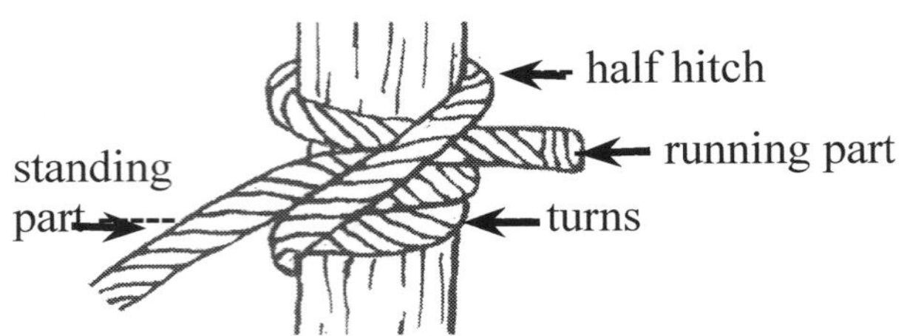

When tied around an object other than its own standing part ---- Rolling Hitch, Magnus Hitch.

(3) Midshipman's Hitch:

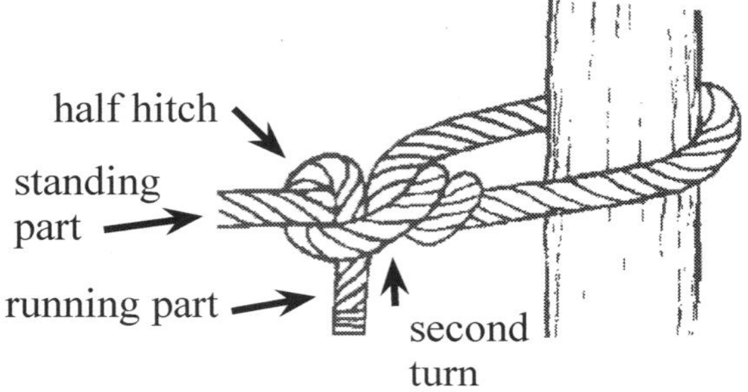

When tied so that the second turn is between the first turn and the standing part ---- Midshipman's Hitch (see direction for Midshipman's Hitch).

(4) Adjustable Jam Hitch:

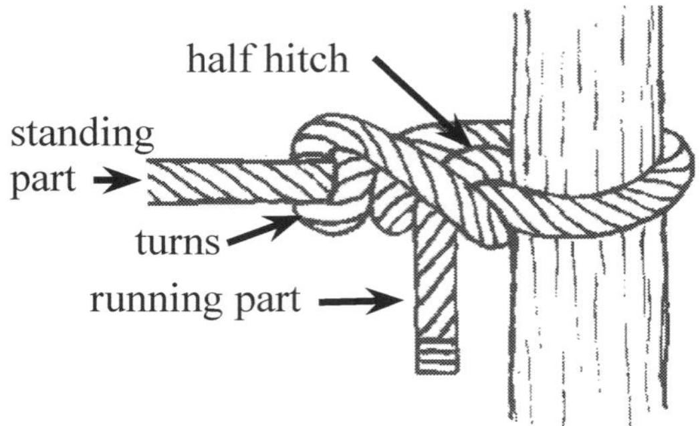

When tied with the two turns outside the loop and the Half Hitch inside the loop.

Use ---- To tie-up a bundle so that the knot can be tightened by sliding the knot toward the bundle and loosened by sliding the knot away from the bundle.

Narration ---- (For knotboard) **(1)** Take a bight around the pole. (The eye of the this bight becomes the eye of the Taut Line Hitch) **(2)** Take a bight around the standing part. **(3)** Pass the running part through the eye of the bight (between standing part and the pole). This forms a Half Hitch around the standing part; pull tight. **(4)** Take a second bight around the standing part in the same direction; **(5)** this results in two complete turns around the standing part. **(6)** Pull tight. **(7)** Go to the outside of the loop. **(8)** Take another bight around the standing part. **(9)** Pass the running part between itself and the first Half Hitch; this forms the second Half Hitch. **(10)** Pull tight.

[NOTES]

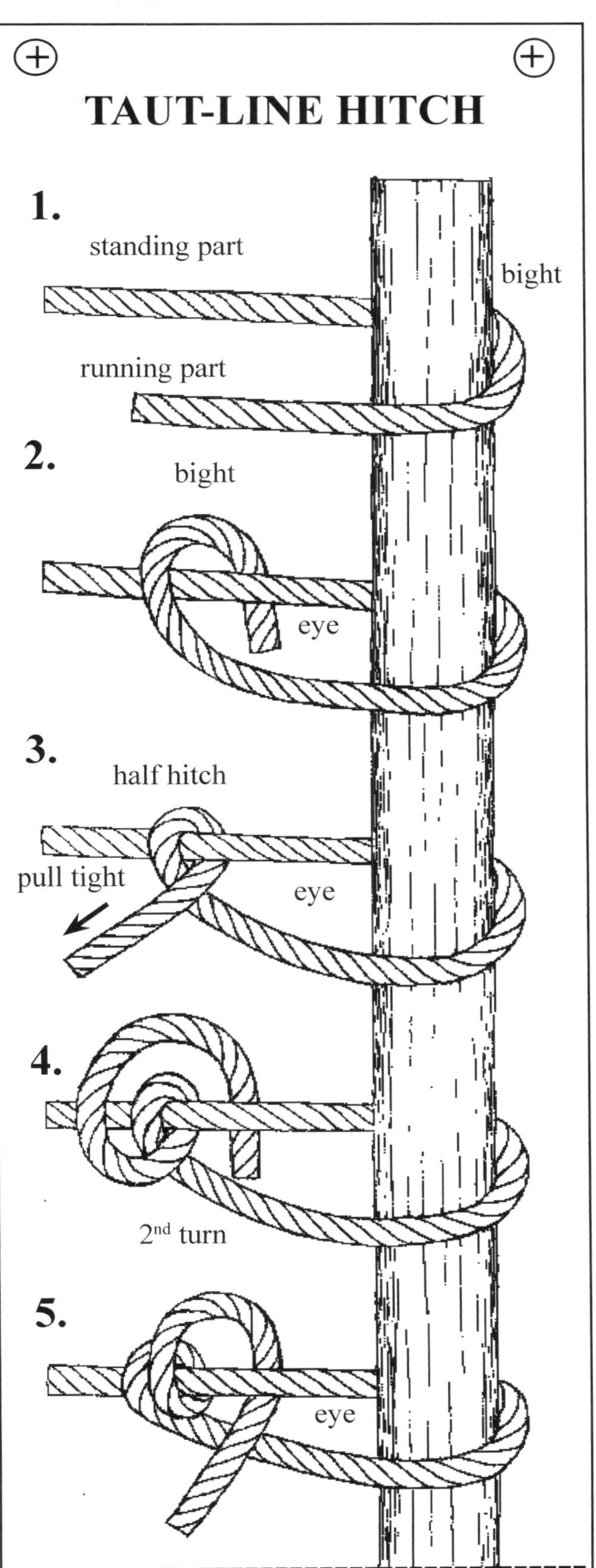

6.

pull tight

7.

8.

bight

9.

2nd half hitch

10.

pull tight

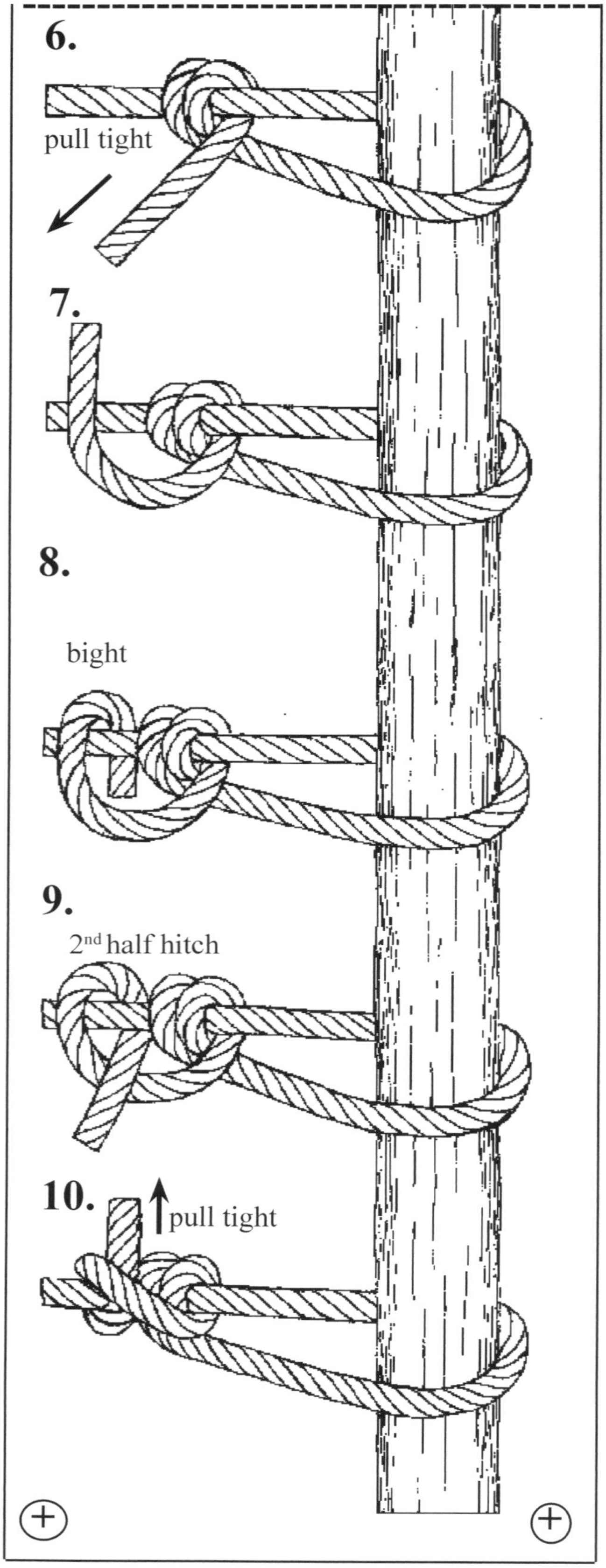

MIDSHIPMAN'S HITCH:

Description ---- Two Half Hitches with an overlapping extra turn.

Use ---- To adjust the tension on a guy line when very smooth rope is being used.

Comments ---- The Midshipman's Hitch is harder to adjust than the Taut-Line Hitch, therefore it is the ideal knot for adjusting the tension on synthetic rope guy lines.

Narrative ----

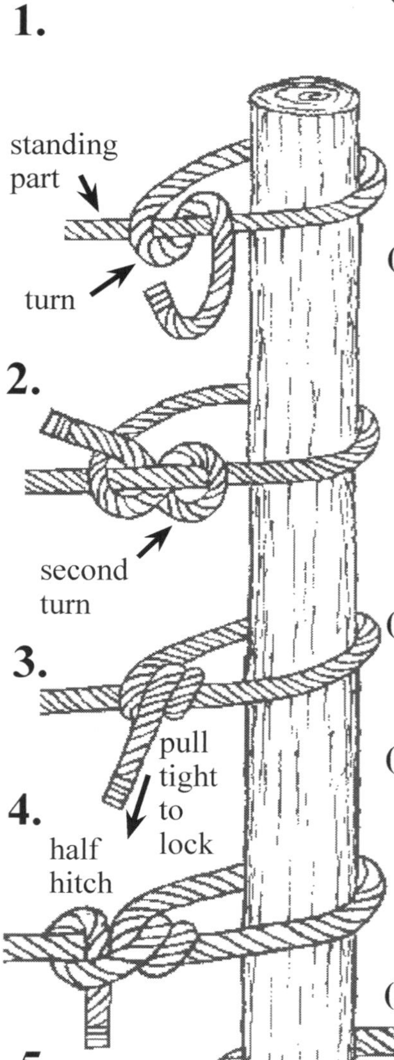

1.

standing part

turn

(1) After taking a bight around an object, take a turn around the standing part so that the turn is inside the loop.

2.

second turn

(2) Take a second turn around the standing part so that the running end crosses the first turn and is between the first turn and the beginning of the knot.

3.

pull tight to lock

(3) Pull the second turn tight to lock it in place.

4.

half hitch

(4) Take a Half Hitch around the standing part so that it is outside the loop.

(5) Opposite side.

5.

opposite side.

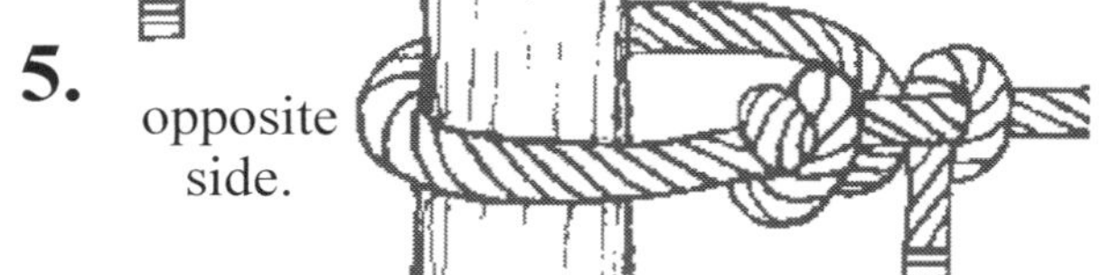

ANCHOR HITCH:

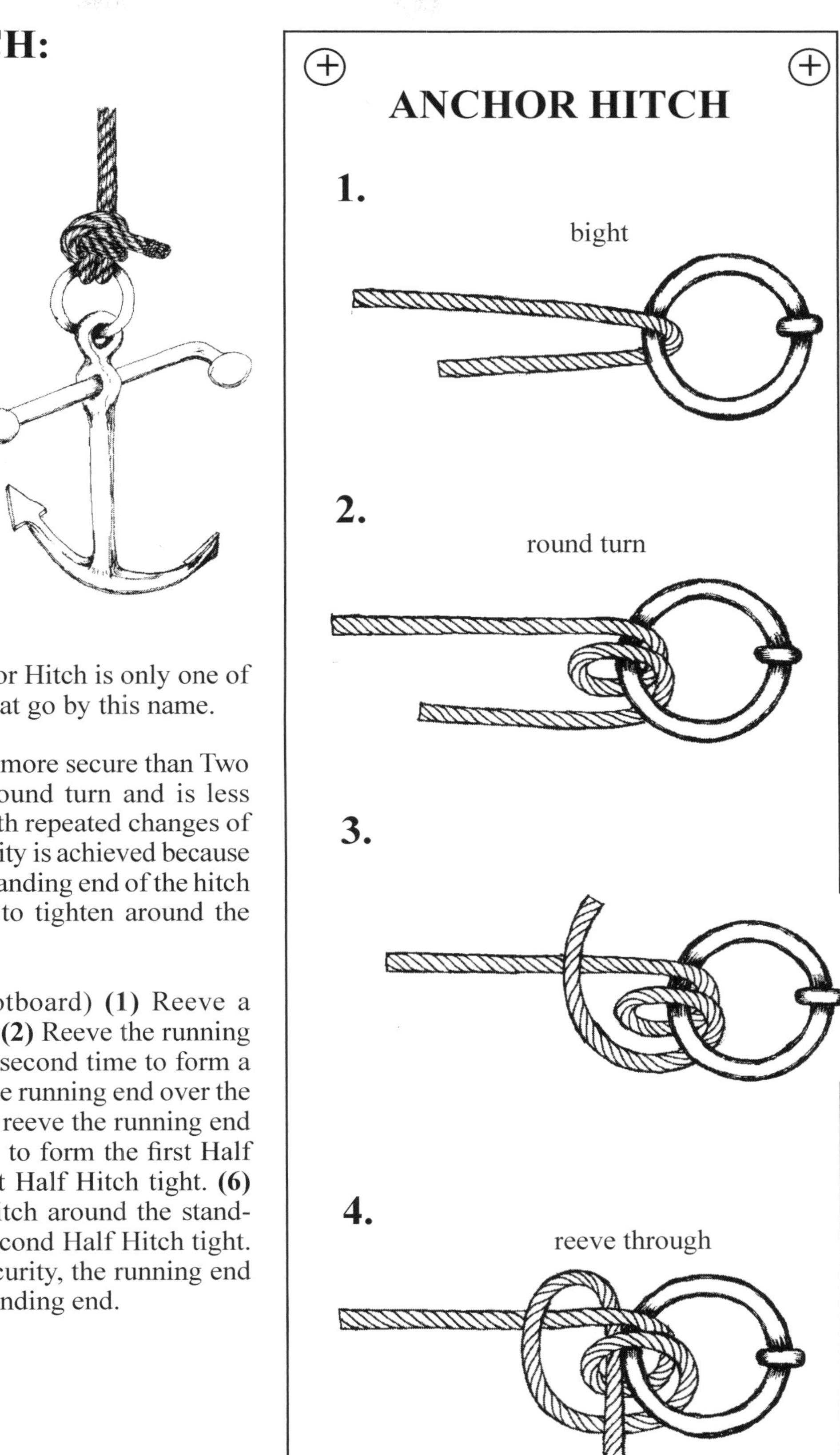

Description ---- A round turn with Two Half Hitches with the first Half Hitch reeved through the round turn.

Use ---- To secure a rope to an anchor ring or chain. It also makes a secure hitch for tying a rope to the handle of a bucket or anything similar.

Other Names ---- Anchor Bend, Fisherman's Bend.

Comments ---- This Anchor Hitch is only one of several related knots that go by this name.

The Anchor Hitch is more secure than Two Half Hitches with a round turn and is less likely to work loose with repeated changes of tension. The extra security is achieved because tension placed on the standing end of the hitch causes the round turn to tighten around the running end.

Narration ---- (For knotboard) **(1)** Reeve a bight through the ring. **(2)** Reeve the running end through the ring a second time to form a round turn. **(3)** Cross the running end over the standing end. **(4)** Then reeve the running end through the round turn to form the first Half Hitch. **(5)** Pull the first Half Hitch tight. **(6)** Take a second Half Hitch around the standing end. **(7)** Pull the second Half Hitch tight. **[NOTE]** For added security, the running end can be seized to the standing end.

5. pull 1st half hitch tight

6.

2nd half hitch

7.

pull tight

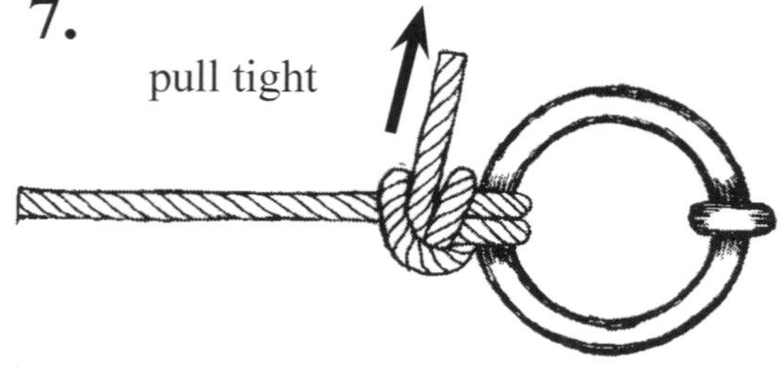

[NOTE]

for added security seize running end to standing end

[NOTES]

TIMBER HITCH:

Description ---- A sliding loop formed by taking a bight around the standing part and wrapping the running part around the standing part.

Use ---- For temporarily attaching a rope for lifting or dragging logs, timbers and other bulky objects.

Comments ---- Easily tied and untied; very secure when under tension especially when used with a Half Hitch.

Other Names ---- Lumberman's Knot, Countryman's Knot; when used with a Half Hitch... Killeg Hitch.

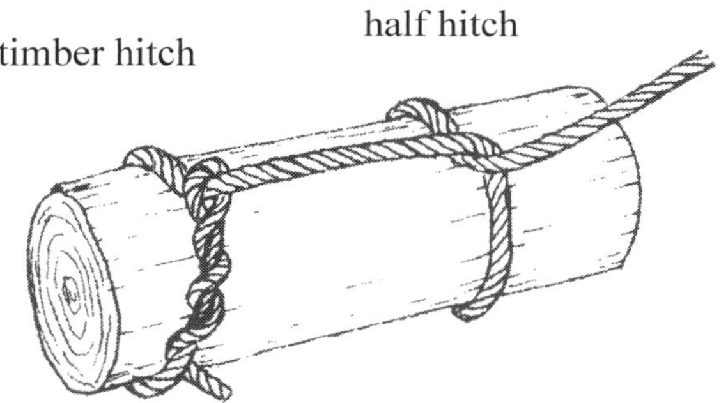

Narration ---- (For knotboard) **(1)** Take a bight around an object with the running part. **(2)** Place the running part across the standing part to form the eye of the hitch. **(3)** Take a bight around the standing part. **(4)** Form a Half Hitch around the standing part by reeving the running part through the eye of the hitch. **(5 and 6)** Pass the running part behind the standing part so that the first turn will be in the direction of the lay of the rope. **(7 and 8)** Take a second and a third turn around the standing part. **(9)** Pull tight.

[NOTE] When using smooth synthetic rope take several extra turns to ensure the security of the Timber Hitch.

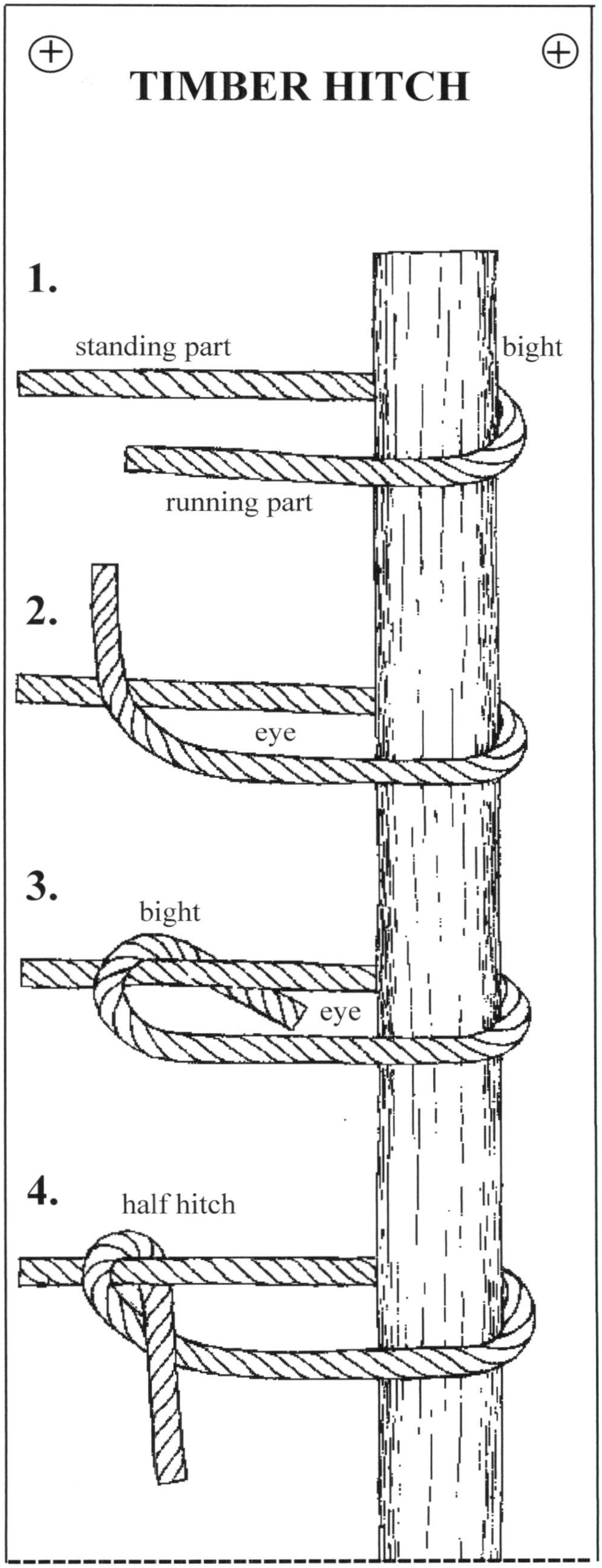

TIMBER HITCH

1.
standing part
bight
running part

2.
eye

3.
bight
eye

4.
half hitch

5.

standing part

6.

1st
turn

7.

2nd
turn

8.

3rd
turn

9.

pull tight

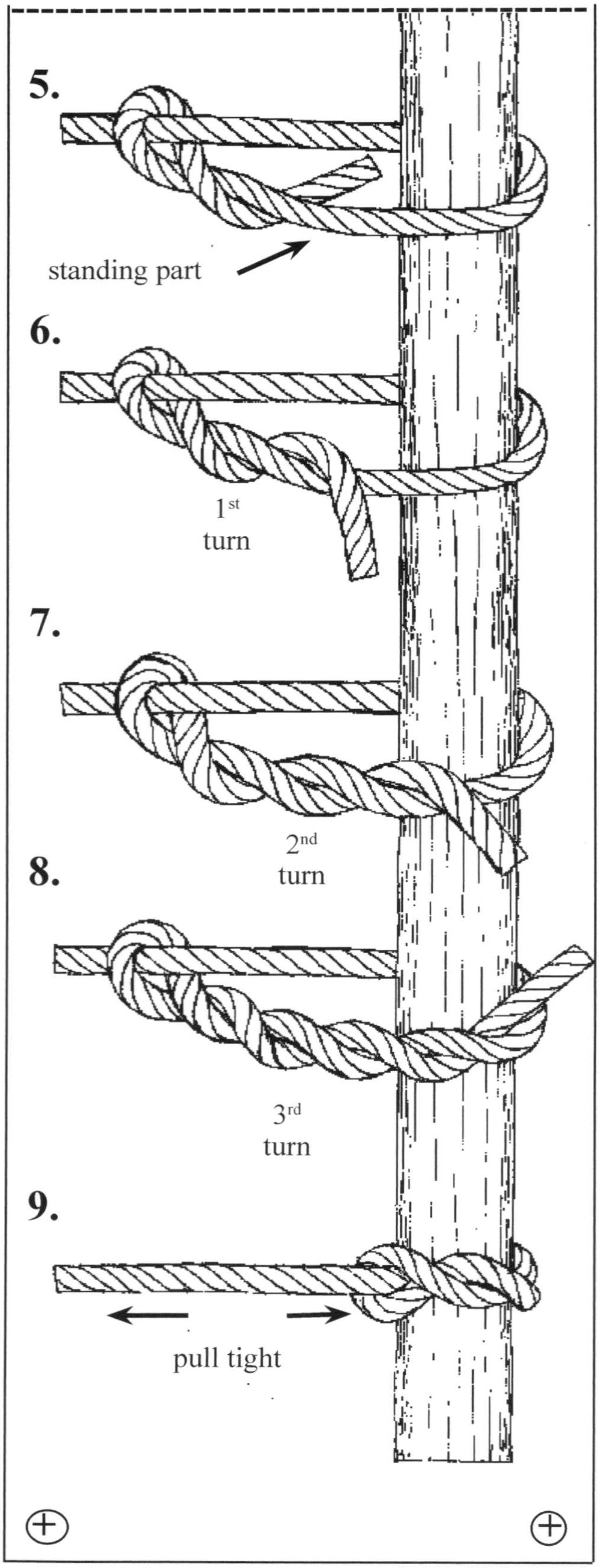

[NOTES]

MARLIN SPIKE HITCH:

Description ---- A loop formed by a Half Hitch around a bight in the standing part of the rope.

Use ---- To temporarily hold a toggle (a Marlin Spike) so that a rope can be pulled tight; as a mooring hitch that can be dropped over the end of a stake or pole; to hold the rungs of a rope ladder.

Comments ---- A secure temporary hitch that can be easily spilled by removing the toggle. The Marlin Spike Hitch gets its name from the practice of using it around a Marlin Spike or similar tool to tighten knots and servings.

Other Names ---- Slip Noose; especially when the Half Hitch is pulled closed around the bight.

Narration ---- (For knotboard) **(1)** Form an overhand loop. **(2)** Then form a bight in the standing part. **(3)** Place the bight under the overhand loop. **(4)** Then reeve the bight through the underhand loop. **(5)** Pass a toggle through the eye of the bight **(6)** and pull tight.

MARLIN SPIKE HITCH

1. overhand loop

standing part

2. bight

3.

4.

5.

toggle

6.

pull tight

pull tight

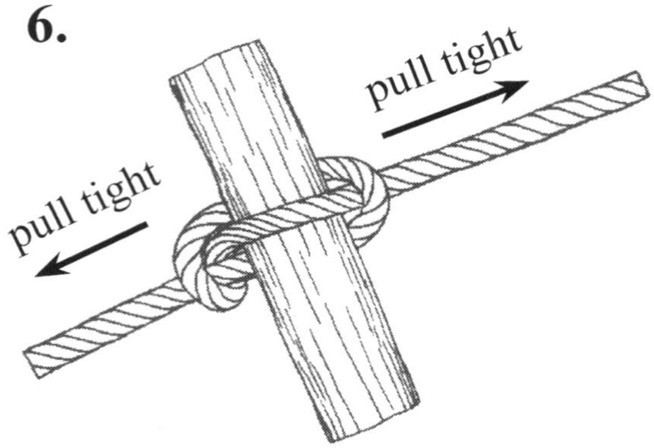

MARLIN SPIKE LADDER

SLIP NOOSE:

Description ---- An Overhand Knot tied around its standing part.

Use ---- As a sliding loop for a snare; as a toggled stopper knot.

Comments ---- Related to the Overhand Knot. Often confused with the Slip Knot.

Narration ---- Tie by folding an overhand loop over the standing part and pulling a bight of the standing part through the eye of the overhand loop. (See Marlin Spike Hitch.)

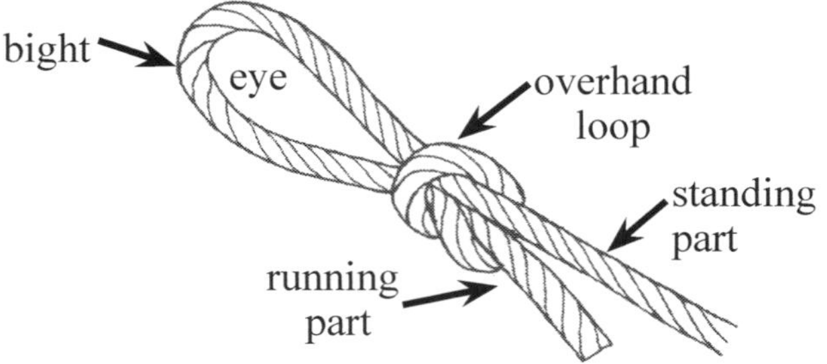

SLIP KNOT:

Description ---- An Overhand Knot tied around its running part.

Use ---- As a Stopper Knot.

Comments ---- Related to the Overhand Knot. Often confused with the Slip Noose.

Narration ---- Tie by folding an overhand loop over the running part and pulling a bight of the running part through the eye of the overhand loop. (See Marlin Spike Hitch.)

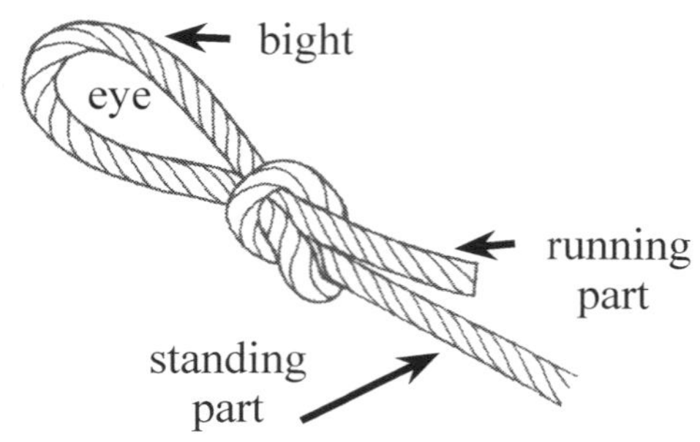

MOORING HITCH:

Description ---- An underhand loop toggled to the standing part with a bight made in the running part.

Use ---- To securely tie off a rope so that it can be quickly untied; especially when tying a small boat to a dock or piling.

Comments ---- A secure knot that is easily tied or untied in wet or dry rope. When properly tied a nonclosing loop is formed. This allows the hitch to move up or down a piling as the water level changes.

Narration ---- (For knotboard) **(1)** Take a bight around an object. **(2)** Form an underhand loop in the running part. **(3)** Place the eye of the underhand loop over the standing part. **(4)** Pull a bight of the standing part through the eye of the underhand loop. **(5)** Pull the underhand loop tight around the bight. **(6)** Place the running part under the eye of the bight. **(7)** Pull a bight of the running part through the eye of the standing part bight. **(8)** Pull on the standing part to tighten the standing part bight around the running part bight.

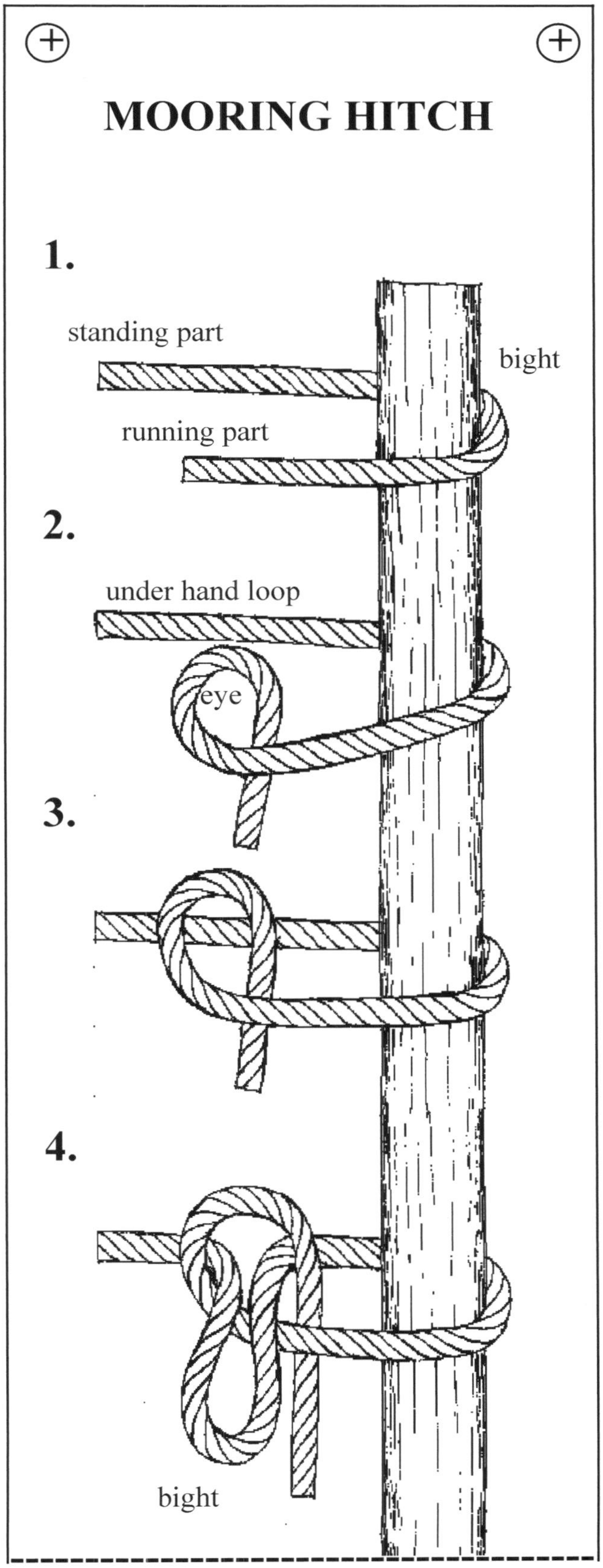

MOORING HITCH

1.

standing part
bight
running part

2.

under hand loop
eye

3.

4.

bight

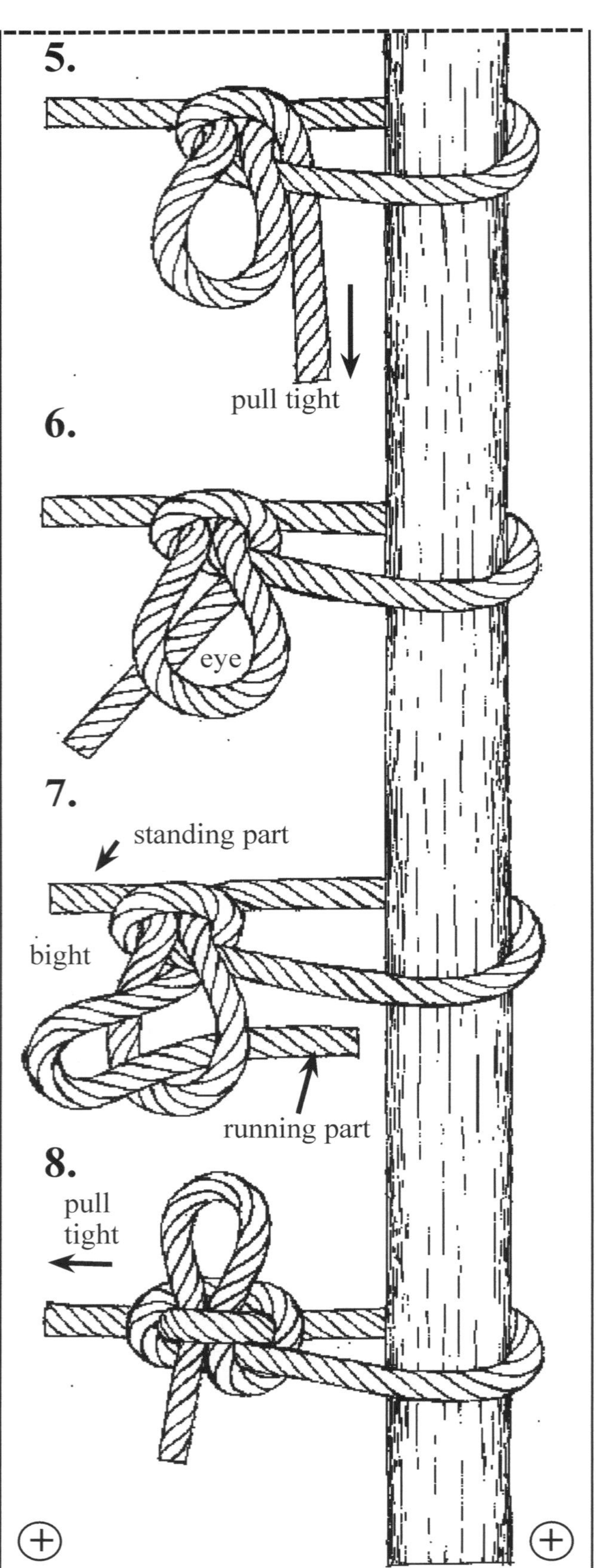
5.
pull tight
6.
eye
7.
standing part
bight
running part
8.
pull
tight

[NOTES]

TURK'S HEAD:

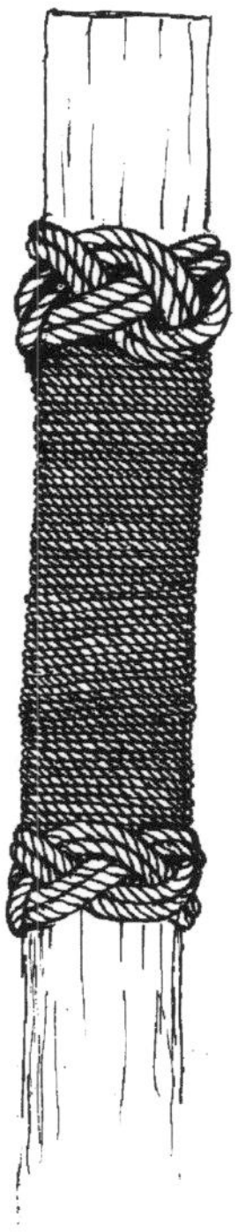

Description ---- Three strand braid worked in a continuous circle.

Use ---- (1) As a decorative knot around a staff or railing. **(2)** Worked tight around a checked or cracked tool handle or canoe paddle to reinforce them. **(3)** As a neckerchief slide or woggal.

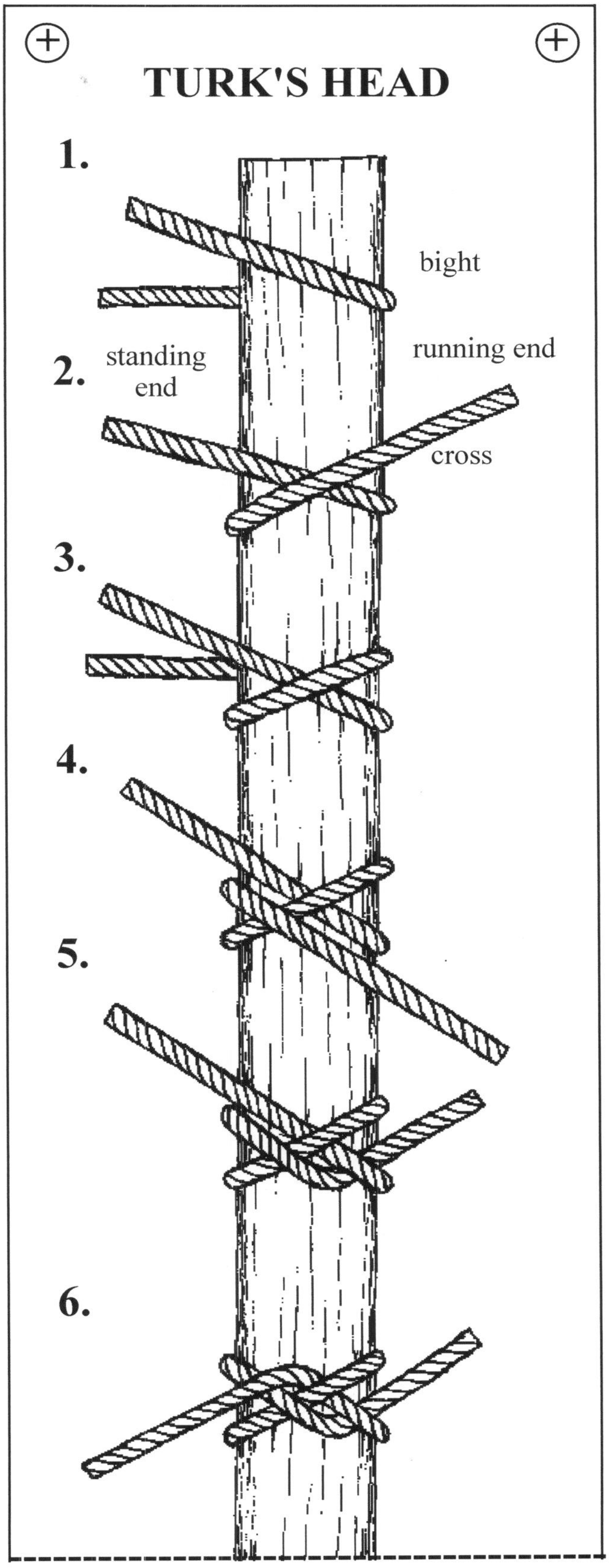

Comments ---- The form of Turk's Head shown here is a Five Crown Turk's Head. This is only one of a group of knots that go by the name Turk's Head.

The crown number is determined by counting the number of bights at the edge of the knot. To make a larger loop, increase the size of the wraps made in steps 1 - 4 and then, at step 7 use three strand braiding to increase the number of crowns. The number of crowns can be increased by increments of three so that the number of crowns in a larger loop can be 8, 11, 14, etc.

TURK'S HEAD

1. bight
2. standing end, running end, cross
3.
4.
5.
6.

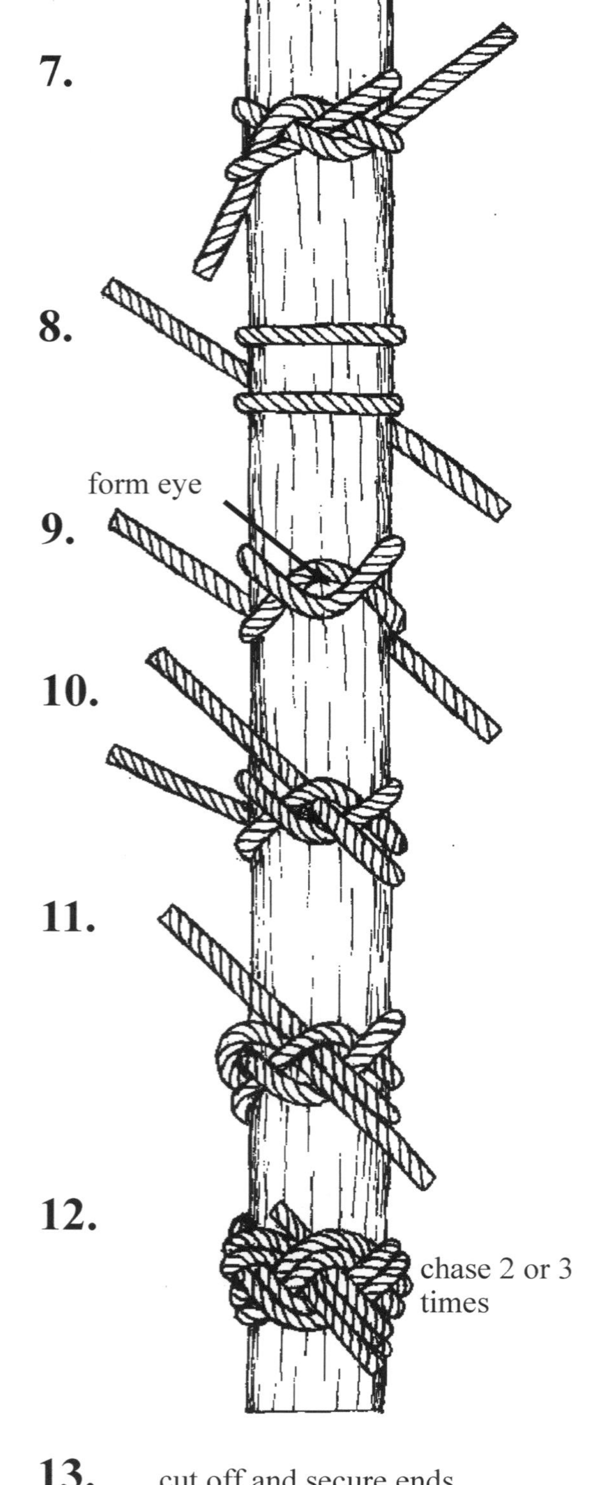

[NOTE] The size of the finished Turk's Head depends on the size of the rope used and the number of times the strand is chased.

Other Names ---- Three Lead by Five Bight Turk's Head, ordinary Turk's Head.

Narration ---- (For knotboard) **(1)** Start at the center of the line by taking a bight around an object (the fingers of the left hand work well). **(2)** Complete the round turn and cross the running end over the standing end. **(3)** Take a second bight around the object so that the running end is between the standing end and the first wrap. **(4)** Lay the running end across the first wrap then **(5)** tuck the running end under the standing end. **(6)** Lay the standing end across the second wrap and **(7)** tuck it under the first wrap. **(8)** Rotate the knot around the object so that you are looking at the opposite side. **(9)** Cross the second wrap over the first wrap. **(10)** Reeve the standing end through the eye formed between the two wraps. **(11)** Reeve the running end through the eye between the two wraps so that the ends are parallel and in opposite directions. **(12)** Chase (follow) the strand of the knot two or three times. **(13)** Cut off and secure the ends.

[NOTE] To determine the length of line to use, wrap the line around the object four times for a single strand knot. Add three and one half wraps for each time you intend to chase the original strand.

[NOTES]

MONKEY'S PAW:

Description ---- Two forms of the Monkey's Paw are presented here. The first is formed from four interlocking loops: a Four Crown Turk's Head. The second is constructed from three interlocking coils.

Use ---- The core determines what the Monkey's Paw can be used for. When tied over a stone or heavy ball, the Monkey's Paw can be used to add weight to a heaving line. If tied with small cord over a cork ball, the Monkey's Paw makes a good float for boat keys or other small items used around a waterfront. Tied over a ball of twine or other soft material, the Monkey's Paw can be used as a weight on the end of a rope for the game Jump the Shot. A Monkey's Paw can also be used as a toggle or button.

Comments ---- Neither form of the Monkey's Paw has an advantage over the other. The form you choose to use is a matter of personal preference.

Core Size ---- The diameter of the core should be between three and four times the diameter of the rope being used.

MONKEY'S PAW: TURK'S HEAD

Narration ---- (For knotboard) **(1)** Form an overhand loop. **(2)** Form a second overhand loop

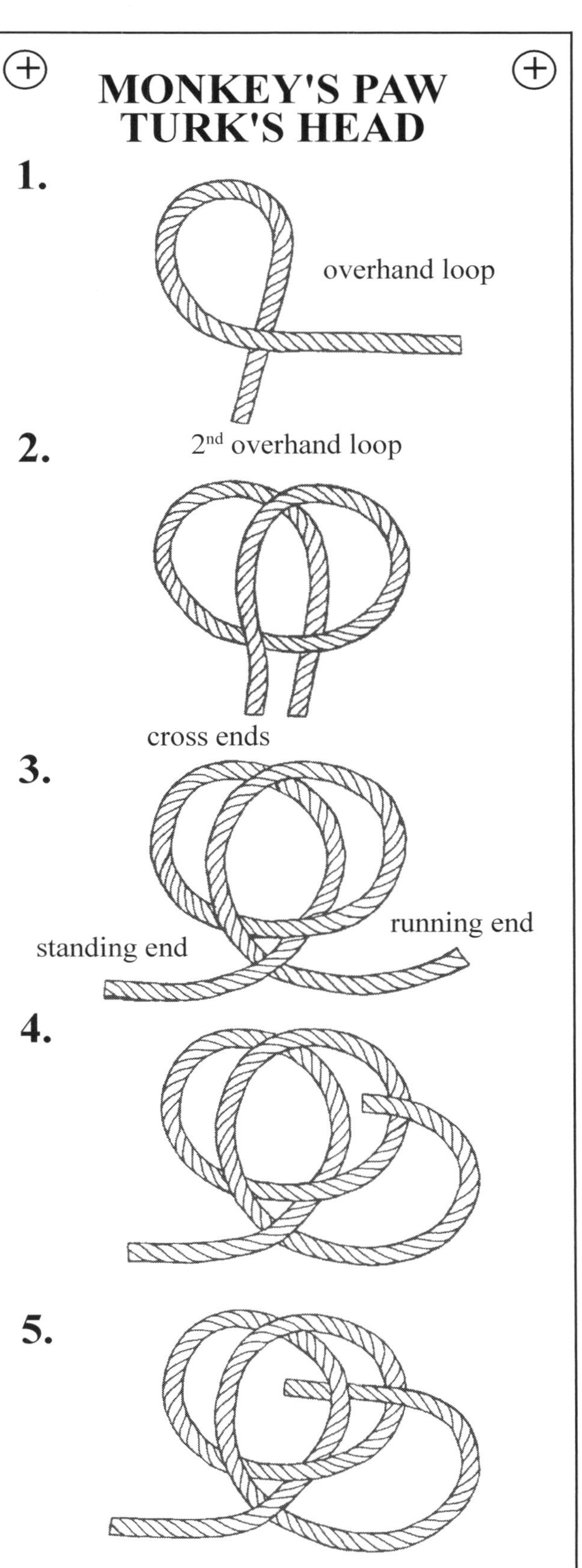

6.

7.

8.

3rd loop

9.

4th loop

10. chase 2 to 3 times

11. work tight over a core

over the left edge of the first overhand loop. **(3)** Cross the standing end over the running end. **(4)** Weave the running end across the loops by placing the running end over the right side of the top loop **(5)** then under the right side of the bottom loop **(6)** next, over the left side of the top loop **(7)** and finally under the left side of the bottom loop. **(8)** Pull the running end through until the third loop is equal to the size of the first two loops. **(9)** Add the fourth loop by placing the running end parallel to the standing end. **(10)** Chase the original pattern 2 to 3 times. **(11)** Work tight over the core.

MONKEY'S PAW: COIL STYLE

Narration ---- (For knotboard) **(1)** Form the first coil by stacking three loops on top of each other. **(2)** Insert core into center of coil. **(3)** Start second coil by forming a small loop at the bottom of the first coil. **(4)** Pass the running end behind and **(5)** across the front to the first loop of the second coil. **(6)** Add the second and third loops of the second coil. **(7)** Start the third coil by reeving the running end through the top of the first coil and **(8)** then reeve the running end through the bottom of the first coil. **(9)** Add the second and third loops of the third coil. **(10)** Work all coils tight over the core.

[NOTE] Join the two ends of the Monkey's Paw with an Eye Splice, a Short Splice, or a Seizing.

MONKEY'S PAW
COIL STYLE

1. form 1st coil

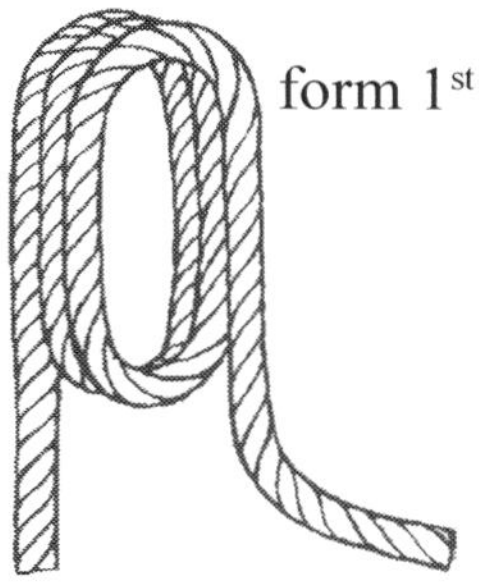

2. insert core

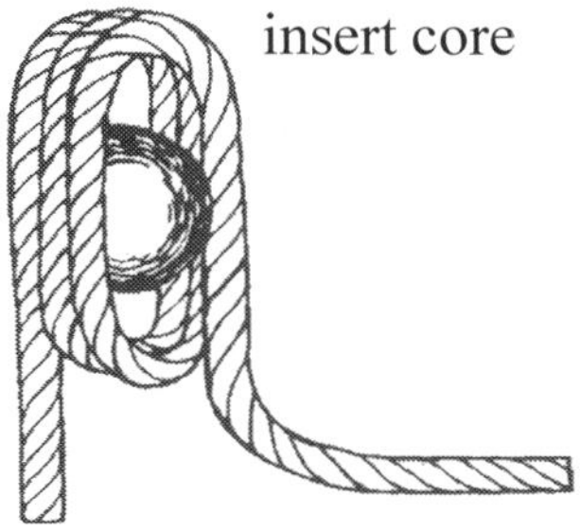

3. start 2nd coil
form small loop

4.

5. 1st loop

6. 2nd and 3rd loops

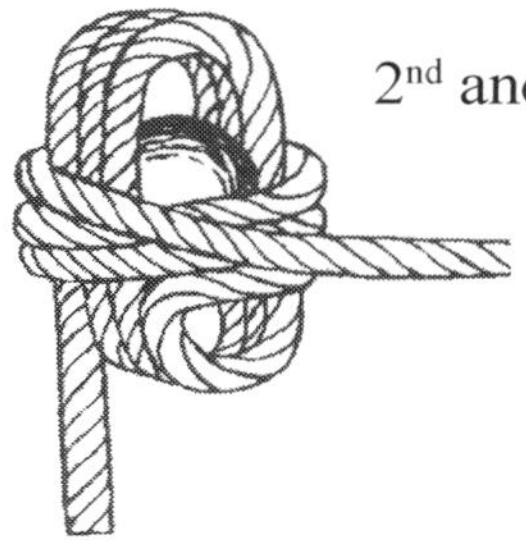

7. start 3rd coil
reeve through

8. reeve through to form 1st loop

9. add 2nd and 3rd loops

10. work tight over core

BOATSWAIN'S WHISTLE KNOT:

Description ---- A two lead knot that is built up from two interlocking underhand loops to look like a Turk's Head Knot when it is worked tight.

Use ---- As a decorative knot to attach a whistle or a knife to a lanyard; ---- to form a toggle or button.

Other Names ---- Sailor's Knife Lanyard Knot, Marlin Spike Lanyard Knot, Single-Strand Diamond Knot, Two Strand Diamond Knot, Pipe Lanyard Knot.

Narration ---- (For knotboard) **(1)** Use the left hand to hold the middle of a strand of rope so that the loop of the bight is to the back of the hand and the two leads are between the fingers and hanging down across the palm. **(2)** Use the bottom lead to lay an underhand loop over the standing end of the top lead. **(3)** Form a bight in the bottom lead so that its running end is under the running end of the top lead. **(4)** Weave the running end of the bottom lead over the right edge of the top underhand loop, then under the standing end of the bottom lead, and over the left edge of the top underhand loop. This forms two interlocking underhand loops. **(5)** Form the next bight by placing the running end of the top lead under the top edge of the top underhand loop. **(6)** Reeve the running end of the top lead to the outside of the standing end of the bottom lead and up through the middle of the interlocking underhand loops. **(7)** Form the next bight by placing the running end of the bottom lead under the bottom edge of the bottom underhand loop. **(8)** Reeve the running end of bottom lead to the outside of the standing end the of the bottom lead and up through the middle of the interlocking underhand loops. **(9)** Work the knot tight.

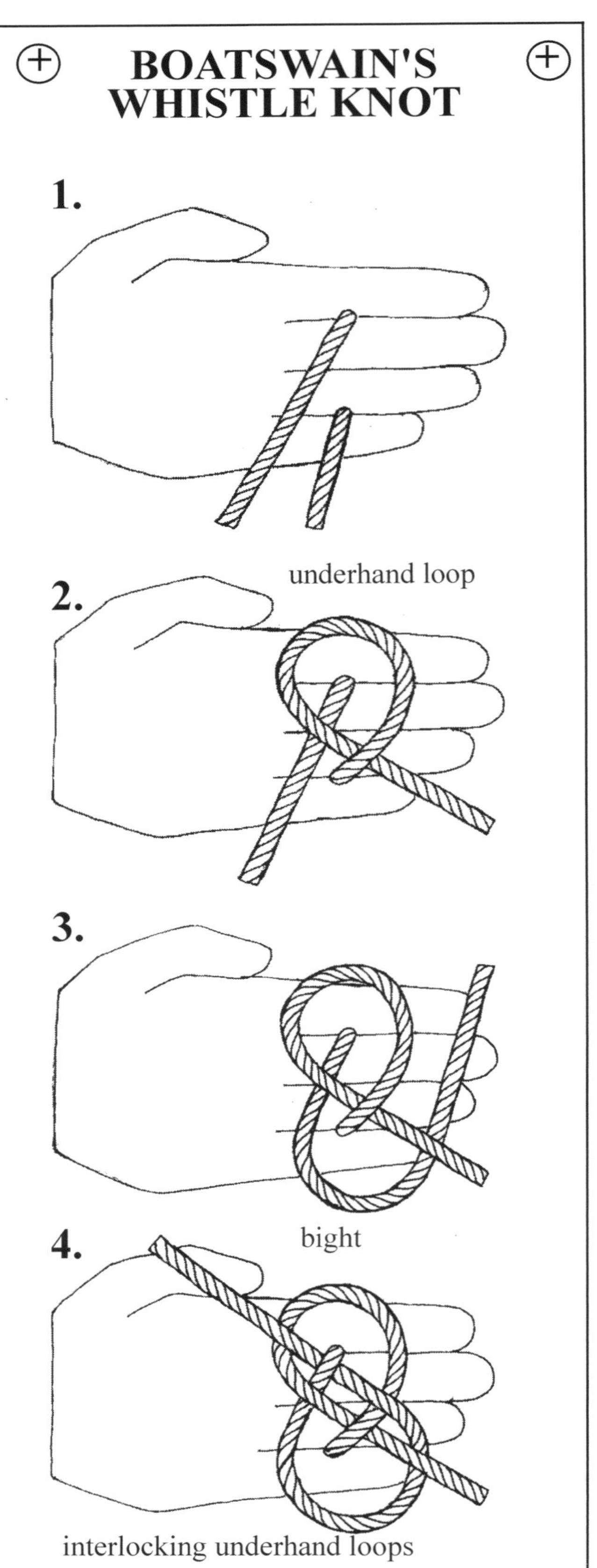

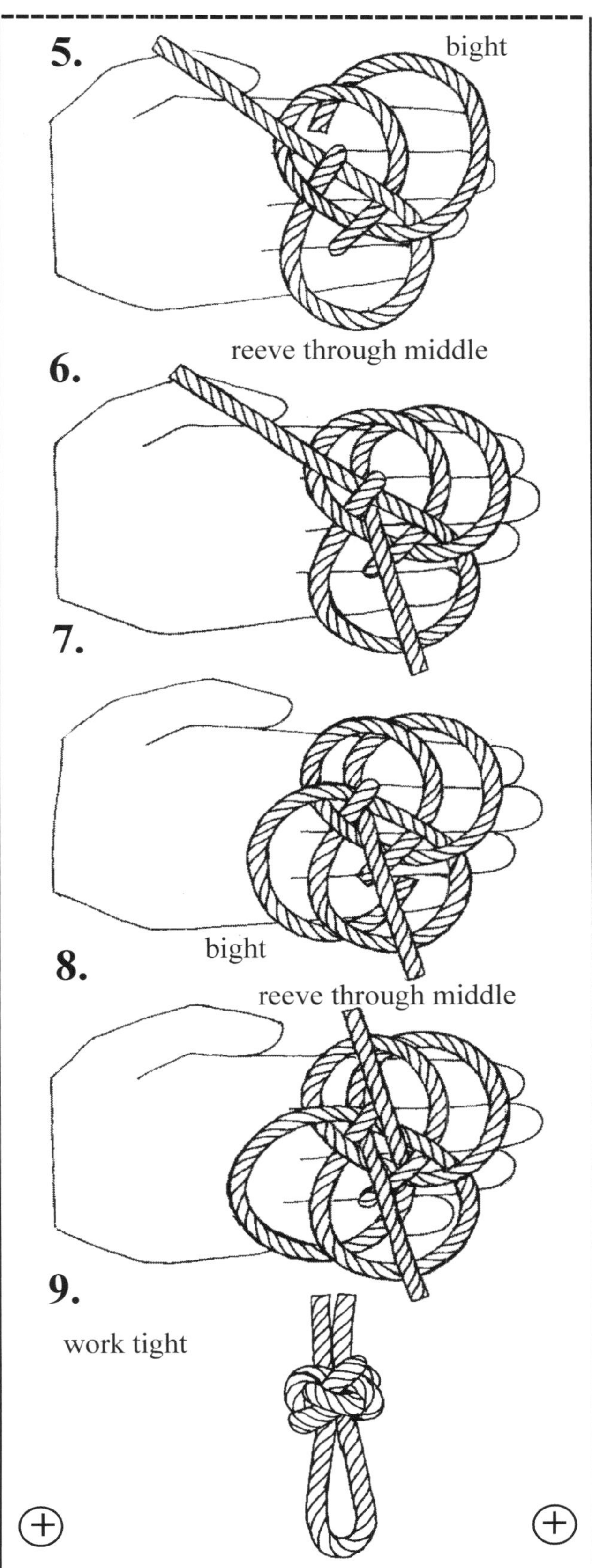

Boatswain's Whistle Knot Doubled:

Use ---- Doubling the Boatswain's Whistle Knot increases its size. The increase in size makes it more effective as a toggle or button. Doubling also gives a variation in appearance when doing decorative work.

Narration ---- (For knotboard) **(1)** Follow steps 1 --- 4 from the knotboard for the BOATSWAIN'S WHISTLE KNOT. **(2)** Form the next bight by placing the running end of the top lead under the top edge of the top underhand loop. **(3)** Weave the running end of the top lead to the inside of the standing end of the bottom lead and across the middle of the interlocking underhand loops. **(4)** Form the next bight by placing the running end of the bottom lead under the bottom edge of the bottom underhand loop. **(5)** Weave the running end of the bottom lead to the inside of the standing end of the bottom lead and across the middle of the interlocking underhand loops. **(6)** Chase the top lead with the bottom lead. End by bringing the top lead up through the middle. **(7)** Chase the bottom lead with the top lead. End by bringing the bottom lead up through the middle. **(8)** Work the knot tight.

[NOTES]

BOATSWAIN'S WHISTLE KNOT DOUBLED

1.

Follow steps 1 -- 4 from the knot board for the

BOATSWAIN'S WHISTLE KNOT

2.

top underhand loop

bottom lead

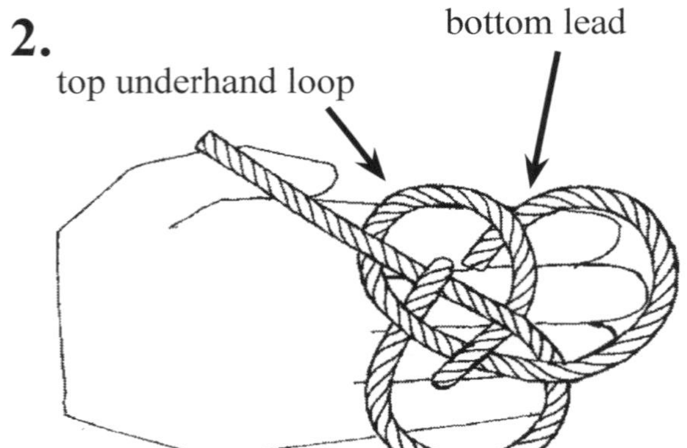

3.

weave inside lead

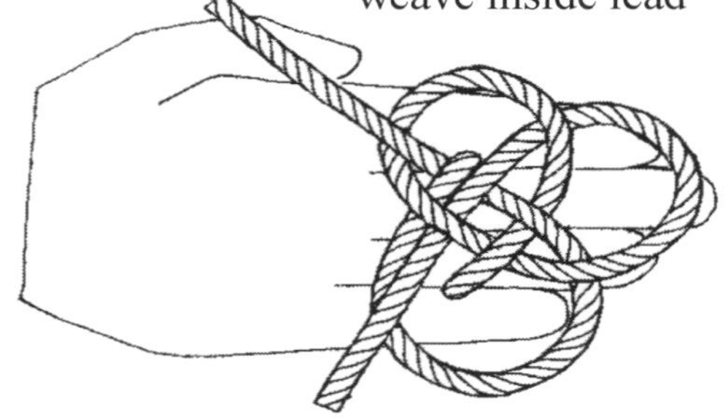

4.

top lead

bottom underhand loop

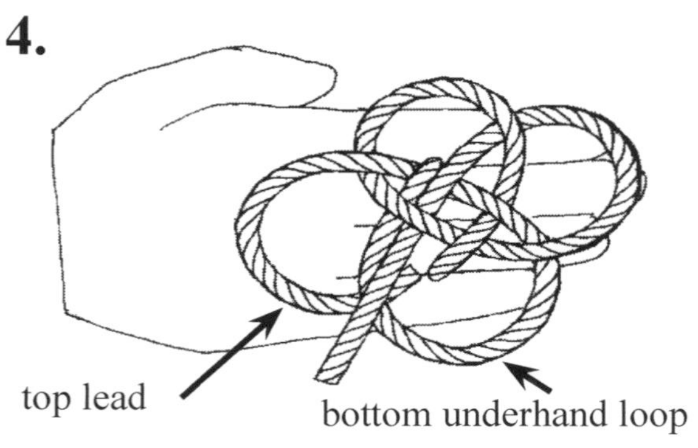

5. weave inside lead

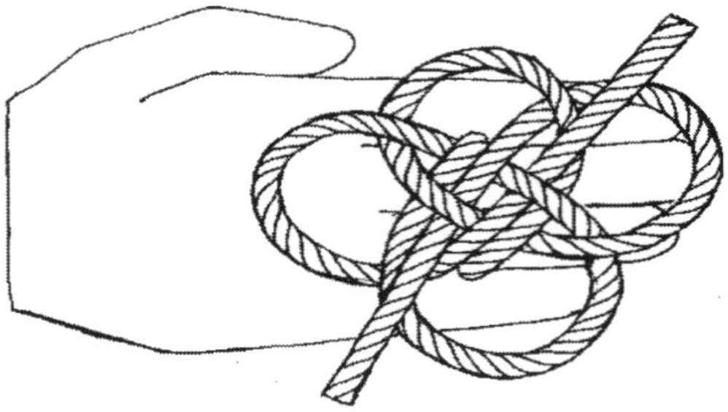

6. chase top lead

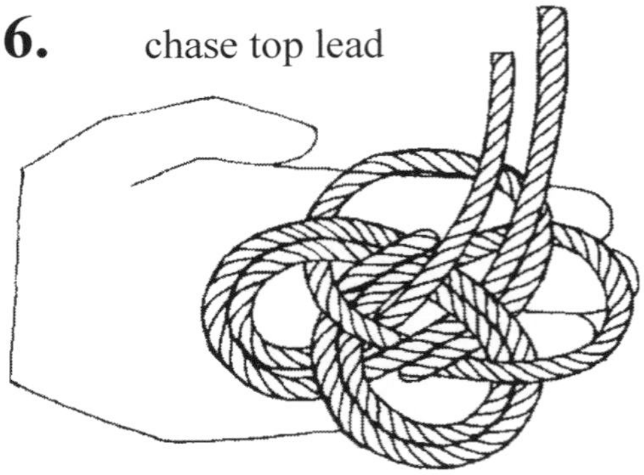

7. chase bottom lead

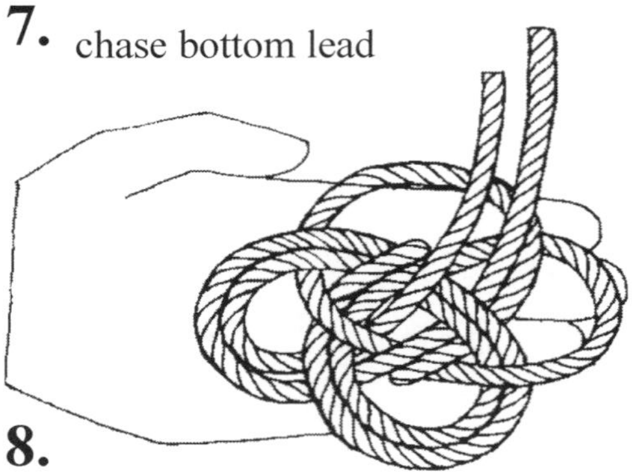

8.

work tight

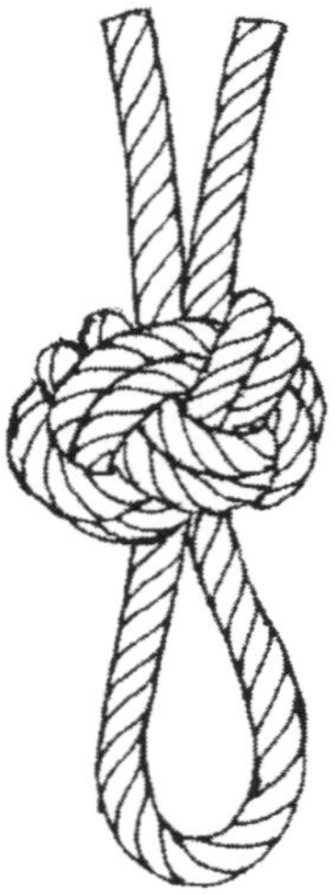

JUG KNOT:

Use ---- To provide a convenient carrying handle for jug or bottle; ---- to attach a tool, such as a hammer to a security line to prevent accidental dropping; ---- to add a wrist loop to a walking staff; ---- to repair a wrist loop handle on a ski pole; ---- to attach a safety line to a canoe paddle; **.....** use your imagination, but be sure that you keep safety in mind.

Other Names ---- Jar Knot, Moonshiner's Knot, Hackamore, Bridle Knot.

Comments ---- The most common use is to provide a loop handle attached to the neck of a bottle. The loop handle makes it easy to carry several bottles with one hand. If a toggle or a two strand button knot such as Boatswain Whistle Knot is added to the free end of the rope, the loop of the Jug Knot can be use to toggle the bottle to a belt so that the bottle can be used as a canteen.

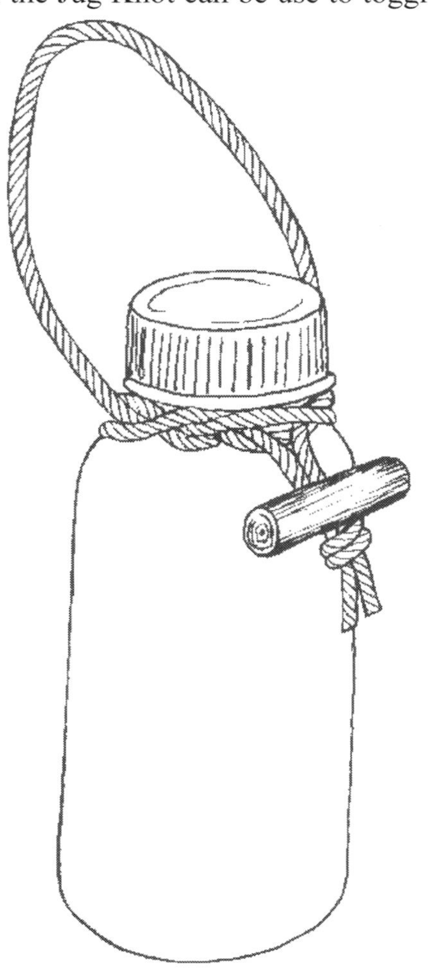

Plastic bottles with screw-on lids such as soda, sport drink, and mineral water bottles make strong, lightweight containers for carrying water on hikes and camp outs. 2 and 3 liter soda bottles are large enough to use as water containers around the camp kitchen. Smaller bottles (8 to 16 oz.) can be used as personal water bottles or canteens. These bottles can be made even more convenient by using a Jug Knot to attach a loop handle.

To help keep your water cool and refreshing in hot weather, place a sock over the bottle, wet the sock when you fill the bottle; evaporation will do the rest.

In cold weather, carry your water bottle under your coat. A dry sock placed over the bottle will help keep the water from freezing.

To protect your health, wash and disinfect your water bottle with a chlorine bleach solution and don't share your water bottle with others. Show them how to make a water bottle of their own.

Narration ---- (For knotboard) **(1)** Form a bight in the middle of a 24 to 30 inch long by 3/16 inch diameter rope. **(2)** Fold the bight down over the standing ends to form two loops. **(3)** Place the right hand loop over the right hand side of the left hand loop. **(4)** Weave the middle of the bight under the left standing end, **(5)** then over the left hand edge of the right hand loop. **(6)** Next go under the right hand edge of the left hand loop. **(7)** Finally pass the bight over the right hand side of the right hand loop. **(8)** Turn the top of the right hand loop down under the knot. **(9)** Turn the top of the left hand loop down over the knot. **(10)** Place the knot over the neck of a bottle and work the knot tight so that the bight forms a 4 to 5 inch loop handle and the loose ends are even.

JUG KNOT

1.

bight

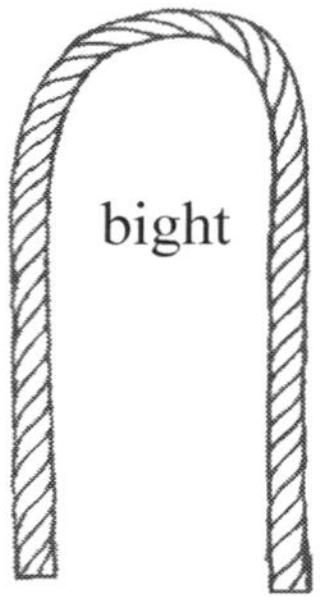

2. fold down

3. cross loops

4.

5.

6.

7.

8.

loop turned down under

9.

loop turned down over

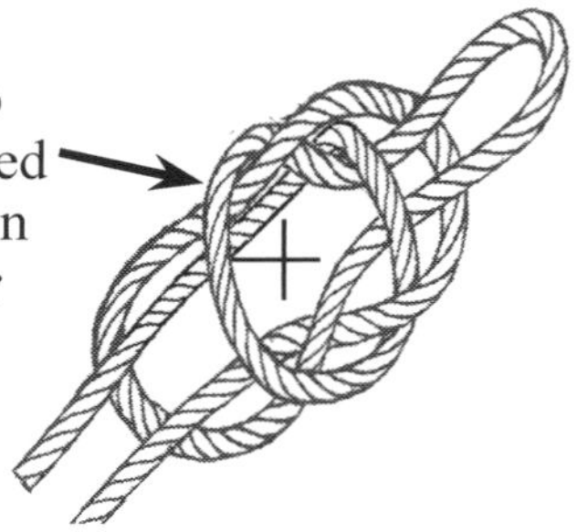

bight

10.

pull tight

pull tight

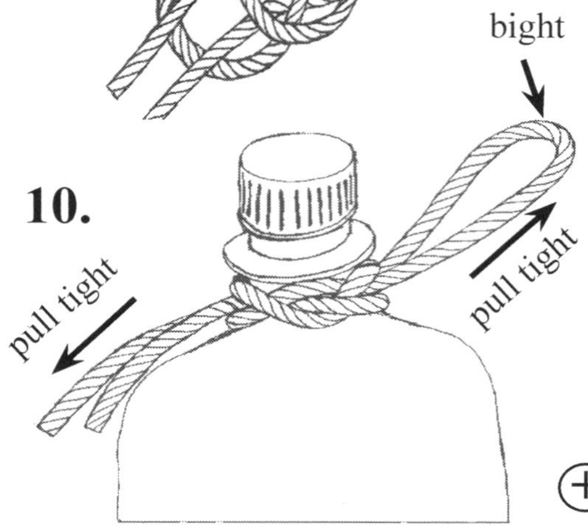

BELAYING TO A CLEAT:

Description ---- A turn secured to a cleat with a figure eight and locked in place with a Half Hitch.

Use ---- To secure a flag lanyard, to moor a boat to a dock.

Comments ---- Belaying to a Cleat is a fast non-jamming method of securing a rope anywhere along its length without reeving any part of the rope through or around anything.

Narration ---- (For knotboard.) **(1)** Take a bight around the first horn of the cleat and pull the line tight. **(2)** Take a bight around the second horn. **(3)** Place the line across the cleat. **(4)** Take a second bight around the first horn. **(5)** Place the line across the cleat a second time. **(6)** Form a loop so that its running end is under its standing end. **(7)** Place the eye of the loop over the second horn of the cleat. **(8)** Pull the loop tight to form a Half Hitch around the horn of the cleat. This locks the rope in place.

[NOTES]

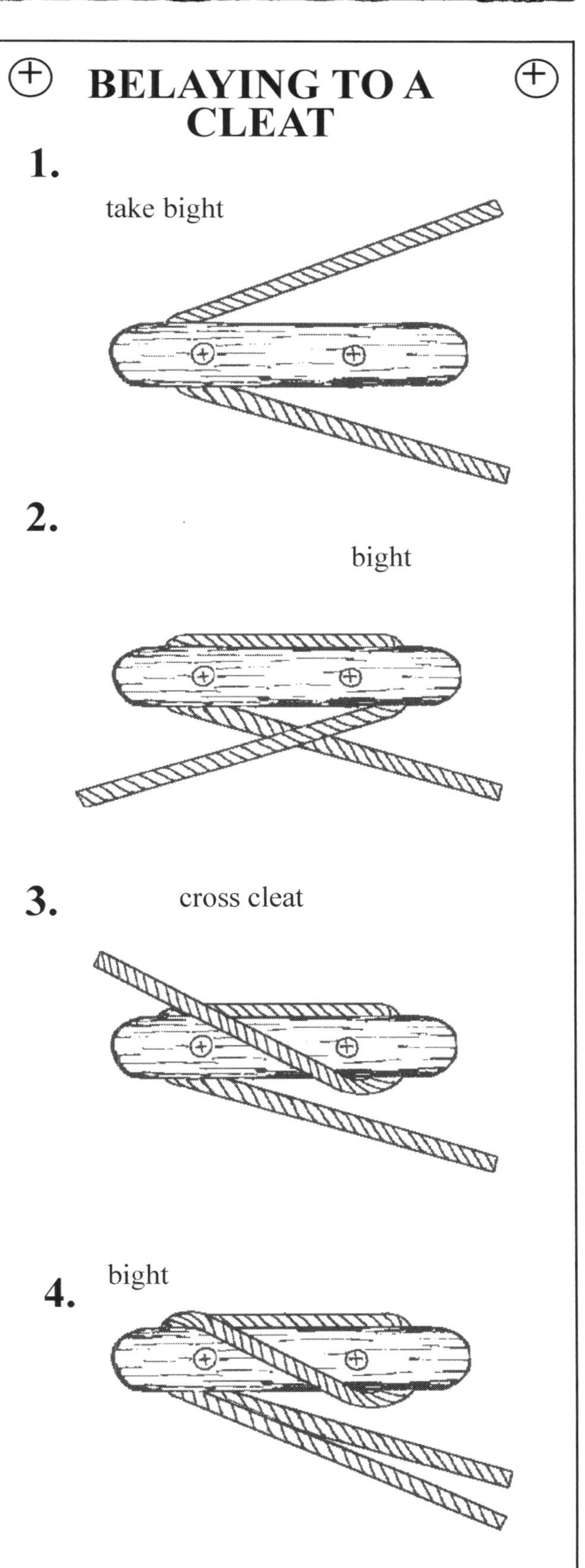

5. cross cleat
6. form loop
7. place over horn
8. pull half hitch tight

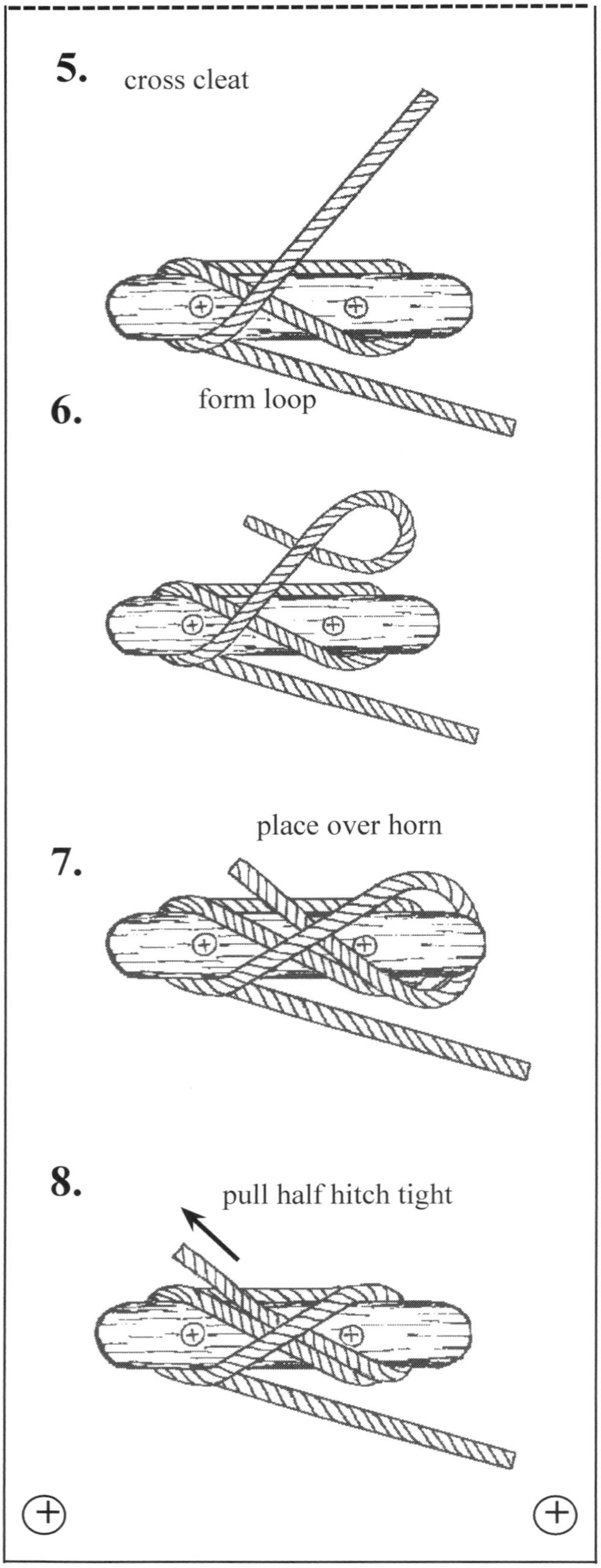

PATTERN FOR CLEAT FOR KNOT-BOARD:

Use this pattern to make 7 hardwood cleats. Attach the cleats to the knotboard with 1 1/2 inch number 8 round head wood screws.

horn
holes for screws
horn

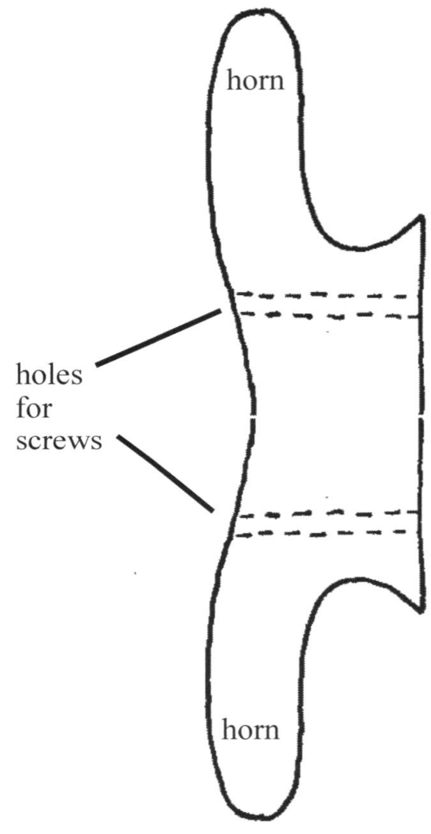

MASTHEAD KNOT:

Comments ----There are several forms of the Masthead Knot, two of which are shown here. The first form of the Masthead Knot was chosen for its symmetry and the ease of transition to the Running Half Hitches used to secure it to the pole. The second form was chosen for the ease with which it can be tied.

Use ---- Aboard a ship, a Masthead Knot was used to rig a temporary mast if the mast was lost in battle or during a storm. On land a Masthead Knot can be used to rig a gin pole or a flag pole.

Other names ---- Jury Mast Knot, Pitcher Knot.

MASTHEAD KNOT (1):

Description ---- A multiple loop knot formed by reeving loosely made loops of two Overhand Knots through each other and then securing the knot to a mast.

Narration ---- (For knotboard:1) **(1)** Loosely tie two Overhand Knots. **(2)** Place the loop of one Overhand Knot on top of the loop of the other Overhand Knot. **(3 and 4)** Reeve the loops of the Overhand Knot through the Half Knot part of the opposite Overhand Knot. **(5)** Place over a pole and draw the three loops up even. **(6)** Secure to the pole with a series of Running Half Hitches above and below the Mast Head Knot.

[NOTE] A fourth loop may be formed by tying or splicing the ends together. If a fourth loop is made, nail a cleat to the pole to prevent the Mast Head Knot from slipping.

[NOTE] Attach the guy lines to the loops with Becket Hitches.

MASTHEAD KNOT (1)

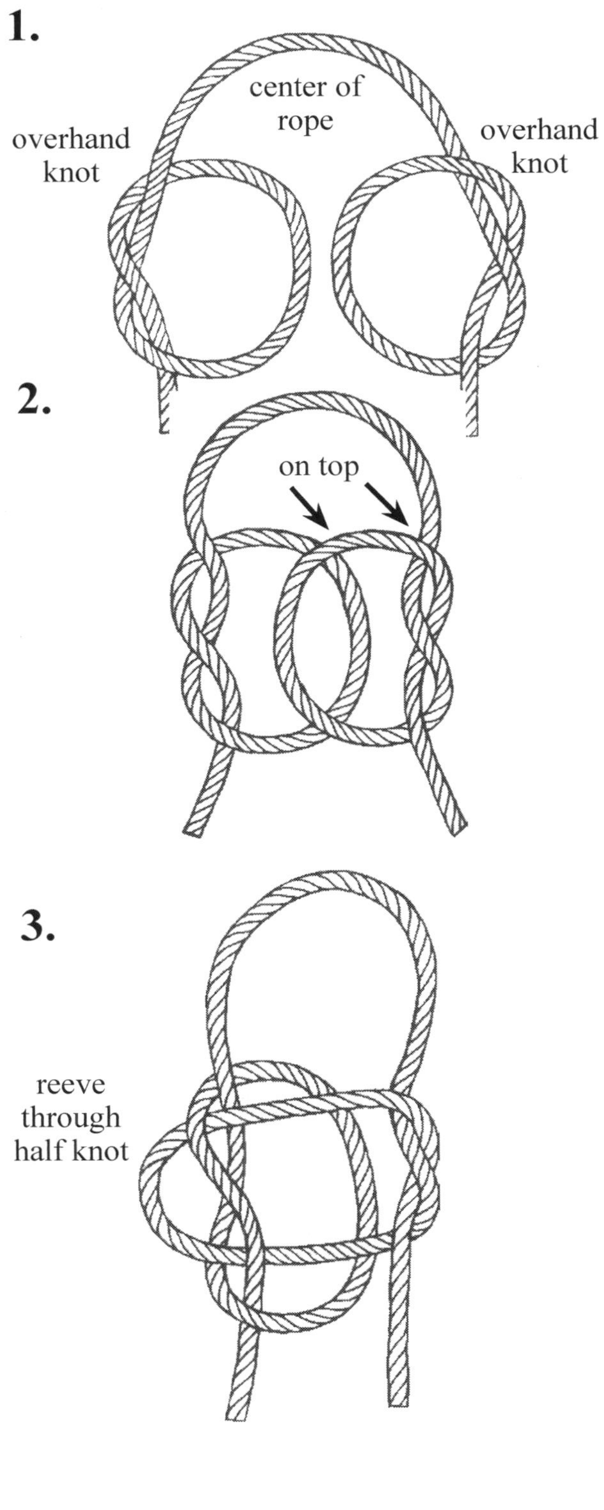

1.

overhand knot

center of rope

overhand knot

2.

on top

3.

reeve through half knot

4.

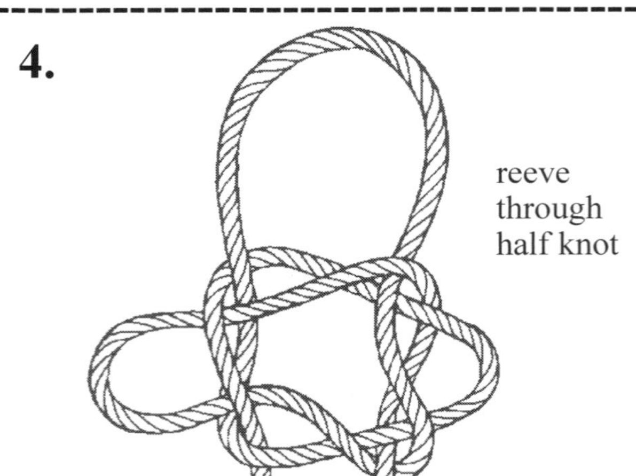

5. place over pole and draw up even

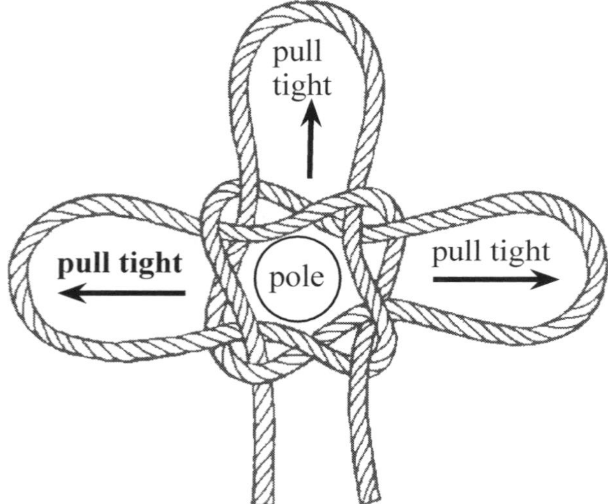

6. secure to pole with running half hitches

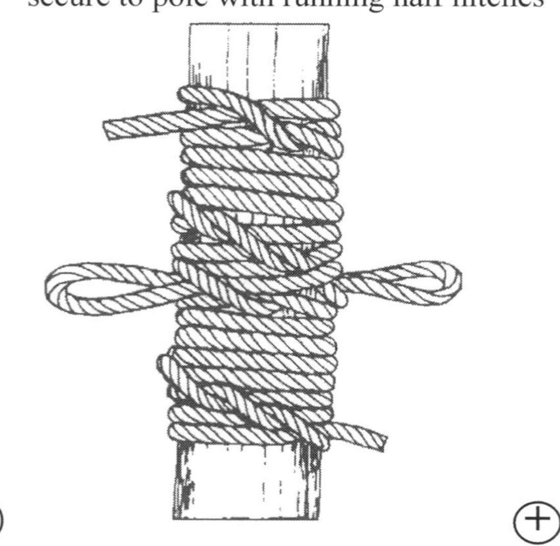

MASTHEAD KNOT (2):

Description ---- A multiple loop knot formed by weaving three overlapping overhand loops together and then securing the knot to a mast.

Narration ---- (For knotboard.) **(1)** Form an overhand loop near the center of the rope. **[NOTE]** The size of the loop is determined by the size of the pole that the finished knot is to be placed over. **(2)** Form a second larger overhand loop at the center of the rope. **(3)** Place the left edge of the second overhand loop under the right edge of the first overhand loop. **(4)** Form a third overhand loop. **(5)** Place the left edge of the third overhand loop under the right edge of the second overhand loop. **(6)** Start weaving the overhand loops together by placing the left edge of the right overhand loop on top of the right edge of the left overhand loop. **(7)** Continue the weaving by placing the right edge of the left overhand loop over the right edge of the center overhand loop and by placing the left edge of the right overhand loop under the left edge of the center overhand loop. **(8)** Finish the weaving by placing the right edge of the left overhand loop under the right edge of the right overhand loop and by placing the left edge of the right overhand loop over the left edge of the left overhand loop. **(9)** Place over pole and work tight. Knot is prevented from slipping down the pole by nailing cleats to the pole or by cutting a groove for the knot to rest in. **(10)** Secure the end by seizing them to the adjacent loop; Running Half Hitches may also be used.

[NOTE] A fourth loop my be formed by tying or splicing the ends together.

[NOTE] Attach the guy lines to the loops with Becket Hitches.

MASTHEAD KNOT (2)

1. overhand loop

center of rope

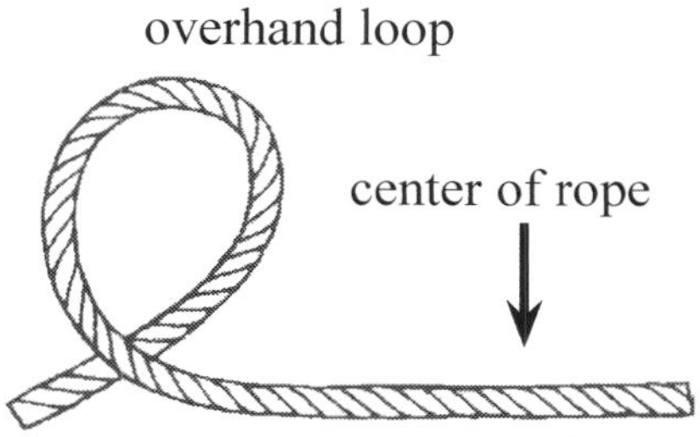

2. 2nd overhand loop

3. place edge under

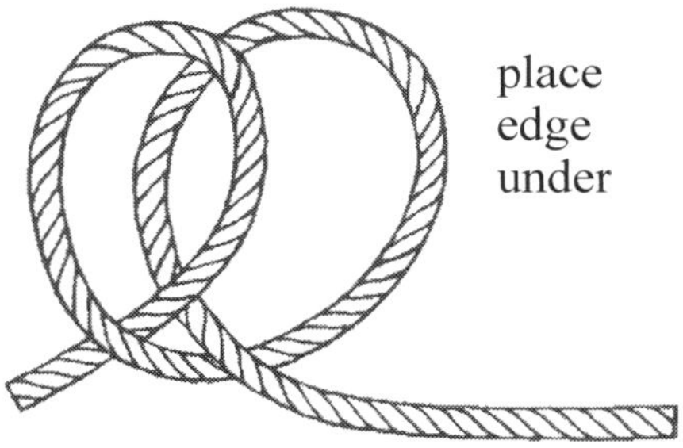

4. 3rd overhand loop

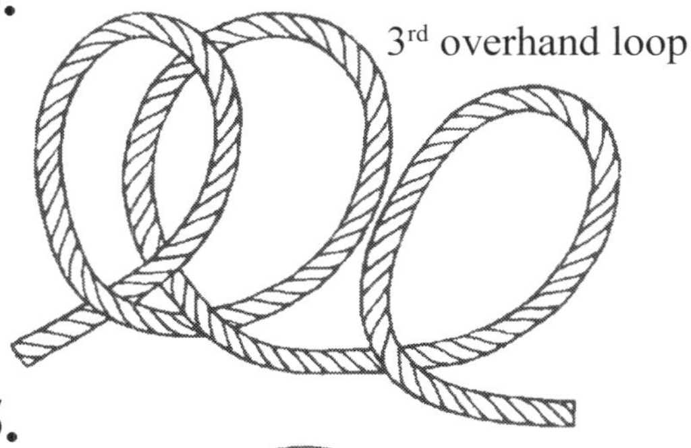

5. place edge under

6. start weaving across

7.

8.

9. place over pole

cleat nailed to pole

cleat

10.

seizing

seizing

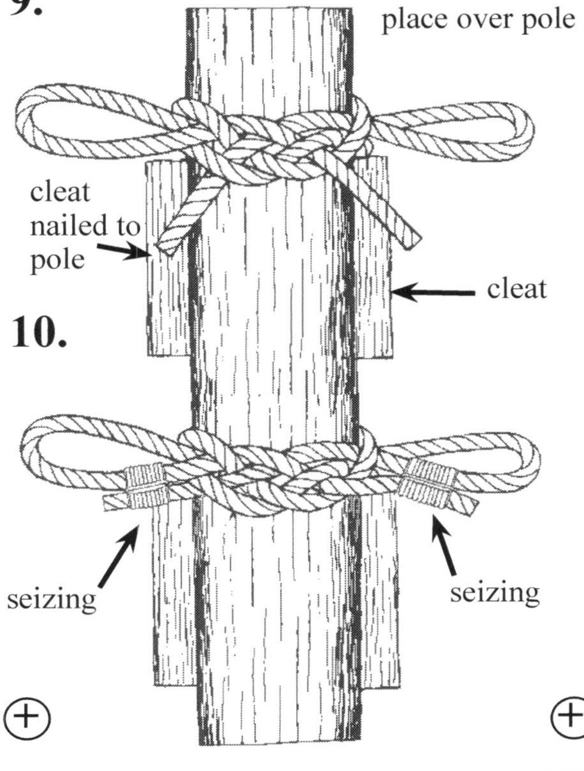

[NOTES]

SPLICING

INTRODUCTION: SPLICING

Splicing is used to join ropes together by interweaving the strands of the rope. Splicing is the safest way to fasten two ropes together or to form a loop. Knots could also be used to do these jobs but knots weaken the rope by as much as 30 to 55 percent of the original strength of the rope. However, with a splice, the rope is 85 to 90 percent as strong as the original rope. Splicing should be used whenever there is a concern about safety or when the loop or joint is going to be left in the rope.

[NOTE] After a splice is started or after each round of tucks, fold the strands back over the work. You will notice that there is one strand going in and one strand coming out between each of the strands of the standing end. If this configuration does not exist you have made a mistake; trace the strands back and correct the mistake or pull the strands out and start over.

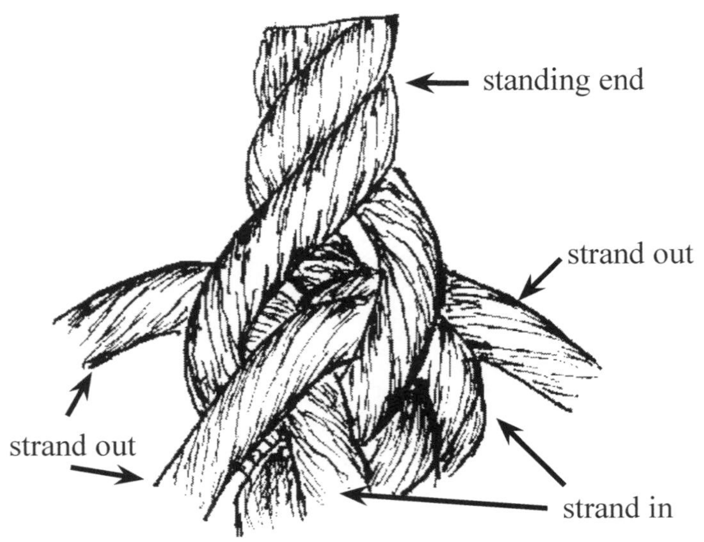

CROWN KNOT:

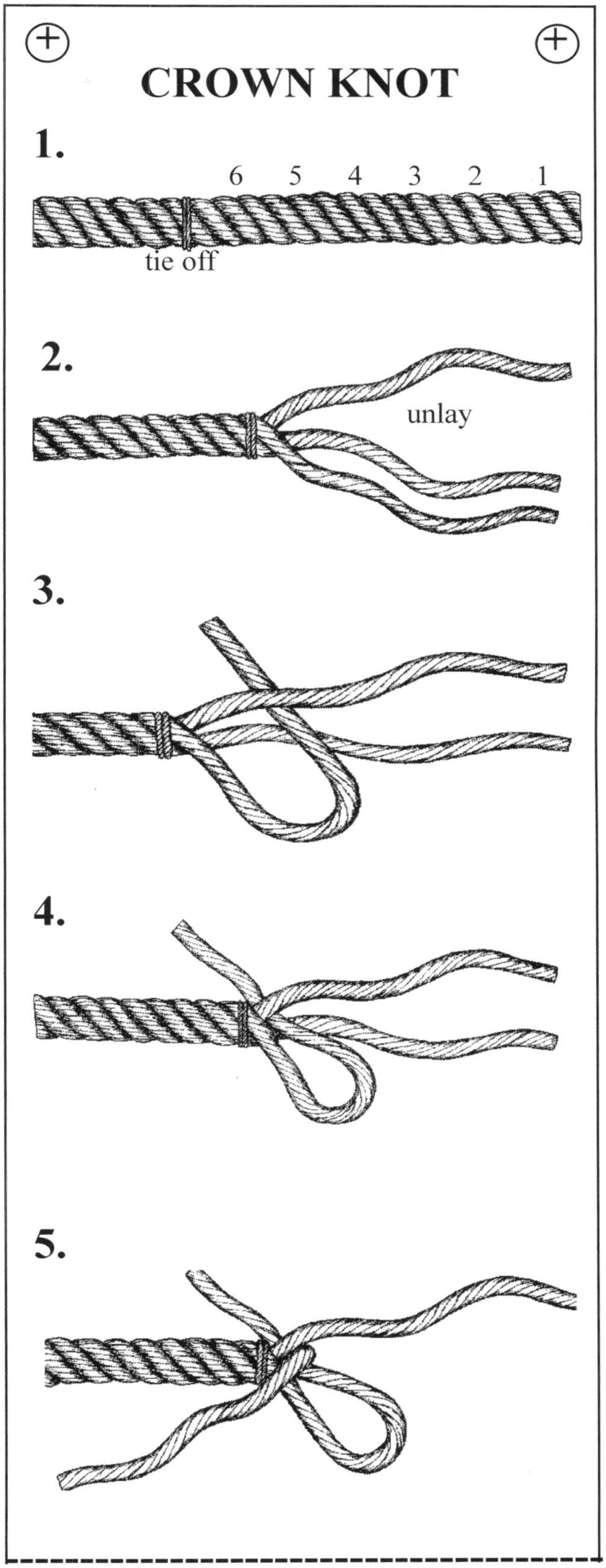

Use ---- To tie off the end of a rope so that it does not unlay. ---- To begin a back splice. ---- As part of several multiple strand knots.

Narration ---- (For knotboard) **(1)** Tie off the rope 6 complete lays from the end. **(2)** Unlay the rope to the tied off point. **(3)** Place the end of one of the unlayed strands between the other two unlayed strands; **(4)** press the strand firmly between the strands so that a loop is formed. **[NOTE]** As you are looking at the end of the rope, work counter clockwise around the rope. **(5)** Fold the second strand over the first strand. **[NOTE]** This will hold the loop in the first strand in place. **(6)** Reeve the end of the third strand through the eye of the loop. **(7)** Pull the third strand snug over the second strand. **[NOTE]** This will hold the second strand in place. **(8)** Pull the first strand loop closed. **[NOTE]** Work and pull all three strands until the knot is even and symmetrical.

CROWN KNOT

1.

6 5 4 3 2 1

tie off

2.

unlay

3.

4.

5.

6.

7.

8.

pull all strands snug and even

[NOTES]

BACK SPLICE:

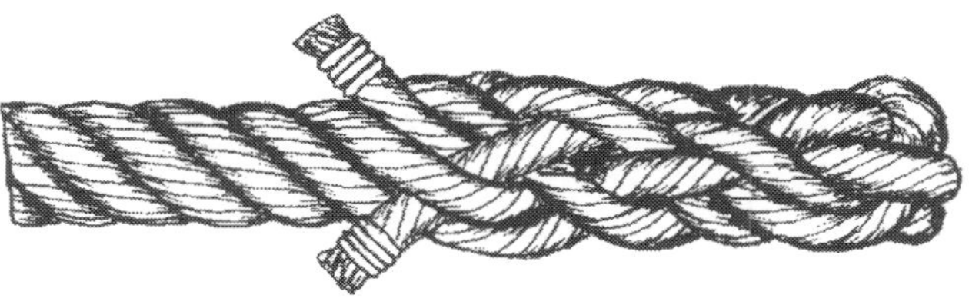

Use ---- To prevent the end of a rope from unlaying.
---- To provide a handle at the end of a rope that can easily be located.

Comments ---- The Back Splice changes the texture, size, and appearance of the end of the rope. These changes make it easier to find the rope by either sight or by feel and act as a handle to make it easier to hold on to the end of the rope. The disadvantage of the Back Splice is that the increased size makes it difficult to reeve the rope through a pulley block or similar restricted space.

Narration ---- (For knotboard) **(1)** Start the Back Splice by tying a Crown Knot. **(2)** The first tuck can be taken with any of the three unlayed strands; working counterclockwise, pass the chosen strand over the main strand next to it and under the next main strand. **(3)** Pull the strand snug. **(4)** As you are looking at the end of the rope, rotate the rope 1/3 of a turn clockwise. **(5)** The second tuck is taken with the unlayed strand that is counterclockwise to the first strand; pass the second strand over the main strand that is next to it and under the next main strand; the second strand is tucked in where the first strand came out. **(6)** Pull the second strand snug. **(7)** Again, as you are looking at the end of the rope, rotate the rope 1/3 of a turn clockwise. **(8)** The third tuck is taken with the remaining unlayed strand; pass the third strand over the main strand that is next to it and under the next main strand; the third strand is tucked in where the second strand came out and comes out where the first strand went in. **(9)** Pull the third strand snug. **(10)** Add 2 or 3 rounds of tucks.

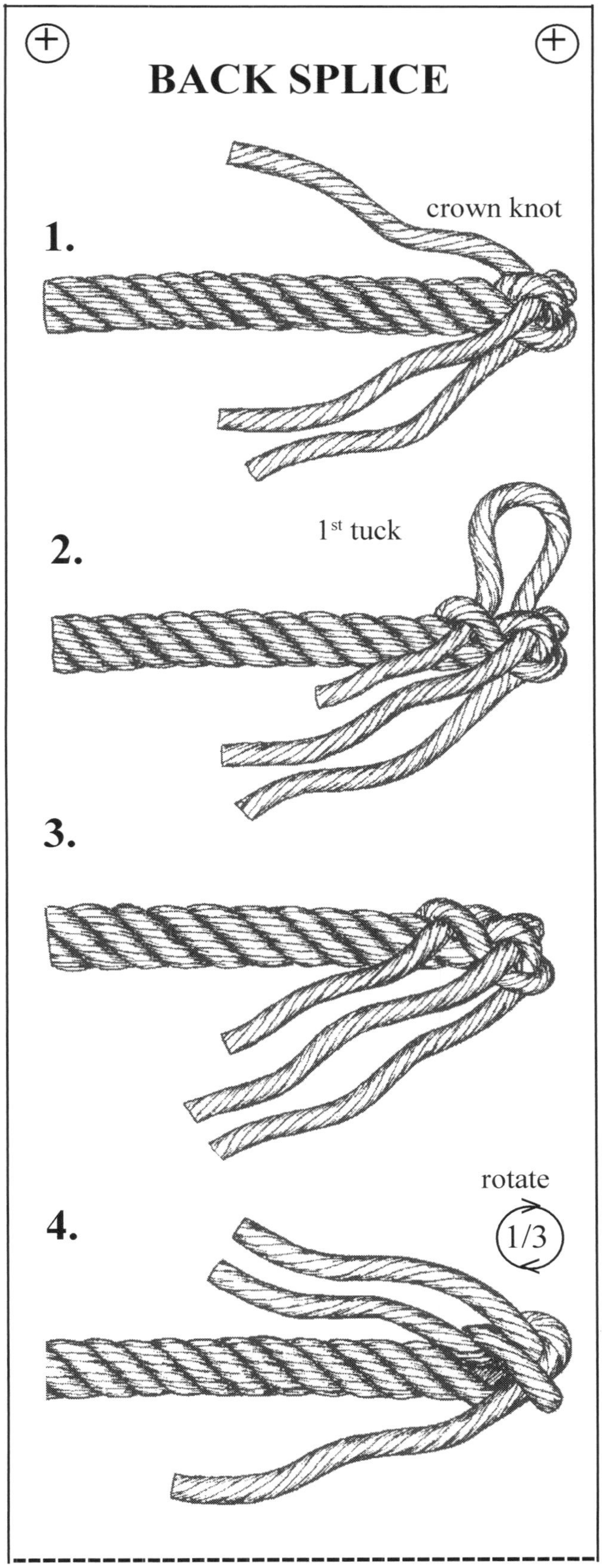

BACK SPLICE

1. crown knot

2. 1st tuck

3.

4. rotate 1/3

5. 2nd tuck

6. pull snug

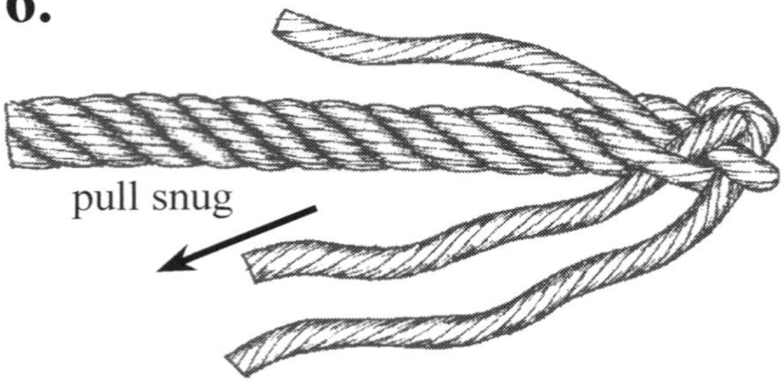

7. rotate 1/3

8. 3rd tuck

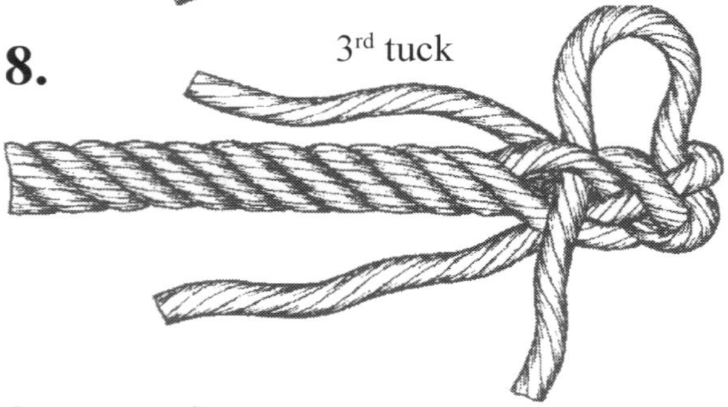

9. pull snug

10. add 2 or 3 rounds of tucks

[NOTE] Fold the unlayed strands back over the work; if the work is done correctly, there should be one strand going in and one strand coming out between each of the main strands.

[NOTES]

EYE SPLICE:

Use ---- To form a permanent loop or eye in the end of a rope.

Comments ---- The loop formed by a well made Eye Splice maintains 85% or more of the original strength of the rope. This makes the Eye Splice the preferred way to form a permanent loop in the end of a rope. However, if the eye is to be subjected to repeated chafing, such as a rope being pulled through it, the eye should be serviced with a wear resistant twine.

Narration ---- (For knotboard) **(1 and 2)** Count back and unlay 5 rounds of the lay of the rope. **(3)** Fan the unlayed end of the rope and place it over the standing part of the rope. The strand to the inside of the eye must look like it is coming out from under the other two strands and the other two strands must be fanned in such a way that they do not cross each other. **(4)** While holding the inside strand in place, stick the middle strand under one of the strands of the standing end of the rope.

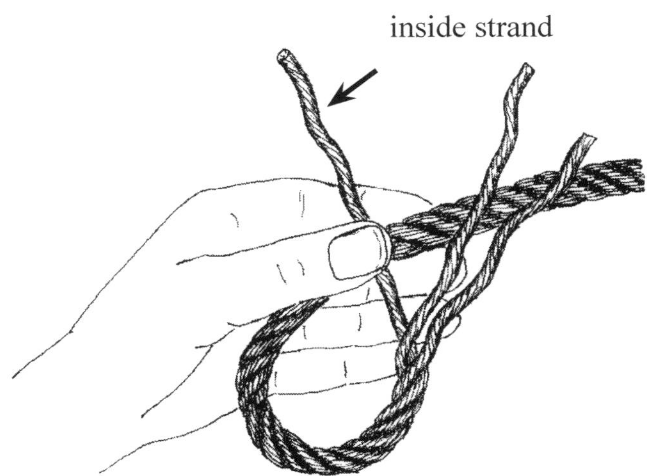

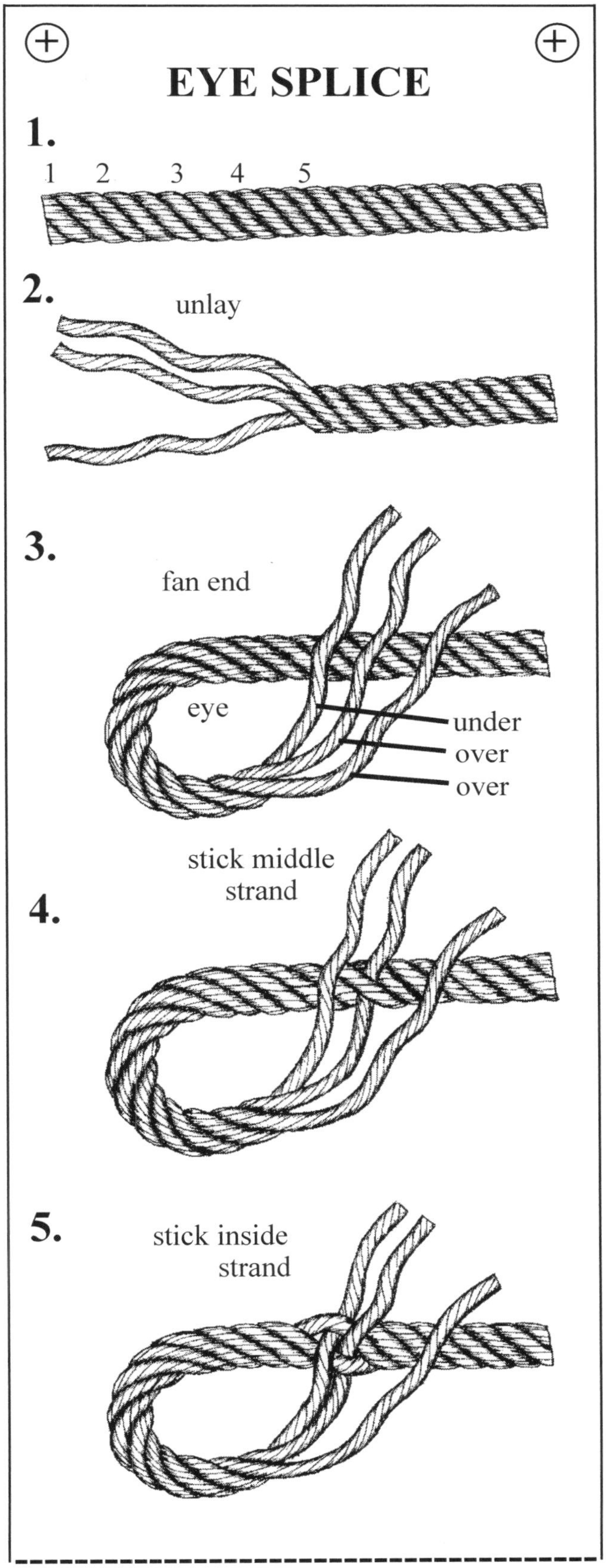

EYE SPLICE

1.

1 2 3 4 5

2.

unlay

3.

fan end

eye

under

over

over

4.

stick middle strand

5.

stick inside strand

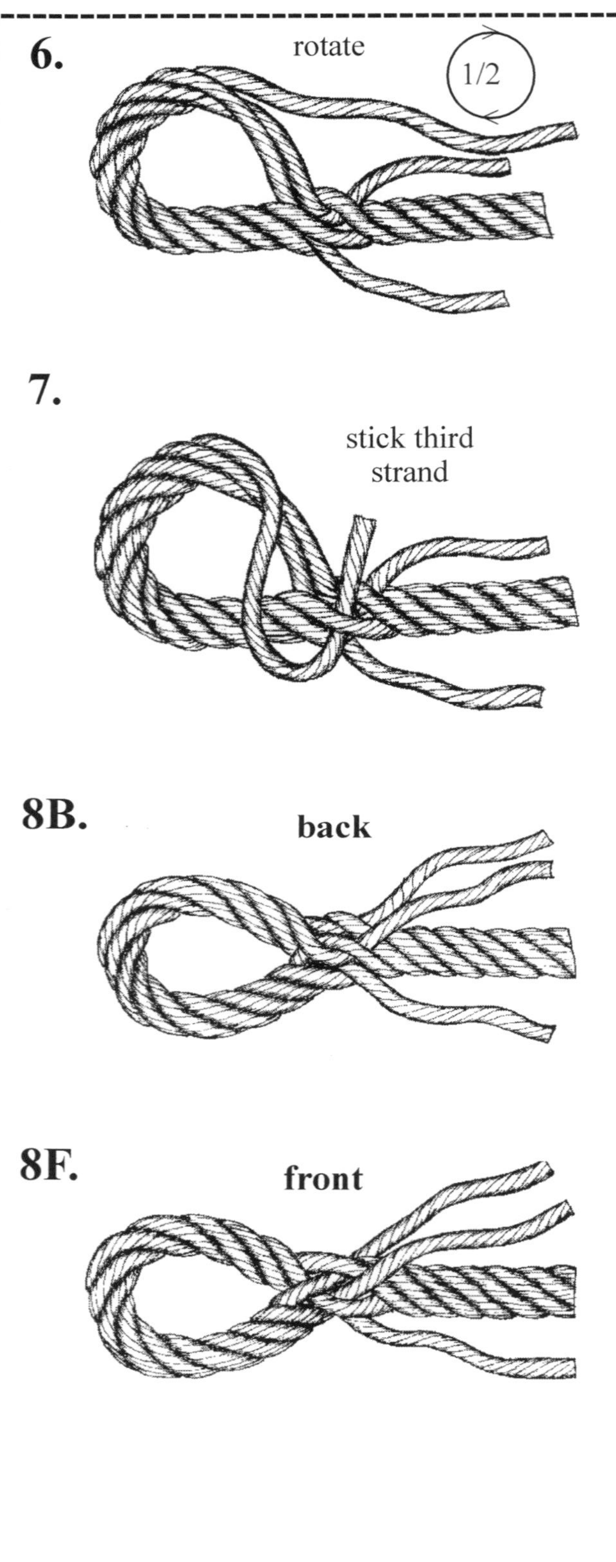

(5) Pass the inside strand over the standing end strand and stick it under the next standing end strand. **[NOTE]** The second strand goes in where the first strand came out. **(6)** Turn the splice over. **(7)** Stick the third strand under the remaining strand of the standing end. **[NOTE]** The third strand is stuck in where the second strand came out and comes out where the first strand went in. **[NOTE]** When the third strand is stuck it appears to go backward but when it is examined closely you will see that it is stuck in the same direction as the other two strands. **(8B and 8F)** Complete first round of the splice by working the strands snug.

[NOTE] When the strands are folded back over the eye, you will notice that there is one strand going in and one strand coming out between each of the strands of the standing end.

[NOTE] Finish the splice by adding several rounds of tucks.

SHORT SPLICE:

Use ---- To join two ropes of the same kind together.
---- To repair a damaged portion of a rope.

Comments ---- Because a well made Short Splice retains 85% of the original strength of a rope, a Short Splice should be used to permanently join two pieces of rope. The disadvantage of the Short Splice is that it increases the diameter of the rope so that it is difficult to reeve the rope through a pulley block or other restricted space.

Narration ---- (For knotboard) **(1)** Unlay the ends of the ropes that are to be joined. **(2)** Arrange the unlayed ends so that they alternate with each other. **(3)** Push the two ends together so that the unlayed strands of each rope are parallel to each other. **(4)** Use a short piece of twine to tie the unlayed strands in place. **(5)** The first tuck can be taken with any of the three unlayed strands. Pass the chosen strand over the main strand next to it and under the next main strand. **(6)** Pull the first strand snug. **[NOTE]** Do not overtighten the strand. Overtightening the strands can cause the splice to be uneven. **(7)** Rotate the top of the work away from you so that the next strand is at the top of the work. **(8)** The second tuck is taken with the next unlayed strand; pass the second strand over the strand that is next to it and stick it under the next strand; the second strand is stuck in where the first strand came out. **(9)** Pull the second strand snug. **(10)** Again, rotate the top of the work away from you so that the third strand is at the top of the work. **(11)** The third tuck is taken with the remaining unlayed strand; pass the third strand over the main strand that is next to it and stick it under the next strand; the third strand is stuck in where the second strand came out and comes out where the first strand went in. **(12)** Pull the third strand snug.

[NOTE] Finish the Short Splice by turning the work end for end and repeating steps 5 through 12. Then add 3 to 4 rounds of tucks to each side.

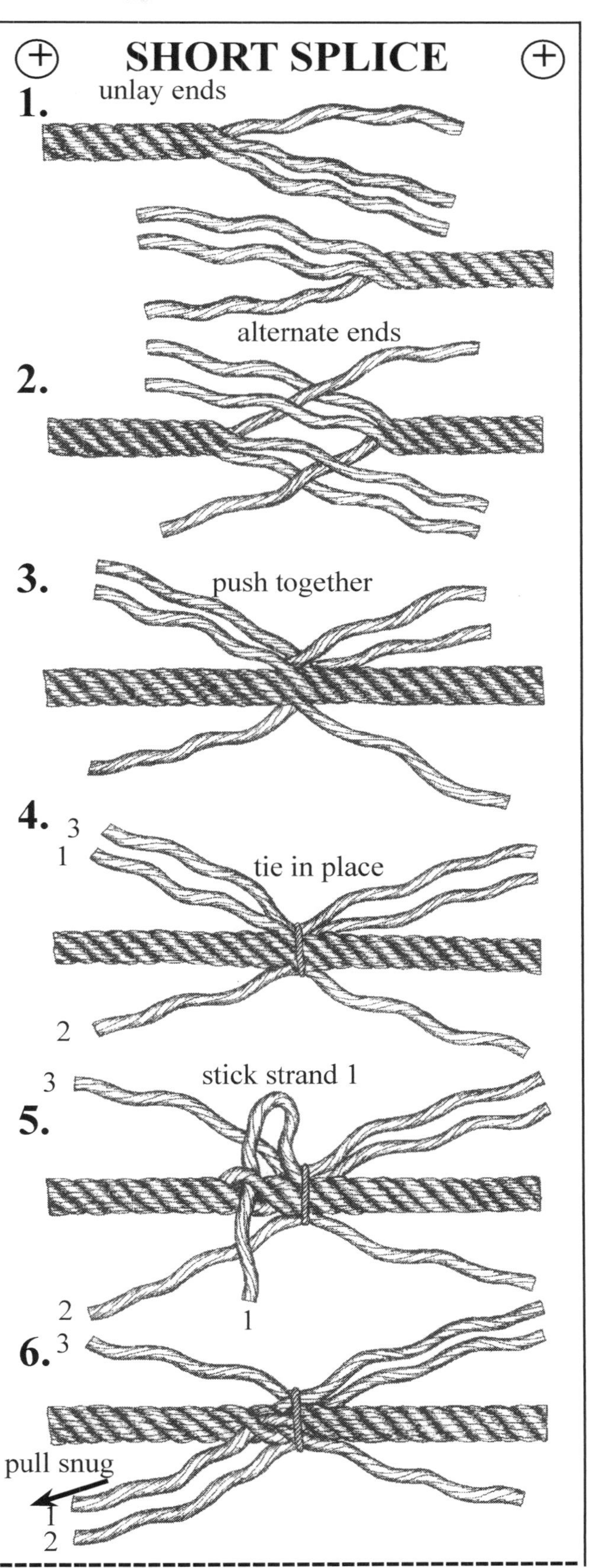

7. rotate

8. stick 2 in where 1 came out

9. pull snug

10. rotate

11. stick 3 in where 2 came out and out where 1 went in

12. pull snug

Repeat steps 5 through 12 on the other side.

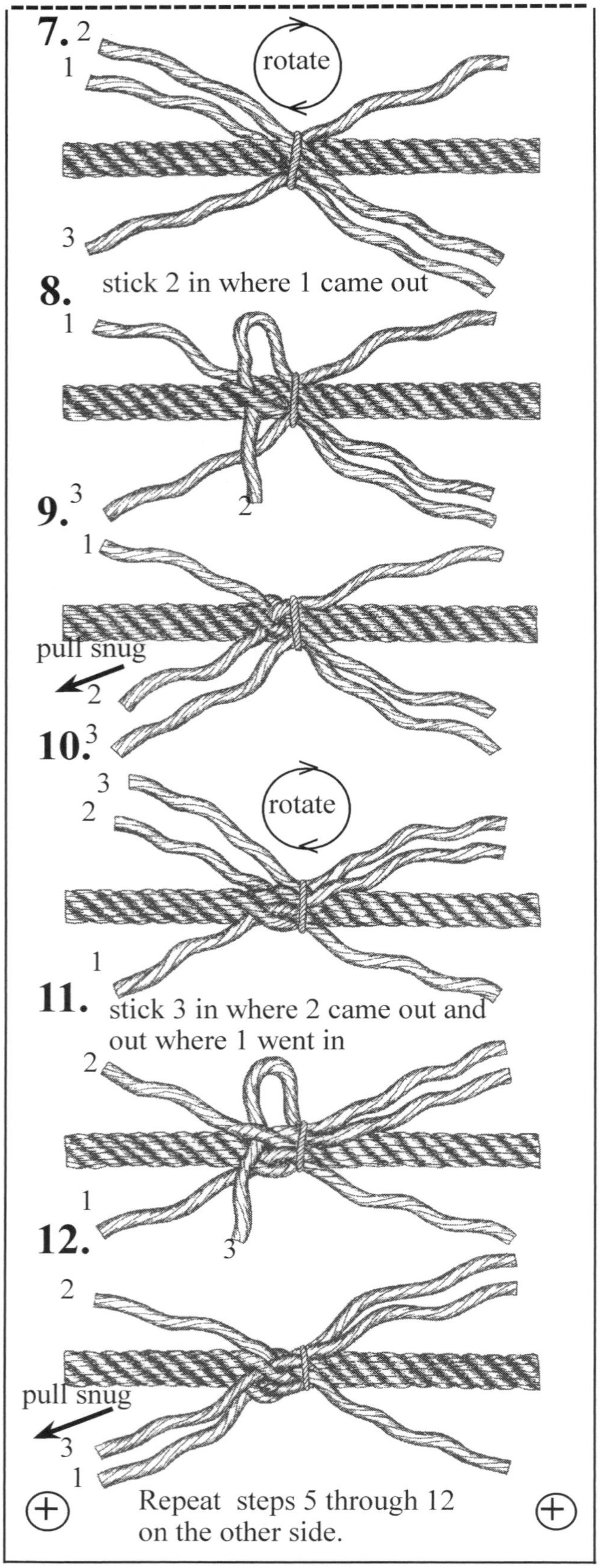

[NOTE] Fold the unlayed strands back over the work; if the work is done correctly, there should be one strand going in and one strand coming out between each of the main strands.

[NOTES]

ADDING ROUND OF TUCKS:

Description ---- When a splice is finished, the spliced portion of the rope should have the appearance of a braided rope.

Use ---- To add length to a splice after the splice is started.

Comments ---- The adding of a round of tucks is the same for the Eye Splice, the Back Splice, and the Short Splice. The number of rounds of tucks that are needed depends on the type of rope that is being spliced. If the rope to be spliced is made of natural fiber, 3 or 4 rounds of tucks will be enough because natural fibers are usually rough and therefore create substantial friction between the strands of the rope. The friction between the strands of the rope is the force that holds the splice together. Synthetic fibers are usually smooth, therefore there is less friction between the strands of a synthetic fiber rope that is being spliced than between the strands of a natural fiber rope that is being spliced. When splicing a synthetic fiber rope, compensate for the reduced friction between the strands of synthetic fiber rope by adding more rounds of tucks. A splice in a synthetic fiber rope should have 5 or 6 rounds of tucks.

Narration ---- (For knotboard) **(1)** Check the splice to make sure that the strands are properly placed and decide which strand is to be the first strand (all the strands are the same until the first tuck is taken.) **[NOTE]** When the strands are folded back over the splice, you will notice that there is one strand going in and one strand coming out between each of the strands of the standing end.

ADDING ROUND OF TUCKS

1.

1
2
3

2.

1 goes in where 2 came out and out where 3 came out

1st tuck
2
3
1

3.

pull snug
1
2
3

4.

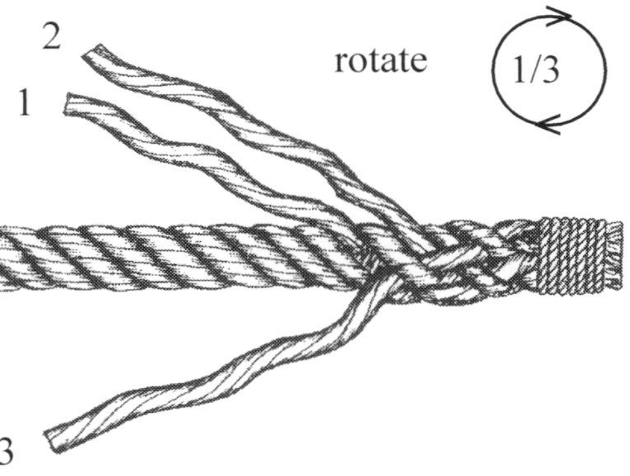

2
1
rotate
1/3
3

5. 2 goes in between 1 and 3

1
2nd tuck
2
3

6.
1
pull snug
2
3

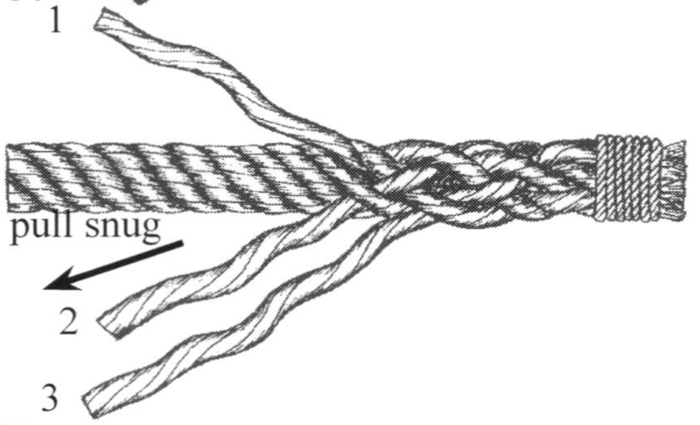

7.
3
2
rotate 1/3
1

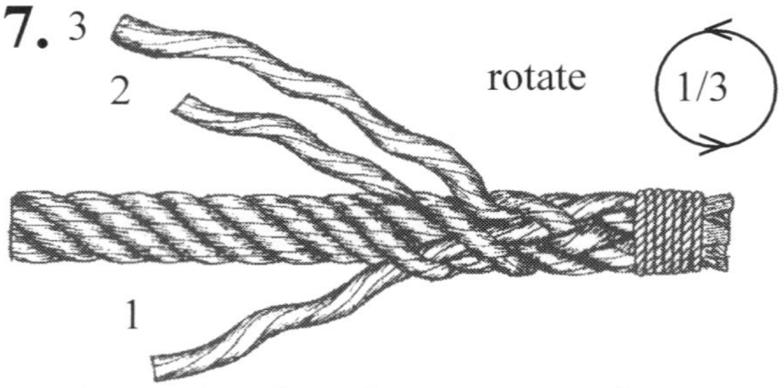

8. 3 goes in where 2 came out and out where 1 went in

2
1
3

9.
2
pull snug
3
1

10. repeat steps 2 through 9 for each round of tucks

(2) Tuck strand 1 in where strand 2 came out and out where strand 3 came out in the previous round of tucks. **(3)** Pull strand 1 snug. **[NOTE]** Twist each strand tight as it is pulled snug. This twisting will result in a neater and more even appearance to the finished splice.

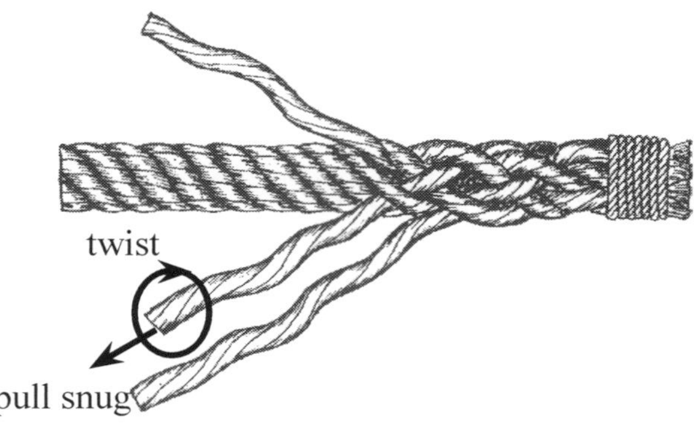

(4) Rotate the work 1/3 of a turn so that strand 2 is at the top front. **(5)** Tuck strand 2 in between strands 1 and 3. **(6)** Pull strand 2 snug. **(7)** Rotate the work 1/3 of a turn so that strand 3 is at the top front. **(8)** Tuck strand 3 in where strand 2 came out and out where strand 1 went in. **(9)** Pull strand 3 snug. **(10)** Repeat steps 1 through 9 for each additional round of tucks.

[NOTES]

SLIDING EYE SPLICE:

Use ---- A Sliding Eye Splice is used to make an adjustable eye at the end of a rope. The Sliding Eye Splice can be used in much the same way that a Taut-line Hitch is used. It can also be used to make an adjustable length toggle rope, or the eye can be slid tightly around a tool handle to form a temporary safety line.

Comments ---- The Sliding Eye Splice should not be used in place of a standard Eye Splice, because the Sliding Eye Splice is not as strong as a standard Eye Splice and may reduce the strength of the rope by as much as 50%.

STEP 1: Open the lay of the rope by grasping the rope so that there are 4 to 5 strands between your hands and then twisting the ends of the rope in opposite directions.

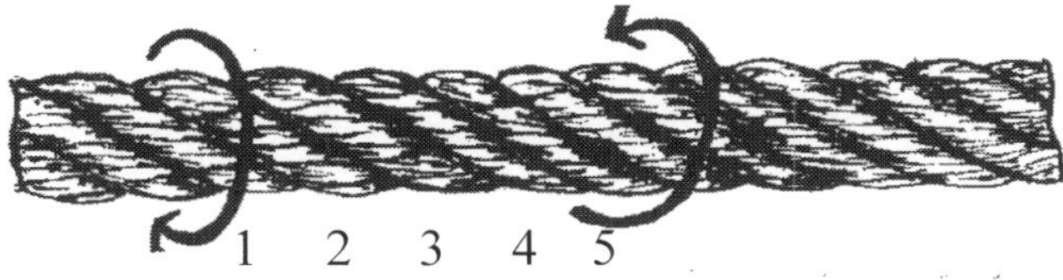

STEP 2: As you twist the rope to open the lay, push the ends of the rope toward each other. This will cause the strands to kink and form loops.

STEP 3: Enlarge the loops formed by the kinks by folding the rope at a 90° angle. Continue to twist the ends of the rope and push toward the loops.

STEP 4: When the loops are large enough, reeve the ends of the rope through the loops to finish the splice.

ENDING A SPLICE:

Comments ---- The way a splice is ended does not affect its strength but it does affect the appearance of the splice. The simplest way to end a splice is to cut the ends of the strands off so that their length is about 1 1/2 times the diameter of the rope. The problem with this is that the ends become frayed and start to look shaggy.

When synthetic rope is used, the end of the strands can be cut off so that their length is about 1/2 the diameter of the rope. The ends are then heat fused.

Whipping each strand close to the rope before cutting off the strand gives the splice a finished look. If synthetic rope is used, the strands can be fused after they are cut off.

Cross Whipping:

Cross Whipping prevents the end of the strands from working out from under the last tuck. Cross Whipping is done by dividing each strand in half and then Whipping the adjacent halves together. If synthetic rope is used, the whipped ends can be fused after they are cut off.

Servicing:

A splice is served by wrapping twine or cord over the splice to secure the ends of the strands and prevent the splice from being chafed.

Preventing chafing of an eye:

If an Eye Splice is to be used where it will be chafed, the rope of the eye can be protected by making the Eye Splice around a metal thimble.

Serving the eye of an Eye Splice with Ringbolt Hitching will also protect an Eye Splice from chafing. The advantages of the Ringbolt Hitching over a thimble are that the eye remains flexible and the eye can be made any size. The disadvantage of the Ringbolt Hitching is that it will not last as long as a metal thimble.

ENDING A SPLICE

cut ends to 1 1/2 times the diameter of the rope

cut ends of synthetic rope to 1/2 the diameter of the rope and heat fuse

whip ends and cut off

CROSS WHIPPING

divide strands, whip adjacent parts together

SERVICING

GRAPEVINE SERVICING

servicing with running half hitches

To protect the eye from chafing:

splice in a metal thimble

service with ringbolt hitching

[NOTES]

GROMMET:

Description ---- A Grommet is a continuous loop of rope.

Use ---- Small Grommets are sewn into canvas or sailcloth to reinforce a hole where a rope is passed through. Larger Grommets are used as block straps or rings for a ring toss game. Still larger Grommets are used as slings or anchor points for guy lines.

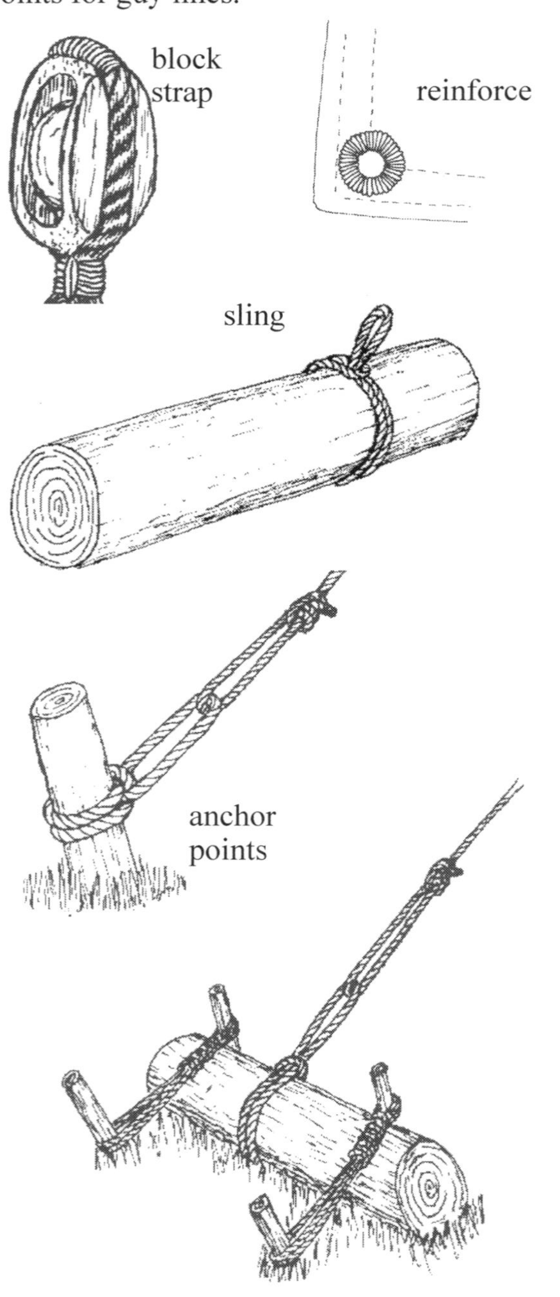

Other Names ---- Strap Loop, Sling.

Comments ---- Grommets can be made in two ways; one, use a Short Splice to join the ends of a rope; two, lay up a single strand of a rope into a multiple strand grommet. The lay up method is shown in the following directions.

STEP 1:

Cut a length of rope that is three times as long as the circumference of the finished Grommet plus 8 to 10 complete turns of the lay of the rope.

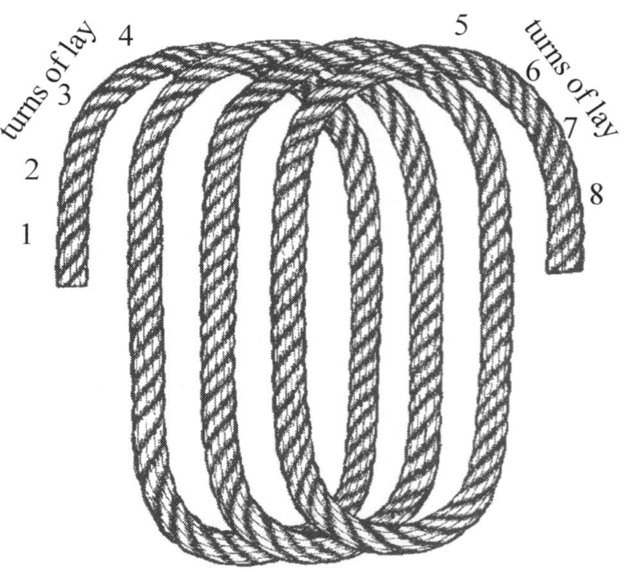

length three times the circumference

STEP 2:

Unlay the rope.

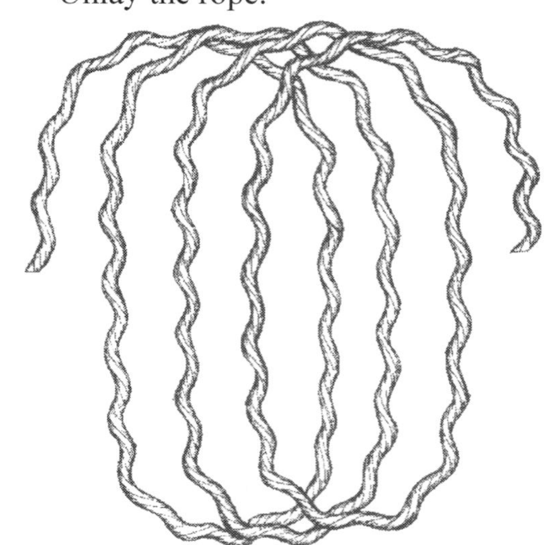

STEP 3:

Lay up the rope. Start at the middle of the strand. Form a loop of the desired size and lay up the rope into a two strand laid rope.

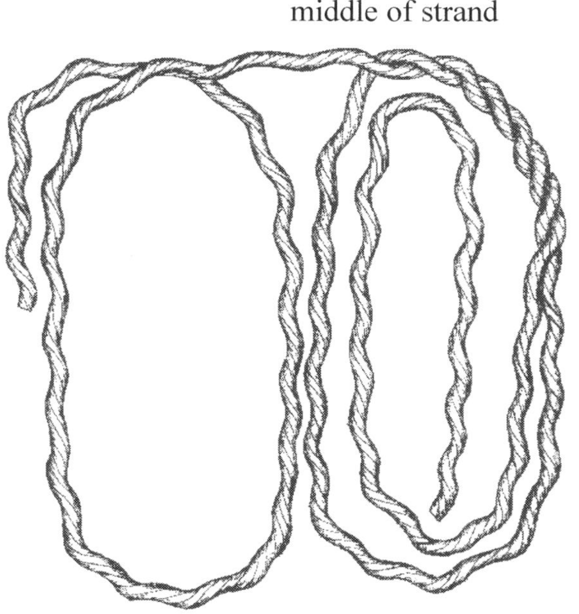

STEP 4:

Be careful to add just enough twist to the strand to make it lay in the same position as it was in the original rope.

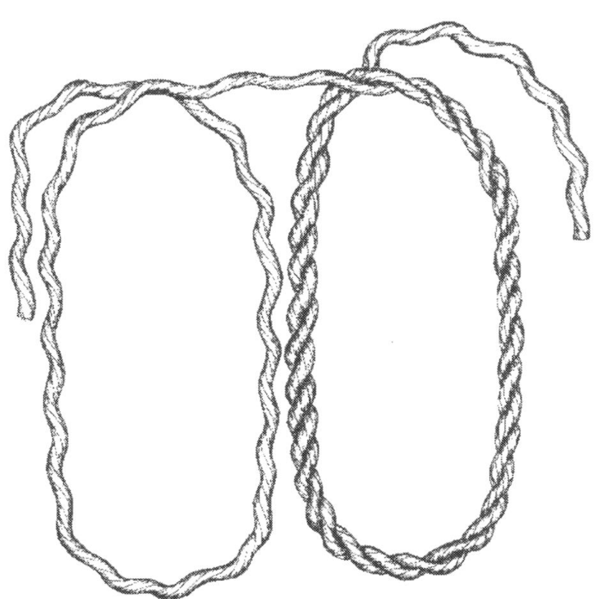

STEP 5:

Start at the middle again and lay up the strand in the opposite direction to form a three strand laid rope.

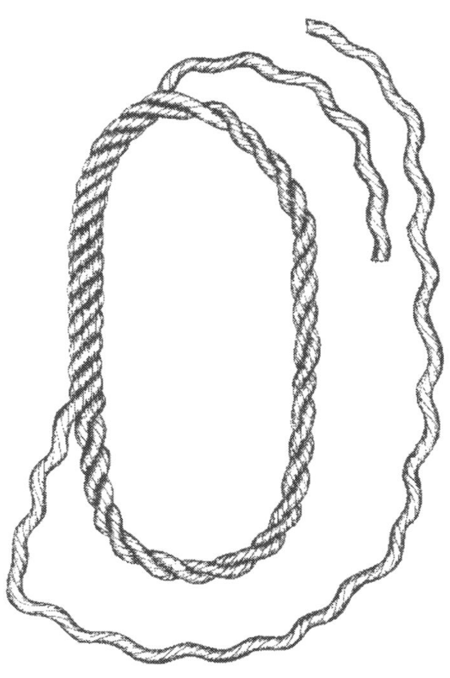

STEP 6:

Be careful to add only enough twist to the strand to make it lay in the same position as it was in the original rope.

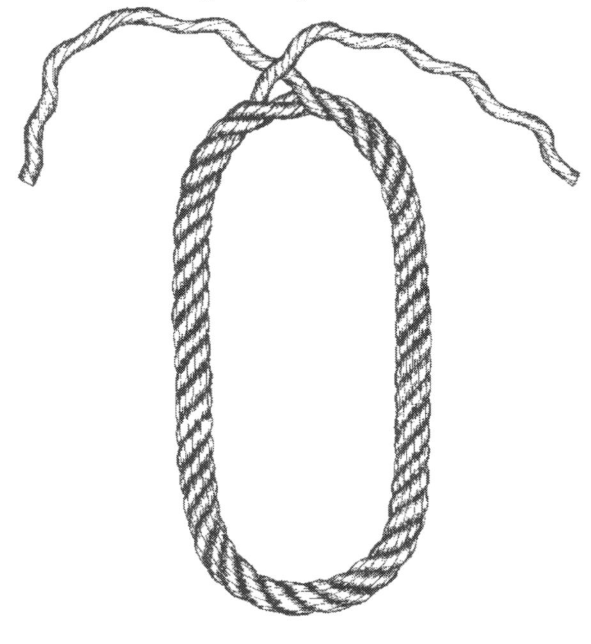

STEP 7:

Join the ends of the strand. The ends of the strand are joined in the same way that a strand in a Long Splice would be joined. The method shown here is only one of several accepted methods.

1. Complete the laying up of the strand.

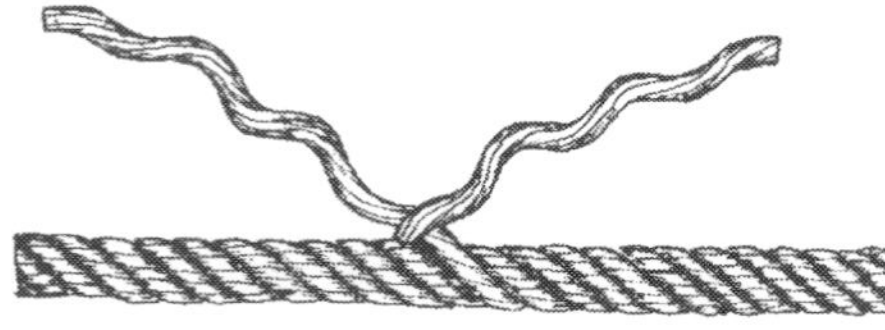

2. Tie a Half Knot with the lay of the strand.

3. Pull the Half Knot snug.

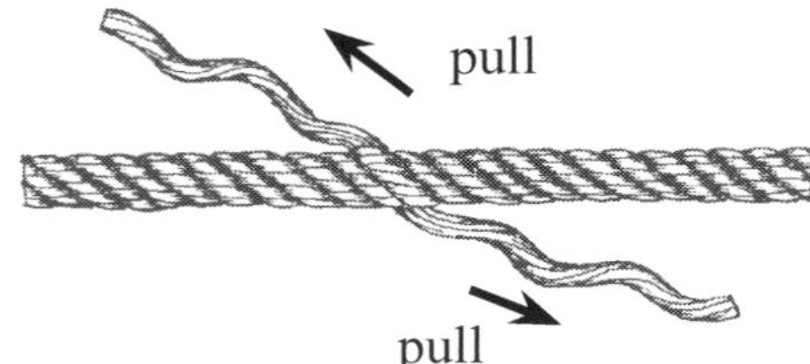

4. Turn the work over.

5. Tuck the strand under the next strand so that it is tucked with the lay of the strand.

6. Pull snug.

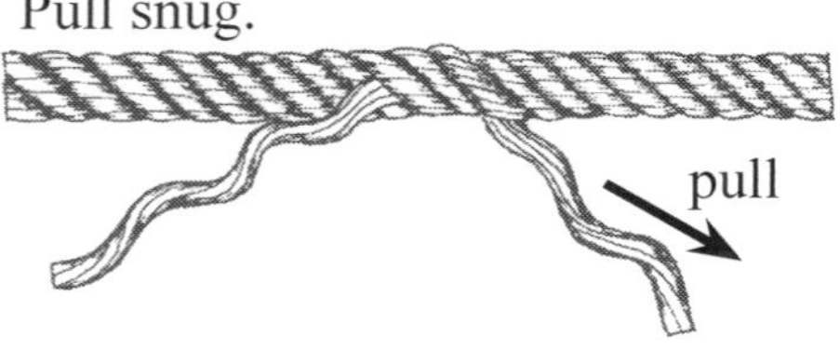

7. Divide the strand in half.

8. Using one half of the strand, go over the next strand of the rope and tuck the half strand under the second strand of the rope so that it is tucked opposite the lay of the strand.

9. Pull snug.

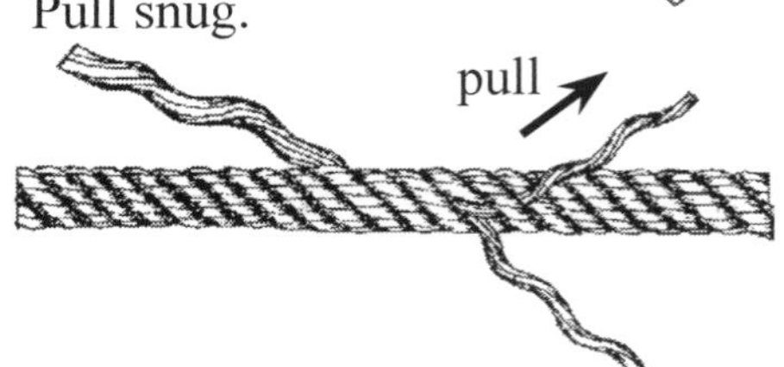

10. Tuck the half strand under the next strand of the rope so that it is with the lay of the strand.

11. Pull snug.

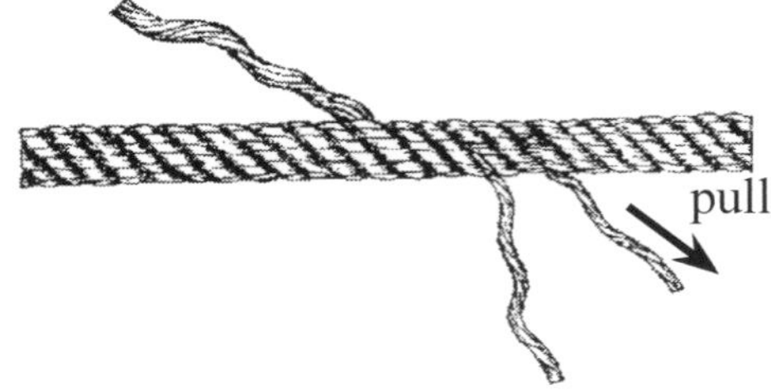

12. Secure the other end of the strand by repeating steps 3 through 11. Trim the half strands so that they stick out a distance equal to their diameter. (Fuse the ends of synthetic rope.)

LASHINGS

INTRODUCTION: LASHING

Lashings are used to join poles or spars when building pioneering structures. These structures can be functional; such as tables, bridges, and towers, or decorative; such as gateways. The only limit as to the type of structure is the imagination of the builder.

Correctly tied lashings in pioneering structures are essential for safety. When young people see an interesting structure, they charge up and over with no thought as to the soundness of the structure. This places the responsibility for a safe structure directly on the builder.

SQUARE LASHING:

Use ---- To bind poles that are in contact and cross each other at any angle from 45° to 90°.

Comments ---- The Square Lashing gets its name from the fact that the wrapping turns are at 90° or "square" to the poles.

Traditional Square Lashing is the most frequently used and the most secure form of lashing. If tied properly, the Square Lashing will remain tight and secure, but, as with all lashings, if any steps are omitted or done carelessly, the lashing will loosen and create a dangerous situation.

The Square Lashing can be used to bind poles together that contact and cross each other at any angle from 45° to 90°. If the angle of contact is less than 45°, a Shear Lashing should be used.

When tying a Square Lashing, the poles and the rope must be positioned properly to achieve the maximum strength. The cross pole

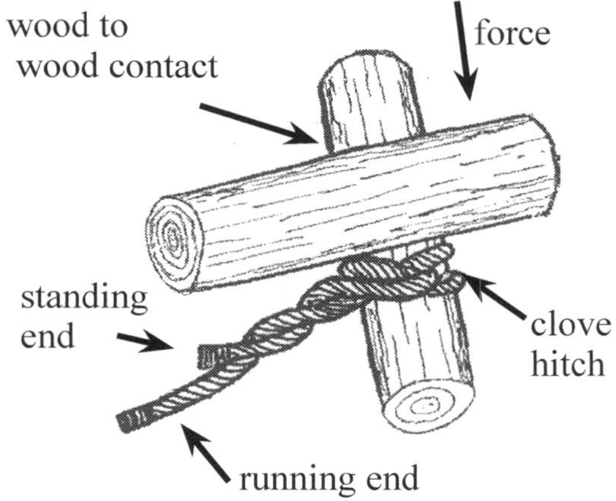

should be positioned so that the force applied to the cross pole is directed toward the pole it is lashed to; this allows the wood to wood contact to bear part of the load. If the force tends to separate the poles, only the rope will be supporting the load. The beginning Clove Hitch should be tied to the pole that is closest to parallel to the direction of the force and to the side of the cross pole that is opposite to the direction of the force. In most cases the force applied to a structure is due to gravity; therefore downward. This means that the beginning Clove Hitch is usually tied to the vertical pole and under the cross pole. Secure the running end of the rope by wrapping it around the standing end.

Narration ---- (For knotboard) **(1)** Tie a Clove Hitch to the vertical pole. **(2)** Wrap the running end of the rope around the standing end. **[NOTE]** The wrapping of the standing part around the running part is to secure the Clove Hitch so that it will not slip around the pole and loosen the lashing from the inside. **(3)** Bring the running end up and over the cross pole; then around the vertical pole; and back down over the cross pole. **(4)** Pass the rope behind the vertical pole and back up in front of the cross pole; this completes the first wrapping. **[NOTE]** Notice that the rope goes around the pole perpendicular, at 90°, to the length of the pole. This 90° angle gives the Square Lashing its name. **(5)** Take two more wrapping turns for a total of three wrappings: pull each turn tight. **[NOTE]** When the wrappings are taken around the vertical pole, the rope should be to the inside of the previous wrapping turn and the wrappings around the cross pole should be to the outside of the previous wrapping turn. When this pattern of taking the wrapping turns is followed, the rope strands remain parallel; this ensures the maximum contact between the wood and the rope. Also, if the strands are not kept parallel, the additional friction between the crossed strands will make it difficult to properly tighten the wrapping turns. **(6)** Start

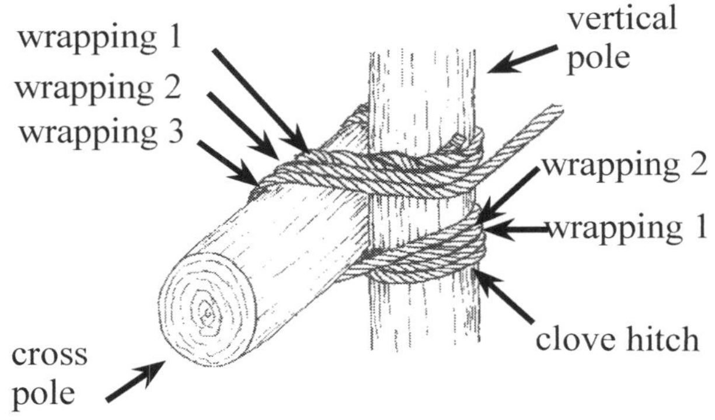

the frapping turns by taking one complete turn around the cross pole. **[NOTE]** The turn around the cross pole prevents the rope from crossing the wrapping turns on a diagonal. If the change of direction between the wrapping turns and the frapping turns is made by passing the rope diagonally across the wrapping turns, the increased friction between the rope strands will make it difficult to pull the wrapping turns tight. A diagonal across the wrapping turns will also allow unnecessary movement within the completed lashing, which could cause chafing of the rope. **(7)** Take at least two frapping turns; keep the turns parallel to each other; pull each turn tight as it is made. **[NOTE]** Keeping the frapping turns parallel prevents unnecessary friction between the turns making it easier to tighten the frapping turns. **(8)** When the last frapping turn is in place, take a Half Hitch around the cross pole; work the Half Hitch tight. **[NOTE]** To prevent the rope from crossing the wrapping turns diagonally when tying the Half Hitch, take the rope past the cross pole on the same plain as the frapping turns, then around the cross pole. **[NOTE]** To work the Half Hitch tight, first pull the running end toward the standing end. This will tighten the frapping turns.

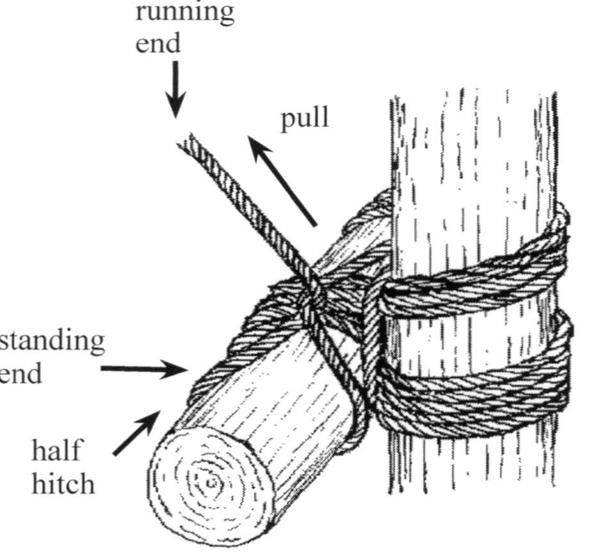

Next, while keeping tension on the running end, pull it in the opposite direction so that the loop of the Half Hitch will slip around the pole. This takes up any slack left in the rope.

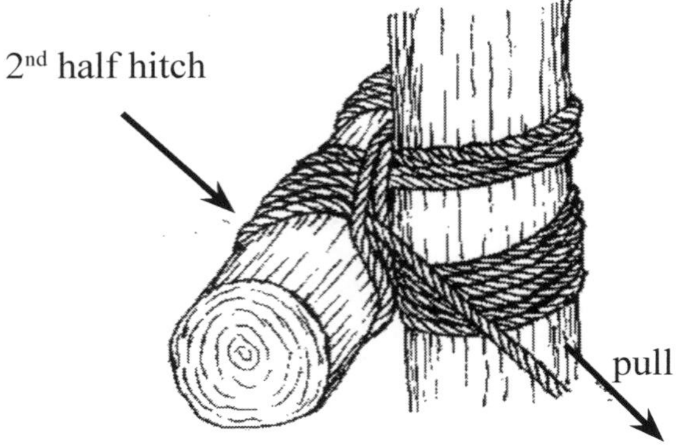

Work the running end back and forth in this way until the Half Hitch is locked tight against the lashing. If this Half Hitch is not locked against the lashing the ending Clove Hitch can slip around the pole allowing the lashing to loosen. **(9)** Add a second Half Hitch to form a Clove Hitch around the cross pole; work Half Hitch tight.

[NOTE] If smooth rope is being used, a third Half Hitch added to the Clove Hitch will help ensure that the lashing will stay securely in place.

[NOTES]

SQUARE LASHING

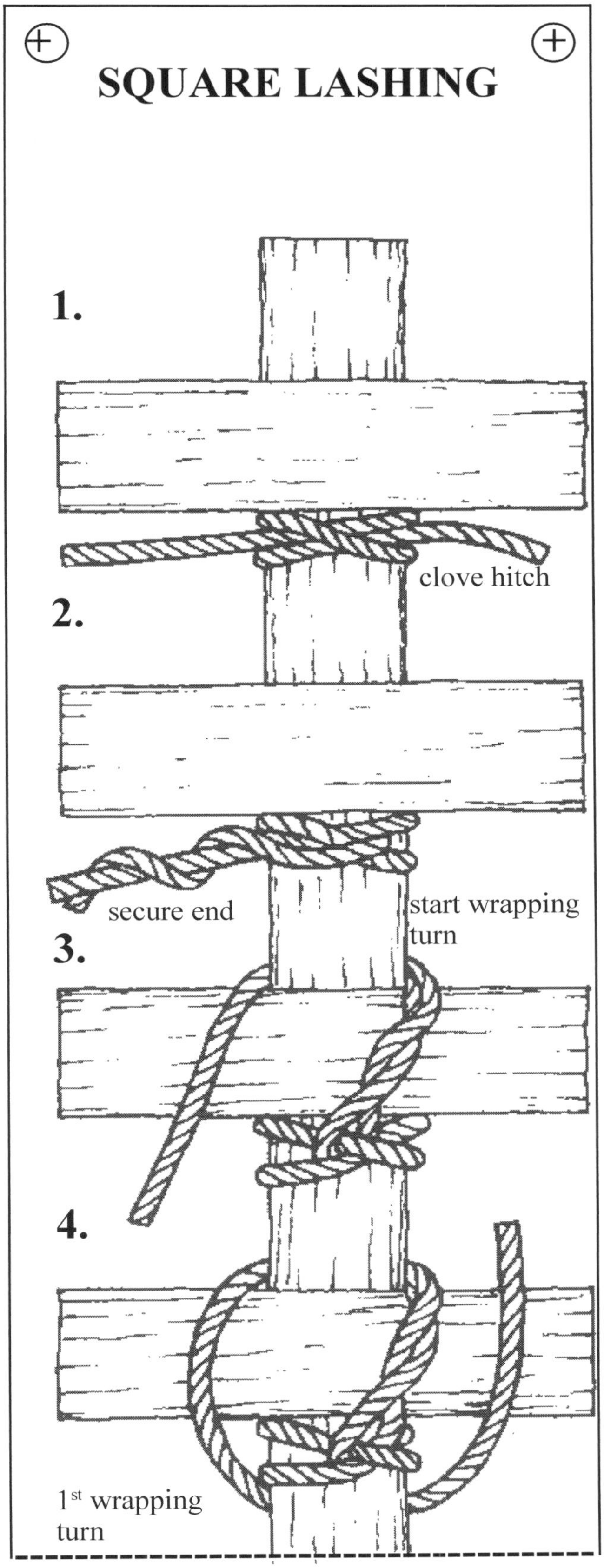

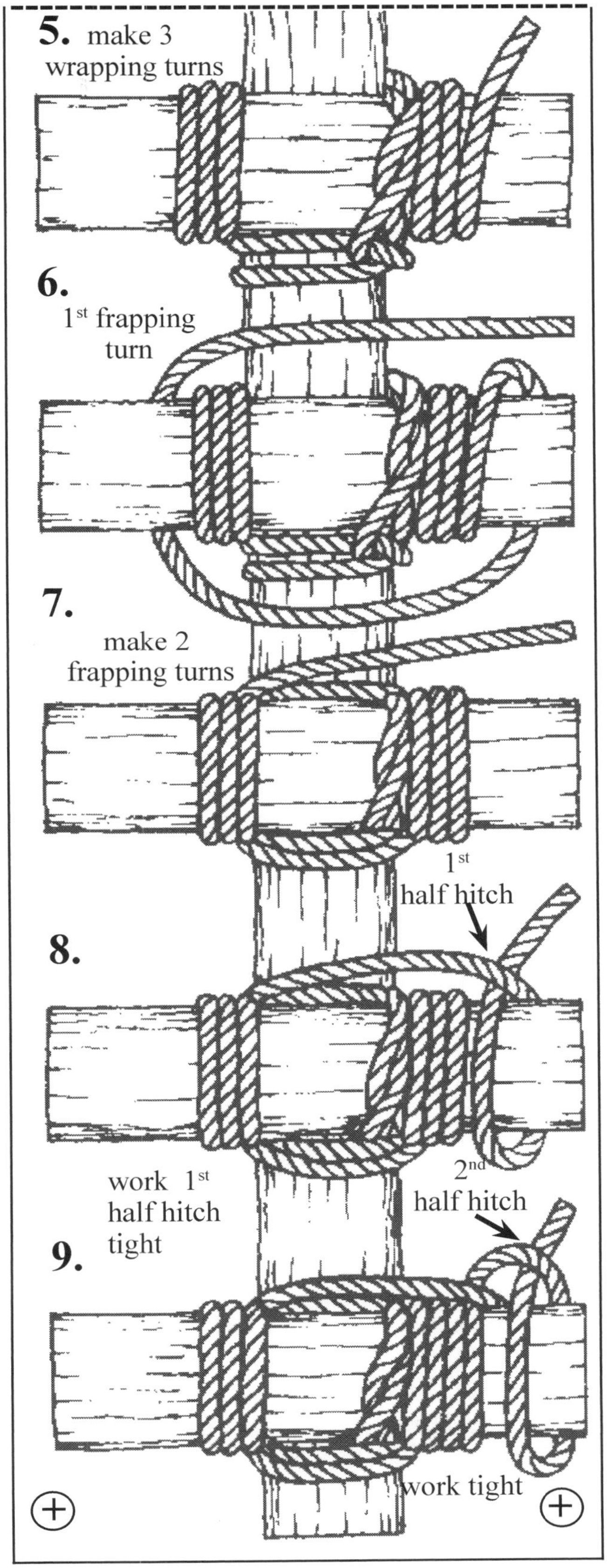

JAPANESE SQUARE LASHING:

Comments ---- The Japanese Square Lashings are a group of similar lashings that are all tied in a similar manner. The main difference is in the way each lashing is started.

The simplest and easiest form of the Japanese Square Lashing is tied by looping the center of the rope around the vertical spar and carrying the strands parallel to each other while taking the wrapping turns. The frapping turns are taken by separating the ends of the rope and taking them in opposite directions.

The Mark II Japanese Square Lashing is tied by looping the center of the rope around the upright spar and then forming the wrapping turns by taking the ends of the rope in opposite directions.

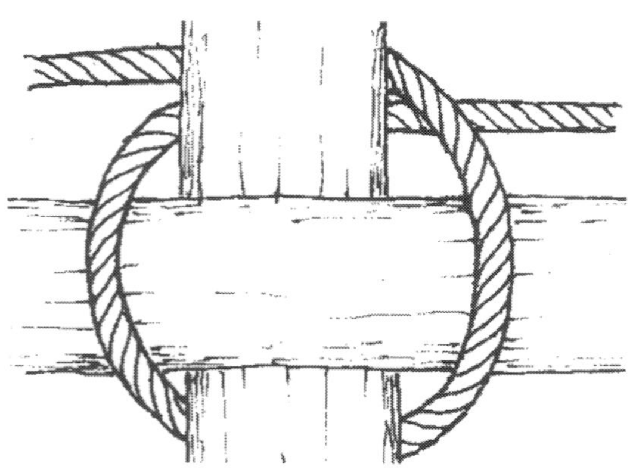

The Mark III Japanese Square Lashing is the same as the Mark II but a Clove Hitch is tied around the upright spar when starting the lashing.

The Mark III is the most secure of the three Japanese Square Lashings because the Clove Hitch helps to prevent the lashing from shifting along the vertical spar.

Narration ---- (For Japanese Square Lashing knotboard) **(1)** Start the lashing by looping the center of the rope around the vertical spar so that the loop is under the horizontal spar. **(2)** Start the wrapping turns by leading the ends around the spars so that the two strands of the rope are parallel to each other. **(3)** When making the wrapping turns, the two strands of the rope are led around the spars at 90^0 to the spars; do not allow the strands to cross; be sure to keep the strands parallel. **(4)** Complete the wrapping turns by leading the rope strand around the vertical pole. **(5)** Start the frapping turns by separating the strands so that one strand is above the horizontal spar and the other strand is below the horizontal spar. **(6)** Lead the frapping strands in opposite directions. **(7)** Make two complete frapping turns; pull each turn tight as it is made; tie the first Half Knot of the ending Square Knot. **(8)** Tie the second Half Knot of the Square Knot to complete the lashing. **(9)** For safety add Half Hitches; the Half Hitches prevent the Square Knot from upsetting.

JAPANESE SQUARE LASHING

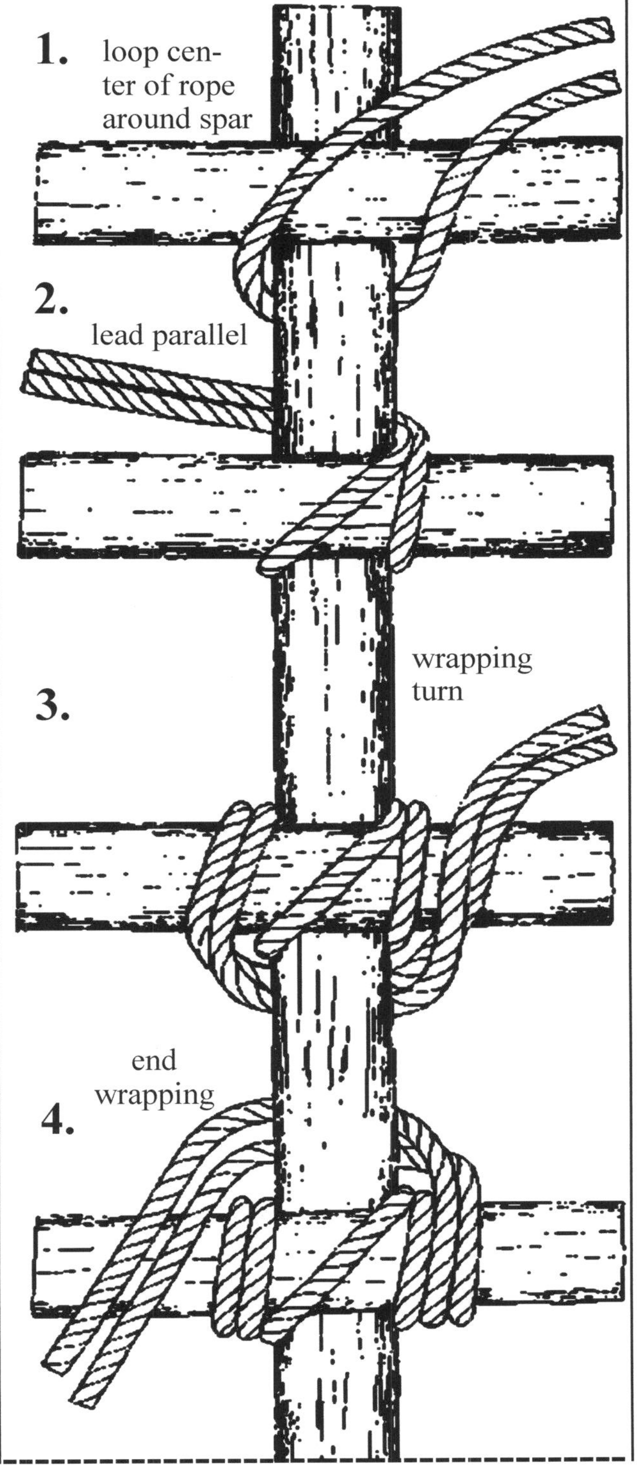

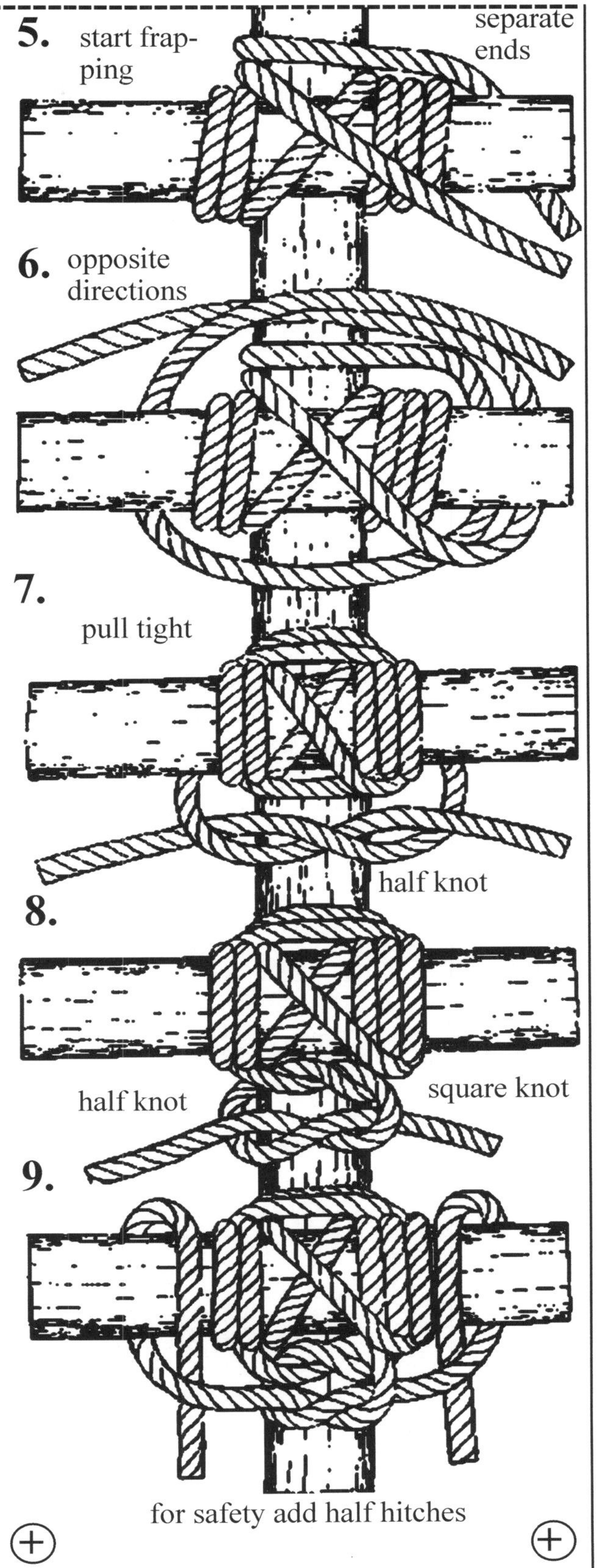

JAPANESE SQUARE LASHING MARK II

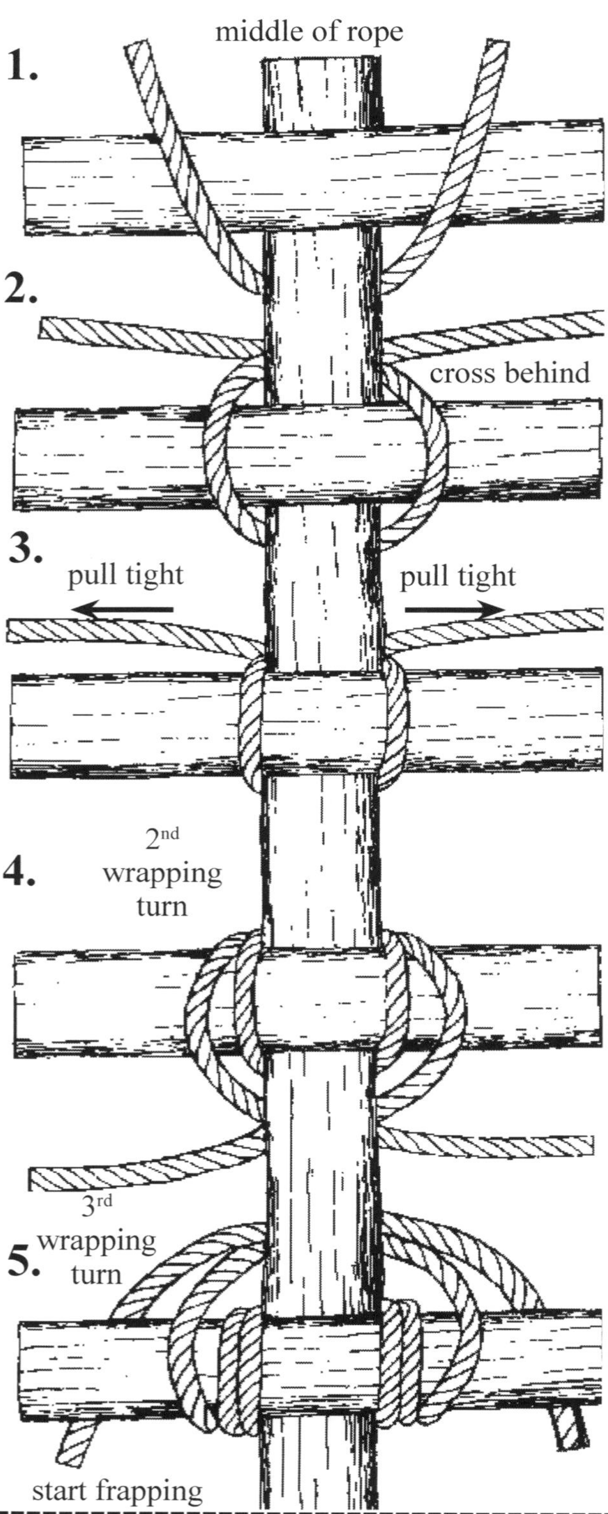

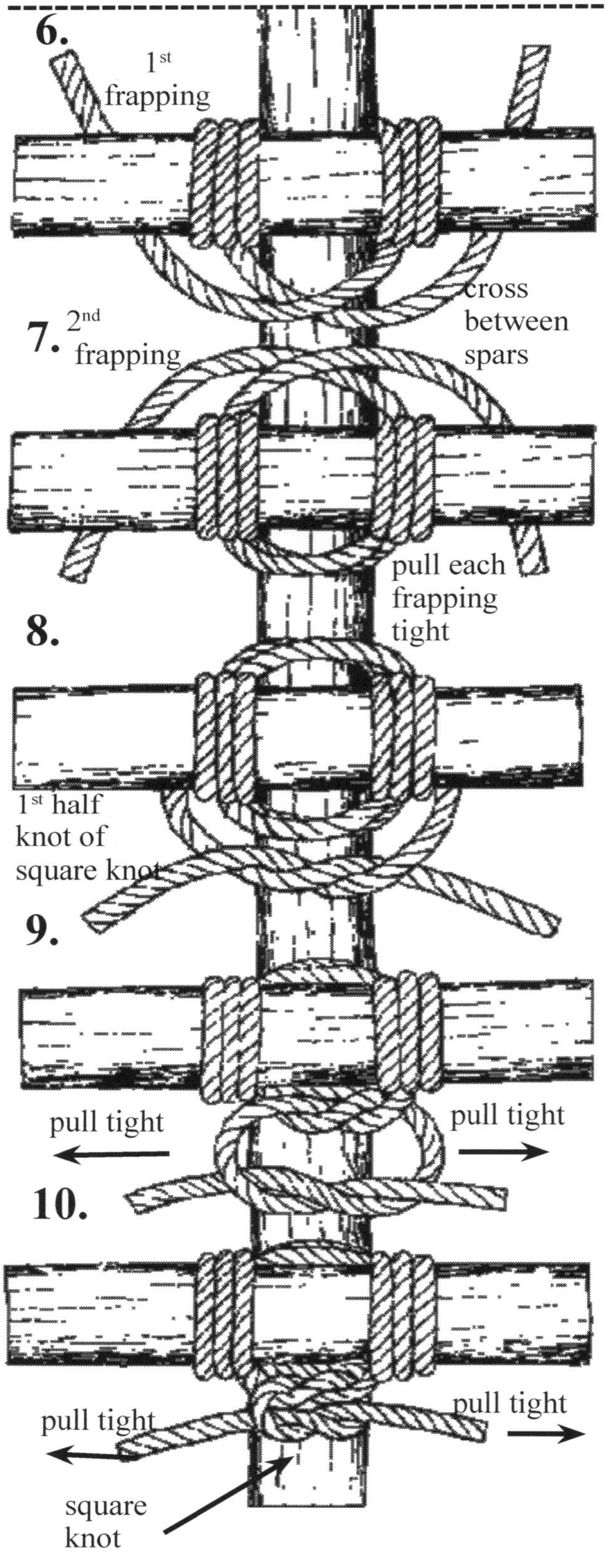

Narration ---- (For Mark II knotboard) **(1)** Start the lashing by tying the center of the rope around the vertical spar with a Clove Hitch so that the Clove Hitch is under the horizontal spar. **(2)** Make the first wrapping turn by leading the ends up over the front of the horizontal spar and then in opposite directions behind the vertical spar. **(3)** Pull the strands tight but do not allow them to cross each other. **(4)** Add the second wrapping turn by leading the ends of the rope down over the front of the horizontal spar and then in opposite directions behind the vertical spar. **(5)** Complete the frapping turns by leading the ends of the rope up over the front of the horizontal spar and then in opposite directions behind the vertical spar. Position the strands of rope for starting the frapping turns by leading them behind the horizontal spar. **[NOTE]** When pulled tight, the strands will cross behind the vertical spar.

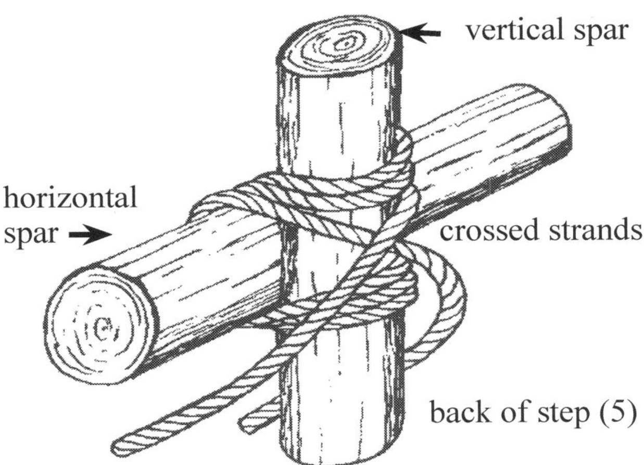

(6) Lead the frapping strands in opposite directions below and in front of the vertical spar and then behind the horizontal spar. **(7)** Make the second frapping turn by leading the ends above and in front of the vertical spar and then behind the horizontal spar; pull each turn tight as it is made. **(8)** End the second frapping turn by tying the first Half Knot of the ending Square Knot. **(9)** Complete the ending Square Knot by adding a second Half Knot. **(10)** Pull the Square Knot tight. **[NOTE]** For safety, add Half Hitches around the horizontal spar to either side of the Square Knot. The Half Hitches prevent the Square Knot from upsetting.

MODIFIED SQUARE LASHING:

Use ---- To bind poles that are in contact and cross each other at any angle from 45° to 90°.

Comments ---- The Modified Square Lashing is similar to the traditional Square Lashing. The main difference is the start and the end. At the start, the standing end of the beginning Clove Hitch is left free. At the end, the standing end and the running end are used to tie a Square Knot.

Narration ---- (For knotboard) **(1)** Start with a Clove Hitch around the vertical pole and under the horizontal pole; the standing end of the Clove Hitch should be about twice the length of the diameter of the poles. **(2)** Bring the running end up and over the cross pole; then around the vertical pole; and back down over the cross pole and behind the vertical pole. This completes the first wrapping. **(3)** Pull the wrapping turn tight. **(4)** Take two more wrapping turns for a total of three wrappings; pull each turn tight. **(5)** Start the frapping turns by leading the running end in front of the vertical pole; complete this frapping turn by leading the running ends between the poles. **(6)** Pull this frapping turn tight. **(7)** Make the second frapping turn; pull tight. **(8)** Make the first Half Knot of the ending Square Knot; pull Half Knot tight to tighten the frapping turns. **(9)** Make the second Half Knot of the ending Square Knot. **[NOTE]** For safety add Half Hitches around the horizontal spar to either side of the Square Knot. The Half Hitches prevent the Square Knot from upsetting.

MODIFIED SQUARE LASHING

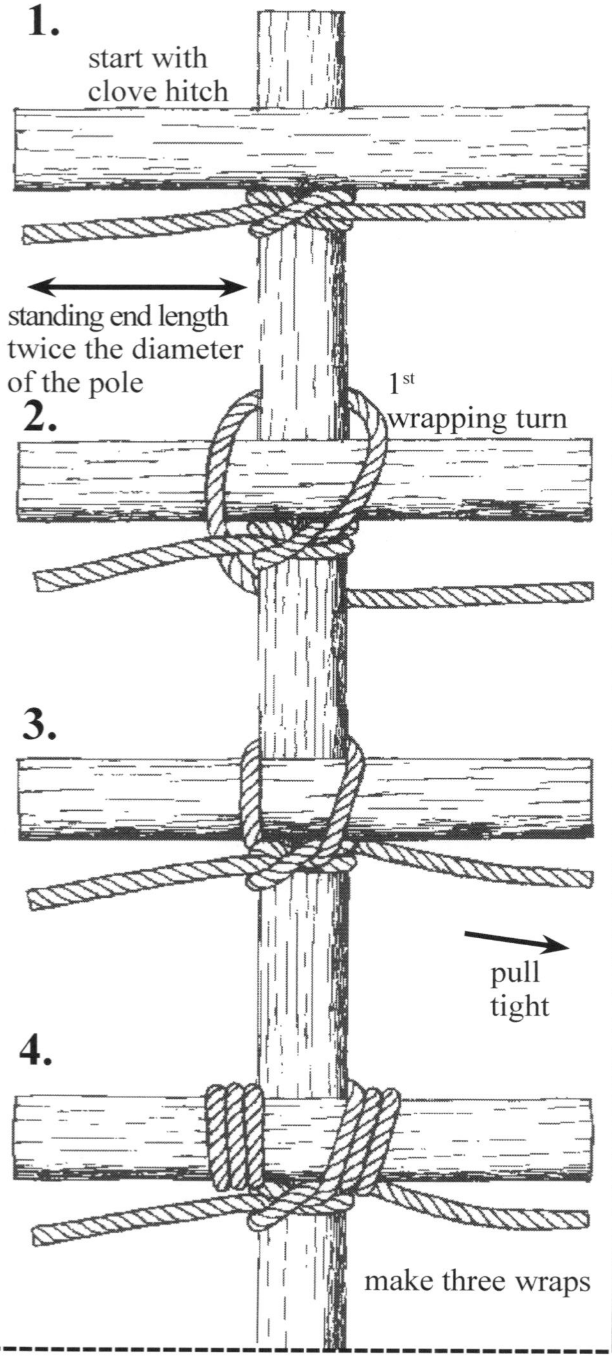

1. start with clove hitch

standing end length twice the diameter of the pole

2. 1st wrapping turn

3. pull tight

4. make three wraps

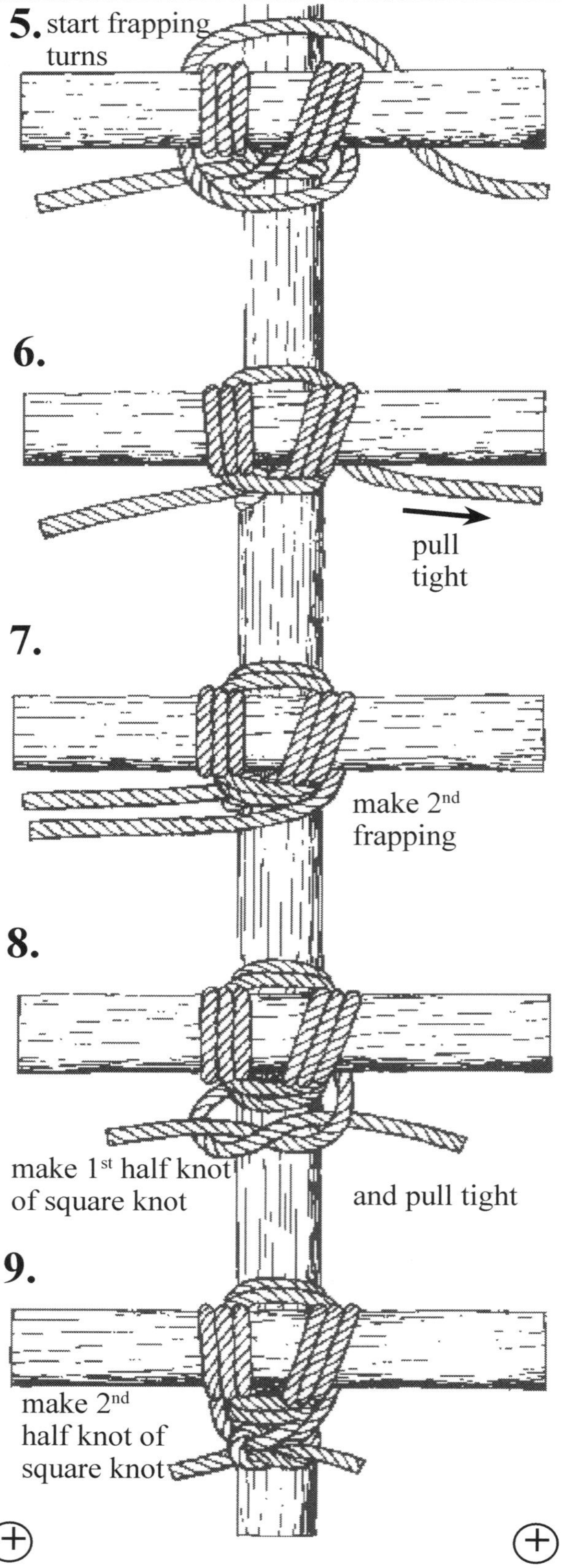

5. start frapping turns

6. pull tight

7. make 2nd frapping

8. make 1st half knot of square knot and pull tight

9. make 2nd half knot of square knot

HALF KNOT SQUARE LASHING:

Use ---- To bind poles together that are in contact and cross each other at any angle from 45° to 90°.

Advantages ---- The Half Knot Square Lashing can be tied faster than the traditional Square Lashing and is as secure as the Traditional Square Lashing when the ropes are tightened by hand and the poles have a small diameter (less than 3 inches).

Comments ---- The Half Knot Square Lashing gets its name from the fact that the wrapping turns are at 90° to the poles and each turn is held tight by a half knot. ----The Half Knot Square Lashing can be used to bind poles together that cross and contact each other at any angle from 45° to 90°. If the angle of contact is greater than 45°, a Shear Lashing should be used. ---- When tying a Half Knot Square Lashing, the poles and the rope must be positioned properly to achieve the maximum strength. The cross pole should be positioned so that the force applied to the cross pole is directed toward the pole that it is lashed to. This allows the wood to wood contact to bear part of the load. If the force tends to separate the poles, only the rope will be supporting the load. The beginning Clove Hitch should be tied to the pole that is closest to parallel to the direction of the force and to the side of the cross pole that is opposite to the direction of the force. This means that the beginning Clove Hitch is usually tied to the vertical pole, and under the cross pole.

STEP 1: Tie the center of the rope to the vertical pole and under the cross pole.

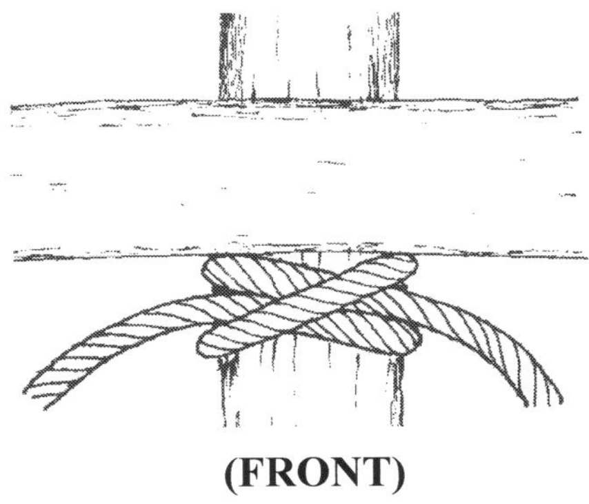

(FRONT)

STEP 2: Take the ends of the rope up and over the cross pole; tie a Half Knot as the ends of the rope cross behind the vertical pole; pull tight.

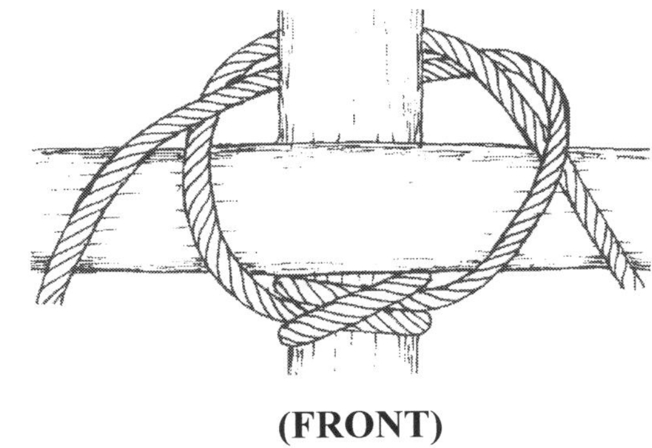

(FRONT)

[NOTE] Half Knot is tied behind the vertical pole.

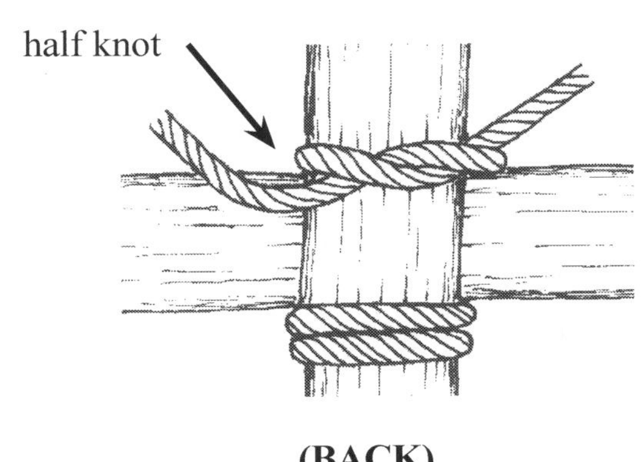

(BACK)

STEP 3: Take the second wrapping turn by passing the ends of the rope down over the cross pole and tying a Half Knot as the ends of the rope cross behind the vertical pole; pull the Half Knot and wrapping turn tight so that the second Half Knot is above the Clove Hitch and the second wrapping turn is parallel to the outside of the first wrapping turn.

(FRONT)

[NOTE] Position of second Half Knot.

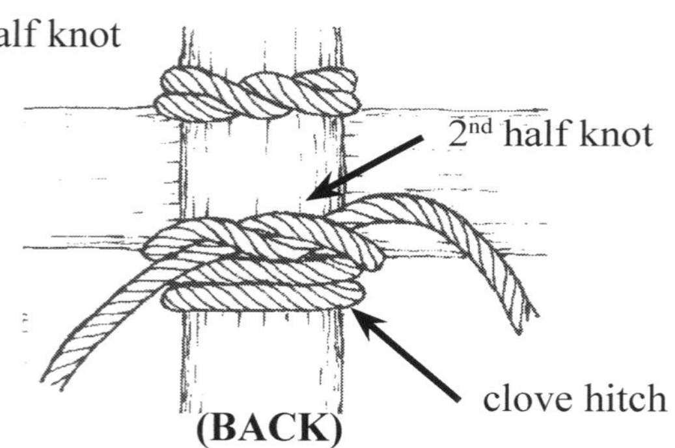

(BACK)

STEP 4: Tie the third wrapping turn by taking the rope ends up and over the cross pole and tying a Half Knot as the ends of the rope cross behind the vertical pole. Pull the Half Knot and the wrapping turn tight so that the Half Knot is between the first two Half Knots and the wrapping turn is parallel to the outside of the first two wrapping turns.

(FRONT)

[NOTE] When pulled tight, the third Half Knot is positioned between the first two Half Knots.

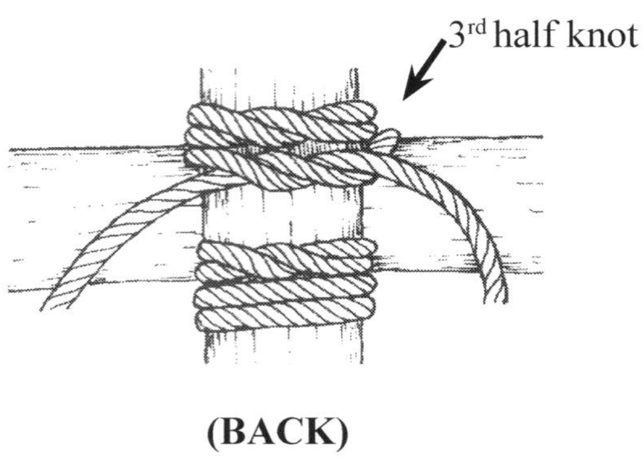

(BACK)

STEP 5: Start the frapping turns by taking the ends of the rope down behind the cross pole and tying a Half Knot under the cross pole and in front of the vertical pole.

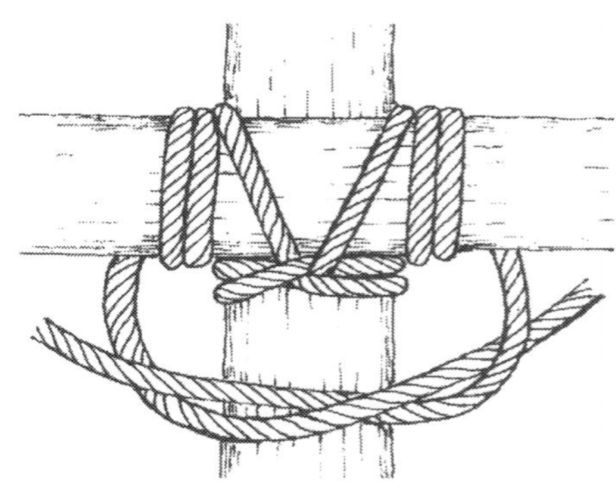

(FRONT)

STEP 6: Pull the Half Knot tight.

(FRONT)

[NOTE] When the Half Knot that begins the frapping turns is pulled tight, the third wrapping turn and third Half Knot are pulled even tighter.

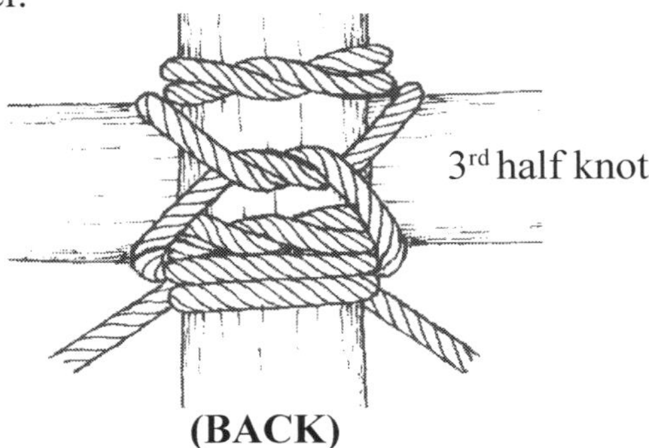

(BACK)

STEP 7: Take the first frapping turn by reeving the ends of the rope upward between the poles and over the wrapping turns; tie a Half Knot above the cross pole .

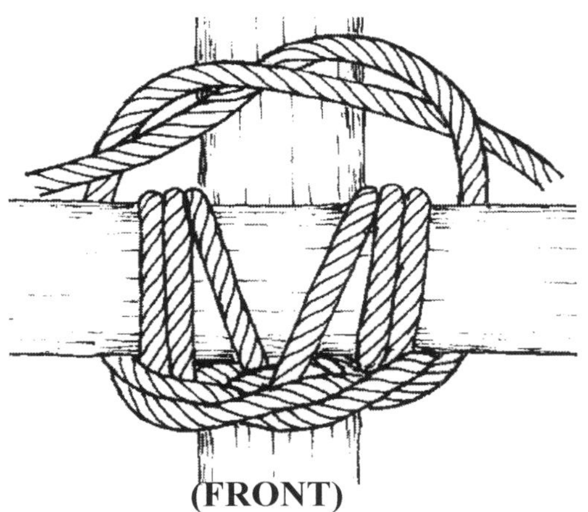

(FRONT)

STEP 8: Pull the Half Knot tight. Take the second frapping turn by reeving the ends of the rope downward between the poles and tie a Half Knot under the cross pole.

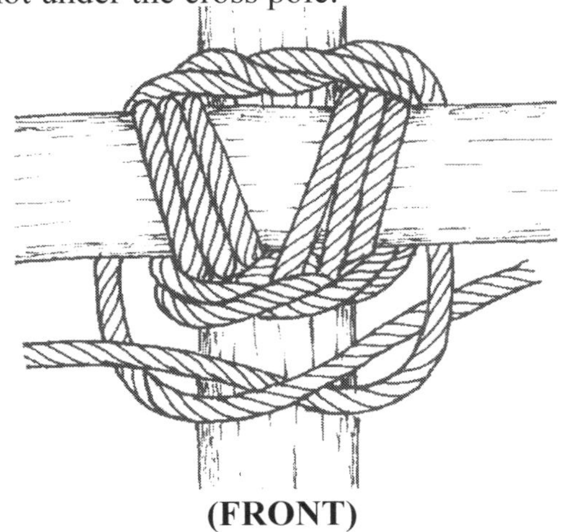

(FRONT)

STEP 9: End the lashing by tying another Half Knot in the opposite direction to the last Half Knot to form a Square Knot.

(FRONT)

[WARNING] A Square Knot can be easily upset to form a Lark's Head by pulling on one of the rope ends; therefore, the Half Knot Square Lashing should not be used on a structure that will be climbed on unless the rope ends are secured to prevent the Square Knot from being upset.

The ends of the rope can be secured by taking a Half Hitch around the cross pole with each end of the rope.

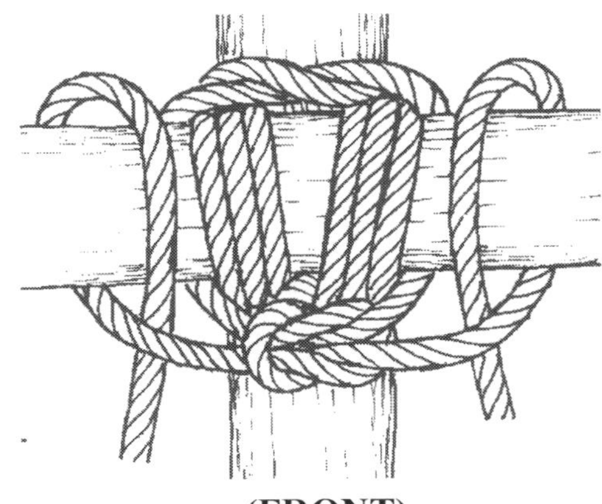

(FRONT)

When tying each Half Hitch, take the end of the rope under and around the cross pole. After the Half Hitch is formed, lock it tight against the lashing by working the Half Hitch tight.

(FRONT)

To make the lashing even more secure, a second Half Hitch may be added to form a Clove Hitch.

[NOTE] The Half Knot Square Lashing is based on a combination of features of the Japanese Square Lashing Mark III and the West Country Round Lashing.

[NOTES]

DIAGONAL LASHING:

Use ---- The Diagonal Lashing can be used to bind poles that cross each other from 90° to 45° but do not touch when their ends are lashed in place in a structure.

Comments ---- The Diagonal Lashing gets its name from the fact that the wrapping turns cross the poles diagonally.

If the angle between the poles is less than 45°, a Shear Lashing should be used.

The Diagonal Lashing makes use of the Timber Hitch to pull poles together that are not touching each other. The Timber Hitch allows the poles to be drawn together without changing their relative positions. **[NOTE]** If a Square Lashing were used to bind poles that do not touch, the beginning Clove Hitch would pull the cross pole toward the Clove Hitch causing unnecessary bowing of the cross pole and could also produce a force that would act along the length of the pole to which the Clove Hitch is tied. These additional forces, if strong enough, can place unnecessary strain on other lashings within the structure, causing the structure to twist and fail.

Narration ---- (For knotboard.) **(1)** Tie a Timber Hitch diagonally around both poles. **(2)** Start the wrapping turns on the opposite diagonal to the Timber Hitch by pulling the rope tight so that the poles contact each other. **(3)** Take 3 to 4 wrapping turns; keep the wrapping turns parallel; pull each wrapping turn tight. **[NOTE]** If the wrapping turns are allowed to cross, the increased friction between the strands of the rope will make it difficult to tighten the wrapping turns. **(4)** Start the second set of wrapping turns by going past and around the last pole. **[NOTE]** Going around the pole with the rope allows the direction of the rope to be changed without crossing the first set of wrappings on a diagonal. **(5)** Take 3 to 4 wrapping turns; be sure to keep the wrapping turns parallel; pull each wrapping turn tight. **(6)** Start the frapping turns by going past and around one of the poles.

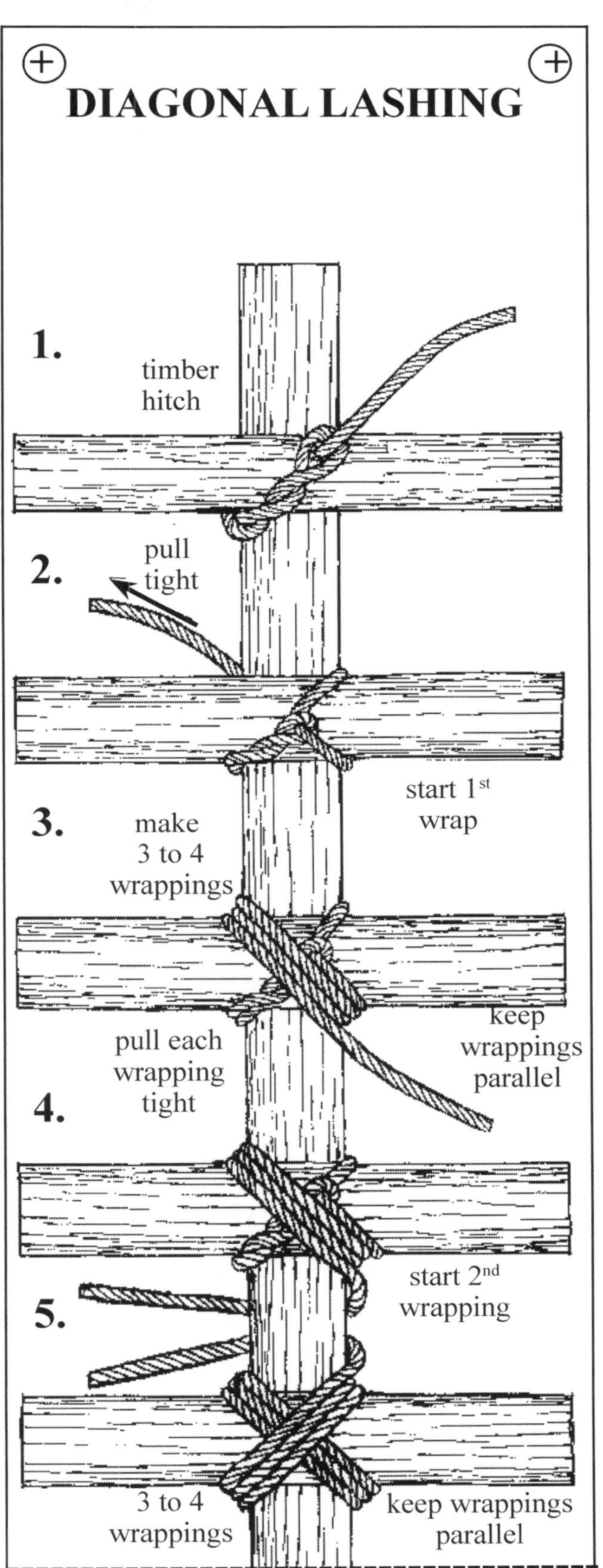

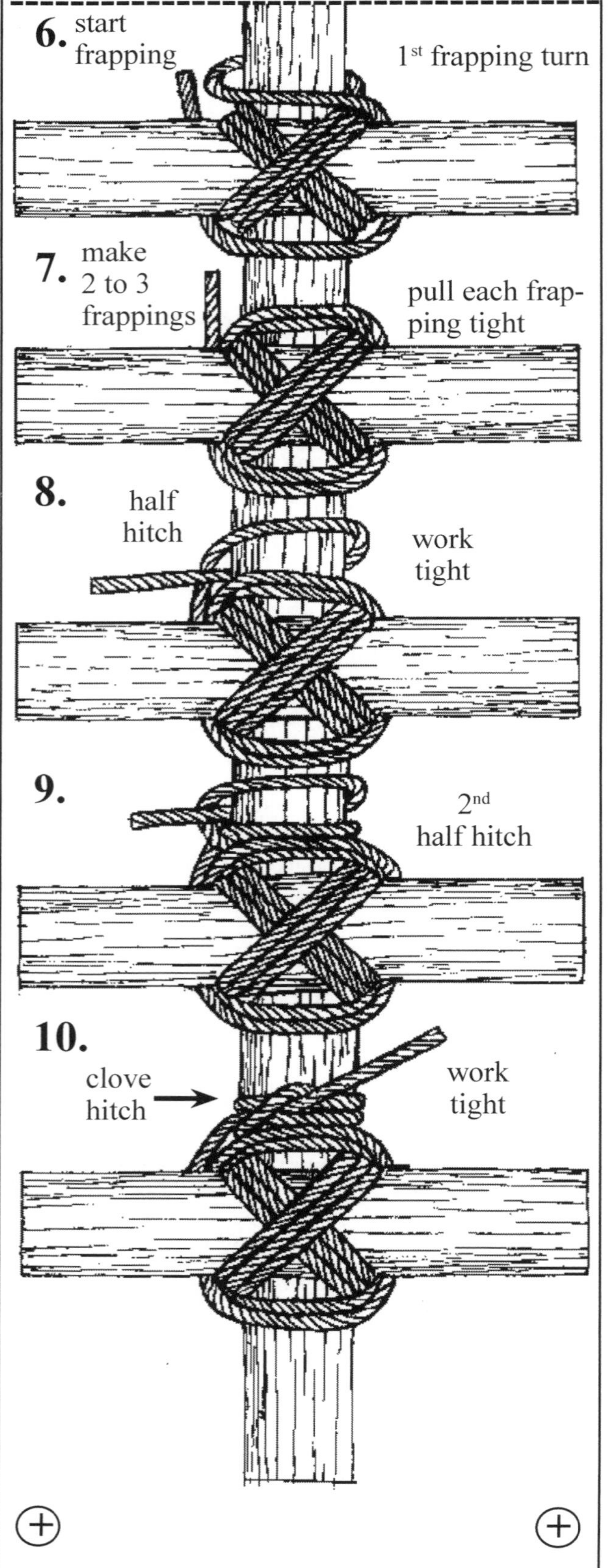

[NOTE] Going around the pole with the rope allows the direction of the rope to be changed without crossing the wrapping turns on a diagonal. **(7)** Take 2 to 3 frapping turns; keep the frapping turns parallel. Be sure to pull each turn tight. **(8)** End the lashing with a Clove Hitch. Take the first Half Hitch of the Clove Hitch by going past and then around one of the poles. Lock the Half Hitch tight against the lashing by working it tight. **(9)** Take a second Half Hitch around the pole. **(10)** Work the second Half Hitch tight against the first Half Hitch so that the Clove Hitch is locked against the lashing.

[NOTE] See the directions for Square Lashing for instructions on working the Half Hitches tight.

[NOTE] If very smooth rope is used, the lashing can be made more secure by adding a third or fourth Half Hitch to the Clove Hitch.

[NOTES]

FILIPINO DIAGONAL LASHING:

Use ---- Filipino Diagonal Lashing is used to bind poles together that cross each other but do not touch when their ends are lashed in place in a structure.

Comments ---- The Filipino Diagonal Lashing gets its name from the fact that the wrapping turns cross the poles diagonally.

The Filipino Diagonal Lashing can be used to bind poles that cross each other from 90° to 45°. If the angle between the poles is less than 45°, a Shear Lashing should be used.

The Filipino Diagonal Lashing makes use of a bight looped around the cross point of the poles. The loop allows the poles to be drawn together without changing the relative positions of the poles.

Narration ---- (For knotboard.) **(1)** Form a bight in the center of the rope; loop the rope around the cross point of the poles; reeve the end of the rope through the eye of the bight. **(2)** Pull poles together. **(3)** Make the first wrapping turn by leading the rope around the poles on the opposite diagonal to the starting loop. **(4)** Pull wrapping turn tight. **(5)** Lead rope behind the poles to change the direction of the rope for the start of the second wrapping. **(6)** Make the second wrapping on the same diagonal as the starting loop. **[NOTE]** For added strength, two turns may be made on each diagonal. **(7)** To start the frapping turns, separate the rope strands; lead one strand over and one strand under the top pole. **(8)** Make the first frapping turn by leading the strands in opposite directions across the wrapping turns so that the frapping turn is between the poles. **(9)** Add a second frapping turn. **(10)** End the lashing by pulling the frapping turns tight and tying a Square Knot.

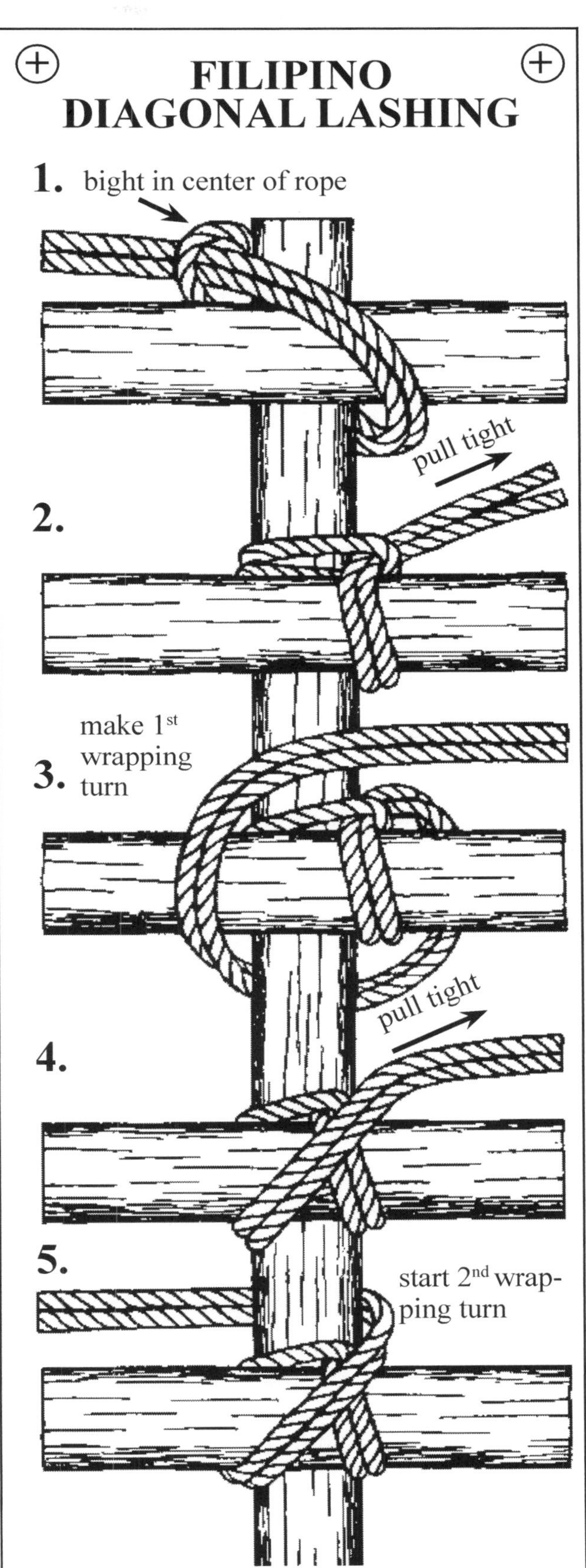

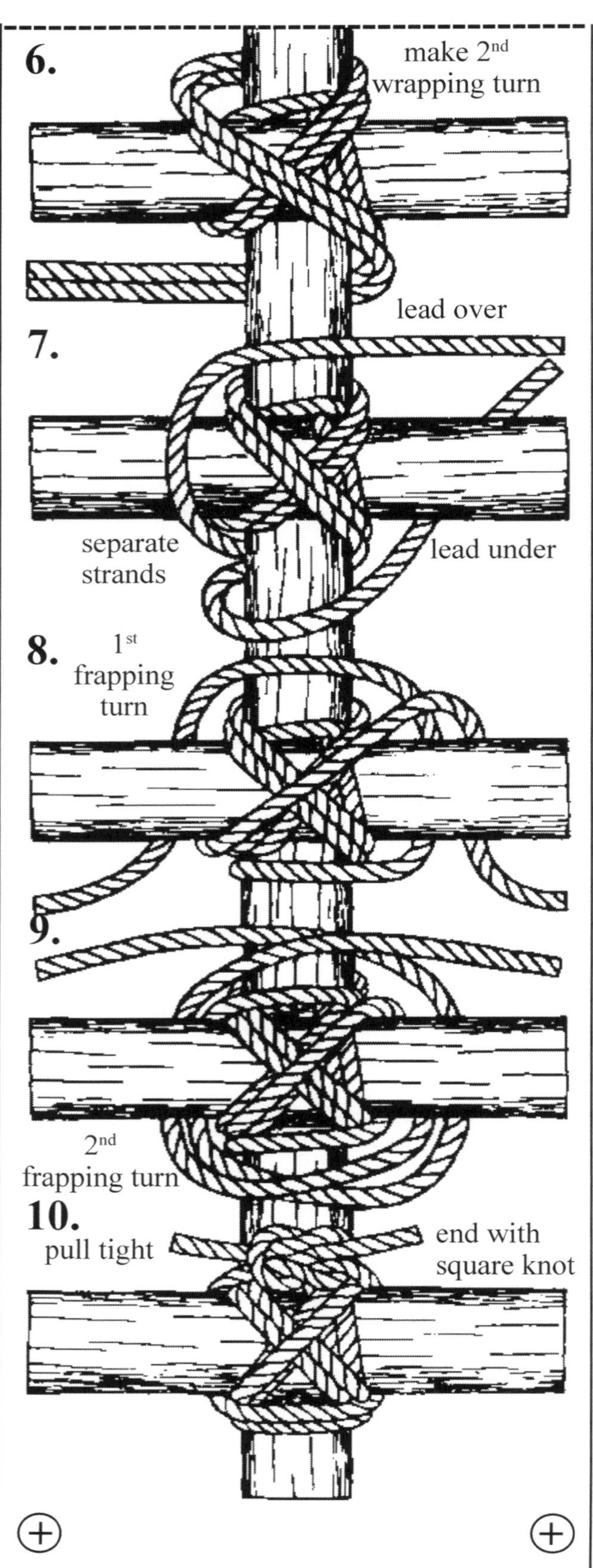
6.
make 2nd wrapping turn
lead over
7.
separate strands
lead under
8.
1st frapping turn
9.
2nd frapping turn
10.
pull tight
end with square knot

[NOTES]

SHEAR LASHING:

Use ---- To form a flexible joint between two poles. ---- To lash two poles together that cross each other at an angle of less thAn 45°. ---- To construct shear legs.

Names ---- The Shear Lashing is named for the scissors like action that can take place between two poles when the Shear Lashing is used to bind them together.

Some sources also include "Round Lashing" in the category "Shear Lashing". Round Lashing is used to join poles together so that the poles are parallel to each other and little or no flexibility exists between the poles. (See ROUND LASHING)

Comments ----The Shear Lashing can be tied with racked wrapping turns or with plain wrapping turns. The wracked wrapping turns are taken by weaving the rope around the poles; this causes the rope to be in contact with the entire circumference of the pole. Therefore, Shear Lashing tied with racked wrapping turns is the most secure form of Shear Lashing and should be the form used to support heavy loads. The Shear Lashing made with plain wrapping turns is faster to tie and is easiest to use.

[NOTE] If the Shear Lashing is intended to bind poles together that cross each other and have already been lashed in place within a structure, a Shear Lashing tied with plain wrapping turns should be used. A Shear Lashing tied with plain wrapping turns can also be used for supporting light loads.

SHEAR LASHING: WITH RACKING TURNS

Narration ---- (For knotboard) **(1)** Tie a Clove Hitch around one of the poles. **(2)** Secure the standing end by wrapping it around the running end. **(3)** Take the first wrapping turn by weaving the rope around the poles. **(4)** Take a total of 5 to 8 wrapping turns. **[NOTE]** The greater the number of wrapping turns the stiffer the

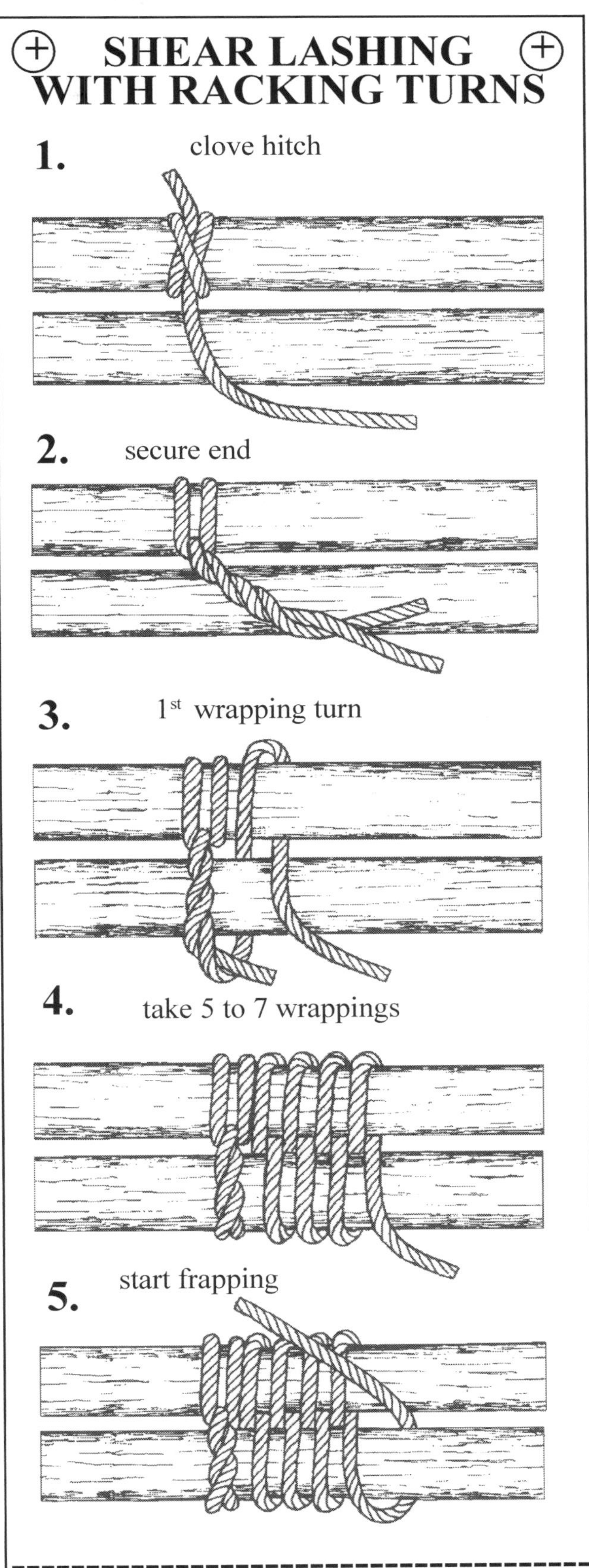

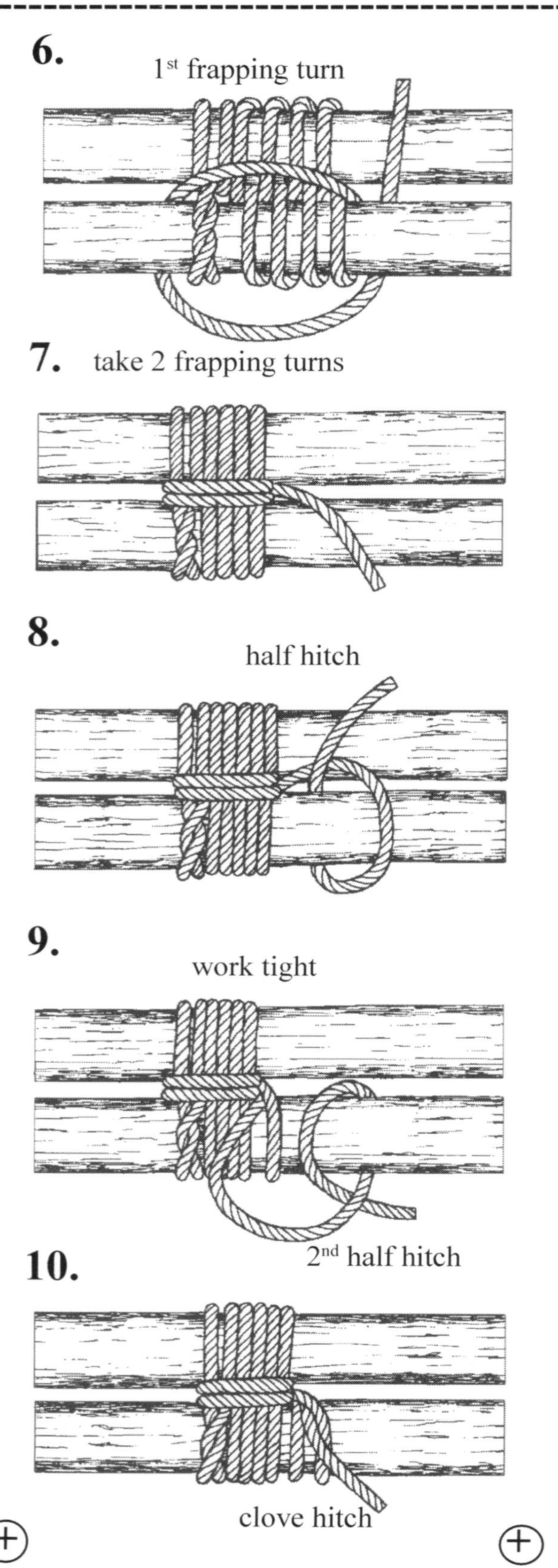

lashing will be. **(5)** Start the frapping turns by reeving the rope between the poles. **(6)** Take the first frapping turn so that the frapping turn passes over the wrapping turns between the poles. **(7)** Take a total of 2 to 3 frapping turns; pull each turn tight as it is made. **(8)** End the lashing with a Clove Hitch; tie the first Half Hitch of the Clove Hitch by reeving the rope between the poles and around the second pole; work tight. **[NOTE]** If the first Half Hitch of the Clove Hitch is not worked tight so that it is locked tight against the lashing, the lashing can loosen and fail. **(9)** Take the second Half Hitch of the Clove Hitch. **(10)** Work the second Half Hitch tight to finish the ending Clove Hitch. **[NOTE]** If the rope being used is smooth, the lashing can be made more secure by adding a third Half Hitch to the Clove Hitch.

SHEAR LASHING: WITH PLAIN TURNS

Narration ---- (For knotboard) **(1)** Tie a Clove Hitch around one of the poles. **(2)** Secure the standing end by wrapping it around the running end. **(3)** Take the first wrapping turn by wrapping the rope around both poles. **(4)** Take a total of 5 to 8 wrapping turns. **[NOTE]** The greater the number of wrapping turns the stiffer the lashing will be. **(5)** Start the frapping turns by reeving the rope between the poles. **(6)** Take the first frapping turn so that the frapping turn passes over the wrapping turns between the poles. **(7)** Take a total of 2 to 3 frapping turns; pull each turn tight as it is made. **(8)** End the lashing with a Clove Hitch; tie the first Half Hitch of the Clove Hitch by reeving the rope between the poles and around the second pole; work tight. **[NOTE]** If the first Half Hitch of the Clove Hitch is not worked tight so that it is locked tight against the lashing, the lashing can loosen and fail. (See SQUARE LASHING for direction on working the Clove Hitch tight.) **(9)** Take the second Half Hitch of the Clove Hitch. **(10)** Work the second Half Hitch tight to finish the ending Clove Hitch. **[NOTE]** If the rope being used is smooth, the lashing can be made more secure by adding a third Half Hitch to the Clove Hitch.

SHEAR LASHING WITH PLAIN TURNS

1. clove hitch

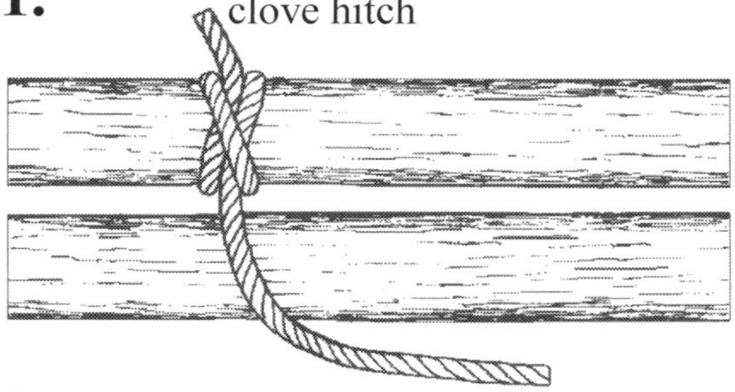

2. secure end

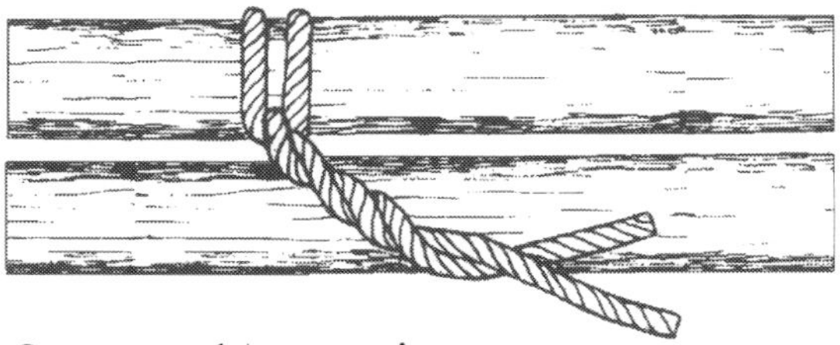

3. 1st wrapping turn

4. take 5 to 8 wrappings

5. start frapping

6. 1st frapping turn

7. take 2 frapping turns

8. half hitch

9. work tight

10. 2nd half hitch

clove hitch

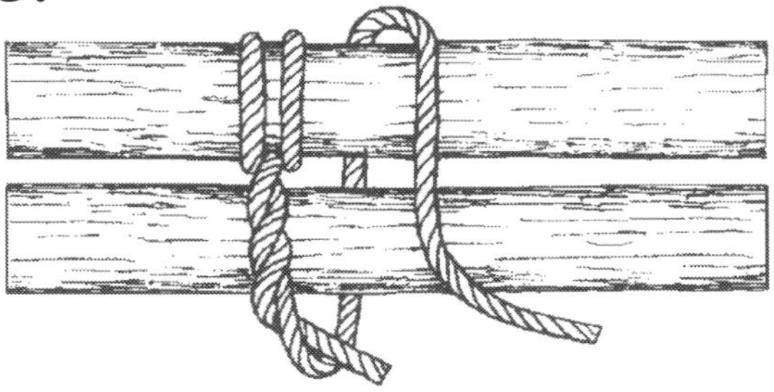

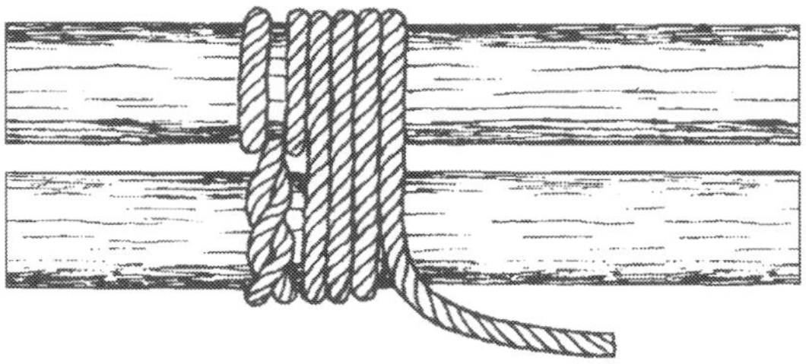

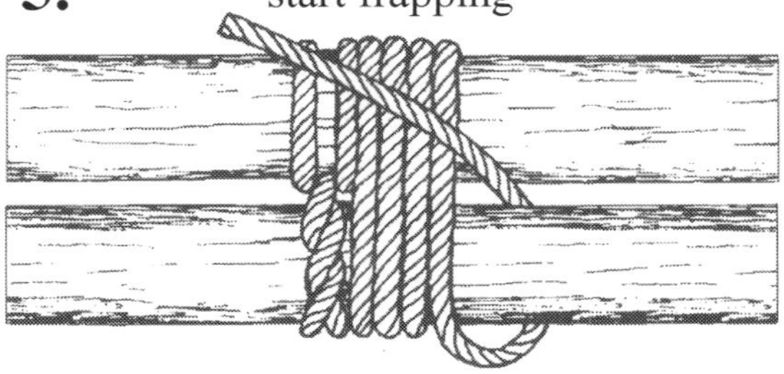

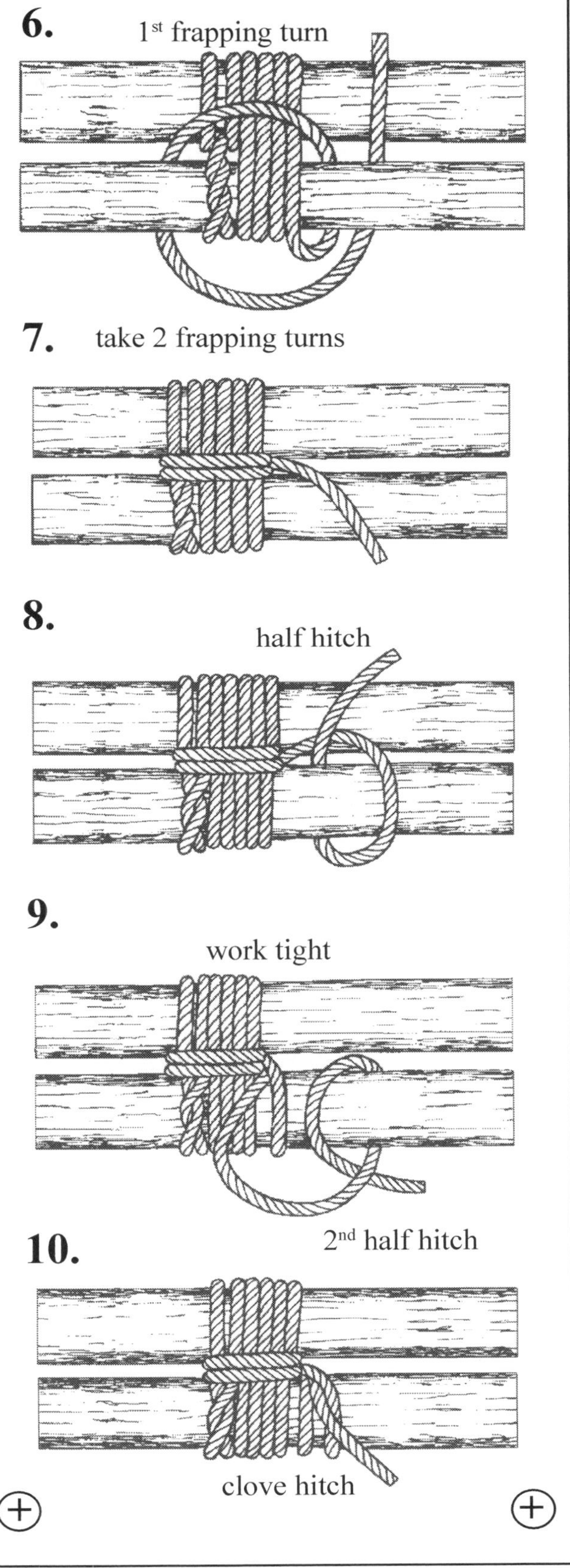

SHEAR LASHING: QUICK

Narration ---- (For knotboard) **(1)** Reeve the standing end of the rope up between the poles; leave the standing end long enough to take the frapping turns. **(2)** Start the wrapping turns around both poles with the running end. **(3)** Take a total of 5 to 8 parallel wrapping turns. **(4)** Start the frapping turns by taking the rope under the pole and reeving it up between the poles. **(5)** Cross the two ends of the rope over the wrapping turns and reeve the ends between the poles. **(6)** Pull the rope strands tight; cross the rope ends over the wrapping turns and reeve the ends up between the poles. **(7)** End the lashing with a Square Knot; tie the first Half Knot of the Square Knot. **(8)** Pull Half Knot tight. **[NOTE]** Pulling the Half Knot tight will tighten both the wrapping turns and the frapping turns. Moving the ends of the rope up and down several times as they are being pulled tight will help ensure the lashing is tight. **(9)** Take the second Half Knot of the Square Knot. **(10)** Pull the Square Knot tight. **(11)** Secure the ends of the rope with Half Hitches.

[WARNING]

A Square Knot can be easily upset into a Lark's Head Knot. If this happens, the entire lashing can loosen and fail. If the Quick Shear Lashing is used on a structure, such as a tower or bridge, the ends of the rope should be secured by taking a Half Hitch or Clove Hitches around one of the poles.

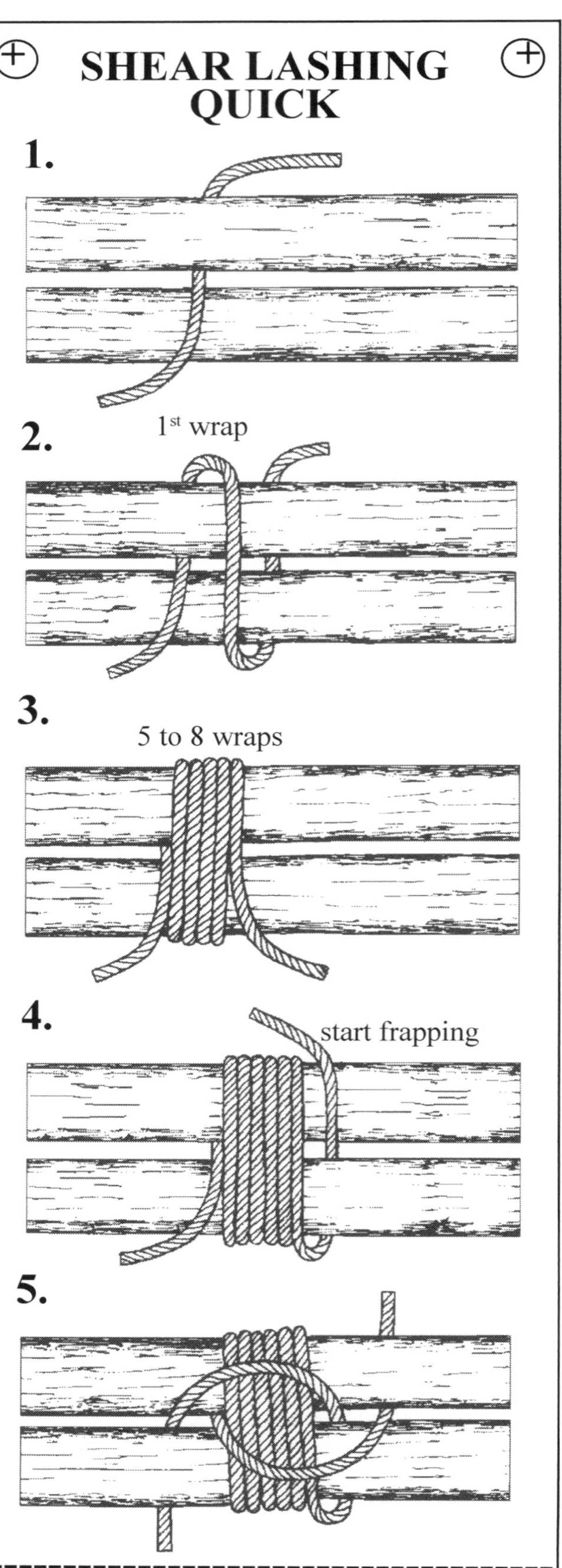

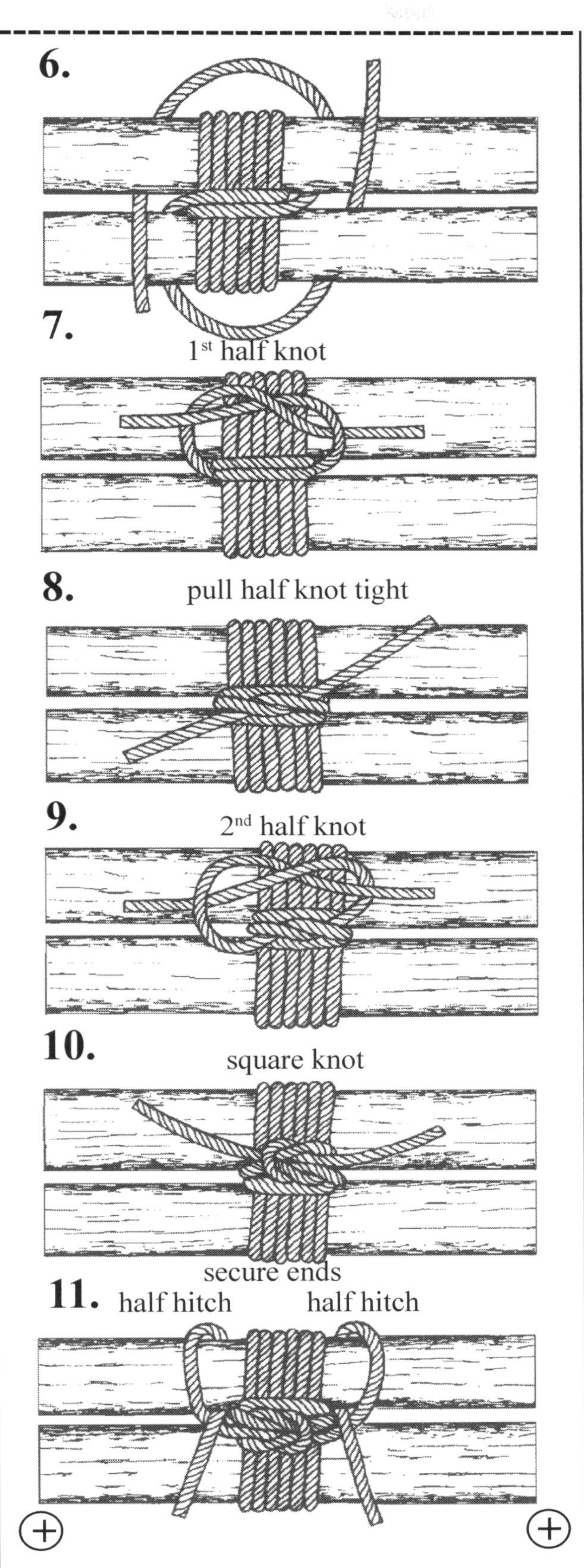
6.
7.
1st half knot
8.
pull half knot tight
9.
2nd half knot
10.
square knot
secure ends
11.
half hitch
half hitch

[NOTES]

TRIPOD LASHING:

Description ---- A Shear Lashing around 3 poles.

Use ---- To bind three poles together, for the construction of a tripod. ---- To bind three poles together that contact at the same point in a structure.

Comments ----The Tripod Lashing is a Shear Lashing that binds three poles together at the same point. ---- The Tripod Lashing gets its name from the fact that its most common use is the construction of a tripod. ----The Tripod Lashing can be used just about anywhere in a structure where three poles cross each other at the same point and at the same time in the sequence of construction. ---- Tripod Lashing takes two main forms; with racked wrapping turns (the rope is woven between the poles) and with plain wrapping turns (the rope is wrapped around the poles without weaving the rope between the poles). When the lashing is made with racking turns, the rope contacts each pole around its entire circumference; this contact makes the Tripod Lashing With Racking Turns the most secure form of Tripod Lashing: therefore, Tripod Lashing With Racking Turns should be used when safety is important. However, for light structures where there would be no danger if the lashing slipped, Tripod Lashing With Plain Turns may be used because it is faster to tie.

Laying Out The Poles ---- For most Tripod Lashings, lay the pole side by side with the butt ends aligned. The alignment of the butts of the pole ensures that the tripod legs are the desired length.

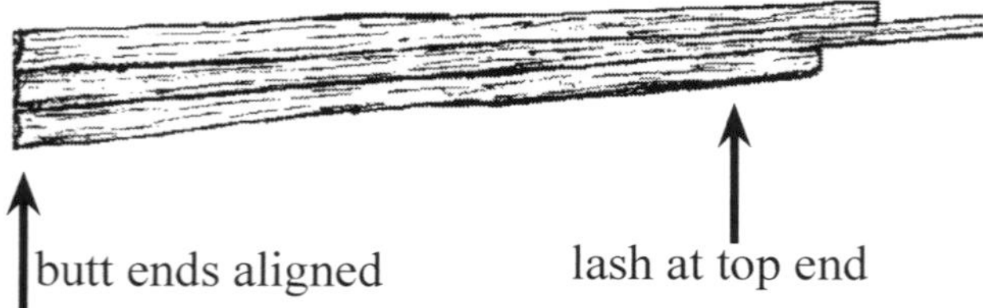

[NOTE] The practice of laying the center pole in the opposite direction to the outside poles creates several problems. When the poles are laid in opposite directions, the wrappings must be put on loosely so that when the center pole is rotated to its proper position the lashing is tightened around the poles. If the wrappings are put on too tightly, the rope is stretched causing damage to the rope fibers therefore weakening the lashing. On the other hand, if the rope is wrapped too loosely, the lashing will not tighten enough when the center pole is rotated and the lashing will be able to slip along the length of the pole. Either way, if the rope is too loose or the rope is too tight, a dangerous situation is created.

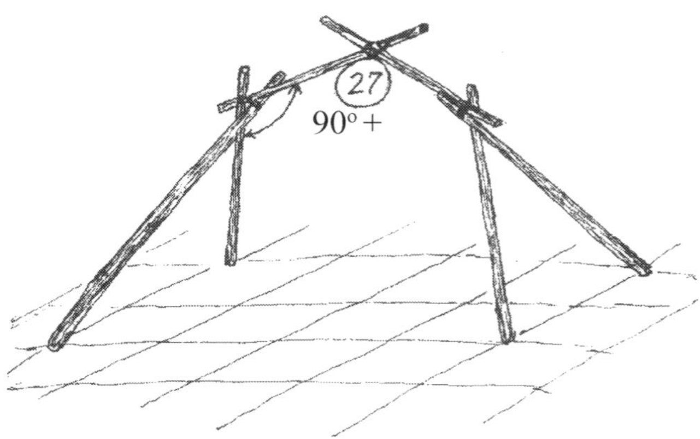

However, if the tripod is to be part of a structure and the center pole will be at an angle greater than 90° to the outside poles, lay the center pole in the opposite direction to the outside poles so that the rotation of the poles at the lashing is less than 90°. See gateway above for an example.

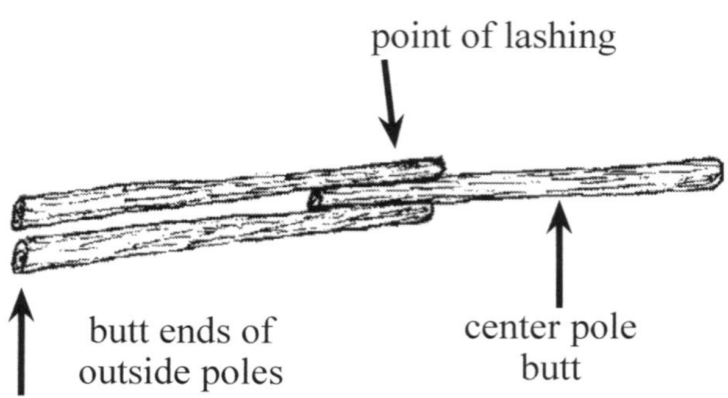

Setting Up A Tripod ---- Set up the tripod by crossing the outside poles so that the cross-point of the poles is under the center pole. Crossing the outside poles under the center pole causes part of the load that is placed on the tripod to be taken up by the wood to wood contact of the poles.

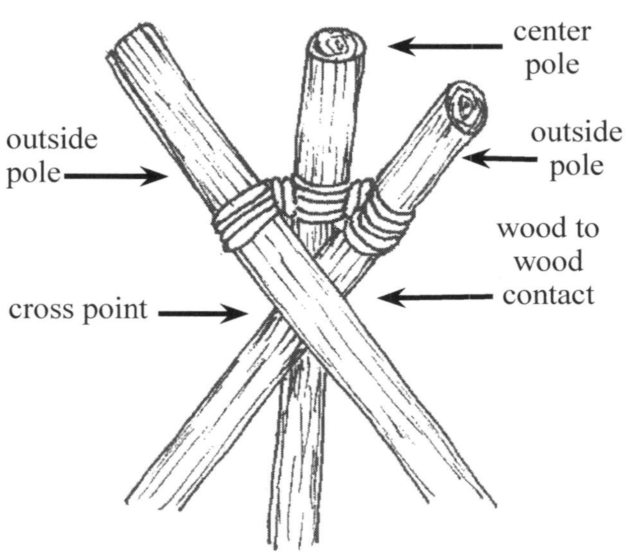

If the outside poles are crossed above the center pole, the rope of the lashing will be required to support all or most of the load; therefore the tripod will not be as strong as when the outside legs are crossed under the lashing.

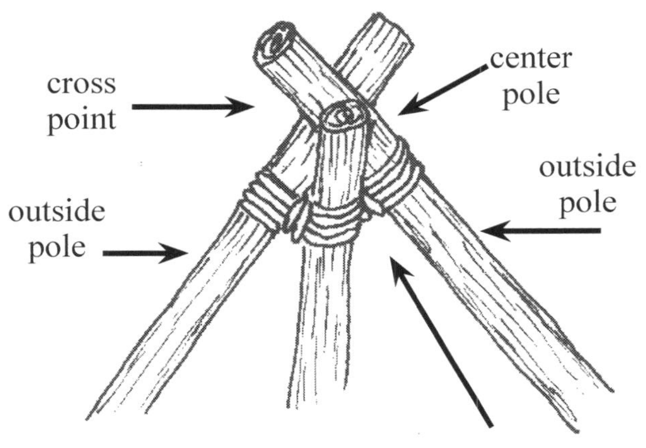

no wood to wood contact,
rope supports load

If a symmetrical arrangement of the poles is needed within a structure, the tripod can be set up by rotating the poles around the lashing. This rotation causes the loss of the wood to wood contact so that the load is supported only by the ropes, and the joint between the poles becomes very flexible; therefore the tripod may be unstable.

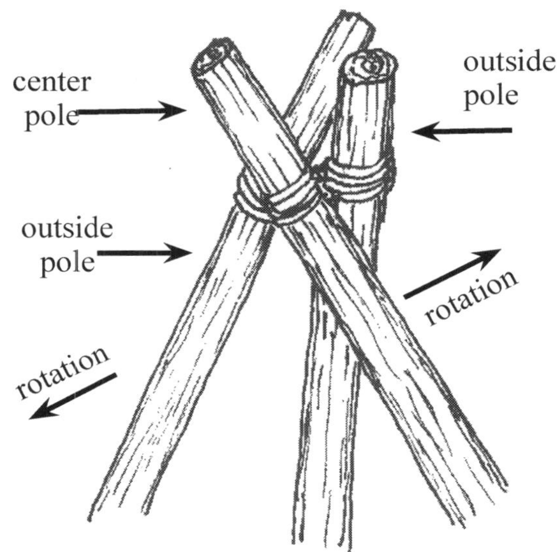

TRIPOD LASHING: WITH RACKING TURNS

Narration ---- (For knotboard) **(1)** Tie a Clove Hitch around one of the outside poles. **(2)** Secure the standing part by wrapping it around the running part. **[NOTE]** Wrapping the standing part around the running part prevents the Clove Hitch from slipping around the pole. If the Clove Hitch slips, the lashing will loosen up from the inside. **(3)** Start the racked wrapping turns by weaving the rope between the poles. **(4)** Take a total of 5 to 7 wrapping turns. Pull each wrapping turn tight as it is made**. [NOTE]** The stiffness of the tripod lashing depends on the number and tightness of the wrapping turns. As the tightness of the wrapping turns or the number of wrapping turns increases, the stiffness of the tripod will increase. **(5)** Take the first frapping turn by taking the rope around the pole that the Clove Hitch was tied to, then between the outside pole and the center pole. **(6)** Take 2 or 3 frapping turns. Pull each frapping turn tight as it is

TRIPOD LASHING WITH RACKING TURNS

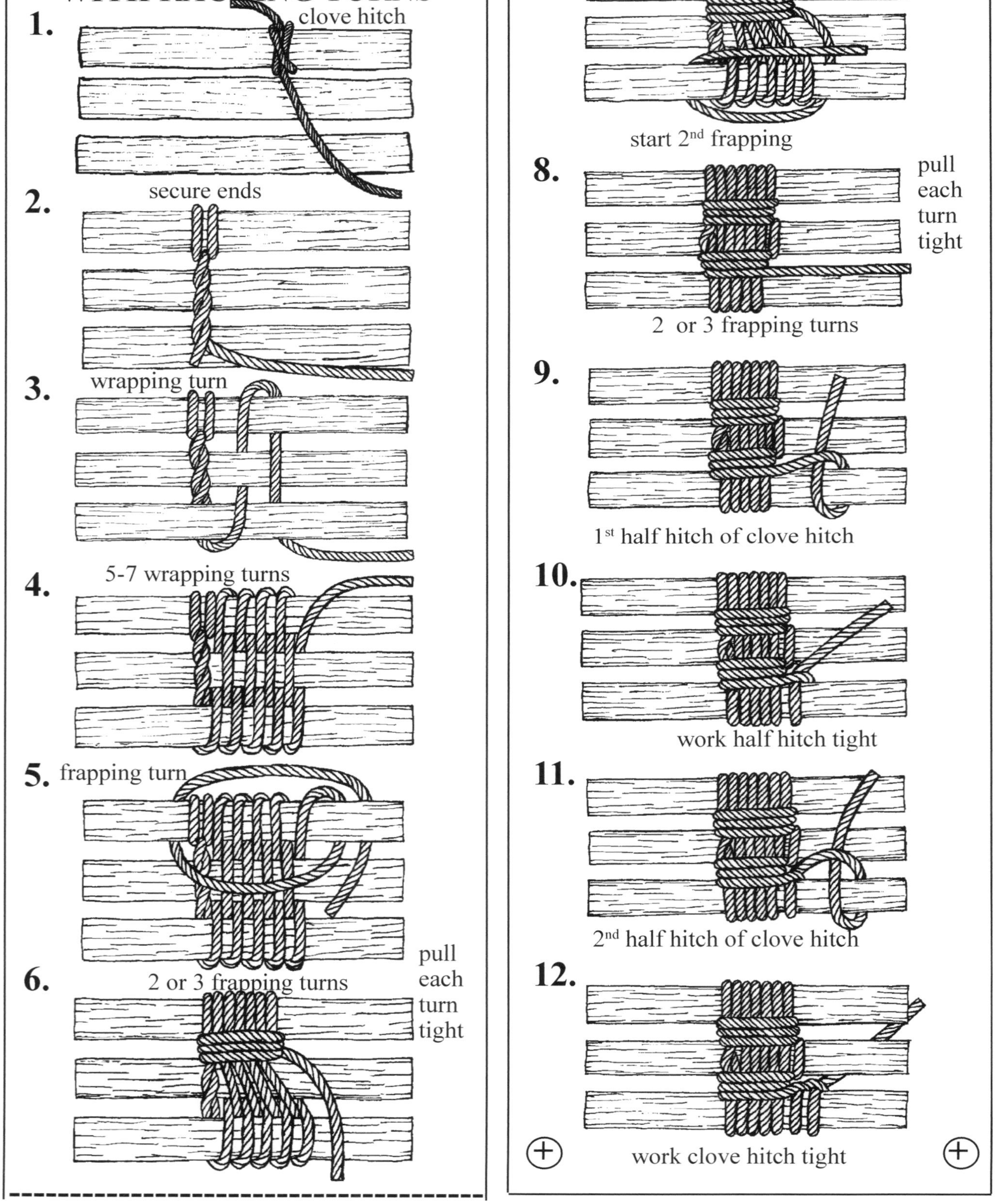

1. clove hitch

2. secure ends

3. wrapping turn

4. 5-7 wrapping turns

5. frapping turn

6. 2 or 3 frapping turns — pull each turn tight

7. start 2nd frapping

8. pull each turn tight — 2 or 3 frapping turns

9. 1st half hitch of clove hitch

10. work half hitch tight

11. 2nd half hitch of clove hitch

12. work clove hitch tight

made. **(7)** Start the second set of frapping turns by taking the rope across the center pole and reeving it between the second outside pole and the center pole. Take the second set of frapping turns in the opposite direction to the first set of frapping turns. **[NOTE]** Taking the second set of frapping turns in the opposite direction to the first set of frapping turns prevents the rope from crossing the wrappings on a diagonal. Unnecessary crossing of the rope increases friction between the strands of the rope making it difficult to tighten the lashing properly. **(8)** Take a total of 2 or 3 frapping turns. Pull each turn tight. **(9)** Take the first Half Hitch of the ending Clove Hitch around the second outside pole by taking the rope past the pole and then around the pole. **(10)** Work the Half Hitch tight so that it is locked against the lashing. **[NOTE]** See the narration for Square Lashing for instructions on working the Half Hitch tight. **(11)** Take the second Half Hitch of the ending Clove Hitch. **(12)** Work the Half Hitch tight to complete the ending Clove Hitch. **[NOTE]** If the Clove Hitch is not worked tight so that it is locked against the lashing, the Clove Hitch will slip around the pole allowing the lashing to loosen. **[NOTE]** If very smooth rope is being used, a third Half Hitch should be added to the Clove Hitch to ensure that the lashing will stay in place.

TRIPOD LASHING: WITH PLAIN TURNS

Narration ---- (For knotboard) **(1)** Tie a Clove Hitch around one of the outside poles. **(2)** Secure the standing part by wrapping it around the running part. **[NOTE]** Wrapping the standing part around the running part prevents the Clove Hitch from slipping around the pole. If the Clove Hitch slips, the lashing will loosen up from the inside. **(3)** Start the wrapping turns by wrapping the rope around the poles. Take a total of 4 to 6 wrapping turns. Pull each wrapping turn tight as it is made**.** **[NOTE]** The stiffness of the Tripod Lashing depends on the number and tightness of the wrapping turns. As the tightness of the wrapping turns increases or the number of wrapping turns increases, the stiffness of the tripod will increase. **(4)** Take the first frapping turn by passing the rope

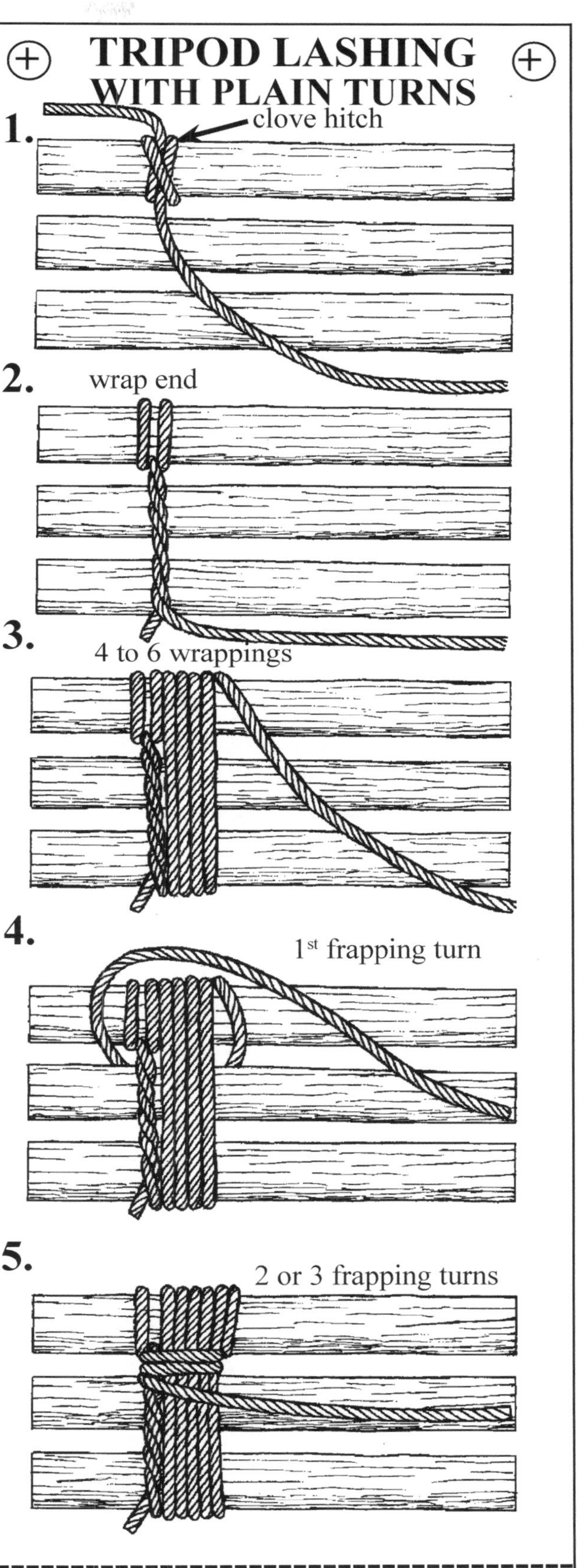

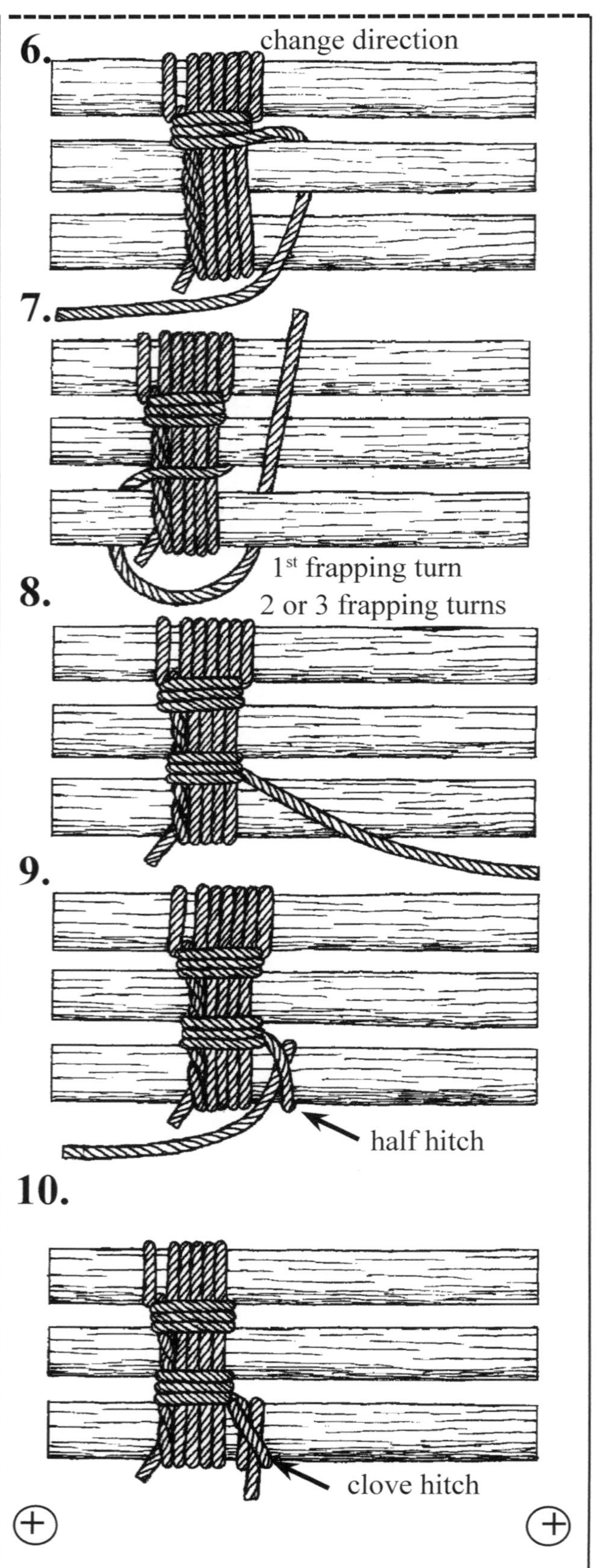

around the pole that the Clove Hitch was tied to, then between the outside pole and the center pole. **(5)** Take 2 or 3 frapping turns. Pull each frapping turn tight as it is made. **(6)** Start the second set of frapping turns by taking the rope around the center pole and reeving it between the second outside pole and the center pole. **(7)** Take the second set of frapping turns in the opposite direction to the first set of frapping turns. **[NOTE]** Taking the second set of frapping turns in the opposite direction to the first set of frapping turns prevents the rope from crossing the wrappings on a diagonal. Unnecessary crossing of the rope increases friction between the strands of the rope, making it difficult to tighten the lashing properly. **(8)** Take a total of 2 or 3 frapping turns. Pull each turn tight. **(9)** Take the first Half Hitch of the ending Clove Hitch around the second outside pole by taking the rope past the pole and then around the pole. Work the Half Hitch tight so that it is locked against the lashing. **[NOTE]** See the narration for Square Lashing for instructions on working the Half Hitch tight. **(10)** Take the second Half Hitch of the ending Clove Hitch. Work the Half Hitch tight to complete the ending Clove Hitch. **[NOTE]** If the Clove Hitch is not worked tight so that it is locked against the lashing, the Clove Hitch will slip around the pole allowing the lashing to loosen. **[NOTE]** If very smooth rope is being used, a third Half Hitch should be added to the Clove Hitch to ensure that the lashing will stay in place.

[NOTES]

TRIPOD LASHING: QUICK

Comments ---- The Quick Tripod Lashing is one of the fastest ways to construct a tripod. However, the Quick Tripod Lashing is not as secure as the more conventional methods, therefore the Quick Tripod Lashing tripod should not be used for heavy loads.

DIRECTIONS ----

STEP 1: Lay the poles side by side with the butt ends aligned. Wrap 5 to 8 wrappings around all three poles.

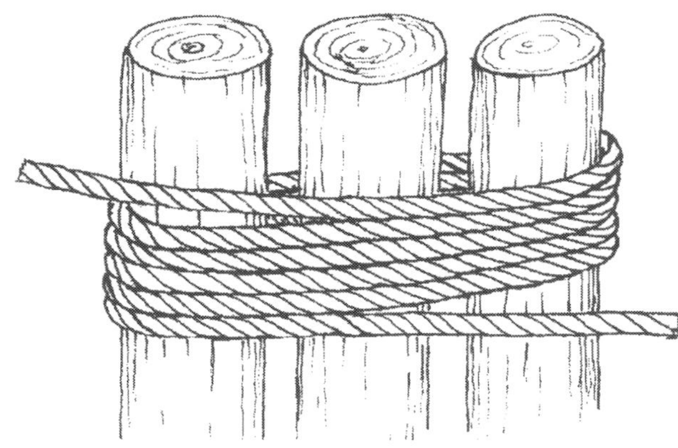

STEP 2: Start the frapping turn by taking each end around an outside pole and then between the outside pole and the center pole.

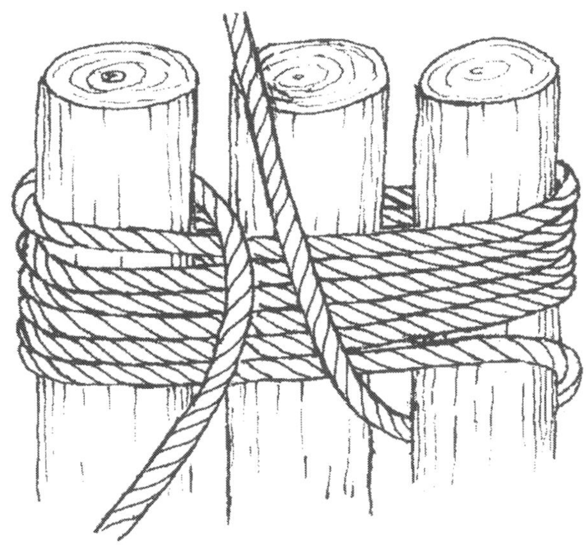

STEP 3: Take 1 or 2 frapping turns with each end. Pull the frapping turns tight; this will also tighten the wrappings.

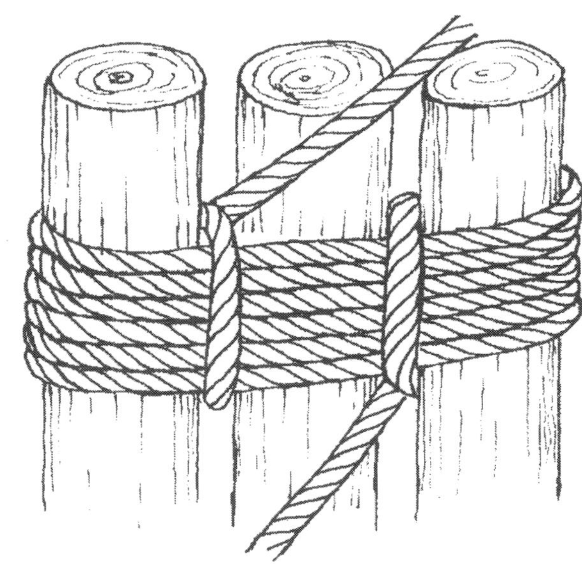

[NOTE] The frapping turns are taken in opposite directions.

STEP 4: End the lashing by tying the ends of the rope together with a Square Knot.

[WARNING]

If one end of the Square Knot is pulled it can be upset into a Lark's Head Knot. When this happens the knot will slip causing the entire lashing to loosen and fail.

ROUND LASHING:

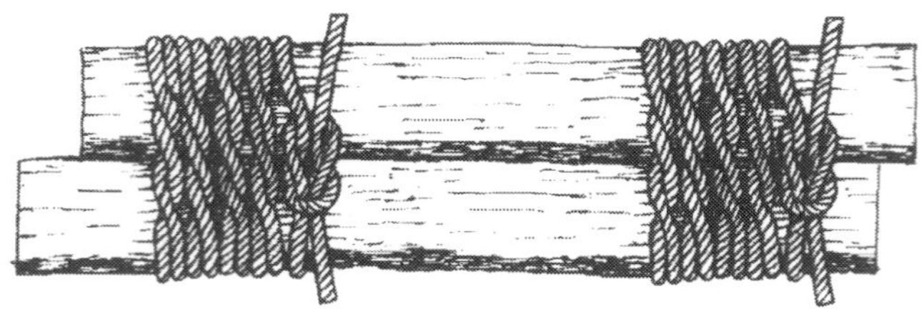

Use ---- To bind two shorter parallel poles together to make a longer pole; ---- to bind several lighter poles together to make a stronger pole.

Several shorter poles can be used in place of a longer pole by overlapping their ends and binding the overlapped portion of the poles together with two or more Round Lashings. Round Lashings can also be use to laminate several light poles together to form a stronger pole or to reinforce a cracked or otherwise weakened pole.

Comments ---- Round Lashings and Shear Lashings are sometimes lumped together as Shear Lashings; this leads to confusion and unsafe constructions when the wrong lashing is used. A Round Lashing forms a rigid joint between parallel poles and are tied without frapping turns. A Shear Lashing, on the other hand, forms a flexible joint and can also be distinguished from Round Lashings by the presence of frapping turns on the Shear Lashing.

ROUND LASHING: TRADITIONAL

Comments ---- The traditional Round Lashing is the easiest and the fastest form of Round Lashing shown in this book.

The traditional Round Lashing, when properly tied and tightened with a rope wrench or other tightening tool, is a rigid and secure form of Round Lashing.

Narration ---- (For knotboard) **(1)** Start the Round Lashing by wrapping the end of the rope around both poles and crossing the running end over the standing end to form the first Half Hitch of a Clove Hitch. **(2)** Tie a second Half Hitch to

ROUND LASHING

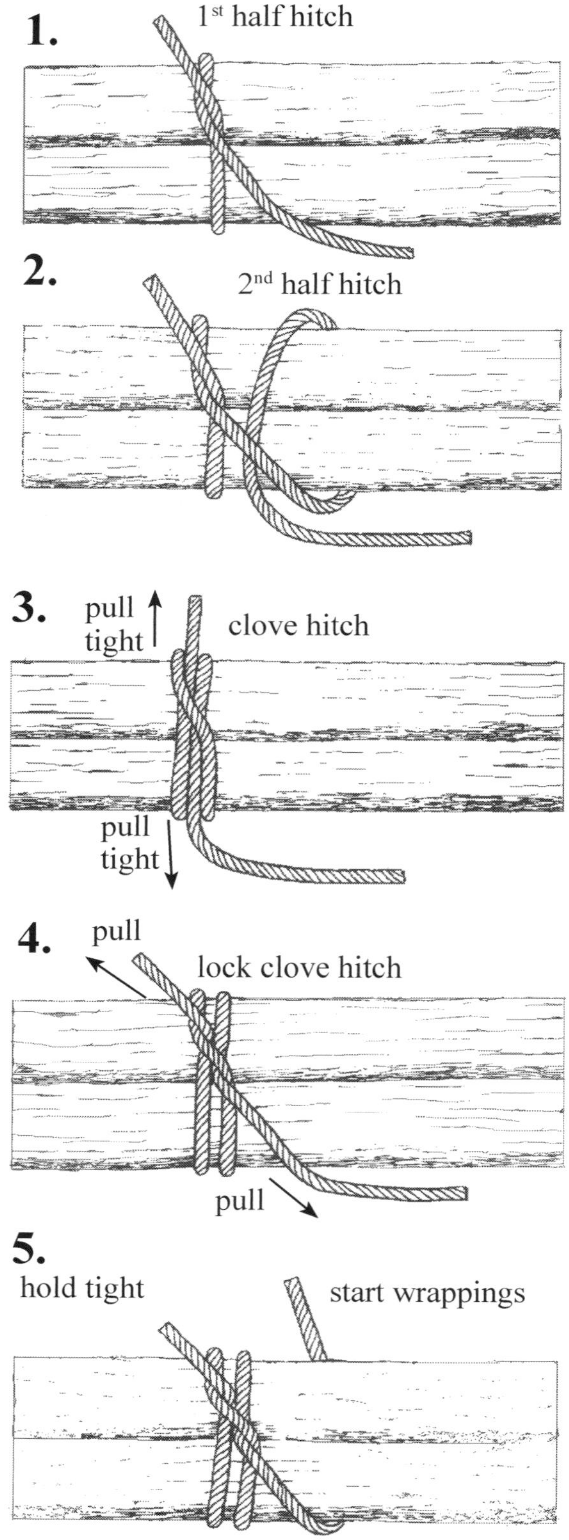

1. 1st half hitch

2. 2nd half hitch

3. pull tight ↑ clove hitch

pull tight ↓

4. pull

lock clove hitch

pull

5. hold tight

start wrappings

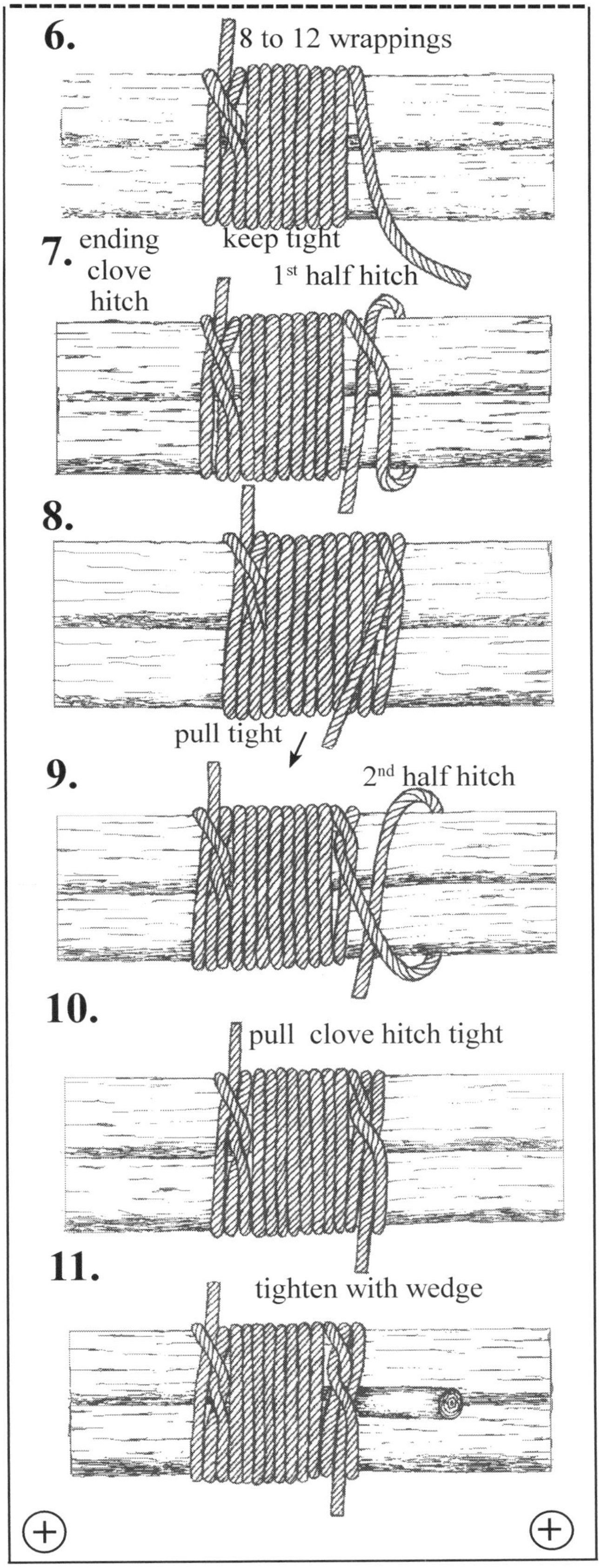

6. 8 to 12 wrappings

7. ending clove hitch keep tight 1st half hitch

8. pull tight

9. 2nd half hitch

10. pull clove hitch tight

11. tighten with wedge

finish the beginning Clove Hitch. **(3)** Pull the Clove Hitch tight. **(4)** Pull the two rope ends to the side to lock the Clove Hitch tight. **[NOTE]** If the poles and/or the rope are very smooth, a round lashing can be made more secure by adding several more Half Hitches to the beginning Clove Hitch. **(5)** While holding the Clove Hitch locked tight, start the wrappings by pulling the rope to the side of the Clove Hitch and wrapping it around both poles. **(6)** Take 8 to 12 parallel wrappings around both poles. **(7)** End the lashing with a Clove Hitch. While holding the wrappings tight, take a Half Hitch around both poles. **(8)** Pull the Half Hitch tight so that it is locked against the wrapping turns. **(9)** Tie the second Half Hitch of the ending Clove Hitch. **(10)** Pull the Clove Hitch tight. **[NOTE]** If the poles and/or the rope are very smooth, a Round Lashing can be made more secure by adding several more Half Hitches to the ending Clove Hitch. **(11)** Tighten the Round Lashing even tighter by driving a small wedge under the wrapping and in the groove between the two poles.

ROUND LASHING: TIGHTENED WITH A WEDGE

Comments ---- All forms of Round Lashing can be made more rigid by driving small wedges under the strands of the lashing so that the wedge fills the groove between the poles. The wedge not only tightens the strand of the lashing but the wedge also helps resist the shearing action between the poles.

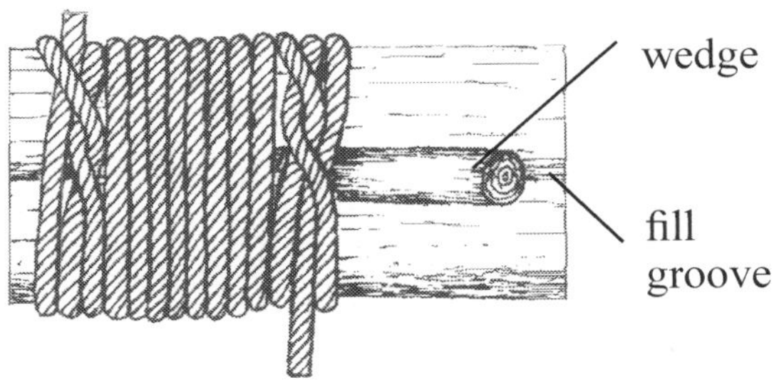

WEST COUNTRY ROUND LASHING:

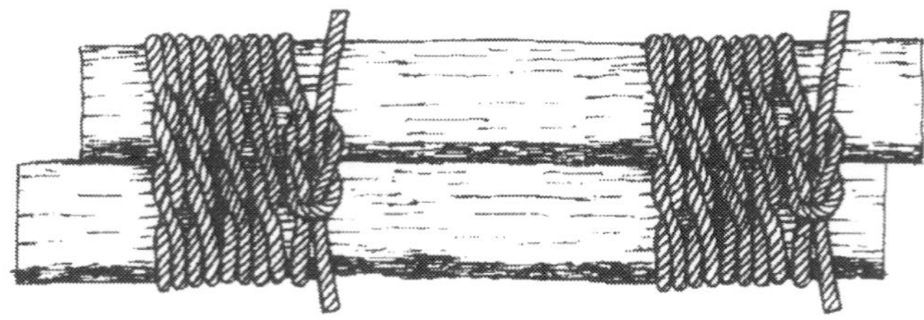

Name ---- West Country Round Lashing is a form of lashing adapted from a form of whipping called West Country Whipping which is tied in exactly the same way as shown here for the West Country Round Lashing.

West Country Round Lashing is also called West Country Shear Lashing but this name contributes to the confusion caused by lumping Shear and Round Lashings together. West Country Round Lashing is used to form a rigid joint between two parallel poles; it does not form the flexible joint of a Shear Lashing and it has no frapping turns.

The West Country Round Lashing has also been called Half Knot Round Lashing and West County Round lashing.

Comments ---- The West Country Round Lashing is a secure and easily tied form of Round Lashing.

If the lashing is to be hand tightened only, the West Country Round Lashing is a good choice.

Narration ---- (For knotboard) **(1)** Start at the middle of the rope. **(2)** Tie the rope around both poles with a Half Knot. **(3A)** Pass both ends of the rope behind the pole and tie them in place with a Half Knot on the back side of the poles. **(3B)** Pull Half Knot tight on the back side of the poles. This completes one set of wrappings. **(4)** Tie 5 to 8 sets of wrappings. **(5)** End the lashing with a Square Knot by taking a second Half Knot in the opposite direction.

WEST COUNTRY ROUND LASHING

1. middle of rope

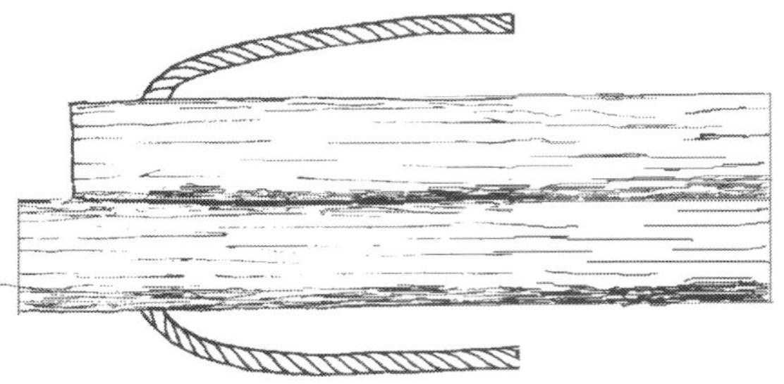

2. half knot

3A. (FRONT)

half knot

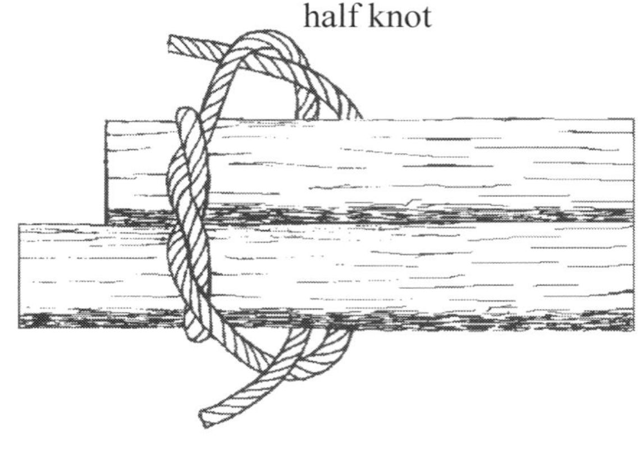

3B. (BACK)

half knot
pulled tight

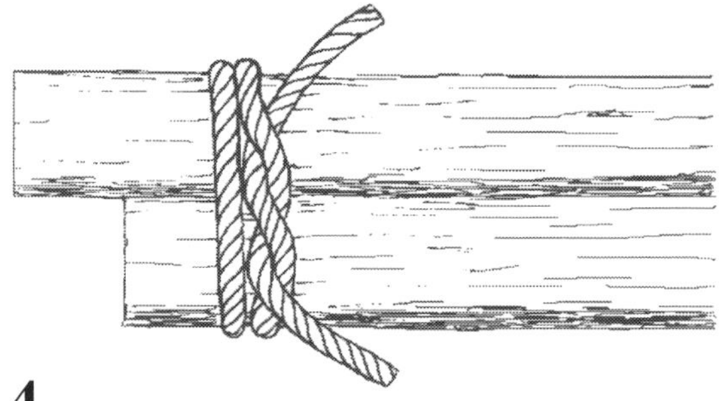

4. 5 to 8 wrappings

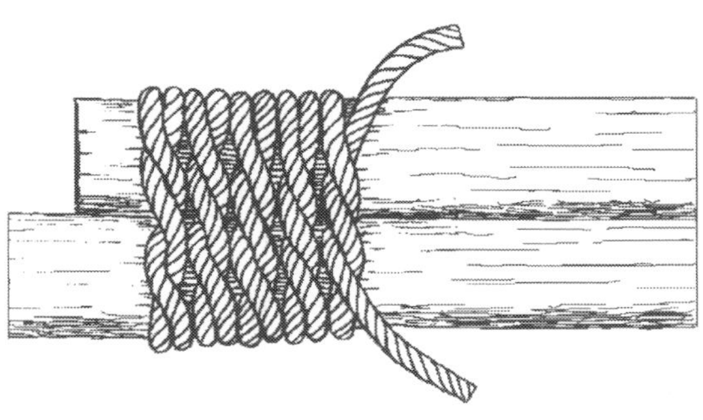

5. end with square knot

2nd half knot

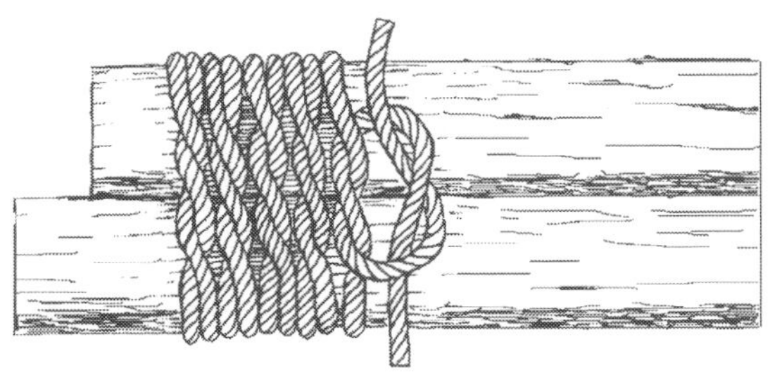

HALF HITCH ROUND LASHING:

Description ---- A series of interlocking Half Hitches.

Comments ---- The Half Hitch Round Lashing is the easiest form of Round Lashing to tie tightly. This is because, as each wrapping is applied, it's tightened and locked in place by the Half Hitch. When the Half Hitches are tightened and locked together, the wrappings cannot slide around the poles and loosen as they sometimes do in the Traditional Round Lashing.

Half Hitch Round Lashing can be easily tightened with a rope wrench; the other forms of Round Lashing can not. The beginning Clove Hitch of the Traditional Round Lashing tends to slip around the poles when a rope wrench is used to tighten the wrappings. The two rope ends of the West Country Round Lashing would require the use of two rope wrenches; this would be awkward and the tightened rope ends would tend to slip past each other in the Half Knot while the next Half Knot is being tied.

Narration ---- (For knotboard) **(1)** Form the first Half Hitch by crossing the ends of the rope so that the running end is in the direction of the additional Half Hitches that will be added. **(2)** Tie a second Half Hitch in the same direction as the first Half Hitch. **(3)** Pull the second Half Hitch tight, this forms a Clove Hitch. **(4)** Push the wrappings together and pull the running ends toward the cross point of the Half Hitch. **(5)** Pull the running end tight in the direction of the wrapping to remove any slack. **[NOTE]** Repeat steps 4 and 5 until all slack is removed. **(6)** Add a third Half Hitch. **(7)** Pull the third Half Hitch tight. **(8)** Push the wrappings together and pull the running ends toward the cross point of the Half Hitch. **(9)** Pull the running end tight in the direction of the wrapping to remove any slack. **[NOTE]** Repeat steps 8 and 9 until all slack is removed. **(10)** Make a total of 10 to 15 Half Hitches; repeat step 6 through 9 for each additional Half Hitch.

HALF HITCH ROUND LASHING

1. half hitch

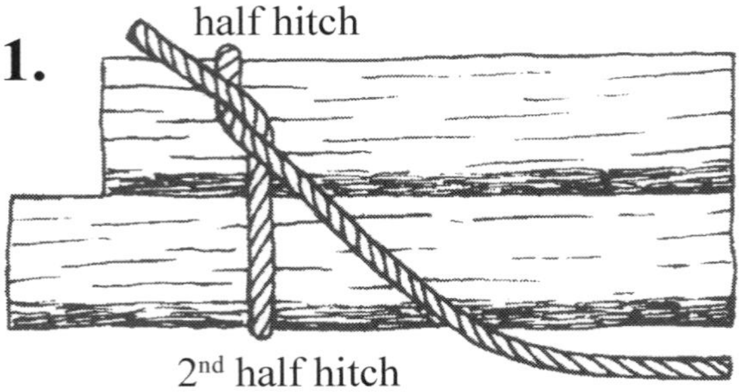

2. 2nd half hitch

3. clove hitch

pull tight

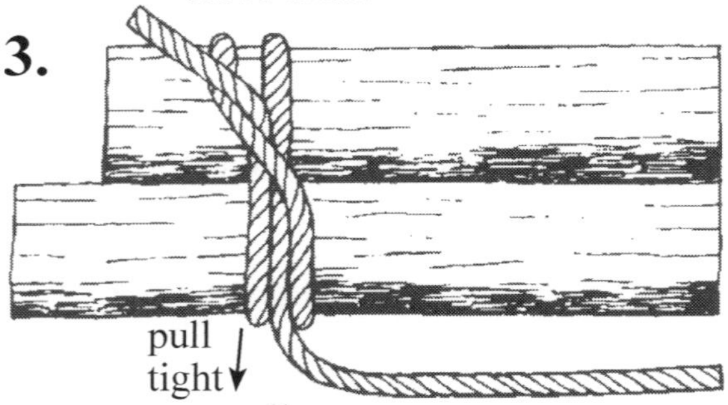

4. pull tight

push strands together

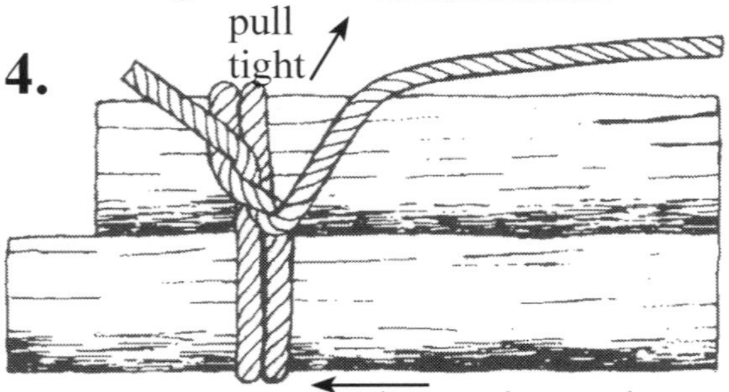

5. pull tight

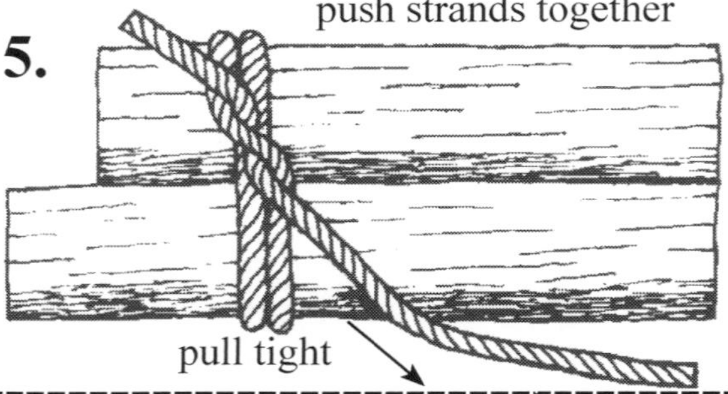

(repeat steps 4 and 5 to remove all slack)

6. 3rd half hitch

7. pull tight

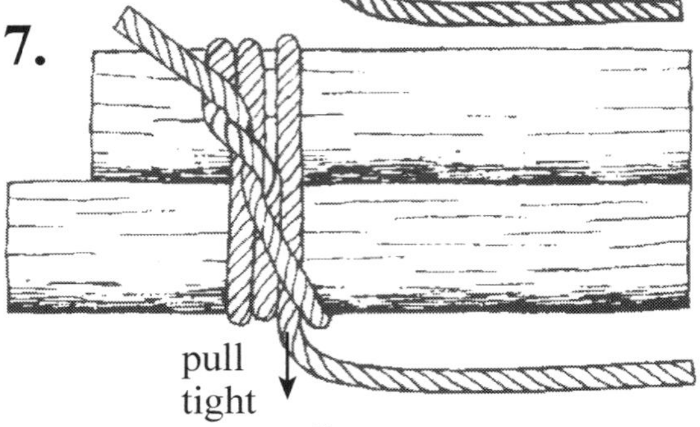

8. pull tight

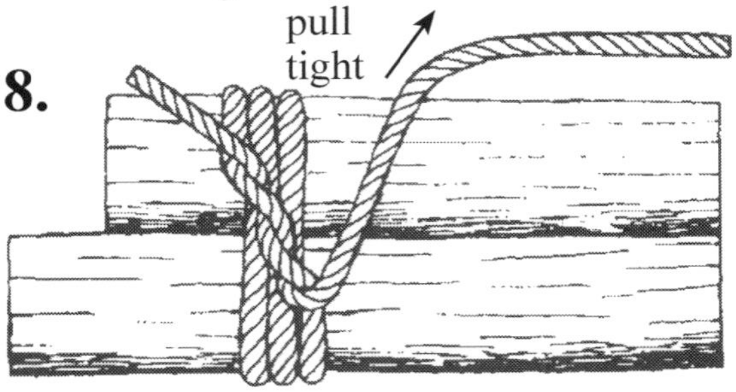

9. pull tight

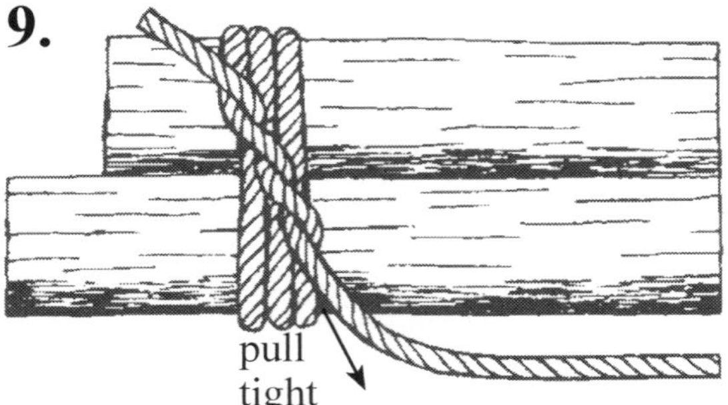

(repeat steps 8 and 9 to remove all slack)

10. make 10 to 15 half hitches

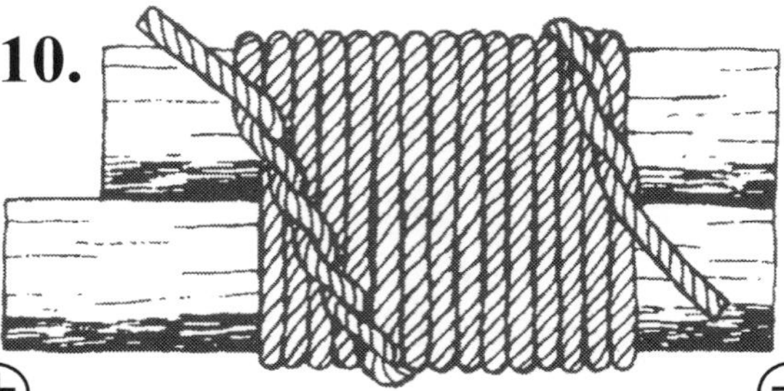

FLOOR LASHING:

Use ---- To lash a series of poles to a set of stringers to form a flat surface such as a deck, a table top, or a roadway.

Comments ---- When using a floor lashing, both ends of the decking poles must be lashed at the same time to ensure a firm even surface.

[NOTE] When placing the decking poles on the stringers, lay the decking poles so that their butt ends are in alternating directions. Alternating the butt ends of the decking poles will compensate for the natural taper of the poles so that the length of the decking along each stringer will be equal.

Narration ---- (For knotboard) **(1)** Tie a Clove Hitch around each stringer. **(2)** Secure the standing end of the rope by wrapping it around the running end in the direction of the lay of the rope. **(3)** Place the decking poles on the stringers and take a bight around the first pole. **(4)** On the inside of the stringer, pull a bight up between the first decking pole and the next decking pole. **(5)** Place the eye of the bight over the end of the decking pole. **(6)** Pull tight. **(7)** On the outside of the stringer, place a bight over the next decking pole. **(8)** Pull tight. **(9)** Repeat steps 4 through 8 until all decking poles are lashed in place. **(10)** Tie the first Half Hitch of the ending Clove Hitch. Work Half Hitch tight. **(11)** Tie the second Half Hitch of the ending Clove Hitch. **(12)** Work Half Hitch tight to form Clove Hitch.

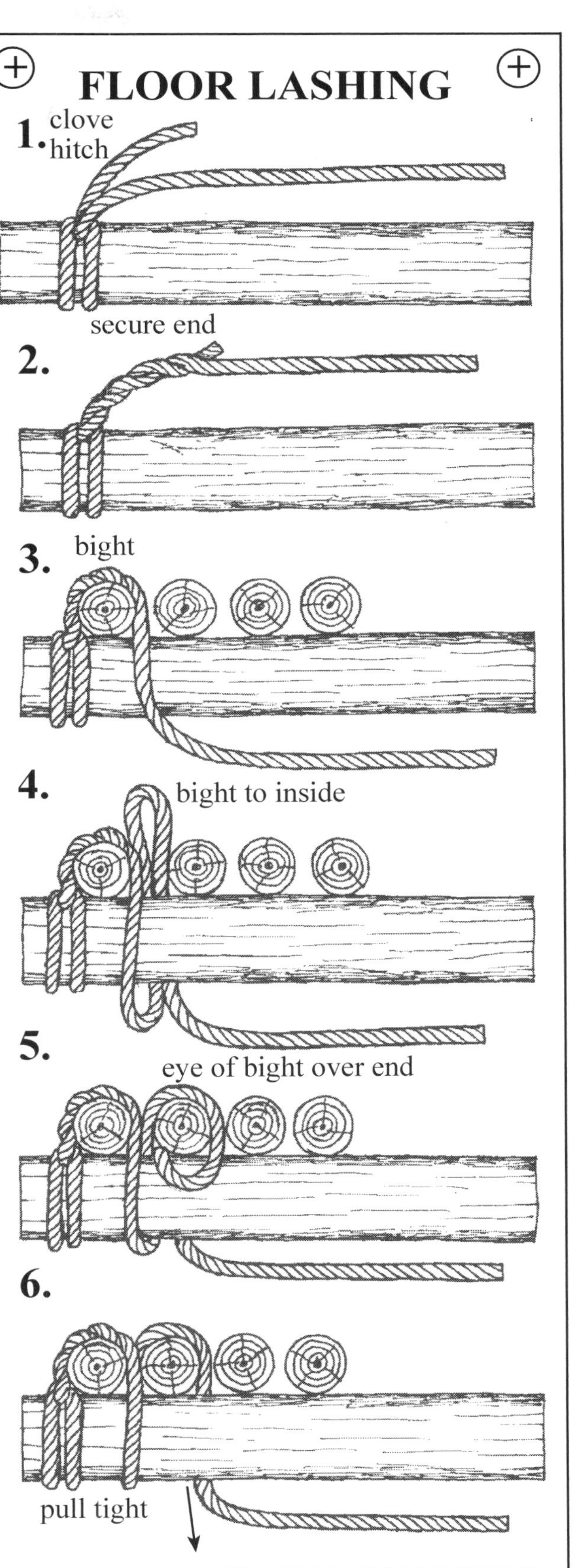

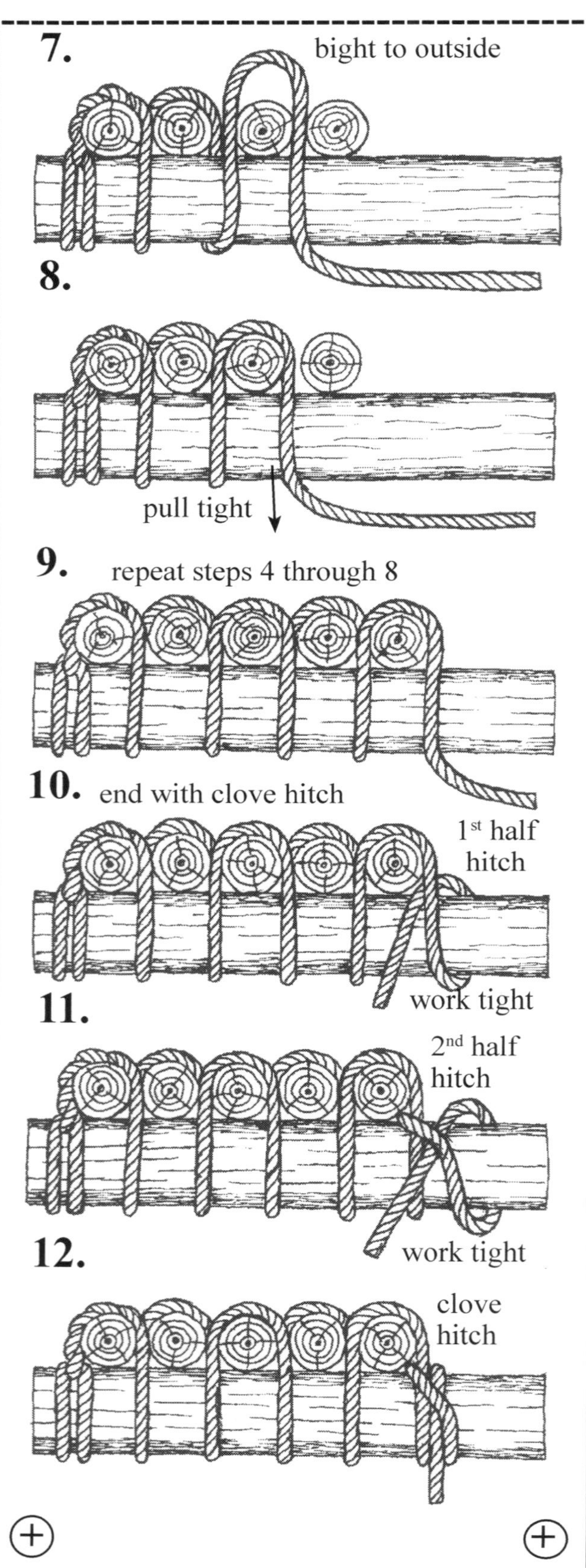
7.
bight to outside
8.
pull tight
9.
repeat steps 4 through 8
10.
end with clove hitch
1st half hitch
work tight
11.
2nd half hitch
work tight
12.
clove hitch

[NOTES]

LADDER LASHING:

Comments:

Ladder Lashing allows for a quick and secure method for constructing a ladder or for constructing a decking with evenly spaced decking pieces.

This form of lashing has several advantages over the traditional Floor Lashing. Less material is required because, unlike Floor Lashing, a space can be left between each piece of the decking. Also, each rung is securely lashed in place by several loops of rope in much the same way as a Square Lashing. A traditional Floor Lashing has only a single loop of rope holding each end of the decking in place. Therefore, if one piece loosens, the entire deck loosens.

The Ladder Lashing has two forms; left and right. Each is a mirror image of the other.

START: The Ladder Lashing is started by using a Clove Hitch stopped with two Half Hitches to secure a rope to the top end of each rail.

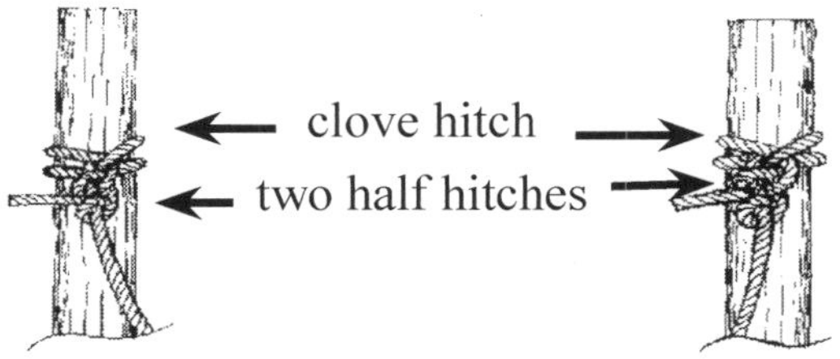

STEP 1: Lay an overhand loop over each side rail so that the running end of each loop is to the outside.

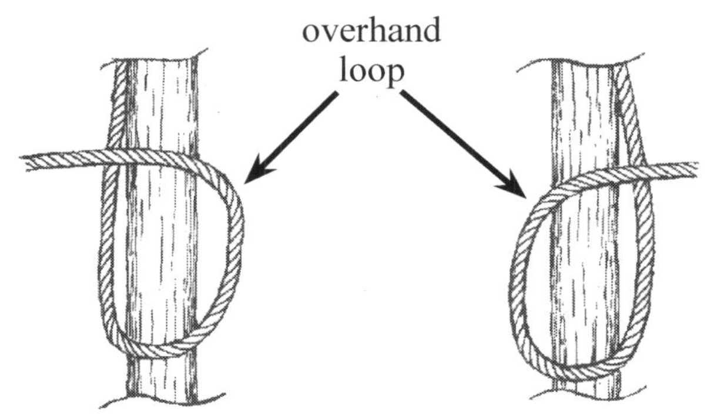

STEP 2: Place a rung across the rails so that the standing part of each overhand loop is over the end of the rung and the running part of each overhand loop is under the rung.

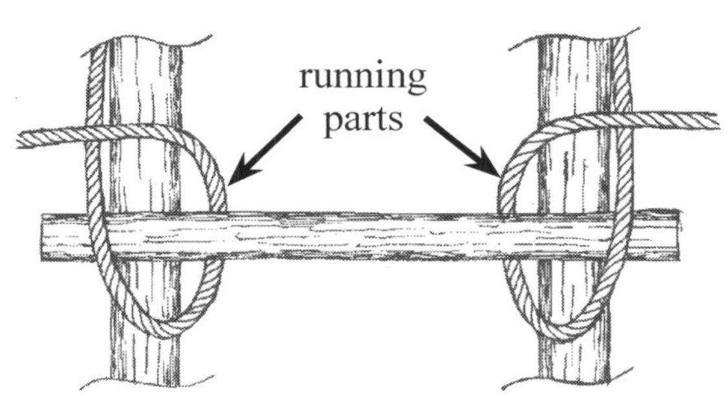

STEP 3: Pull the running part side of each overhand loop behind and to the outside of each rail.

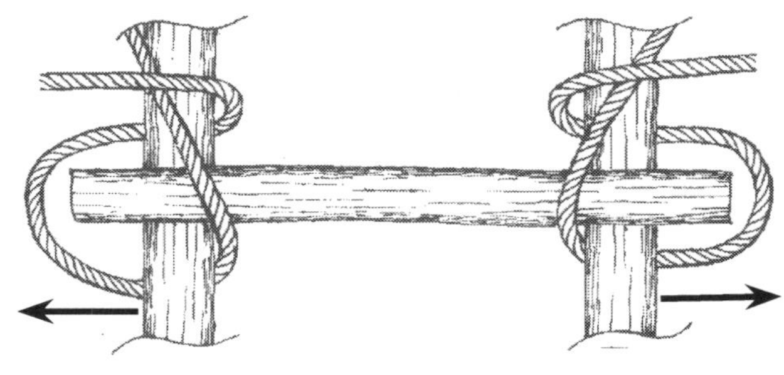

STEP 4: Then pull the loop over the end of the rung.

STEP 5: Work each rope until it is tightened around the rung and the rung is in its desired position.

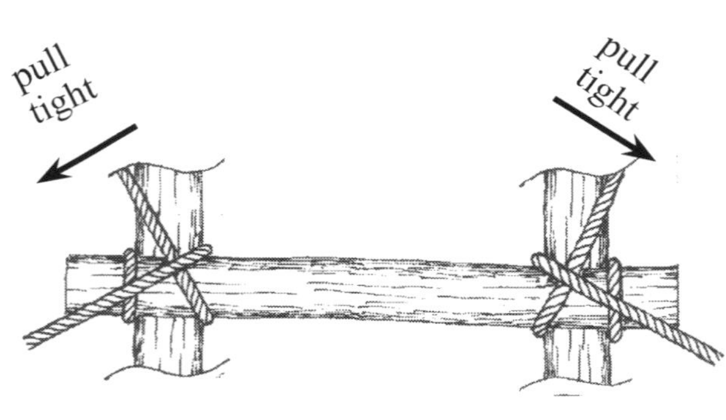

STEP 6: Form an overhand loop in each running part.

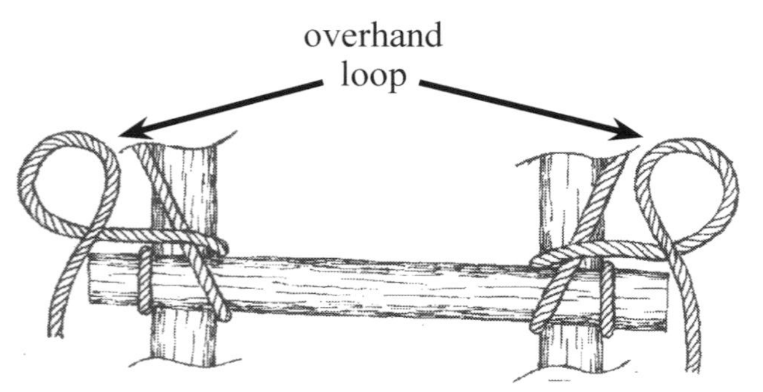

STEP 7: Place an overhand loop over each end of the rung to form a Half Hitch around each end of the rung.

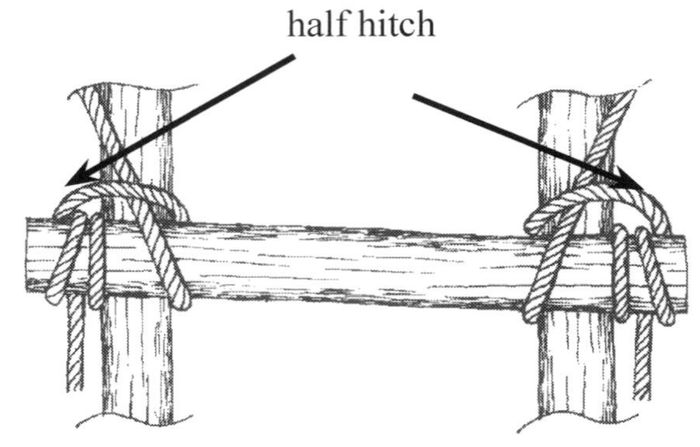

STEP 8: Work the Half Hitch tight.

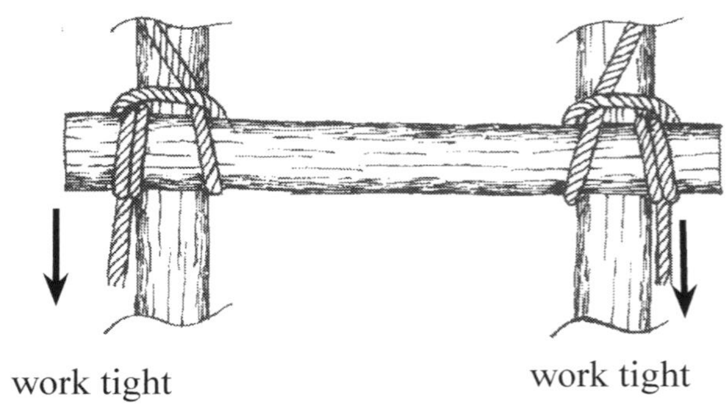

STEP 9: Repeat steps 1 through 8 for each additional rung.

END: Finish the lashing by tying a Clove Hitch around each rail so that the Clove Hitch is directly under the bottom rung.

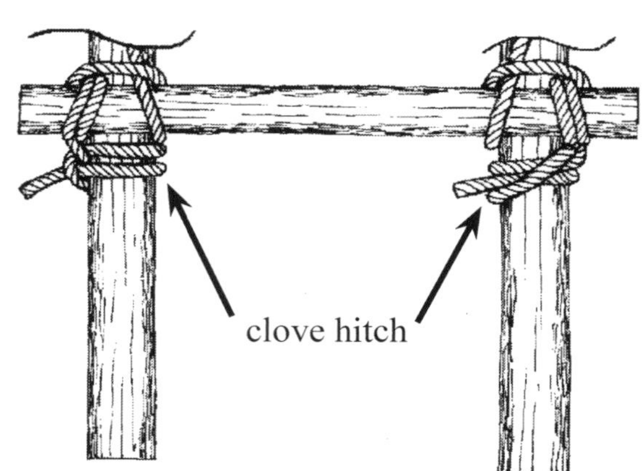

NETTING

NETTING:

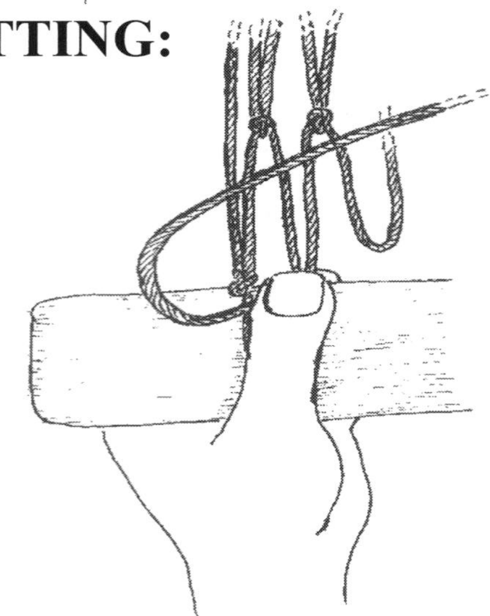

The making of netting is an ancient craft. Many prehistoric cultures used netting for a variety of uses; storage bags, fencing, hammocks, just to name some, and, of course, the obvious use as a fish net. No matter what the netting was used for, the knitting of the mesh was done by tying a series of loops in some type of twine. To form and tie the loops, a knitting shuttle and a spacer (gauge) were frequently used. The basic knot used was the Sheet Bend.

NETTING TOOLS:

The size of the shuttle and gauge that is needed will depend on the project that you are working on. The size of the shuttle and gauge given in the following directions are a convenient size for many projects and are also a good size to use for practicing the craft of netting. Shuttles and gauges of different sizes can be made by changing the size of the materials used.

Knitting Shuttle:

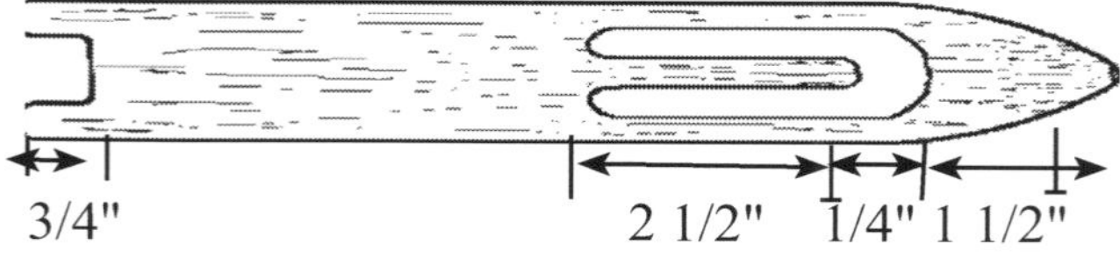

cross sections

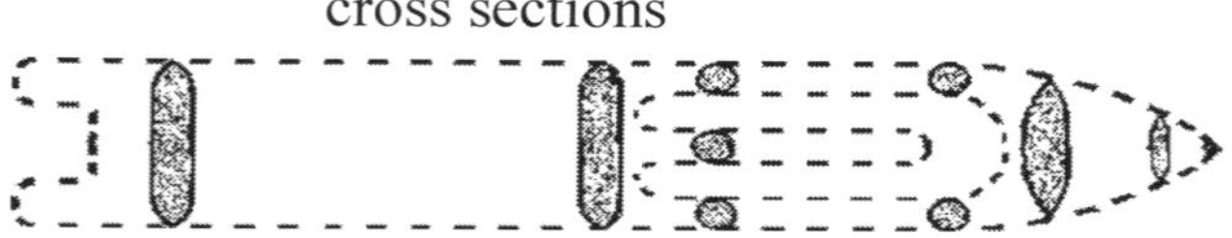

Make the knitting shuttle from a 1/4 inch * 1 inch * 12 inch piece of smooth grained hardwood. Carve and sand the shuttle to the shape shown in the diagram. Leave the shuttle unfinished; varnish or paint has a tendency to become sticky.

Knitting Gauge:

Make the knitting gauge from a 1/4 inch * 1 1/4 inch * 12 inch piece of smooth grained hard wood. Carve and sand the gauge to the shape shown in the diagram. Leave the gauge unfinished; varnish or paint has a tendency to become sticky.

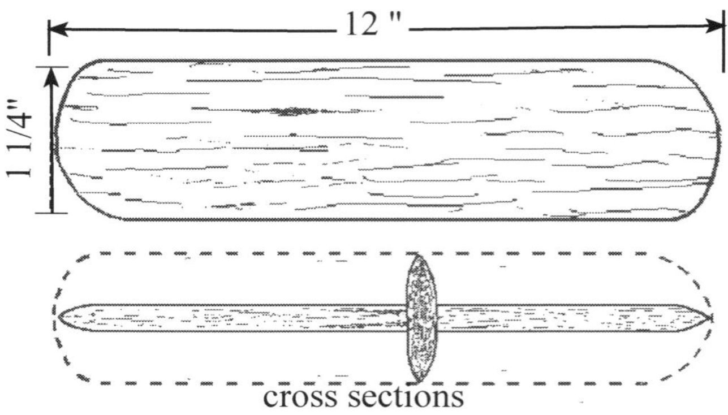

cross sections

Filling The Knitting Shuttle:

STEP 1: Fill the shuttle with twine. Start by tying a Half-Hitch around the tongue of the shuttle and then pass the twine through the notch.

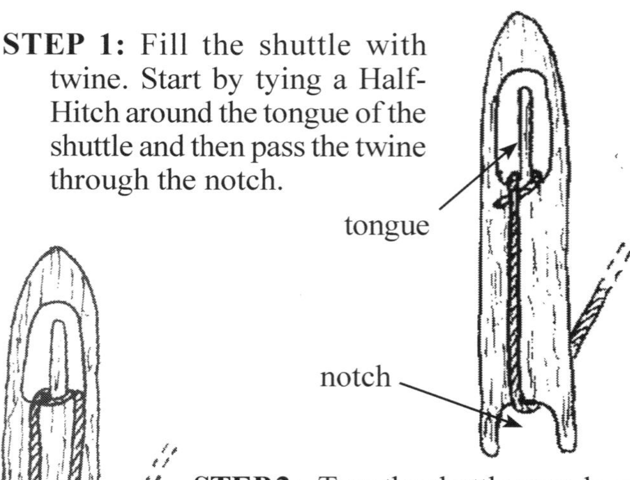

STEP 2: Turn the shuttle over, loop the twine around the tongue and then through the notch.

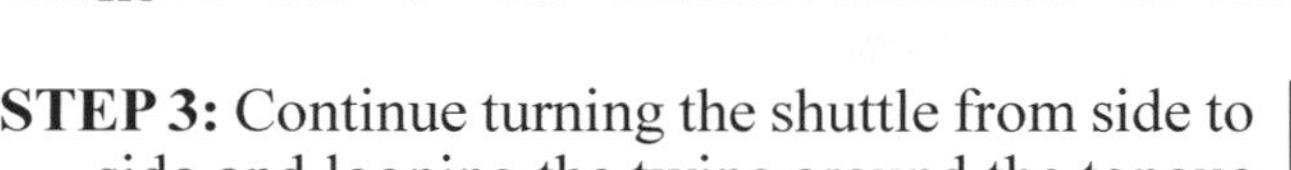

STEP 3: Continue turning the shuttle from side to side and looping the twine around the tongue until the shuttle is filled.

[NOTE] To prevent synthetic twine from fraying, use a candle flame to cut and fuse the ends.

[WARNING] Using a butane cigarette lighter to cut or fuse synthetic rope or twine may cause the lighter to overheat and explode.

DIAMOND MESH NETTING:

Diamond Mesh Netting is the easiest of the two forms of mesh to make. Square Mesh Netting will be dealt with later.

Casting On: To start diamond mesh netting, the first row of mesh loops is cast on to a loop of some kind. The kind of loop used depends on the project; a ring, grommet, frame or loop of twine may be used. The following directions are for casting on to a ring, but the same steps may be used for any starting loop.

STEP 1: Tie the end of the twine to the ring with a Clove Hitch stopped with two Half Hitches.

STEP 2: Place the twine behind the gauge then bring the twine in front of the gauge and to the right.

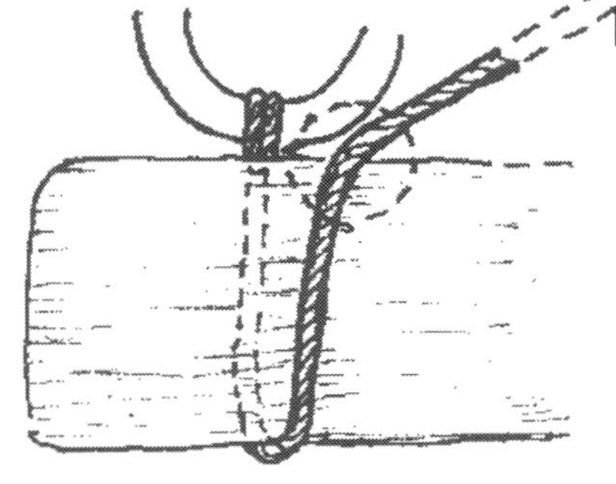

[NOTE]: The dotted circles in each of the diagrams is used to show the position of the thumb and finger of the left hand.

STEP 3: Reeve the twine through the ring from the front to the back so that an overhand loop is formed.

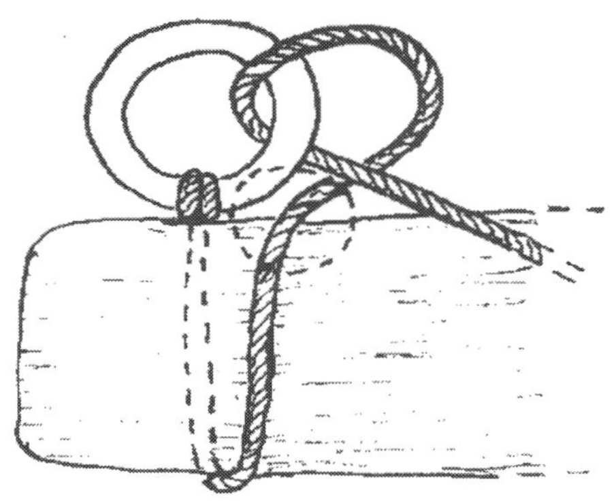

STEP 4: Pull the twine to the left to tighten the twine around the ring and the gauge.

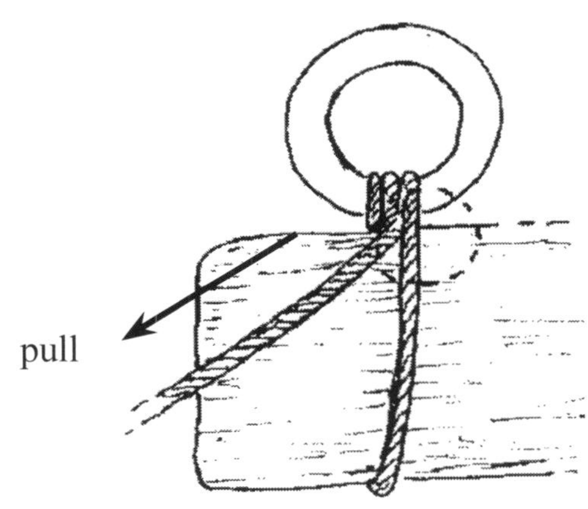

STEP 5: Lay the twine across the ring from left to right.

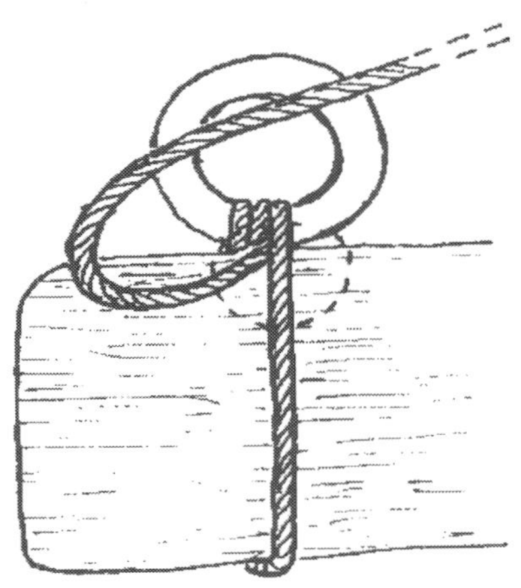

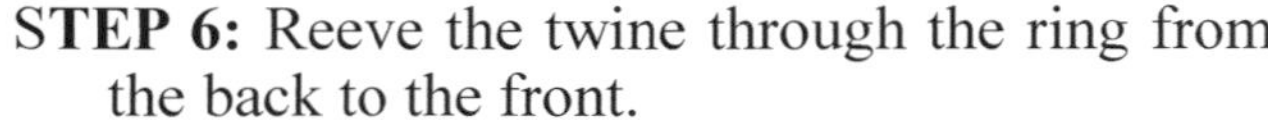

STEP 6: Reeve the twine through the ring from the back to the front.

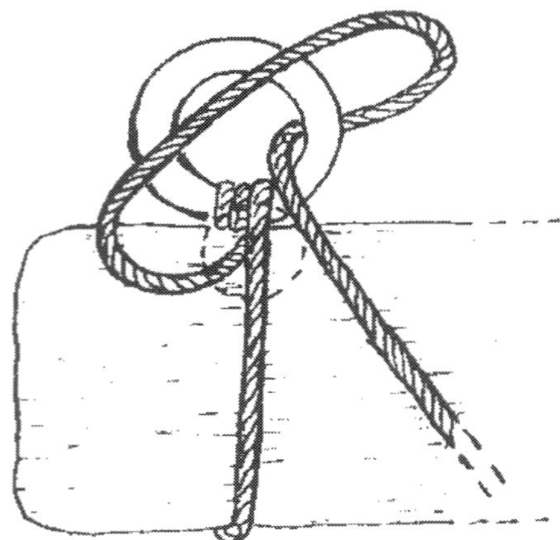

STEP 7: Place the twine behind the gauge; then pull the twine downward to tighten the twine around the ring. This forms a Lark's Head Knot around the ring.

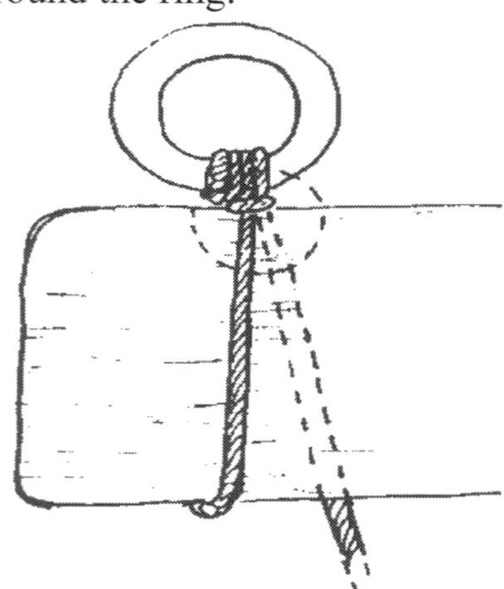

STEP 8: Repeat steps 2 through 7 for each additional loop required for the project.

KNITTING A ROW OF MESH:

Netting is made by knitting rows of mesh using a shuttle and a gauge. The gauge is used to determine the size of the mesh, and the shuttle is used to hold the twine and to form and tie the mesh loops. The basic knot used in netting is the Sheet Bend. The following diagrams illustrate the tying of the Sheet Bend as it is used for knitting a net.

STEP 1: Bring the twine down the front and up the back of the gauge. Pick up the next loop by passing the shuttle through the loop from back to front.

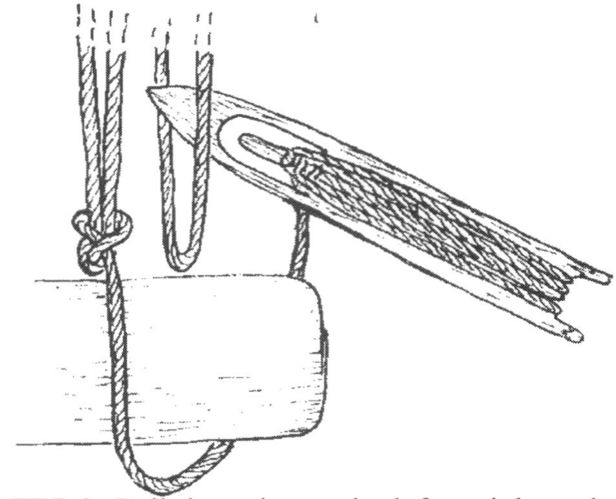

STEP 2: Pull the twine to the left to tighten the twine around the gauge. Use the thumb and finger of the left hand to hold the twine in place.

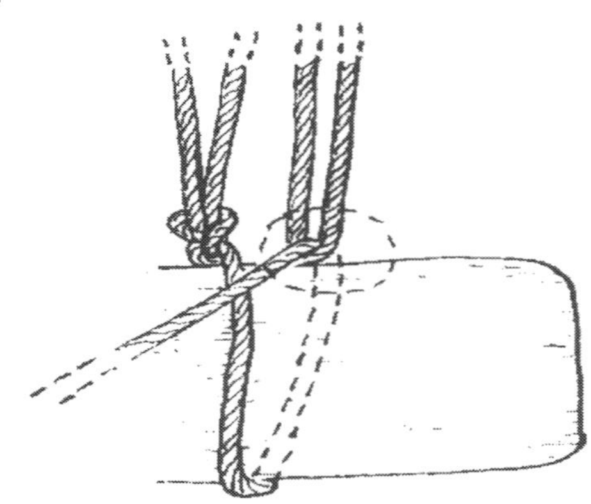

STEP 3: Lay a loop of twine over the loop just picked up.

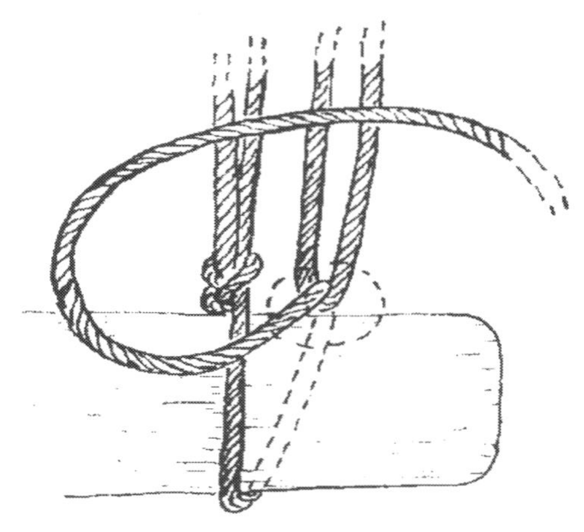

STEP 4: Pass the shuttle in back of the picked up loop and through the loop that was laid on top.

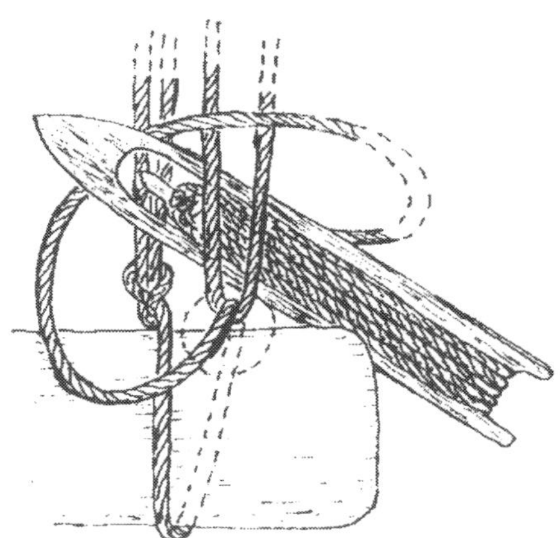

STEP 5: Pull the twine downward and slightly to the right to tighten the knot.

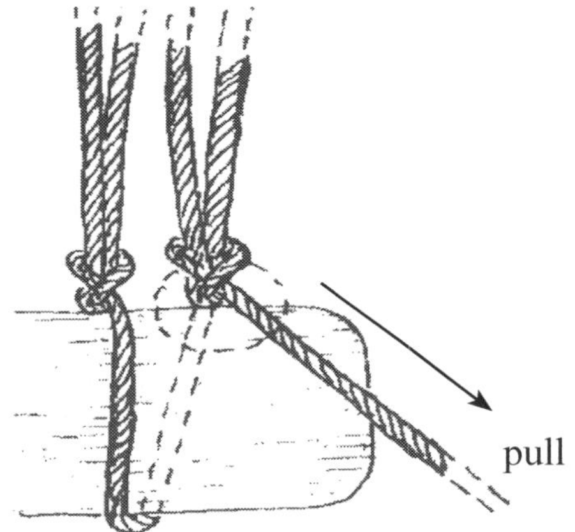

STEP 6: Repeat steps 1 through 5 for each loop in the row.

STARTING A NEW ROW:

STEP 1: When the end of a row of mesh is reached, slide the accumulated loops off the gauge. Turn the work piece over so that the running end of the twine is on the left side of the work piece.

STEP 2: Wrap the twine around the gauge from front to back; pick up the first loop by passing the shuttle through the loop from back to front.

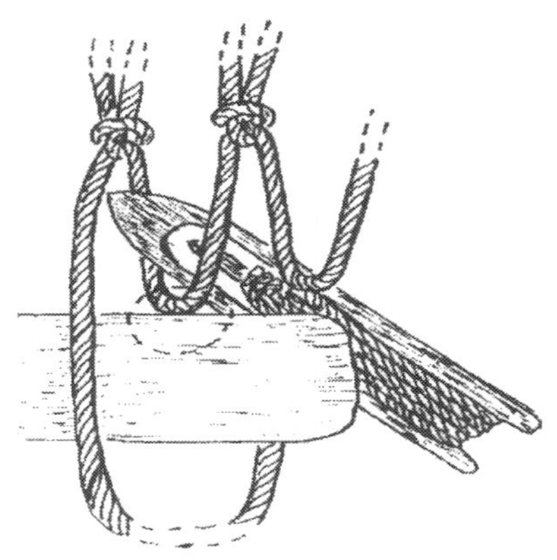

STEP 3: Knit the loop in place by following the directions for knitting a row of mesh.

ADDING A LOOP:

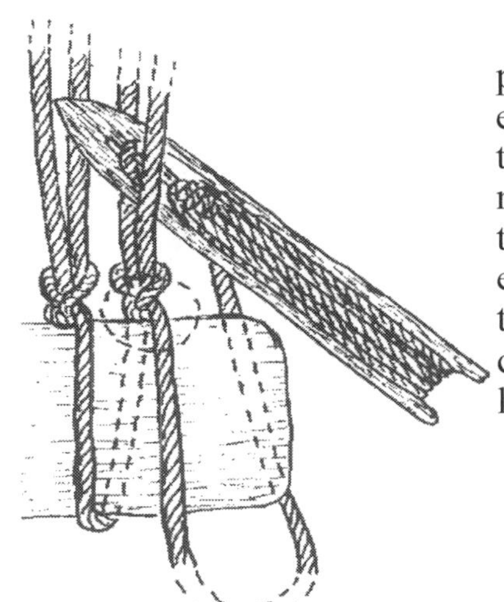

For some projects it is necessary to increase the width of the netting part way through the project. The width of the netting is increased by adding loops of mesh.

A loop is added by picking up the same loop a second time so that two loops are tied to the same loop in the previous row of mesh.

DROPPING A LOOP:

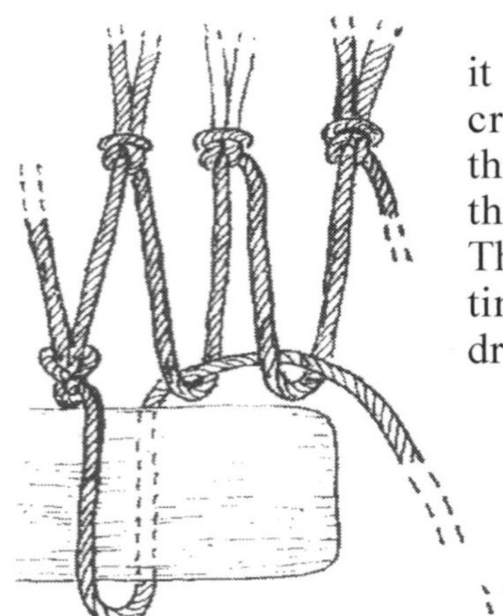

For some projects it is necessary to decrease the width of the netting part way through the project. The width of the netting is decreased by dropping loops.

A loop is dropped by picking up two adjacent loops from the previous row so that one loop in the new row is tied to two loops in the previous row. See diagrams.

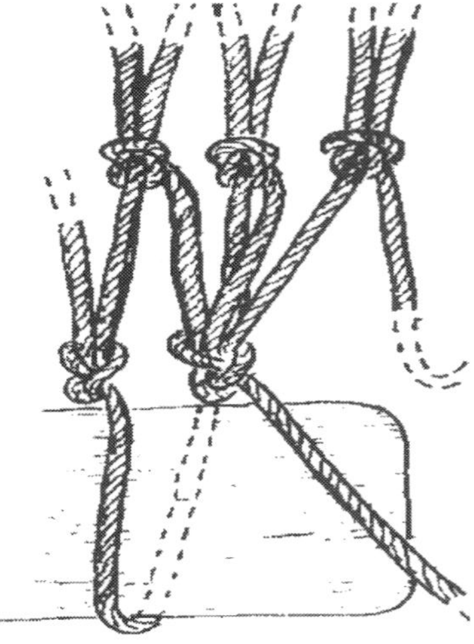

DOUBLE LOOP:

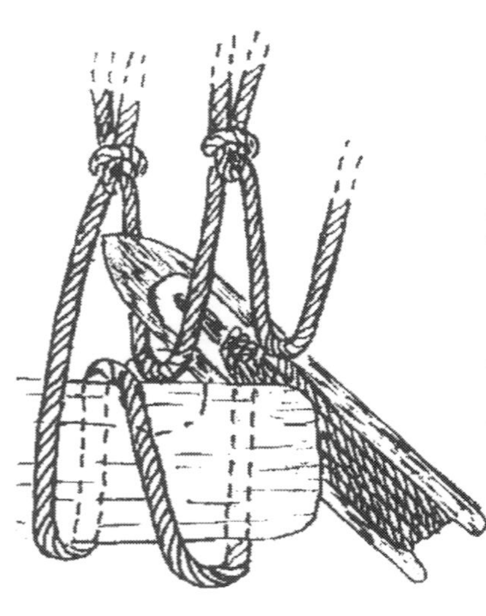

Instead of using a wider gauge, a double loop can be used. The only difference between a double loop and a single loop is the extra wrap around the gauge before tying off the loop.

SQUARE MESH NETTING:

For some projects Square Mesh Netting is required. The difference between Square Mesh Netting and Diamond Mesh Netting is that in Diamond Mesh Netting each new row of mesh is added across the width of the work piece. In Square Mesh Netting, each new row is added diagonally across the work piece.

STEP 1: Tie the running end of the twine (the free end of the twine on the shuttle) to a loop of twine.

STEP 2: Follow the directions for adding a loop to tie two loops around the gauge.

STEP 3: Slide the loops off; turn the work piece over so that the running end is on the left side. Start the next row by picking up the first loop on the left; pull the twine to the left to tighten it around the gauge.

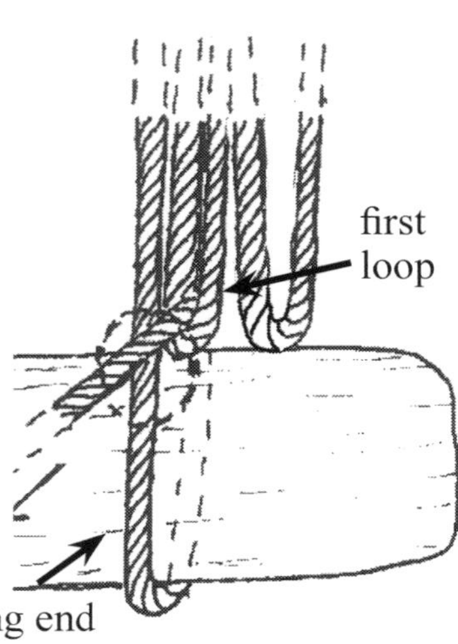

STEP 4: Knit the loop in place so that the outside strand goes through the Sheet Bend.

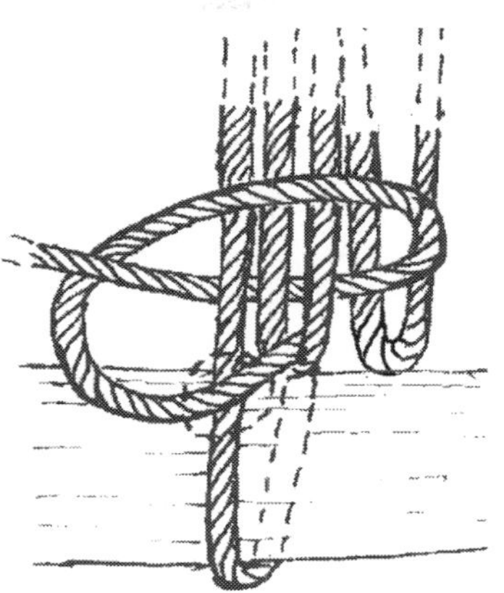

STEP 5: Pull the knot tight.

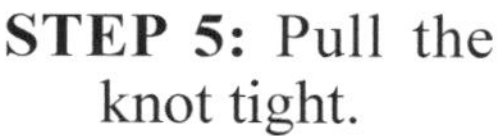

STEP 6: Pick up the second start loop and tie two loops in it; follow directions for adding a loop.

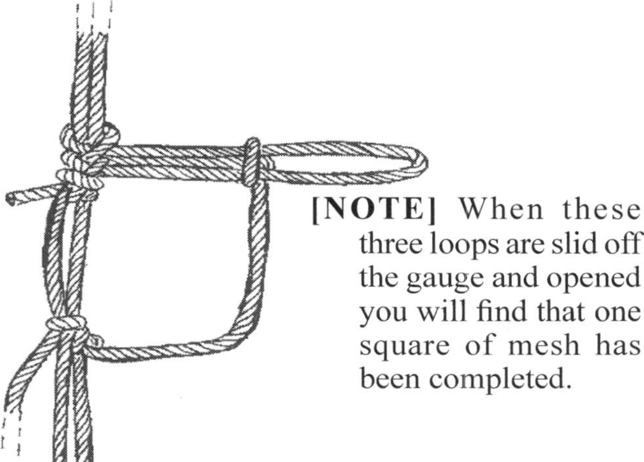

[NOTE] When these three loops are slid off the gauge and opened you will find that one square of mesh has been completed.

STEP 7: Continue to knit additional rows of mesh, (add a loop at the end of each new row) until the work piece has reached the desired width.

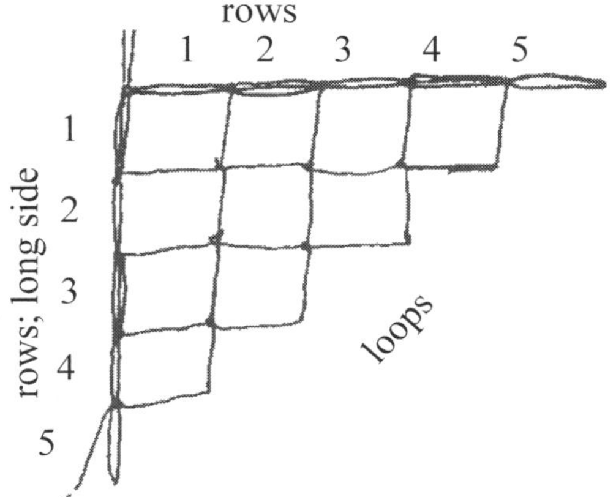

[EXAMPLE] Step 7: If the desired width of the work piece is five squares; knit five rows that have a loop added at the end of each row. This row will have six loops, one more than the desired number of mesh squares, 5.

STEP 8: When the work piece has reached the desired width, end the next row without adding a loop. This forms the second corner of the work piece. **[Note]** This row will have one more loop than the desired number of mesh squares.

[EXAMPLE] Step 8: Knit the sixth row; do not add a loop at the end. This row will have six loops.

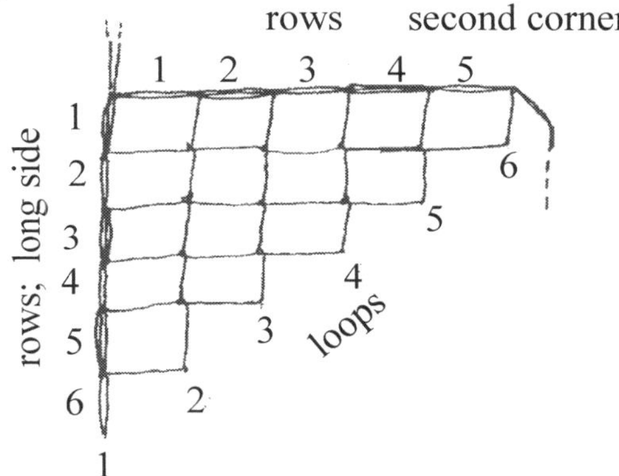

STEP 9: Knit the next row after the second corner, add a loop at the end. **[Note]** This row will have 2 more loops than the desired number of mesh squares and will end on the long side.

[EXAMPLE] Step 9: Knit the seventh row, add a loop at the end of the row. This row will have seven loops, two more than the desired number of mesh squares, 5.

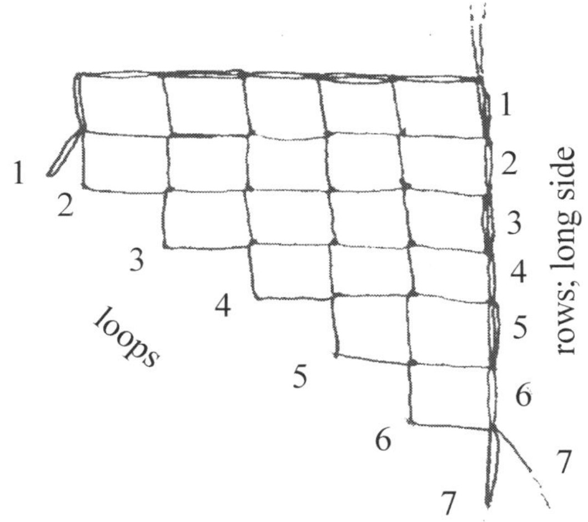

STEP 10: Knit the second row after the corner; drop a loop at the end of the row. **[Note]** This row will have one more loop than the desired number of mesh squares and will end on the side that the second corner is on.

[EXAMPLE] Step 10: Knit the eighth row and drop a loop at the end of the row. This row will have six loops, one more than the desired number of mesh squares, 5.

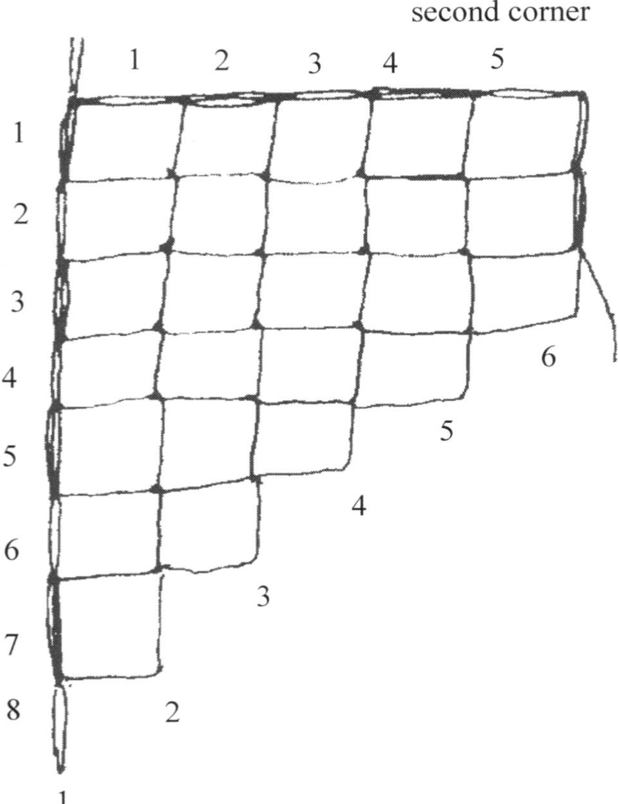

STEP 11: Continue to knit alternating rows as described in steps 9 and 10, until the work piece has reached the desired length. On the next row ending on the long side do not add a loop. This will form the third corner of the work piece.

STEP 12: Continue to knit additional rows, dropping a loop at the end of each row, until only two loops are left.

STEP 13: Hook a finger into the loop that will be the corner square of the finished work piece.

STEP 14: Form a loop as shown in the diagram.

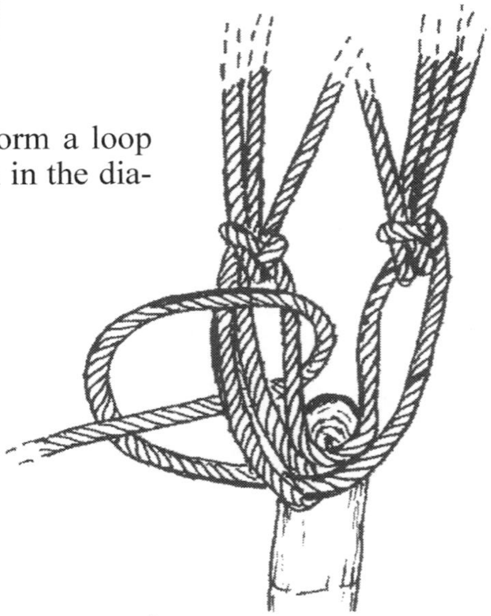

STEP 15: Pull twine tight to form the knot. The knot should take the form of a Sheet Bend.

NET MESH BAG:

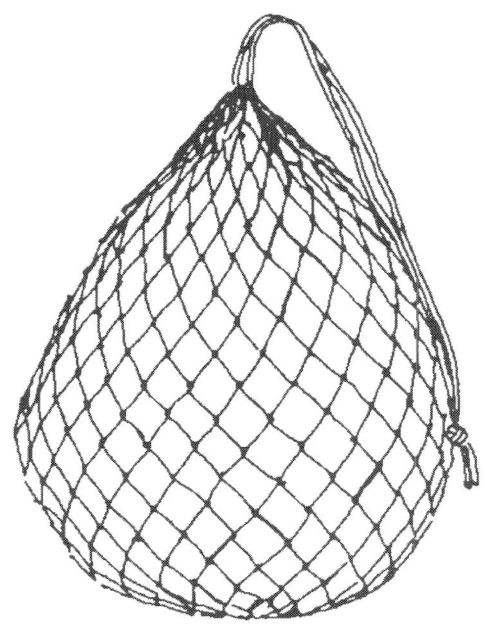

Knitted Mesh Bags have many uses such as; sports equipment storage, laundry bag, tent or tarp bag, bear bag, toy bag, etc.. Even though different uses may require different sized bags with different sized mesh, all of them can be made by using the following set of directions.

STEP 1: Bag Size: The size of a mesh bag is determined by the size of the knitting gauge used, the number of loops that are knitted in each row and the number of rows knitted. **[NOTE]** For the purposes of instruction, a 1 1/4 inch gauge will be used to knit a bag that has a 36 inch circumference and a height of 20 inches.

1A] To determine the number of loops to use for each row, multiply 1.4 times the width of the gauge and divide that answer into the desired circumference; then round the answer to the nearest whole number. (see the following formula):

$$\text{number of loops} = \frac{\text{circumference}}{1.4 * \text{gauge width}}$$

[EXAMPLE]

circumference = 36 inches
gauge width = 1 1/4 inches = 1.25 inches
number of loops = ?

$$? = \frac{36 \text{ inches}}{1.4 * 1.25 \text{ inches}}$$

$$? = \frac{36 \text{ inches}}{1.75 \text{ inches}}$$

? = 20.57
? = 21 loops

1B] To determine the number of rows of mesh, multiply 0.7 times the gauge width and divide the answer into the desired height of the bag; then round the answer to the nearest whole number.

$$\text{number of rows} = \frac{\text{height of bag}}{0.7 * \text{gauge width}}$$

[EXAMPLE]

height of bag = 20 inches
gauge width = 1 1/4 inches = 1.25 inches
number of rows = ?

$$? = \frac{20 \text{ inches}}{0.7 * 1.25 \text{ inches}}$$

$$? = \frac{20 \text{ inches}}{0.875 \text{ inches}}$$

? = 22.85
? = 23 rows

STEP 2: Foundation Loop: A foundation loop is used to start the bag and serves to form the bottom of the bag. Make the foundation loop by tying the ends of a 36 inch strand of twine together. Then fold the twine over on itself so that it forms a three strand loop.

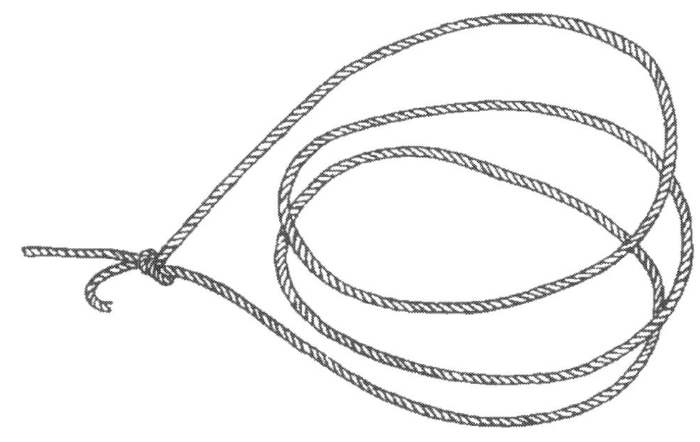

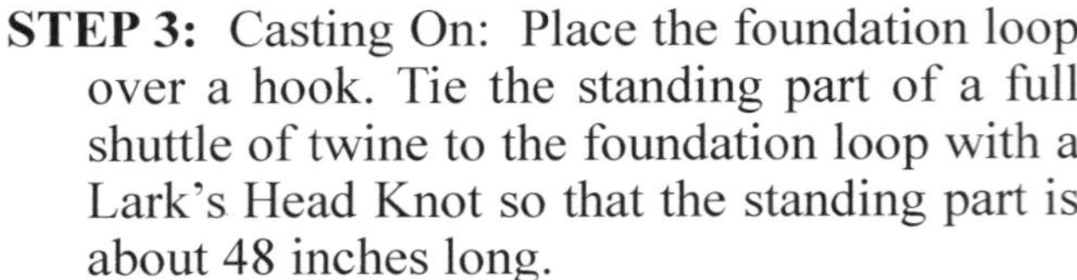

STEP 3: Casting On: Place the foundation loop over a hook. Tie the standing part of a full shuttle of twine to the foundation loop with a Lark's Head Knot so that the standing part is about 48 inches long.

STEP 4: Cast a total of 20 mesh loops on to the foundation loop. (see directions for casting on).

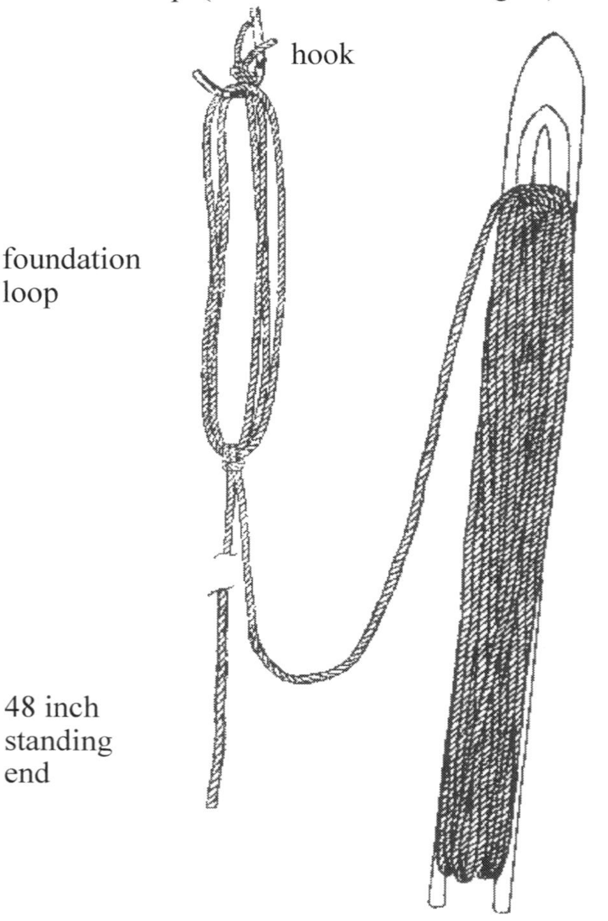

STEP 5: Knit a row of diamond mesh (see directions for Diamond Mesh Netting).

STEP 6: Finish each row of mesh by joining the standing end and the running end together with an Overhand Knot.

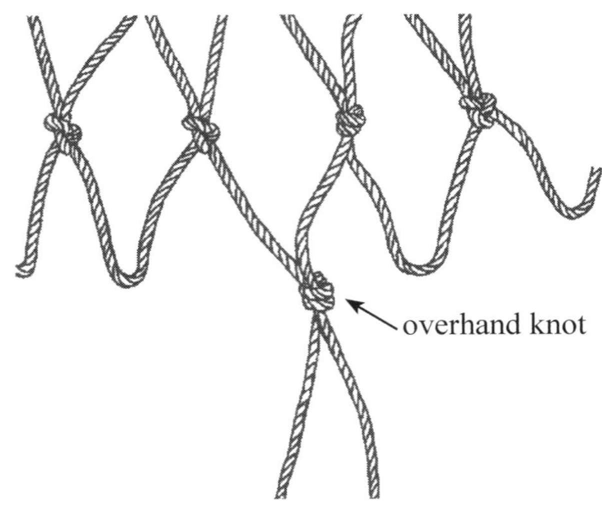

STEP 7: Knit a total of 27 rows of mesh.

STEP 8: Close Foundation Loop: Untie the ends of the foundation loop and pull on the ends of the twine to close the loop so that all the Lark's Head Knots are all adjacent to each other.

STEP 9: Tie the ends of the twine together with a Square Knot.

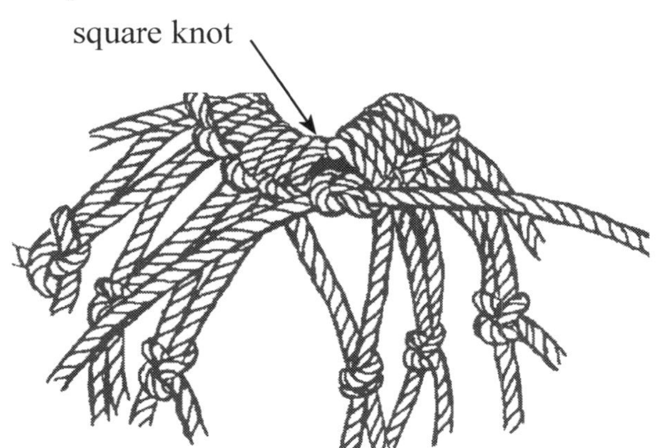

STEP 10: Use a needle to work the ends of the foundation loop through the Lark's Head Knots on either side of the closed end and trim off the ends.

STEP 11: Finish the bag by reeving a drawstring through the final row of mesh loops.

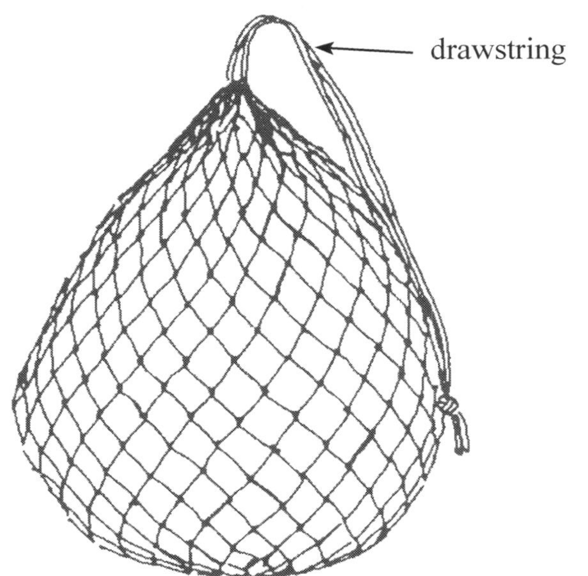

[NOTES]

HAMMOCK:

Hammocks come in a variety of styles. Each style was designed to meet a specific need. The following directions are for a hammock that can be used for camping or storage.

MATERIALS: Any natural or synthetic twine or cord that will securely hold a knot and has a test strength of about 60 pounds or more.

STEP 1: Use an Overhand or Figure-Eight Knot On a Bight to tie a 2 1/2inch loop in the end of the twine. This loop will be slightly larger than the eye of the finished clew at the end of the hammock.

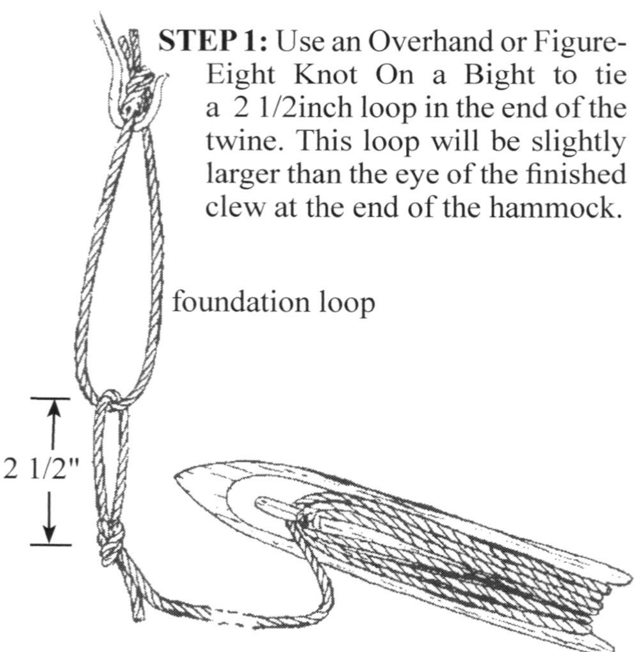

STEP 2: Form a foundation loop by reeving a 2 foot length of twine through the eye of the 2 1/2 inch loop and joining the end with an Overhand Knot. Hang the foundation loop on a hook.

STEP 3: Cast on 12 quadruple mesh loops. Make each of the 12 mesh loops by taking 4 turns around a 2 1/2 inch netting gauge before tying it off to the foundation loop with a Lark's Head Knot or a Clove Hitch.

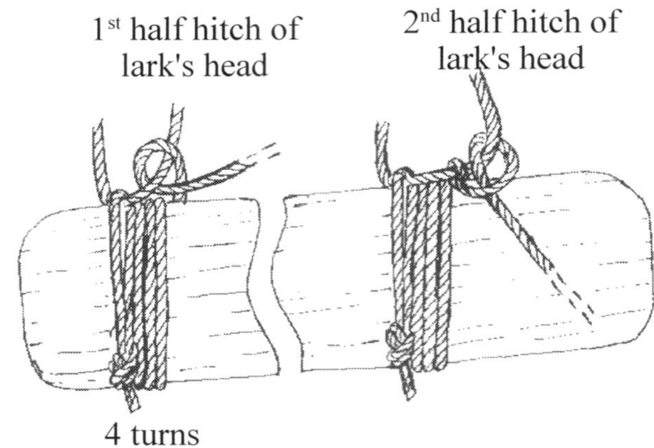

STEP 4: Second row of mesh. Knit two triple length mesh loops to each of the mesh loops in the first row; this will result in the second row having 24 mesh loops. **[NOTE]** The triple length mesh loop is made by taking three turns around the gauge before tying off the new mesh loop.

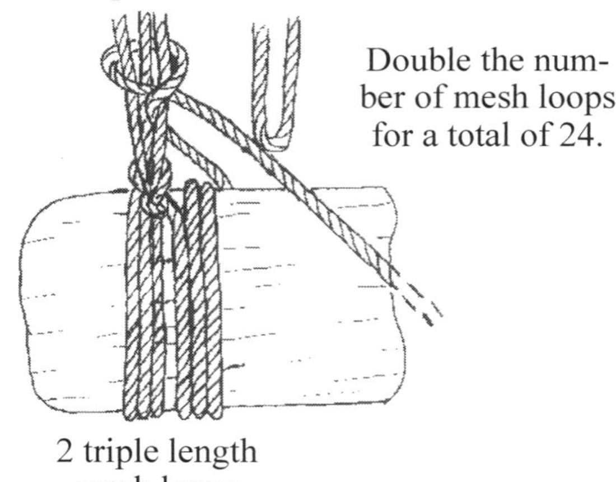

STEP 5: Third row of mesh loops. Knit one double length mesh loop to each of the mesh loops of the second row. When the third row is completed, the total length of the work should be about 2 feet.

STEP 6: Knit 6 feet of single length mesh.

STEP 7: Knit one row of double length mesh.

STEP 8: Knit one row of triple length mesh.

STEP 9: Knit one row of 12 quadruple length mesh. Reduce the number of mesh loops from 24 to 12 by picking up two mesh loops at a time as this row is being knitted.

STEP 10: Tie 2 1/2 inch loop in the end of the twine with an Overhand or Figure-Eight Knot On a Bight. This knot must be tied so that it can be stacked with the last row of mesh when forming the clew.

STEP 11: Form the clew at the end of the hammock.

A] Form the core of the clew by stacking the last row of mesh loops one on top of another. Include the 2 1/2 inch ending loop in this stack.

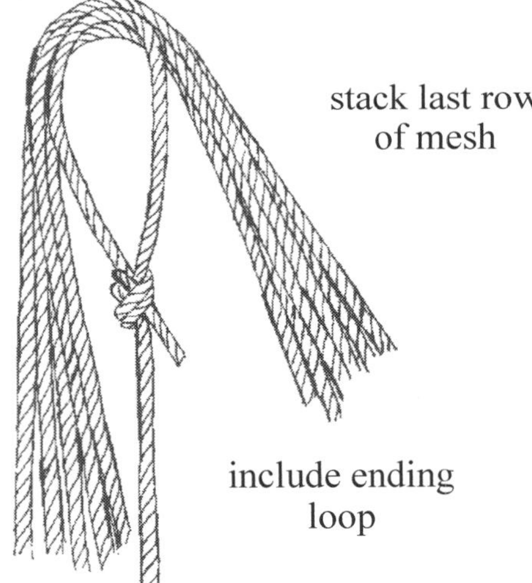

B] Bind the loops together with Ringbolt Hitching.

C] Finish off the eye of the clew by seizing the ends together.

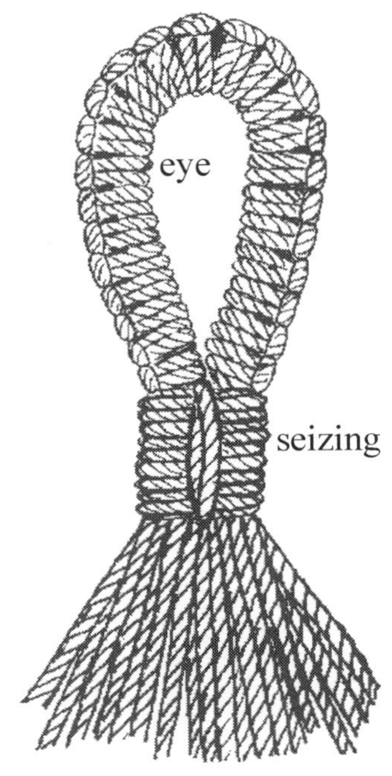

STEP 12: Form a clew at the other end of the hammock by removing the foundation loop and then repeating step 11.

[NOTES]

ROPE MAKING

MATERIALS:

Any of the following materials may be used to make rope: binder twine, bailer twine, plastic twine, jute twine, yarn, string, or plastic bags. Just about any material that is made up of long flexible strands or that can be cut into strands can be used to make rope. However, only twines of proven strength should be used to make rope that will be expected to carry a load or lash a structure.

TYPE OF ROPE:

The type of rope that is explained in this book is three strand laid rope. This type of rope is made by twisting three strands of fiber in one direction and then laying the three strands together by allowing the strands to twist together in the opposite direction.

This twisting and laying can be done by hand but this takes a long time. To speed up the operation a machine is needed.

SIMPLE ROPE MACHINE:

A rope machine consists of two devices; one that twists the three strands, the twisting end; and one that is used to lay the twisted strands together, the laying end.

The following diagrams show a simple rope machine that can be made from scrap lumber and coat hanger wire.

MATERIALS:

2 ----1" * 4" * 30" wood strips ---- [frames]
1 ----1" * 4" * 14" wood strip ----- [paddle]
4 ----9" number 9 steel wire (coat hanger, light rod, etc.) --------------- [cranks]
2 ----6ft. ropes ----------------------- [anchor ropes]

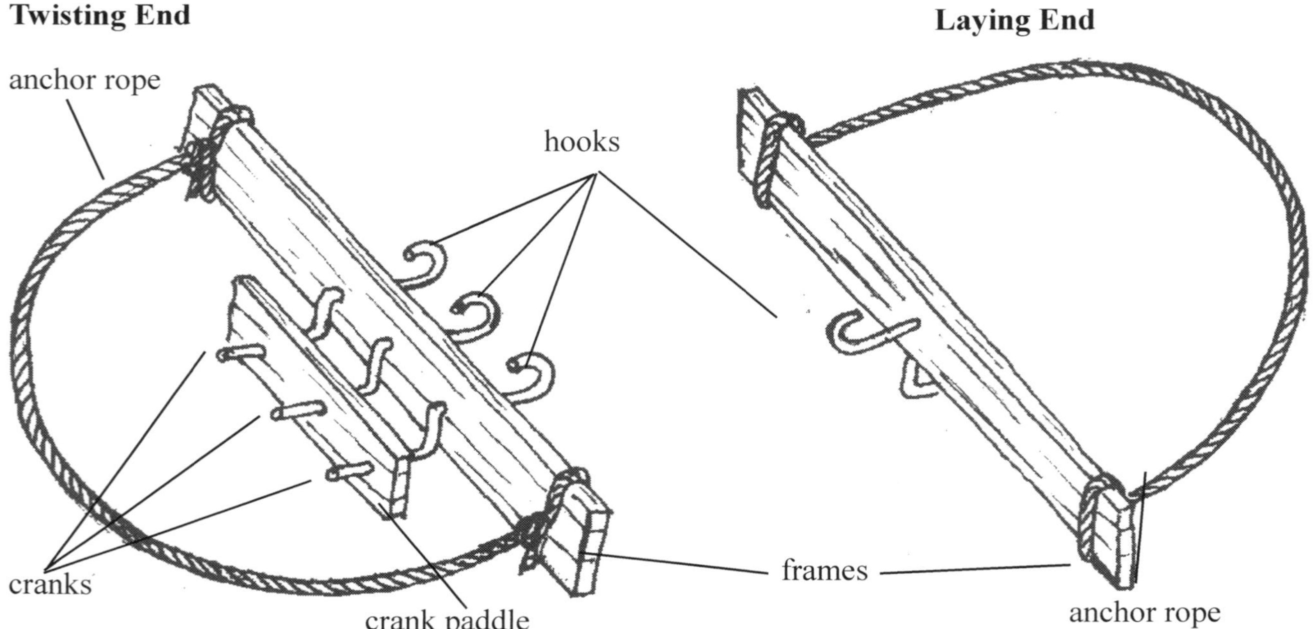

STEP 1: Make 4 cranks.

The cranks are made by bending the 9" long pieces of wire as shown.

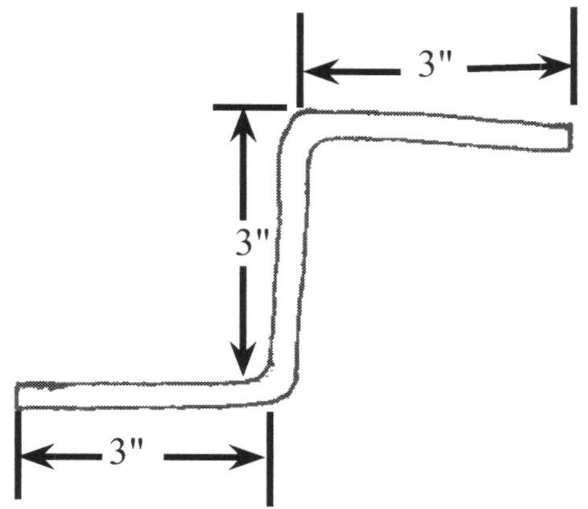

STEP 2: Locate and drill holes.

2A] Mark centers of frame and paddle pieces.

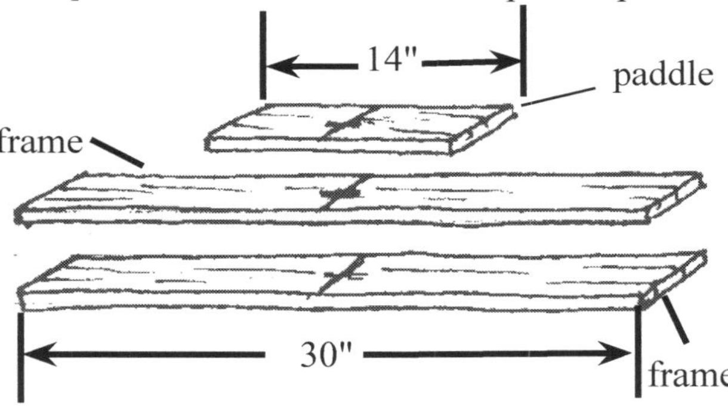

2B] Mark location of holes on the paddle.

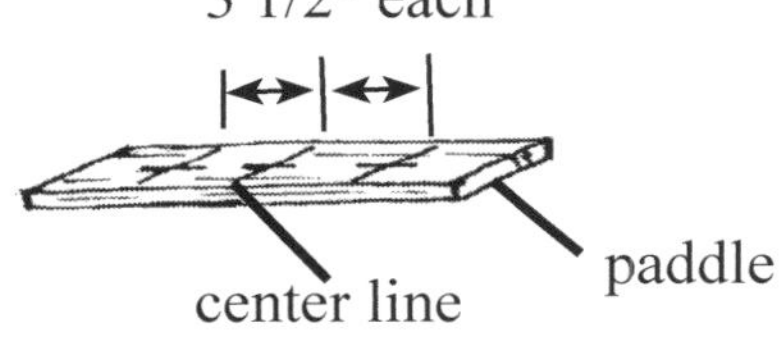

2C] Drill holes.

Place the paddle on top of one of the frame pieces, line up the centers, then drill holes through the paddle and the frame at the same time.

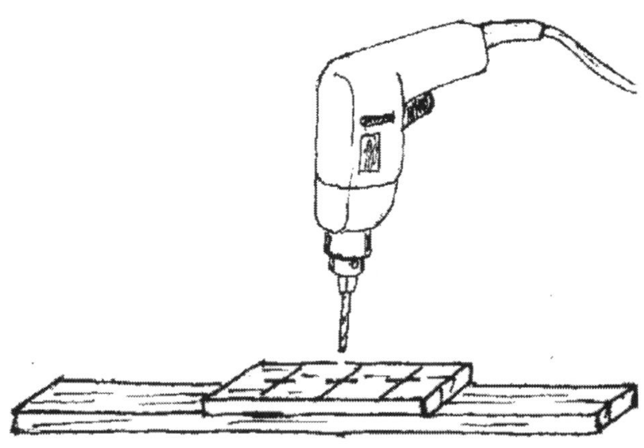

[NOTE] Drill one hole in the center of the second frame.

[NOTE] Holes should be just large enough for the wire to fit through.

STEP 3: Assemble twisting end.

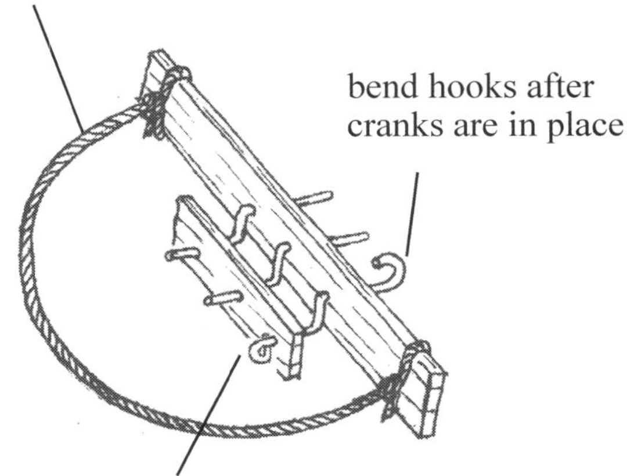

STEP 4: Assemble laying end.

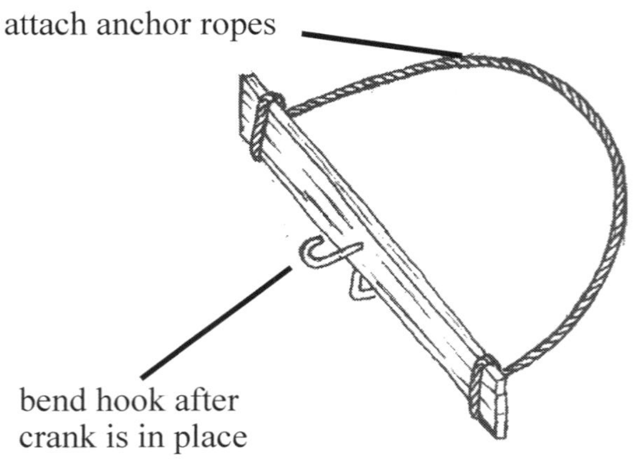

SETTING UP:

After the two ends of the rope machine are positioned, tie the end of the twine to the laying end hook. Then hook the twine over one of the hooks on the twisting end, then back to the laying end hook. Continue back and forth until each of the three hooks on the twisting end have two lengths of twine on it. Be careful to keep the tension equal on all lengths of twine.

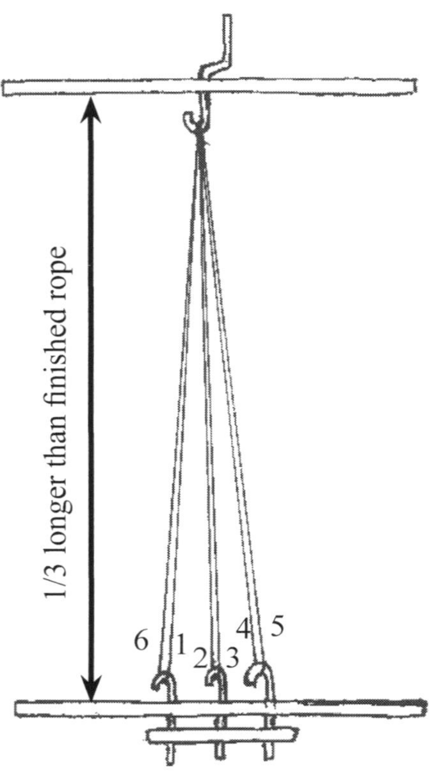

[NOTE] The size of the finished rope depends on the size and number of strands of twine used to make the rope.

[NOTE] If the number of strands is increased by 2 it is unnecessary to cut and tie the twine at both ends.

Twisting the Strands:

After the machine is set up, turn the cranks on the twisting end so that the cranks are turning clockwise as you are looking at the crank handles. It is a good idea to mark this direction on the frame of the machine.

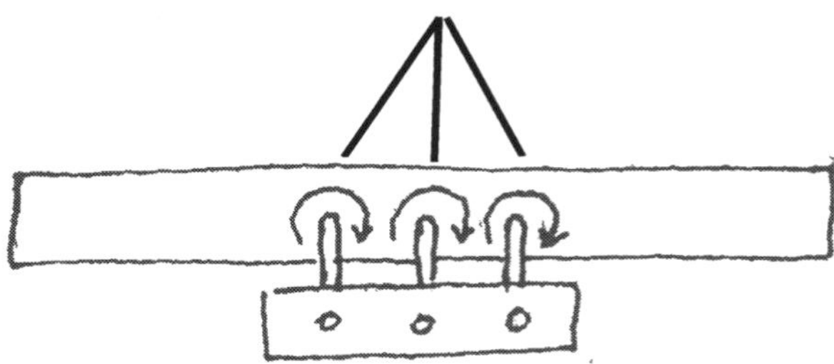

Twist the strands until they become firm and resist further twisting. If the strands are not twisted tight enough the rope will be loose. On the other hand if you twist the strands too tight the strands will kink. Kinked or loose strands will weaken the rope. Experience will teach you when the amount of twist is just right.

[NOTE] During the twisting, the laying end must not be turned.

[NOTE] While twisting and laying, a modest amount of tension must be kept on the rope.

Laying the Strands:

To lay the rope, a rope-wrench will be needed. A rope-wrench can be made from a crotched stick.

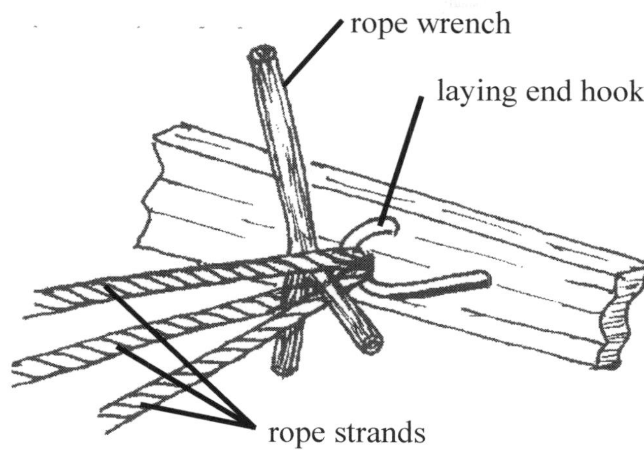

The actual laying of the rope is done by turning the laying end crank in a counterclockwise direction and moving the rope-wrench toward the twisting end.

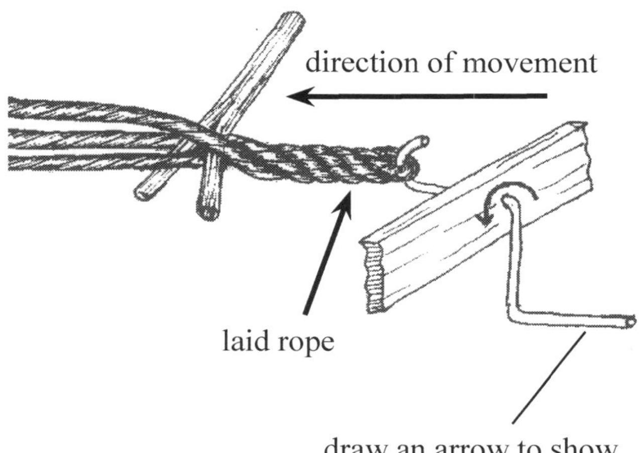

[NOTE] While laying the rope, the twisting end must be turned one turn for each turn of the laying end. This is necessary because as each turn of the lay of the rope is made the strands are untwisted one turn.

[NOTE] If you can push the rope-wrench back toward the laying end you are moving too fast or the strands have loosened and the rope will be loose.

Removing Rope From Machine:

When the rope has been laid, unhook it from the machine and tie an Overhand or Crown Knot in the end of the rope to keep the rope from unlaying.

To set the fiber and even out the twist, the rope should be beaten on the ground, rolled under foot, or stretched after it has been removed from the machine.

[WARNING] Keep long hair and loose clothing away from the rotating strands.

[NOTE] If strands wind together before laying, they must be separated.

[NOTE] If natural fiber twine is soaked in soapy water a tighter rope can be made. The soap also makes the rope last longer.

[NOTE] Wait several days before attempting to splice newly made rope. This allows time for the rope fibers to set into their new shape. When the rope fibers have had a chance to set, the rope is less likely to unlay and the strands of the rope are less likely to untwist while you are working the splice.

[NOTES]

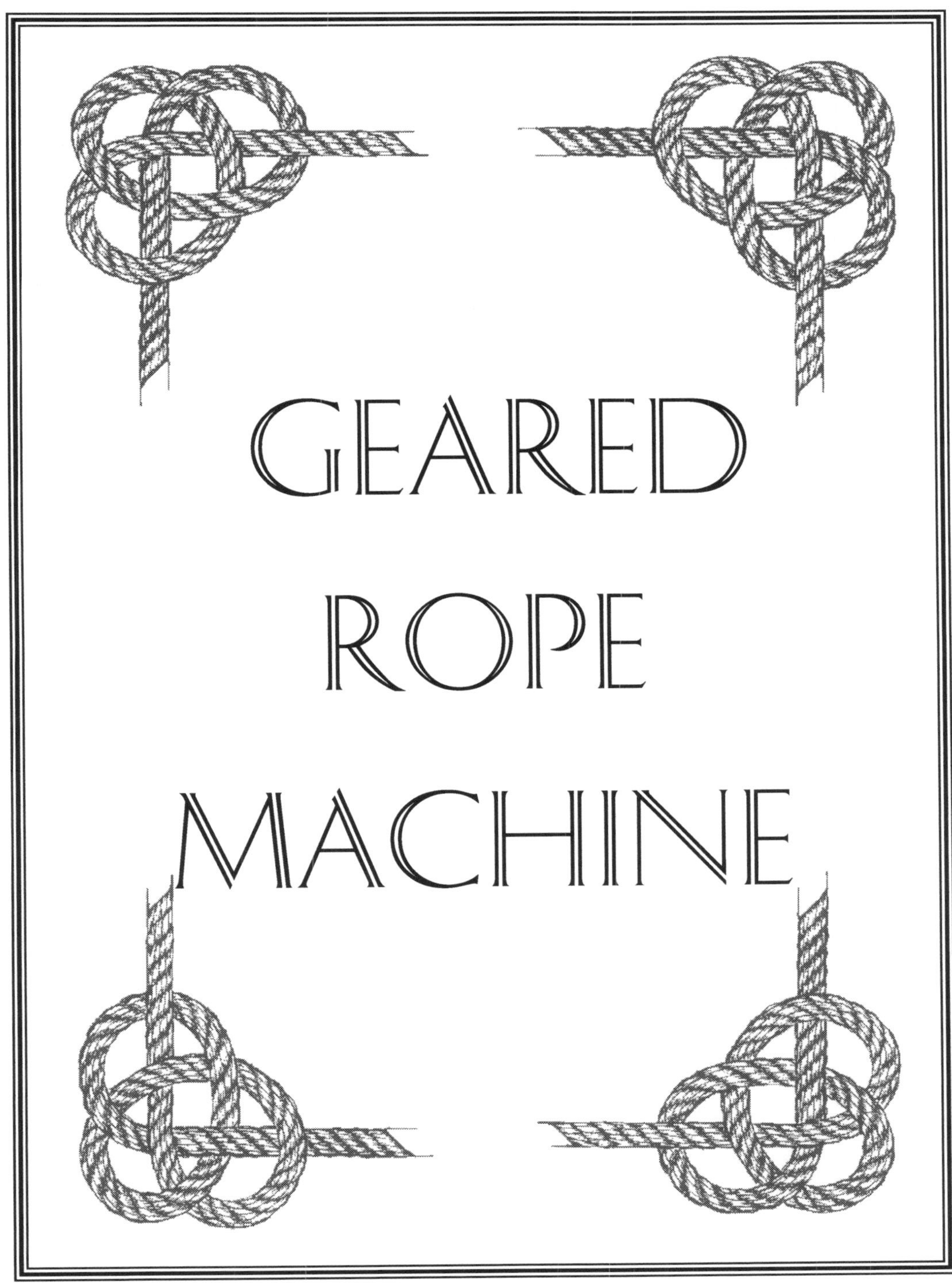
GEARED
ROPE
MACHINE

MATERIALS:

1---- 24" * 24" * 3/4" Plywood

4 ---- 6ft. (2 *4)

32 --- 10D Nails

5 ---- 1" Flat Washers

10 --- 3/8" Flat Washers

1---- 7/16" Flat Washers

4 ---- 3/8" * 6" Eye Bolts

2 ---- 3/8" * 5" Carriage Bolts

1 ---- 3/8" * 6" Machine Bolt

7 ---- 3/8" Nuts

20 --- 1/2" # 10 Wood Screws

3 ---- 1/2" * 8" Pipe Nipples

1 ---- 1/2" * 3" Pipe

5 ---- 1/2" Pipe Flange

1 ---- 24" * 24" Poster Board

FRAME ASSEMBLY:

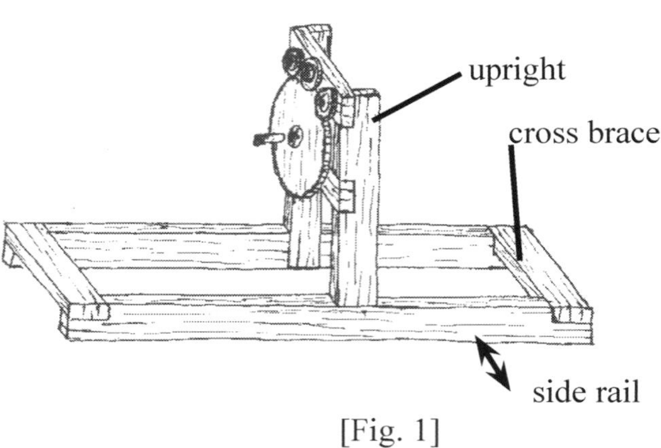

[Fig. 1]

Side Rail:

Make 4 side rails. Two must have the center notch on the right side and two must have the center notch on the left side.

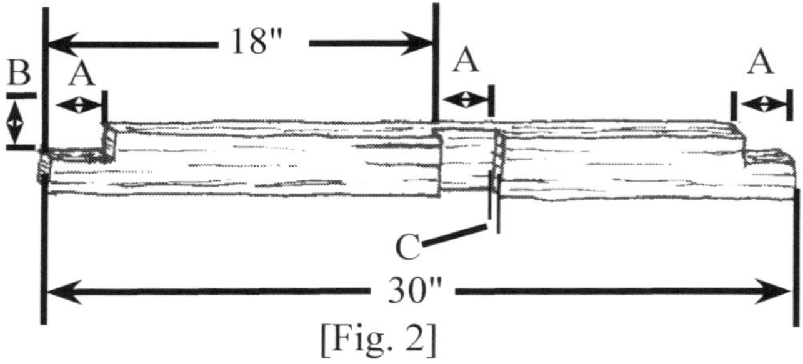

[Fig. 2]

SIZES
- A = width of (2 * 4)
- B = thickness of (2 * 4)
- C = 1/2 thickness of (2 * 4)

[**NOTE**] The size of a (2 * 4) can vary with its source. Rough cut lumber can be a full 2 inches by 4 inches but planed lumber can be as small as 1 1/2 inches by 3 1/2 inches.

Uprights:

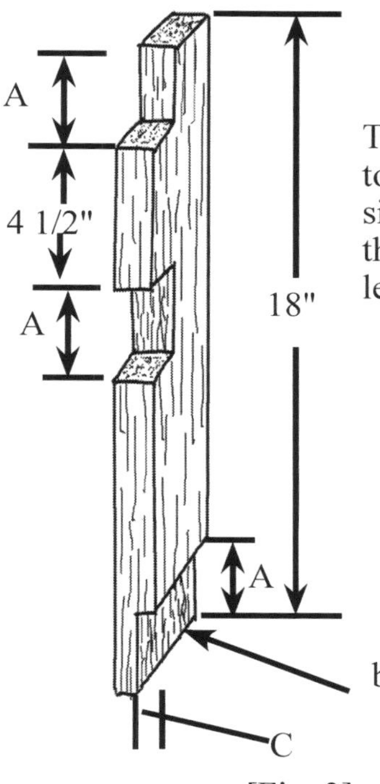

[Fig. 3]

Make 4 uprights. Two must have the bottom notch on the right side and two must have the bottom notch on the left side.

Cross Braces:

Make 8 cross braces. Each brace is made from a 16" length of (2 * 4).

Assemble Frames:

[NOTE] — Frames may be bolted together using 1/4" carriage bolts.

Wood screws or wallboard screws may be used.

TWISTING END:

Location of Gears:

Locate and drill holes for gear axles in one of the frames. See diagram (Fig. 4).

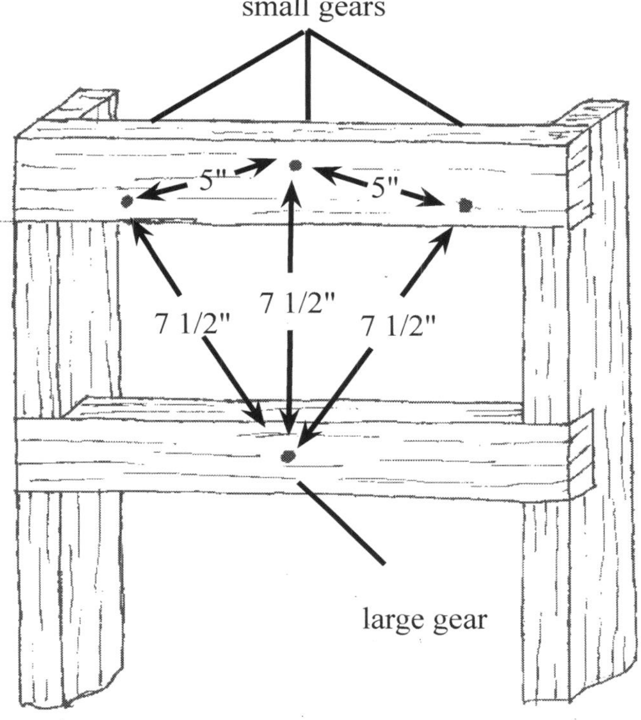

Drill a 7/8" hole at each gear location.

[Fig. 4]

Small Gears:

1. Trace (Fig. 6) to make a pattern for the small gear.
2. Trace pattern 3 times on the plywood.
3. Cut out gears.
4. Drill a 7/8" hole in the center of each gear.
5. Assemble gears and axles as shown in diagram (Fig. 5).

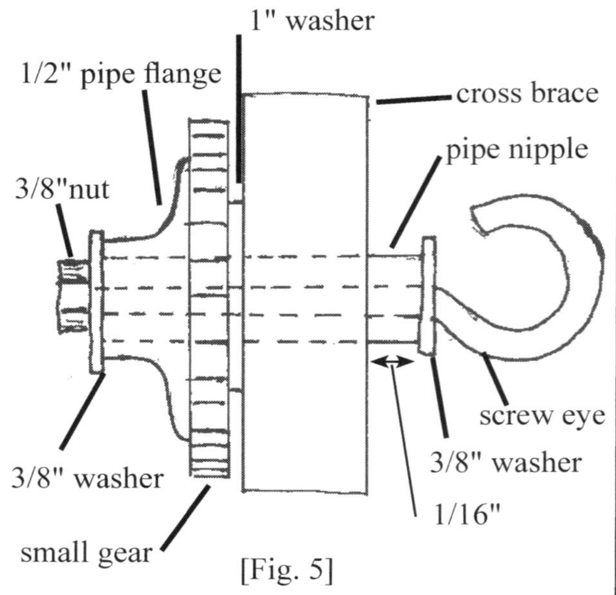

[Fig. 5]

[NOTE]

Each pipe nipple is cut to make two gear axles.

Cut off the end of the pipe nipple so that it sticks out 1/16" beyond the frame.

Attach the pipe flange to the gear with 4 -- 1/2" wood screws.

SMALL GEAR PATTERN:

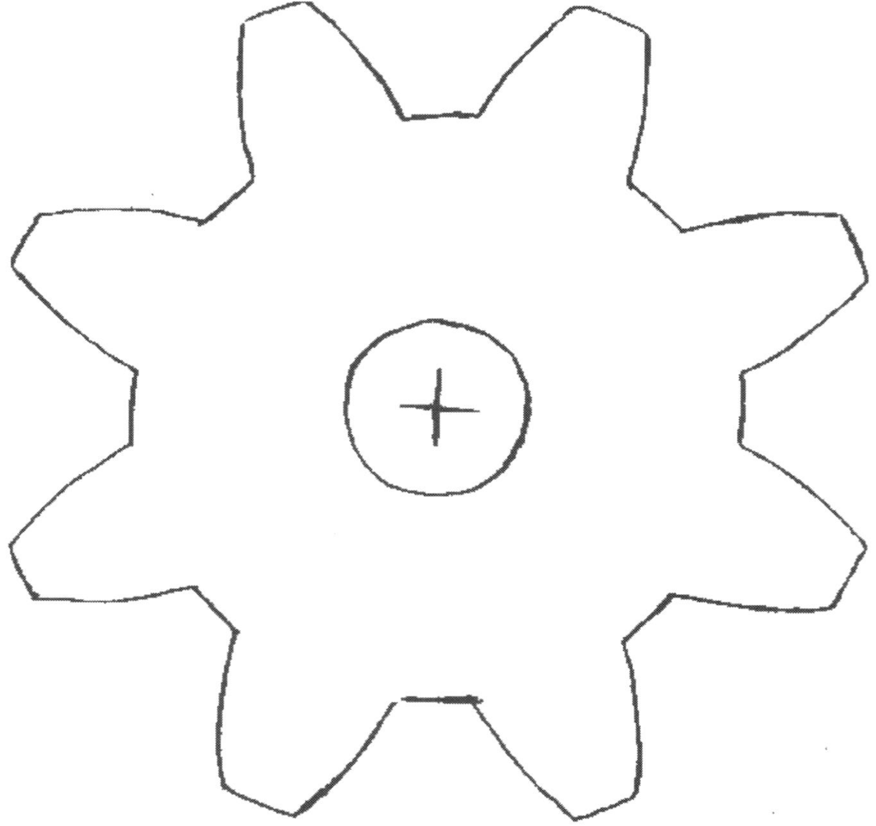

[Fig. 6]

LARGE GEAR PATTERN:

LAYING CRANK CAM:

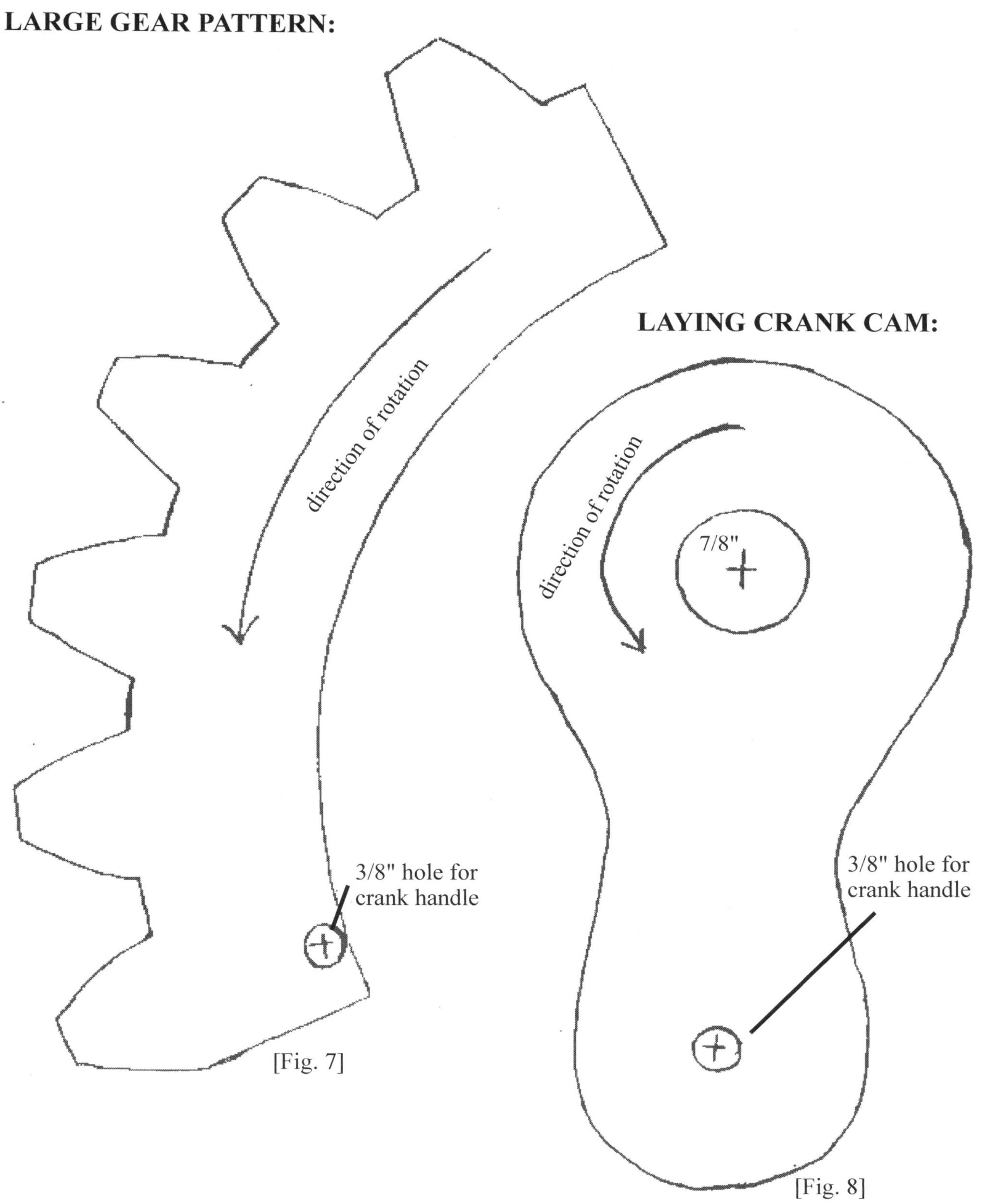

[Fig. 7]

[Fig. 8]

Large Gear:

1. Trace and cut out (Fig. 7).

2. Draw an 8" diameter circle on the poster-board.

3. Use a carpenter's square to divide the circle into fourths (Fig. 9).

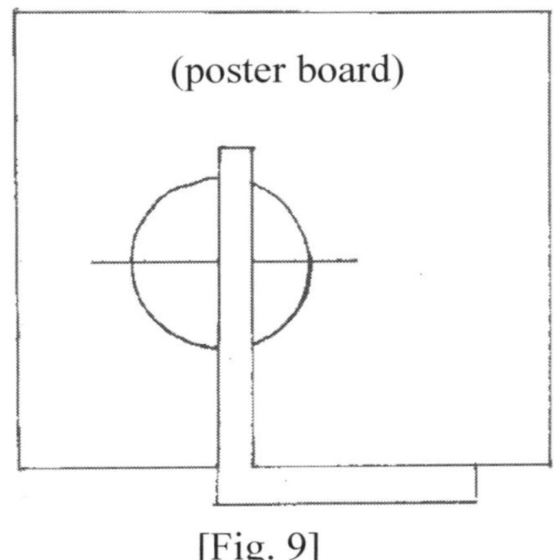

[Fig. 9]

4. Position large gear pattern (Fig. 7) as shown in (Fig. 10), then trace.

5. Repeat step 4 for each of the remaining quarters.

6. Cut out gear pattern.

7. Trace pattern on plywood and cut out gear.

8. Drill a 7/8" hole in center of gear.

9. Drill 3/8" hole for crank handle as shown on (Fig. 7).

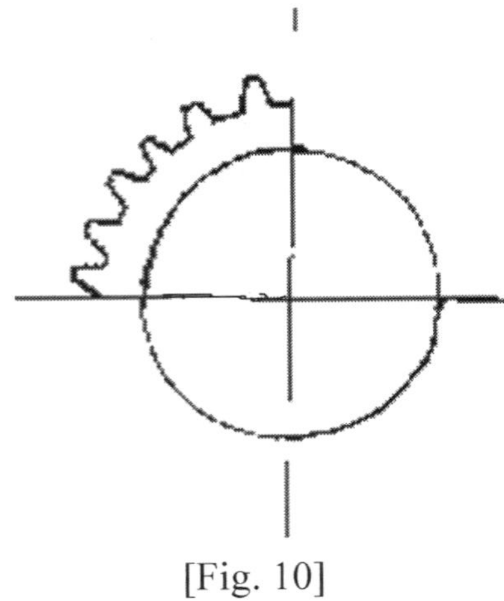

[Fig. 10]

10. Assemble crank handle as shown in diagram (Fig. 11).

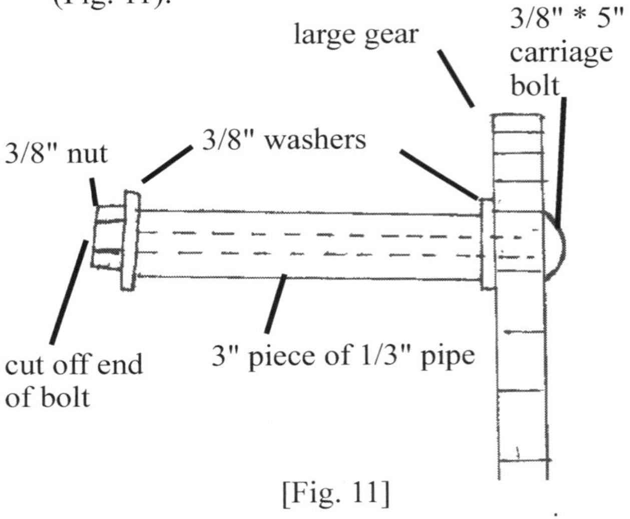

[Fig. 11]

11. Assemble axle for large gear in the same way as axles for small gears, see (Fig. 5). Use a 3/8" * 6" machine bolt and a 7/16" flat washer instead of an eye bolt.

12. Mark direction of rotation of large gear as shown in (Fig. 7).

13. Paint or varnish all wooden parts.

14. Grease or oil axles and gears.

[NOTE] Gears may need to be sanded to remove high spots that cause binding.

LAYING END:

1. Locate and drill 7/8" hole for crank axle at the center of the top brace of the second frame. See (Fig. 12).

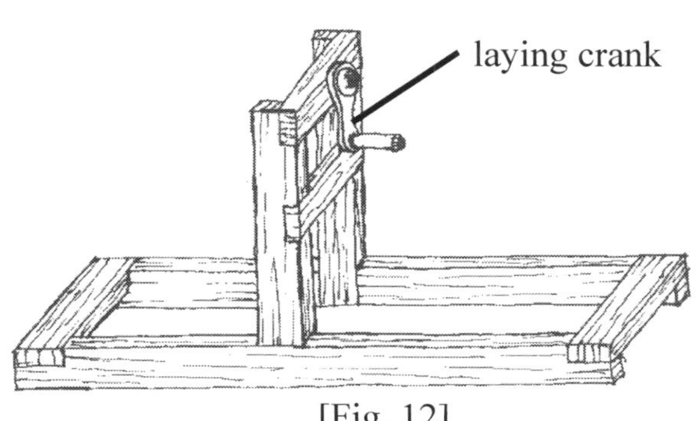

[Fig. 12]

2. Trace and cut out (Fig. 8) to make pattern for cam.

3. Trace cam pattern on plywood and cut out.

4. Drill holes in cam as shown in (Fig. 8).

5. Assemble laying crank as shown in diagram (Fig. 13).

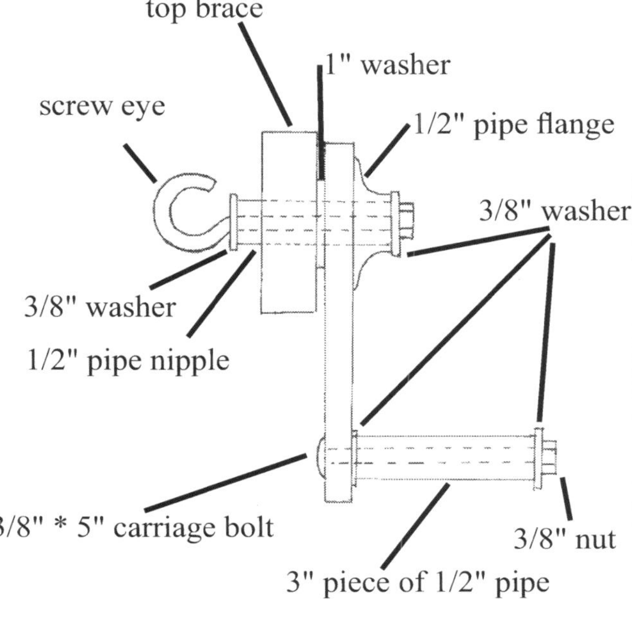

[Fig. 13]

[NOTES]

[NOTES]

TOOLS AND MORE

ROPE WRENCH:

A rope wrench is a simple tool that can be used to tighten the ropes of a lashing. Use a crotched stick that is about 18 inches long and $1^1/_2$ inches in diameter; the crotch should be about 6 inches from the end.

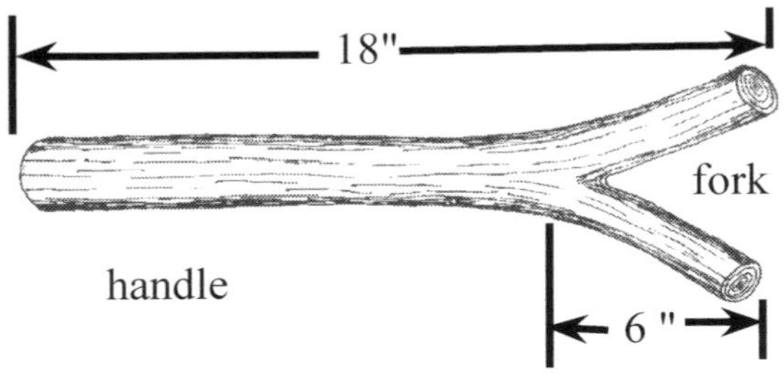

Using A Rope Wrench:

STEP 1: Use the rope wrench by placing it over the pole next to the rope that is to be tightened.

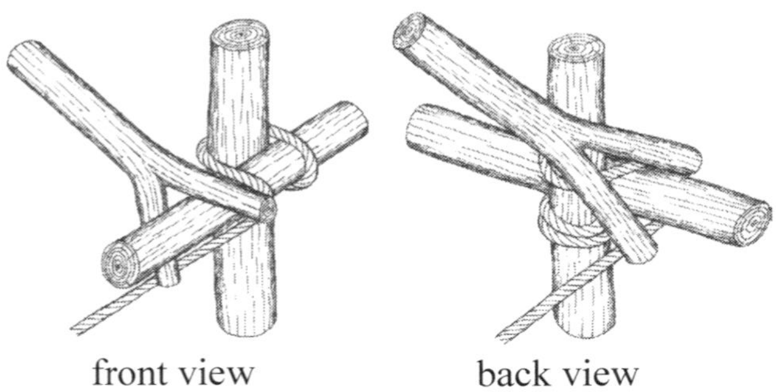
front view back view

STEP 2: Wrap the rope around the fork of the wrench.

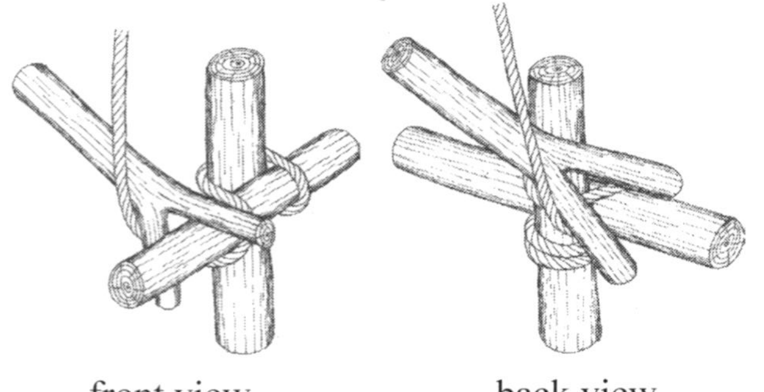
front view back view

STEP 3: Make one or two wraps around the handle of the wrench.

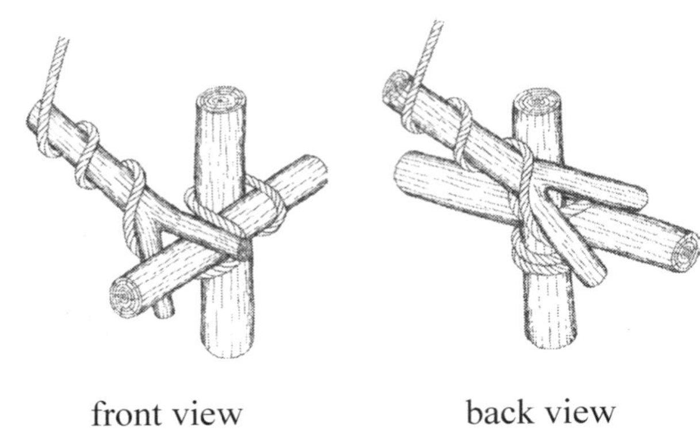
front view back view

STEP 4: Grasp the handle so that you are holding the rope firmly to the handle; then rotate the wrench around the pole.

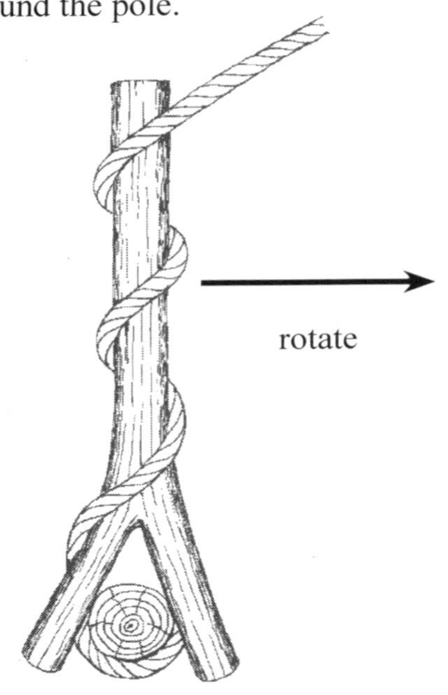

[NOTE] Tighten each turn of a lashing as it is made. The friction between the rope and the pole is too great to tighten more than one turn at a time.

Maintain the tightness of the rope by keeping a small amount of tension on it or by pressing the rope firmly against one of the poles while taking the next turn around the poles.

Be careful that the rope is not tightened so tight that the fibers of the rope begin to break.

FIDS:

A fid is a tool that is used to open the lay of a rope when working a splice or to loosen knots.

MAKING A WOODEN FID:

Split out an 8 inch by 3/4 inch piece of close grained, smooth, hardwood. Carve and smooth the piece to the shape shown in the diagram.

MAKING METAL FIDS:

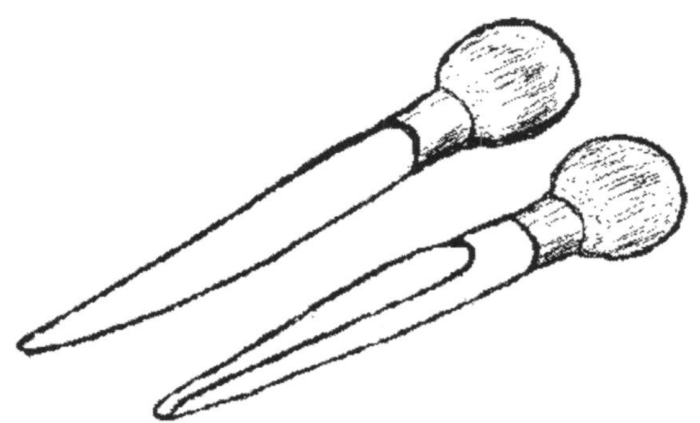

Materials:

1 --- 8 inch * 1/2 inch copper tubing or steel electrical conduit.
2 --- 1 inch diameter * 3 inch long piece of smooth grained hardwood.
2 --- 4D finishing nails.

Construction:

Cut the tubing diagonally into two pieces as shown in the diagram. (Use a hacksaw)

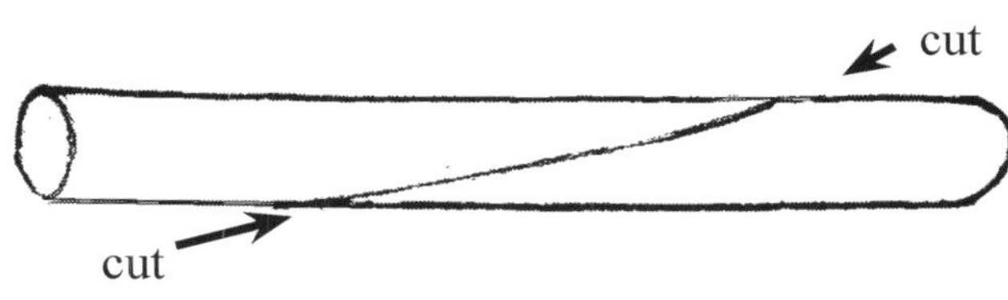

Making a Closed Fid:

STEP 1: Use a triangular file to enlarge the diagonal opening in one of the halves of the tubing. File the opening to the shape indicated by the dotted lines in the diagram.

STEP 2: Close the diagonal opening. Using light taps with a hammer, gently roll the two edges toward each other to form the tubing into a cone. When the two edges of the opening meet, the seam in the tubing should be straight.

STEP 3: Solder the edges of the opening together.

3A] Clean the edges of the opening with steel wool.

3B] Spread soldering paste along the cleaned edges.

3C] Solder the seam. Use a propane torch to apply heat to the side of the fid that is opposite the seam. (Heating the tube from the opposite side will ensure that the metal is heated all the way through so that the solder will flow into the seam and not just spread out on the surface.) As you heat the tubing, test the seam for the proper temperature by touching the solder to the seam. When the solder starts to melt and flow into the seam, move the solder along the seam until the entire seam is filled with solder.

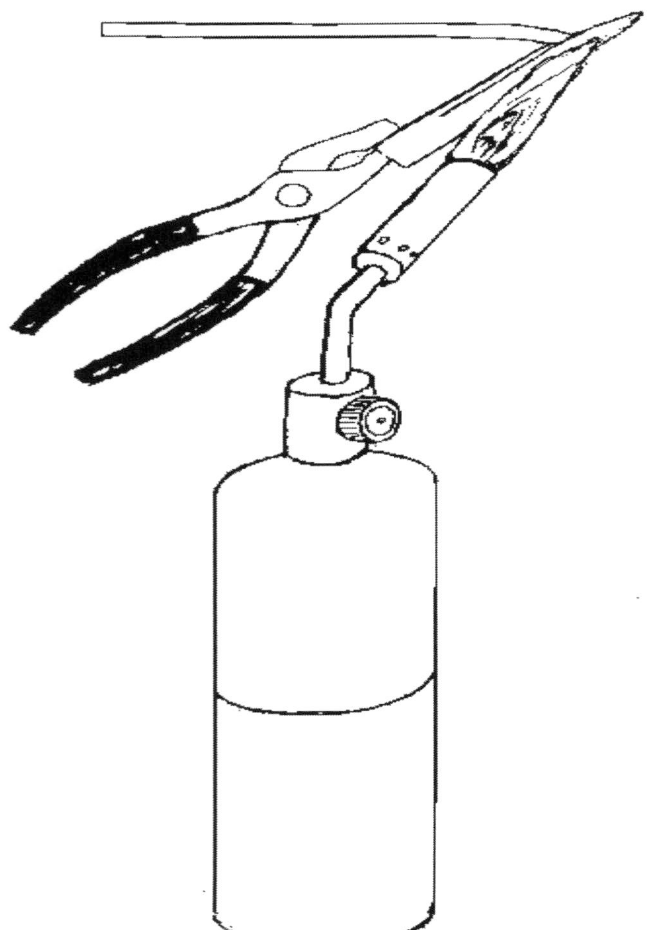

STEP 4: Clean up the seam with steel-wool and a file. Make sure that there are no sharp edges to catch or cut the rope fibers when the fid is being used.

Making an Open Fid:

STEP 1: Enlarge the diagonal opening of the other piece of tubing by setting the tubing on end and forcing a rod into the opening. When the rod is forced into the opening, the cross section of the tubing should become "U" shaped.

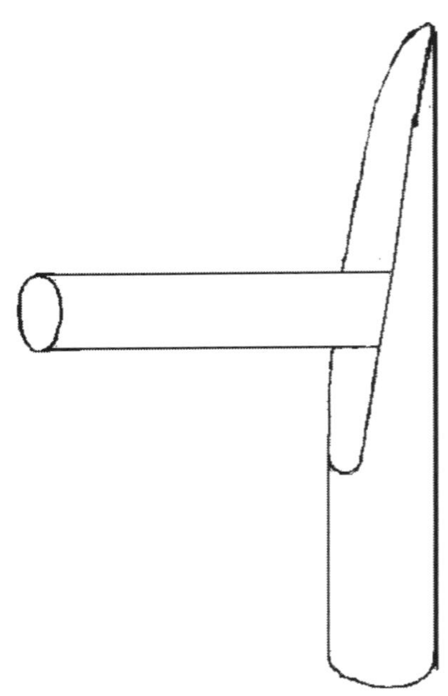

STEP 2: With a round file, enlarge the diagonal opening to the shape shown by the dotted line.

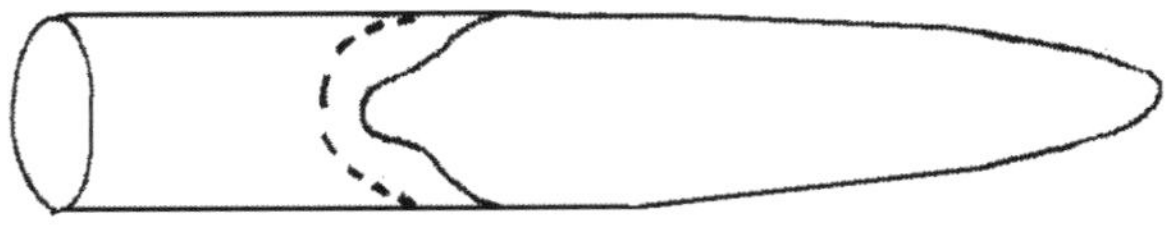

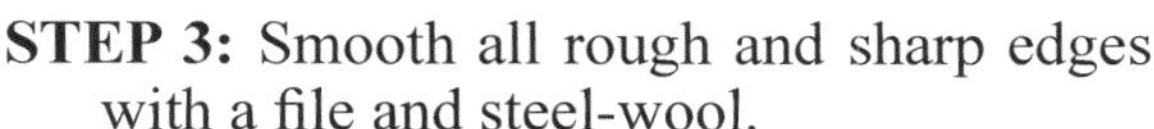

STEP 3: Smooth all rough and sharp edges with a file and steel-wool.

STEP 4: Gently tap the edges of the opening toward each other so that a cross section anywhere along its entire length will be "U" shaped.

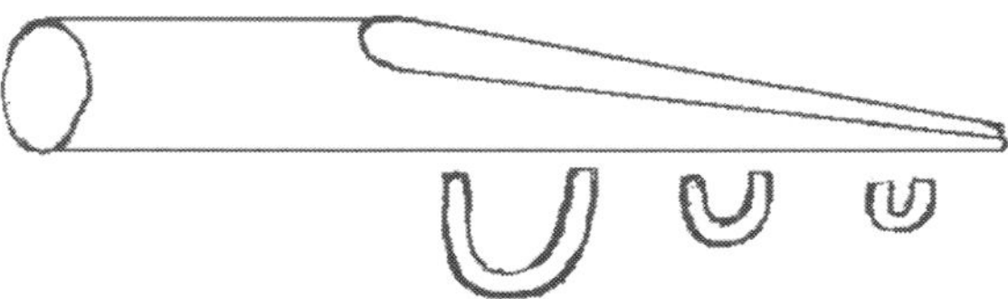

Making Handles For Fids:

STEP 1: Carve one end of a 1 inch diameter * 3 inch long piece of wood so that it will fit snugly into the end of the fid.

STEP 2: Attach handle to fid.

2A] Drill a small hole into the side of the fid about 1/2 inch from the end.

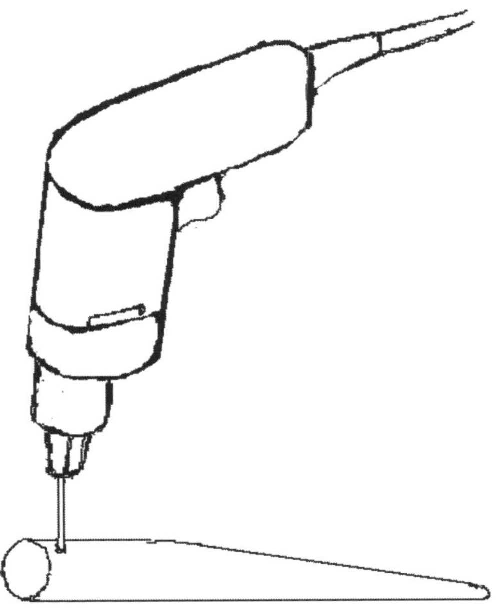

2B] Insert the handle into the end of the fid. Then drive a finishing nail through the hole into the wood of the handle.

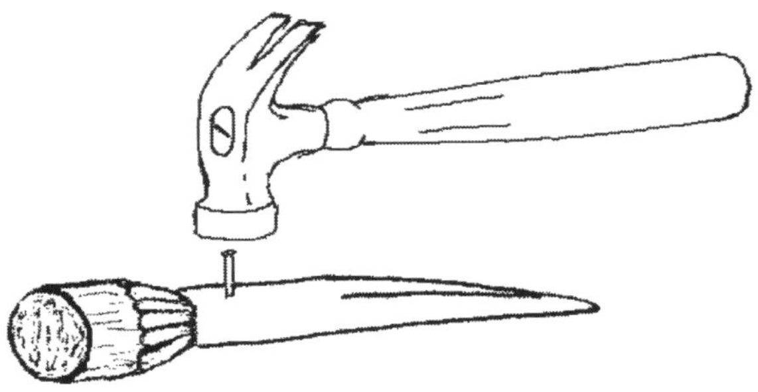

2C] Cut the nail off close to the side of the fid. Then file the nail down so that it is smooth and even with the surface.

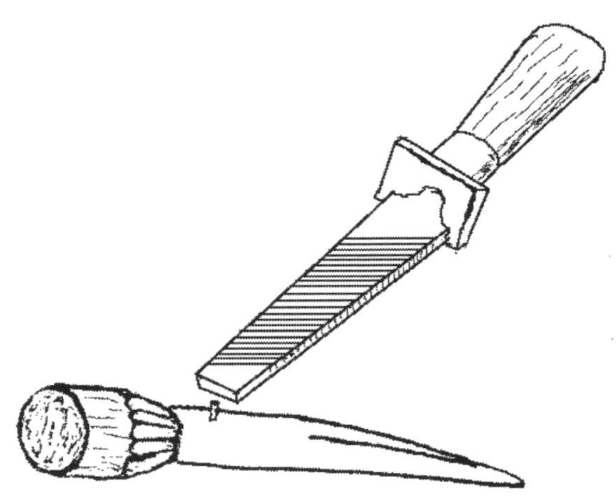

STEP 3: Finish the handle. Here is a chance to be creative. You can carve a simple rounded handle or let your imagination take over.

MAULS:

A maul is a wooden club or hammer that is used for driving stakes or wedges and, for safety reasons, should be used instead of an ax.

Using an ax instead of a maul exposes the user to the danger of being cut by the ax's sharp edge. Even if the edge of the ax is covered by a sheath, a glancing blow can cause the sheath to be ripped off or cut through.

The pole of an ax serves as a counterweight to the blade. This counterweight adds to the balance of the ax head and helps to control and increase the force of momentum delivered to the bit. The ax head is shaped in such a way that the momentum of the ax head is delivered through the thin walls of the eye. However, when an ax is being used as a hammer, this same shape causes the eye of the ax head to spread and the handle to loosen.

The flat surface and angular edges of an ax pole make it difficult to strike a stake squarely. This difficulty in striking a square blow results in most blows delivering some of their force sideways, causing the end of the wooden stake to flare and split very quickly. In addition, when the pole of an ax contacts a stake, the metal surface of the pole lacks the ability to absorb any of the force of the impact and this contributes to the destruction of the stake. A wooden maul, on the other hand, absorbs some of the impact of the initial contact and a maul has no angular edges. Therefore, more of the force of the maul is used to do useful work and less of the force is used up in deforming or splitting the stake.

MAKING A CLUB MAUL:

MATERIALS:

A club maul, for driving tent pegs and other light work, can be made from a piece of hardwood that is about 3 inches in diameter and 18 to 24 inches long.

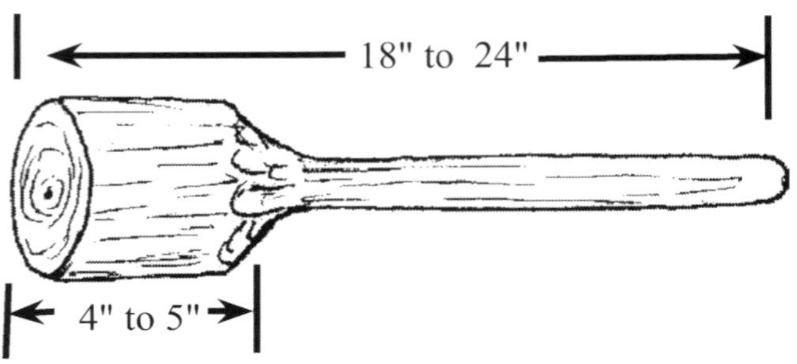

STEP 1: Use an ax to rough out the maul. Form a handle by cutting away one end of the piece of wood so that it is about 1 1/4 inches in diameter. Leave 4 to 5 inches of the other end at its original diameter to form the head of the maul.

STEP 2: Smooth the handle with a knife.

MAKING A HAMMER MAUL:

MATERIALS:

To make the head of a hammer maul you will need a 4 inch diameter, 10 inch long piece of hard, dense, unchecked, well seasoned, hardwood such as elm, black gum or hophornbeam.

For the handle you will need a piece of well seasoned ash, hickory, or similar straight grained wood; 1 1/2 inch diameter and 3 to 4 feet long.

MAKING A MAUL:

STEP 1: Square the ends of the head with a saw.

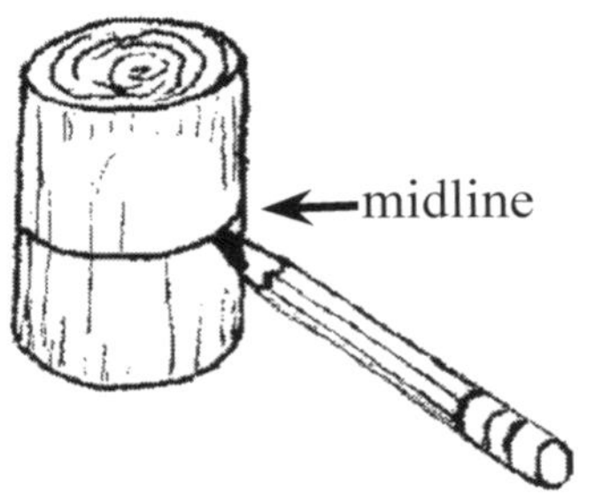

STEP 2: Find and mark the midline between the two ends.

STEP 3: Locate the center of the handle hole on each side of the maul head.

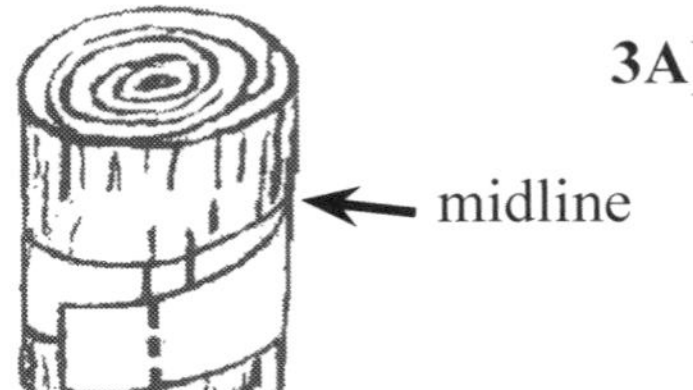

3A] Wrap a strip of paper around the maul head. Cut the strip of paper off so that the two ends just meet.

3B] Locate handle hole by folding the strip of paper in half to mark its mid point, then unfold it and wrap it around the maul head again. Mark the midline at the fold and at the ends of the strip of paper.

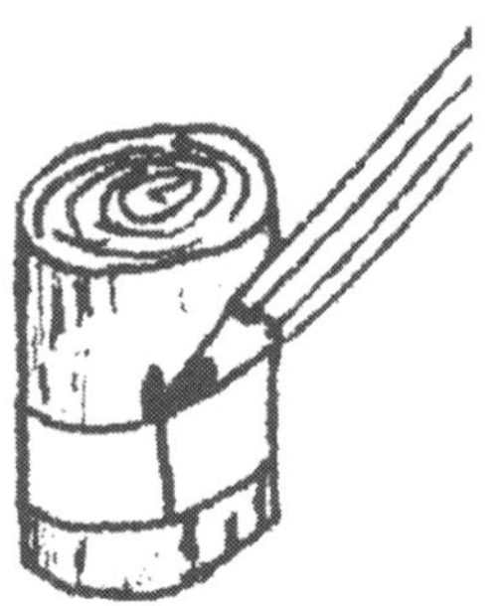

STEP 4: Drill the handle hole in the head. Use a 1 1/4 inch drill bit to drill a hole halfway through the head from one side, then finish drilling the hole from the other side of the maul head.

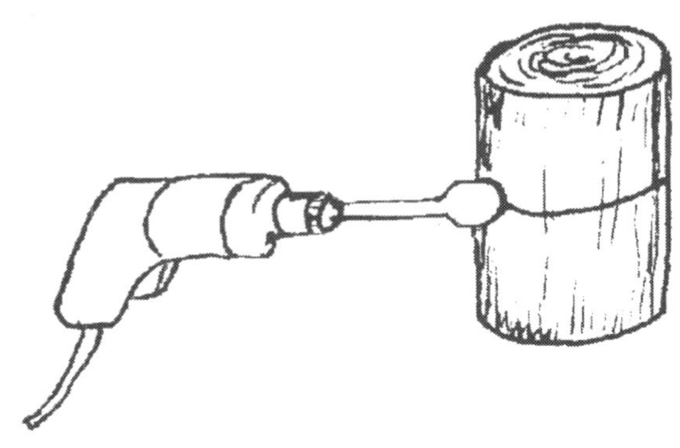

[NOTE] If the holes do not line up in the middle, use a chisel or wood rasp to cut away some of the excess wood.

STEP 5: Make maul handle.

5A] Cut a saw kerf in the one end of the handle. The depth of the kerf should be equal to 1/2 the diameter of the maul head.

5B] Use a knife to shave the end of the handle down until it can be easily driven through the head with light blows of a light wooden block.

STEP 6: Attach the maul head to the handle.

6A] Make a hardwood wedge that is 1 1/4 inches wide, 3 inches long, and 1/4 inch thick at its large end.

6B] Drive the handle into the maul head, making sure that the saw kerf is lined up across the maul head.

6C] Then drive the wedge in place.

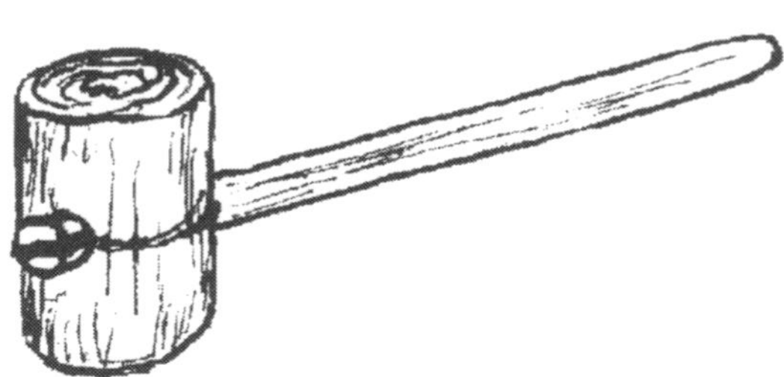

STEP 7: Reinforce the maul head to keep it from splitting by wrapping several turns of rope or wire around each end of the maul head. These turns can be held in place with staples.

Another method of reinforcing the head would be to drive a braided ring or a grommet over each end of the head.

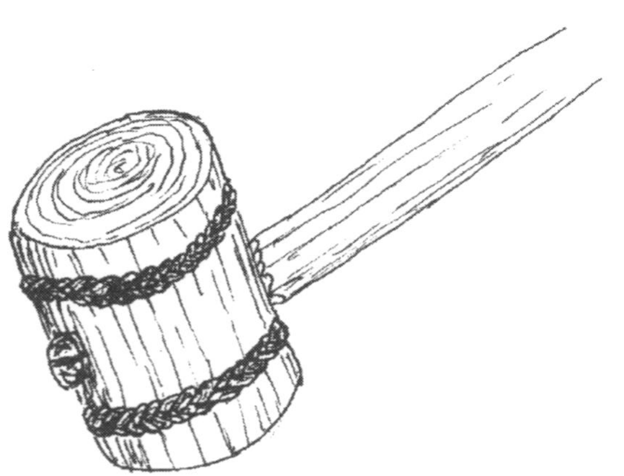

MAUL --- DOVETAIL HANDLE:

MATERIALS:

1 ----- Piece of seasoned hardwood that is 2 1/2 inches to 3 inches in diameter and 5 to 7 inches long for the head.
1 ----- Piece of seasoned hardwood that is 1 1/2 inches to 2 inches in diameter for the handle.

CONSTRUCTION:

STEP 1: With a saw, cut 3 kerfs as shown at the center of the side of the head.

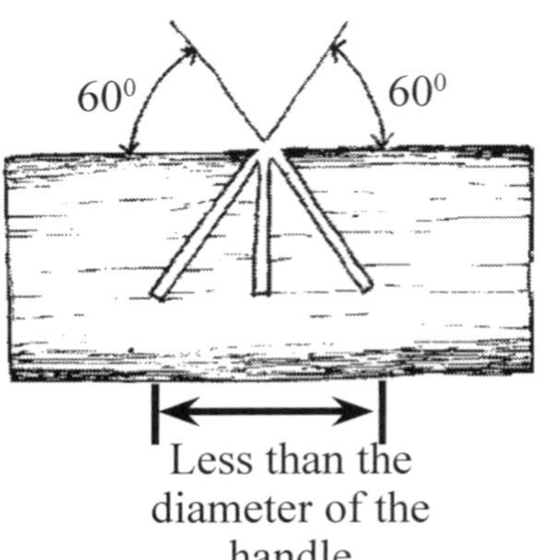

[NOTE] The width of the bottom of the dovetail notch must be less than the diameter of the handle.

STEP 2: Use a knife or chisel to remove the wood to form the dovetail notch.

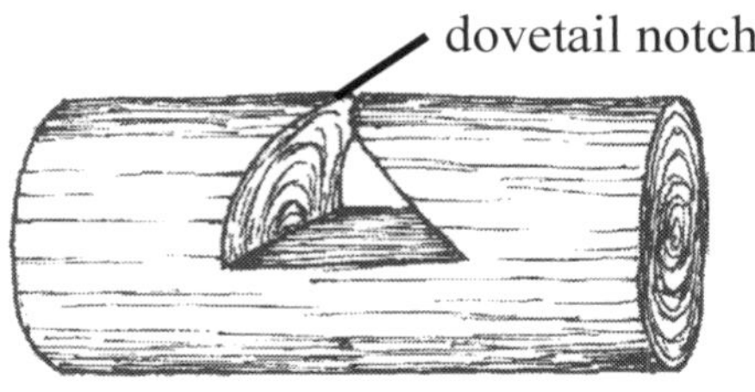

STEP 3: Shape and fit handle to head.

3A] Flatten one side of the end of the handle.

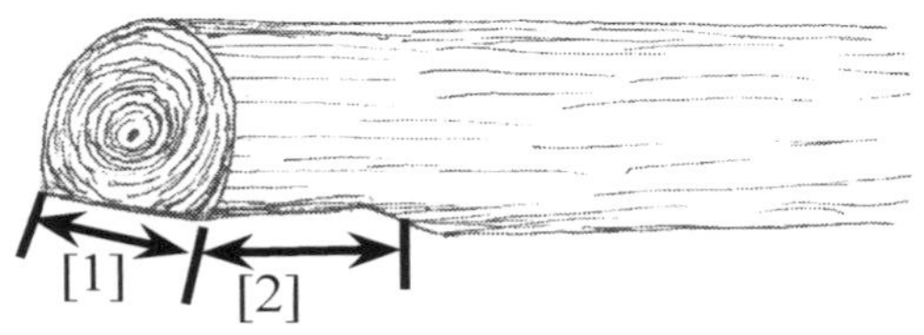

[1] Equal to or greater than the width of the bottom of the dovetail notch.

[2] Equal to the diameter of the head.

3B] Fit the handle to the bottom of the dovetail notch. Gradually remove the surplus wood until the flattened part of the handle is the same width as the width of the dovetail notch.

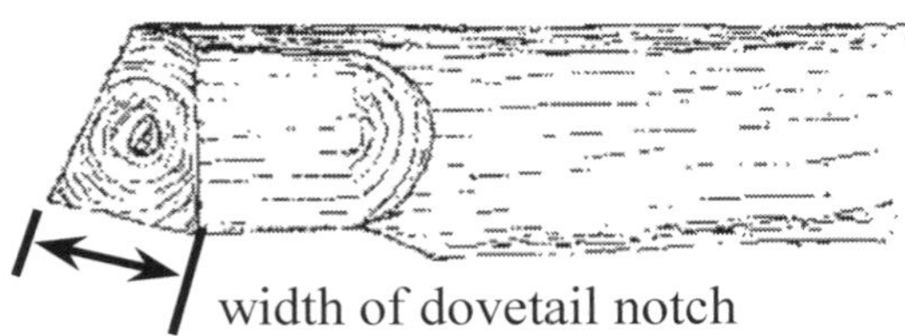

3C] Flatten the remaining two sides of the handle. Gradually remove the surplus wood until the handle fits snugly into the dovetail notch in the head.

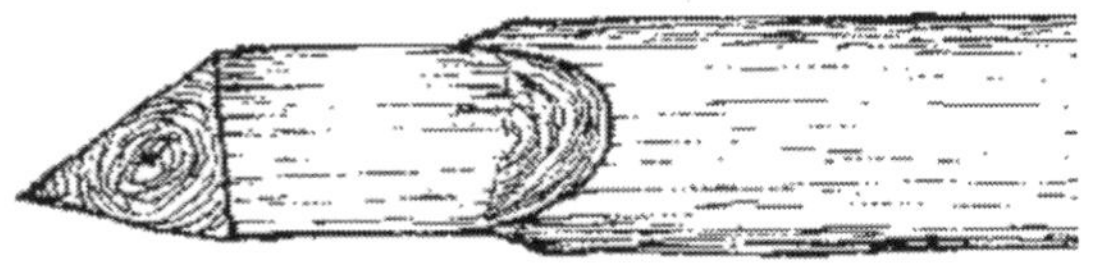

3D] Tap handle firmly into dovetail notch.

Dovetail Maul Used as Rope Wrench:

The Dovetail Maul makes a good rope wrench. Pass the rope over the head of the maul and then take several wraps around the handle. The rope is then tightened by rotating the maul so that the rope wraps part way around the head of the maul. (see ROPE WRENCH page 178 for more details)

CAMP SAW:

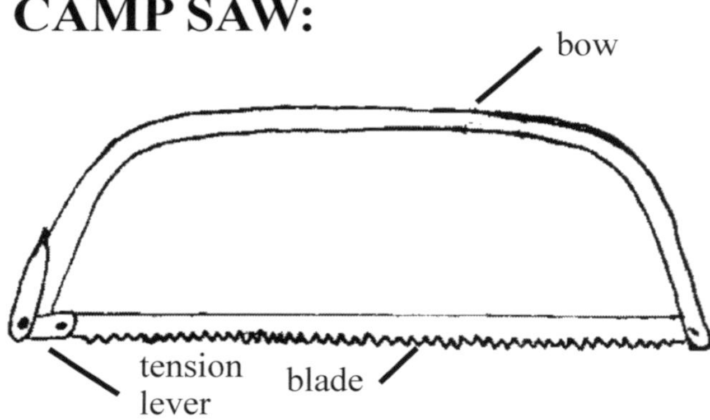

A camp saw is a crosscut saw; that means it is designed to cut across the fibers of the wood. Another design feature is that it will cut on both the push and the pull strokes. There are two types of teeth on the camp saw blade: cutting teeth and rakers. The cutting teeth are designed to cut the wood fiber off on either side of the of the kerf or saw cut. To do this, the cutting teeth are divided into two groups. One group of cutting teeth is set or bent slightly to the side so that they cut off the wood fiber on the right-hand side of the kerfs. The other group of teeth is set to the other side so that they cut the wood fiber on the left-hand side of the kerf. The rakers are designed to chisel off and carry out the wood fibers from the bottom of the kerf after the cutting teeth have cut them loose from the edges of the kerf.

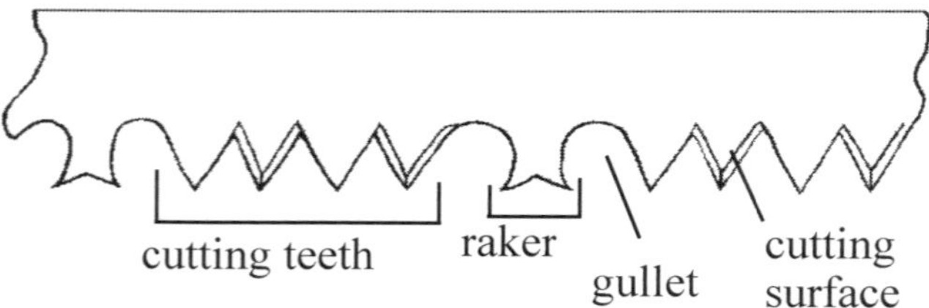

TERMINOLOGY:

blade — A thin metal strip with cutting teeth on one edge and holes in the end for mounting it in the bow.

bow (frame) — The part of the camp saw that supports and applies tension to the blade.

cutting surface — The surface produced on a cutting tooth when it is filed to sharpen it.

cutting teeth — The sharp pointed teeth that cut through the wood fiber when the saw is being used.

gullet — The space between the teeth on a saw blade.

join — To file or grind the points of the saw teeth so that they are all the same length.

kerf — The slot or groove made in the wood as a saw is being used.

rakers — The teeth on a saw blade that chisel loose and carry out the wood fibers cut off by the cutting teeth.

saw set — A tool used to set the teeth of a saw.

set — (1) The bending of the cutting teeth to either side in an alternating pattern to widen the kerf and prevent the blade from binding in the kerf. — (2) To bend the teeth of a saw blade in an alternating pattern so as to widen the kerf.

swage — A tool used to change the shape of a saw tooth by placing the tool on the tooth and then striking the tool with a hammer

tension — The pulling force applied to the ends of a saw blade to keep it stiff and straight.

tension lever — A device on one end of a saw bow that applies tension to the saw blade.

CAMP SAW: CARE AND USE

A dull camp saw is a frustrating, dangerous time waster and its blade should be sharpened or replaced as soon as possible. To prevent a saw from becoming dull follow these guidelines:

1. When not in use, hang the saw in a safe place or lay it on a clean, dry surface. Do not lay the saw on the ground. Soil particles can stick to the blade and then grind the sharp edges off the next time the saw is used.

2. After use and before storage, wipe the blade with a cloth saturated with oil. Moisture and chemicals from the wood attack the metal of the blade and cause rust.

3. When transporting or storing a saw, protect the blade with a guard. This will prevent the blade from being damaged by coming in contact with hard surfaces.

4. When using the saw, be sure the wood that is being cut is held firmly on one end and that the piece being cut off can fall freely

away. If the wood that is being cut can move around, this will cause the saw blade to be twisted back and forth bending and weakening the blade. If the wood that is being cut off cannot fall freely away, the kerfs will be forced closed causing the saw blade to jam and twist in the kerfs. Forcing the kerf closed also has a tendency to remove the set from the blade.

CAMP SAW: SAFETY AND USE

A camp saw is easier and safer to use than an ax if the saw is handled properly and kept in good repair. The following suggestions should help make a camp saw your friend rather than a snarling toothed monster that is ready to tear into your flesh.

1. Always keep the cutting edge of the saw pointed away from yourself and others.

2. Set the saw down in a safe place when you are moving a piece of wood.

3. Make sure that the wood is being held firmly and cannot move when you are using the saw.

4. Be sure that the piece of wood that is being cut off can fall away safely. Do not try to secure both ends of the piece of wood. Securing both end of the piece of wood will cause the saw blade to jam in the kerfs.

5. When transporting or storing a saw, place a guard over the blade.

SHARPENING A CAMP SAW: EVALUATING THE BLADE

Sharpening and setting a saw blade will make it last longer and keep it cutting faster and safer. However, before you start to sharpen a blade look it over and try it out so that you can determine whether to replace the blade or sharpen it and what you must do to the blade to put it in good condition.

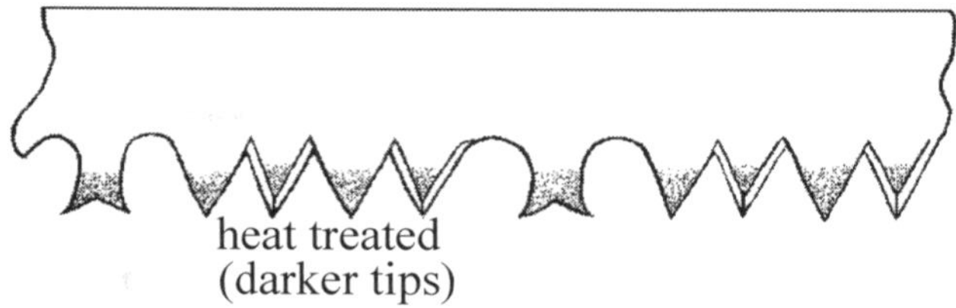

When you look at a new saw blade you will notice that the tips of the teeth are usually darker in color than the rest of the blade. This is the result of heat treating to harden the teeth so that they will remain sharp longer. If the blade has been sharpened several times, this heat-treated surface will have been filed away and the blade should be replaced.

If the saw blade is rusted, clean a part of the blade with steel wool. If the blade is pitted, replace the blade. If the blade is not pitted, finish cleaning it and give it a coat of oil to prevent future rusting.

If the saw cuts quickly at first and then begins to drag and bind in the kerf, the blade will need to be set but may not need to be sharpened.

Examine the saw dust; if the ends of the fibers in the chips appears to have been torn loose rather than cut loose, one of two things may be wrong. The raker teeth may be too long; therefore they are ripping the wood fibers from the bottom of the kerf before the cutting teeth have cut the fiber loose. The other problem may be that the cutting teeth are dull and therefore are tearing the fiber out of the kerf rather than cutting it loose.

If the ends of the wood fiber appear to be cut but the surface of the chip appears to be rough, this may indicate that the raker teeth are dull and are dragging the fiber out of the bottom of the kerfs rather than cutting it loose from the bottom of the kerfs. Another problem may be that the raker teeth are too short and the cutting teeth are not only cutting the fiber loose but are also tearing the fibers from the bottom of the kerfs. If the raker teeth are too short, the easiest thing to do is to replace the blade, but it can be joined and resharpened.

Check the length of the teeth by laying a straightedge on the points of the cutting teeth. If the teeth are of different lengths, the saw blade will need to be joined before it is sharpened.

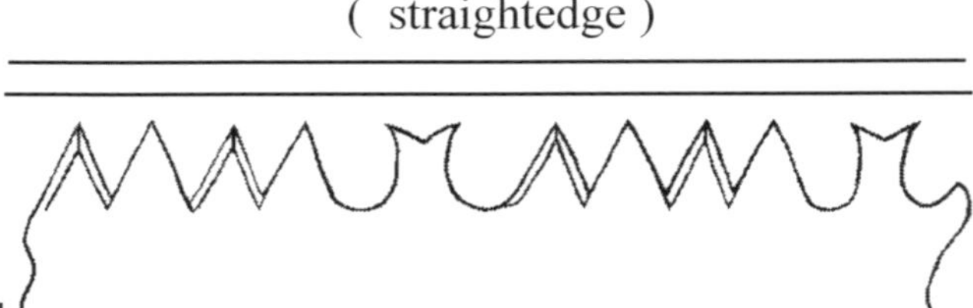

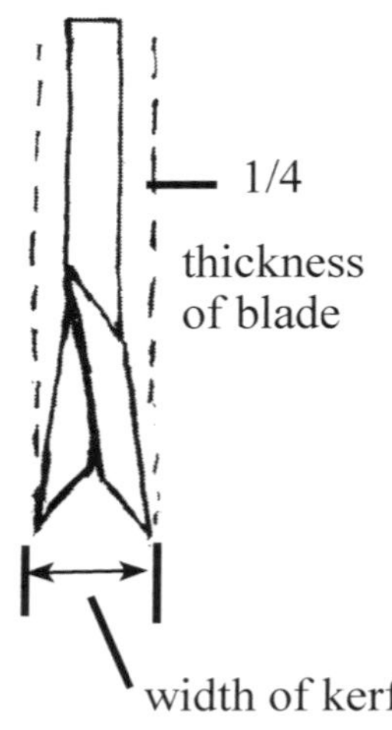

If the kerf tends to drift or curve to one side, this indicates that the cutting teeth on one side of the blade are too long. To correct this, sharpen the teeth that are on the outside of the curve.

SETTING A CAMP SAW:

Set allows the saw to cut a kerf that is wider than the thickness of the blade. This wider kerf is necessary to prevent the blade from binding in the kerfs. Set is produced by bending the cutting teeth in an alternating pattern to the left and right of the blade. To determine which teeth to bend which way, look at the blade from the side. You should be able to see the filed surface on every other cutting tooth. Use a saw set to put set into the blade. Bend each tooth toward its flat side by about 1/4 the thickness of the blade.

Be careful to bend each tooth the same amount so that the teeth cut two parallel lines.

If the teeth are overset (bent too far) place the blade on a flat piece of steel so that the overset teeth are resting on the steel. Then hammer the teeth back in line.

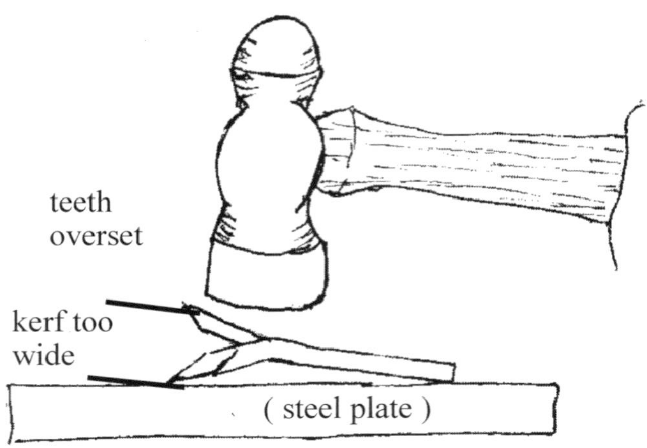

JOINING THE CUTTING TEETH:

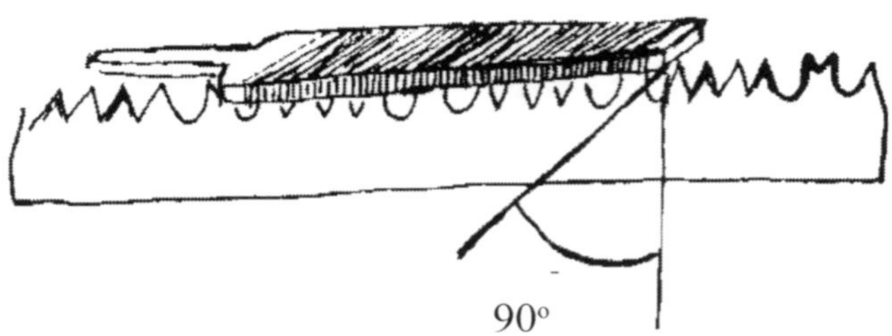

The cutting teeth will cut more efficiently if they are all the same length. If the teeth are not all the same length, they will need to be joined or filed down to the same length.

Join the teeth by placing the blade in a saw vice and then drawing a file across the points of the teeth. The file must be held so that it is parallel to the length of the saw blade and the cutting face of the file is at 90° to the width of the saw blade. Apply light but firm pressure to the file as you draw it over the points of the teeth.

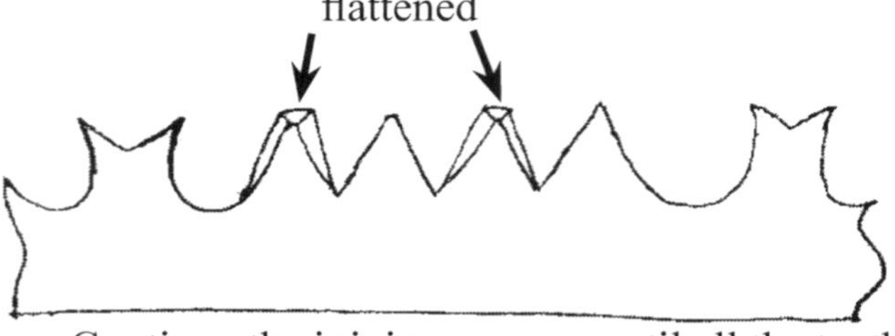

Continue the joining process until all the teeth have been contacted by the file. When the point of a tooth has been contacted by the file, it will have a slightly flattened, shiny, surface. The saw blade is then sharpened to restore the points on the teeth.

The teeth that have been filed off the most when joined will require more filing than the teeth that were just barely contacted by the file.

SHARPENING THE CUTTING TEETH:

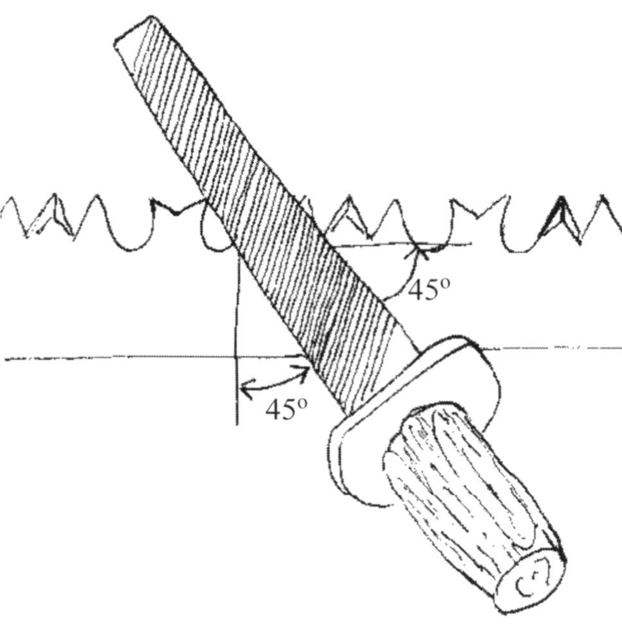

The cutting teeth act like two rows of small knives cutting off the wood fiber on either side of the kerf. Unlike a knife that is sharpened with a double bevel on one edge of the blade, the cutting teeth are sharpened with a single bevel on both edges of the tooth so that it can cut in both directions. One row of teeth is beveled and set to one side and the other row is beveled and set to the other side.

To sharpen the cutting teeth, first place the saw blade in a saw vice. Then hold the file so that it is tilted at 45° to the length and 45° width of the blade. This should line the file up with one set of cutting surfaces. File all the cutting surfaces that are at this angle; be sure to use the same pressure, the same number of strokes, and the same angle on each tooth. Then change the angle of the file to match the angle of the other cutting surface on this set of teeth. After completing one side, turn the saw blade around and do the other side the same way.

SHARPENING THE RAKERS:

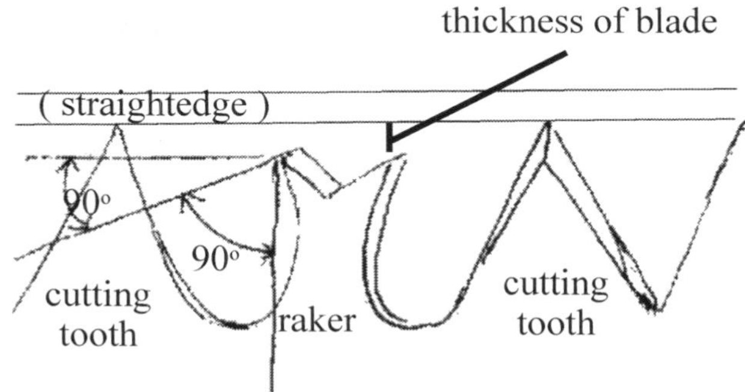

The rakers are designed to act like small chisels that cut the wood fiber loose from the bottom of the kerfs. Each raker is shorter than the cutting teeth, by about the thickness of the blade, and has a pair of cutting edges. One edge cuts on the push stroke and the other edge cuts on the pull stroke. When properly sharpened, each cutting edge is at 90° to both the length and width of the blade. To sharpen the rakers, place the blade in a saw vice. Check the length of the raker by placing a straightedge on the cutting teeth. The distance between the straightedge and the raker teeth should be equal to the thickness of the blade. (A thickness gauge can be made from a piece of old saw blade.) Sharpen each cutting edge by filing the notch in the top of the raker so that the edges are at 90° to both the length and width of the blade. Recheck the length of the raker with the straightedge and gauge. If the

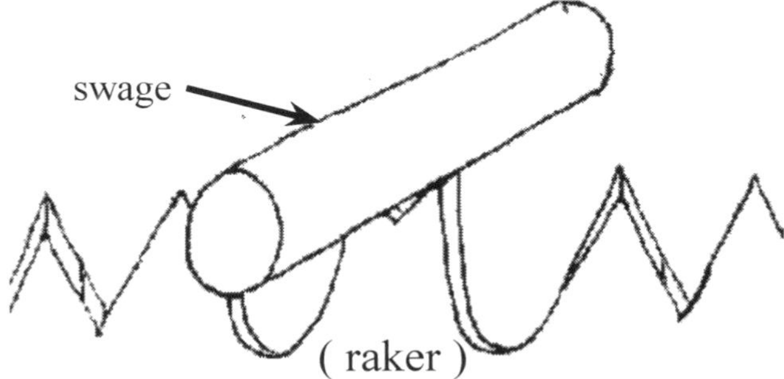

rakers are still too long, continue to file them down or use a swage to turn the cutting edges slightly outward. (A piece of steel rod that is just large enough to contact the cutting edges of the raker can be used as a swage.) Place the swage on the cutting edges so that it is at 90° to both the length and width of the blade and then tap it firmly with a hammer. Then recheck the length of the raker with the straightedge and the gauge.

SHARPENING LARGER SAWS:

One and two man crosscut saws can be sharpened by following the same procedure as described for sharpening a camp saw. However, there is one additional step; the gullet, the space between the teeth, must also be filed.

The gullet is designed to provide a space for the sawdust to collect in as the saw cuts through the wood. The gullet also allows the rakers to carry the sawdust out of the kerfs. If the gullet is too small for the amount of sawdust collected, the sawdust will be packed into the gullet and will not fall out easily when the gullet clears the kerfs. Additionally, the packed sawdust may cause the blade to bind in the kerfs. As the cutting teeth and the rakers are sharpened, they become shorter. This means that the gullet is smaller and needs to be filed out. To do this, make a template of the desired shape from sheet-metal. Using the template as a pattern, reshape and deepen the gullets with a round file.

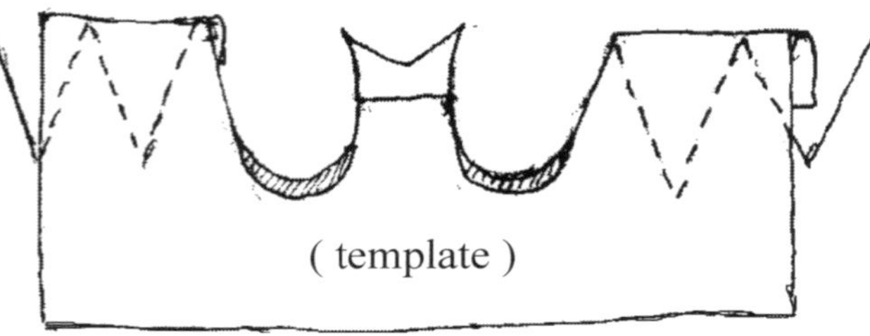

Make the template by folding a piece of sheet metal in half. Place the folded piece behind the saw blade with the folded edge sticking out a distance equal to the amount that is going to be cut out of the gullet. Use a scribe to trace the shape of the gullets onto the sheet metal. Use a file to cut out the template.

To use the template, place it over the saw blade, then use a round file to file the gullet to its new depth.

MAKING A SAW SET:

A saw set is a tool that is used to set a saw or bend the cutting teeth to either side in an alternating pattern to widen the kerf and prevent the blade from jamming in the kerf.

To make a saw set, use a hacksaw to cut a 1/2 inch deep and slightly angled slot in the end of a piece of cold rolled steel that is about 6 inches long and 1 inch wide. Also, cut a groove deep enough in a block of wood so that when the back of the saw blade is placed in the groove the teeth will just stick out of the groove.

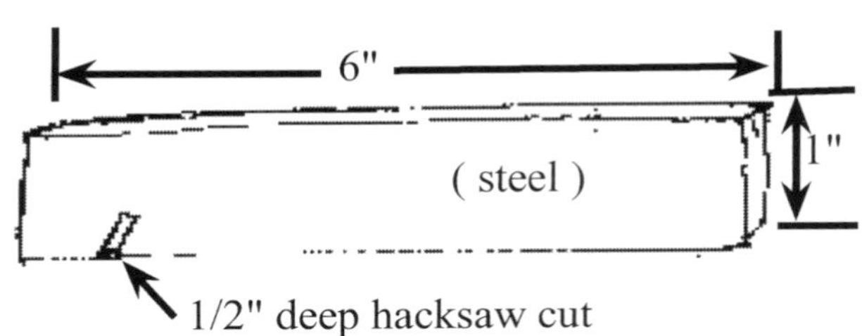

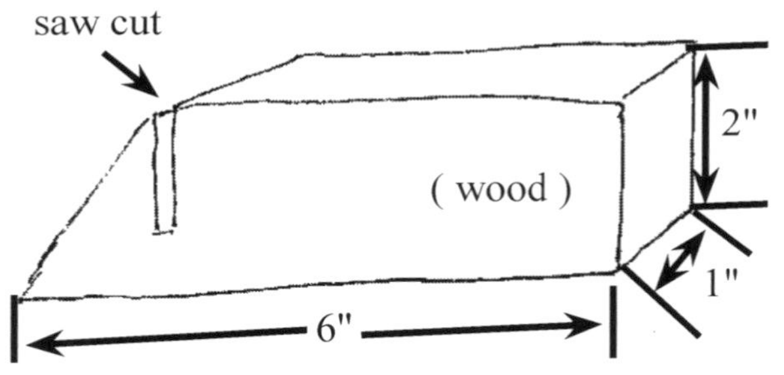

To use the set, place the back of the saw blade in the wooden block, place the set over a tooth and press down.

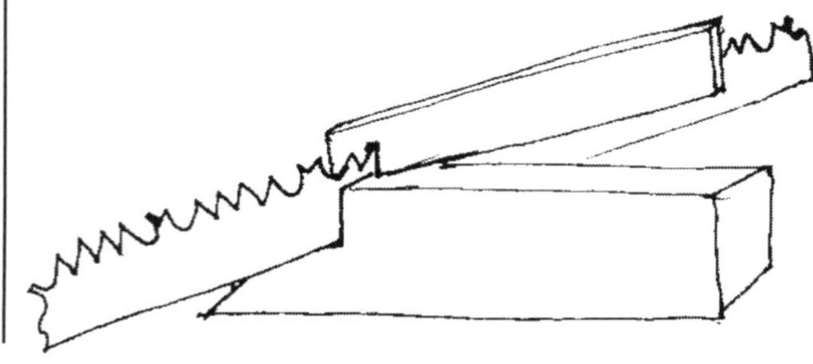

MAKING A SAW VICE:

A saw vice is a tool used to hold a saw blade while it is being worked on. A simple vice that can be used to sharpen a camp saw can be made by following these directions.

MATERIALS:

3 — pieces of wood 24" long by 3" wide
2 — 1/4" diameter times 3" long carriage bolts
2 — 1/4" washers
2 — 1/4" wing nuts
several wood screws
glue

CONSTRUCTION:

(1) Use the wood screws and glue to join two of the pieces of wood together.

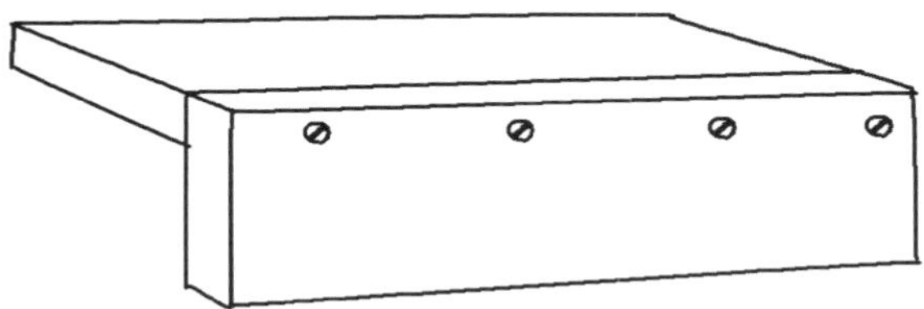

(2) Bevel the edge of the third board at a 45° angle.

(3) Clamp the beveled board and the first assembly together. Drill two holes through the boards for the carriage bolts.

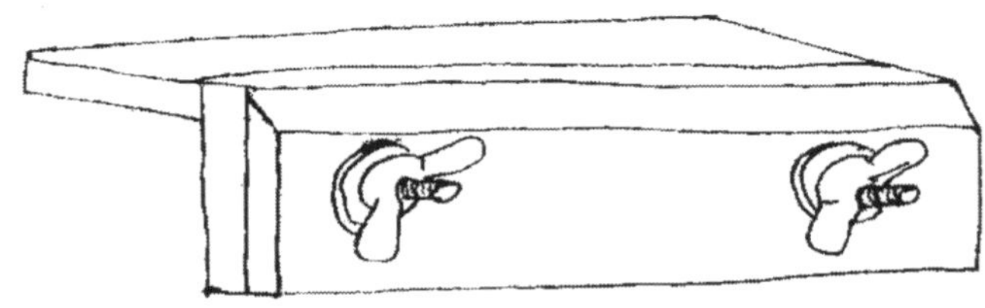

To use the saw vice, clamp it to the edge of a table with two "C" clamps. Clamp the saw blade in the vice so that the saw teeth are just clear of the vice and pointed upward.

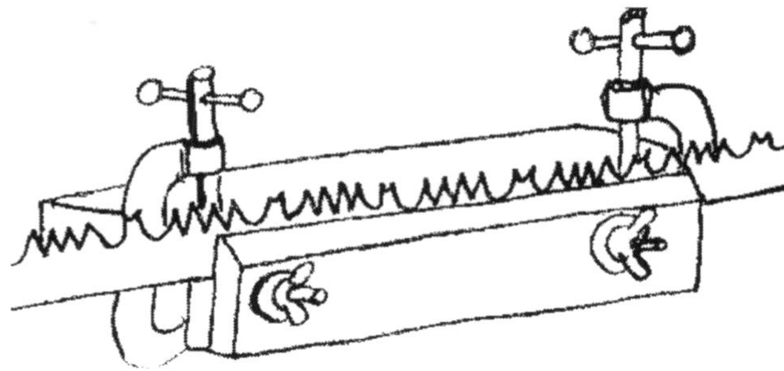

SAW GUARD:

To protect the saw teeth from damage and to protect you from the saw teeth, a saw guard should be used whenever the saw is not in use.

The saw guard should be made from a non corrosive material such as plastic, rubber, or metal. Wood and leather contain chemicals that can cause the saw blade to rust. Rust will cause the blade to lose its sharpness.

PLASTIC PIPE SAW GUARD:

Materials:

1/2" or 3/4" rigid plastic pipe
36" shoelace or similar material

Construction:

1. Cut the pipe to the length of the saw blade.

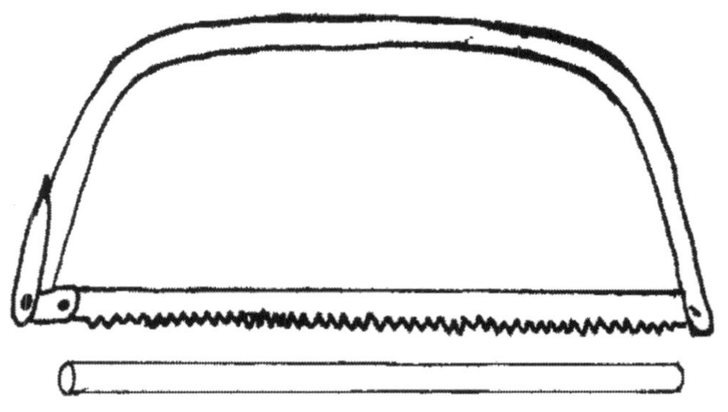

2. Saw a slit the full length of one side of the pipe. (Use a carpenter's hand saw.)

3. Near each end of the pipe, drill two 3/16 inch holes through the pipe so that the holes are at 90° to the slit.

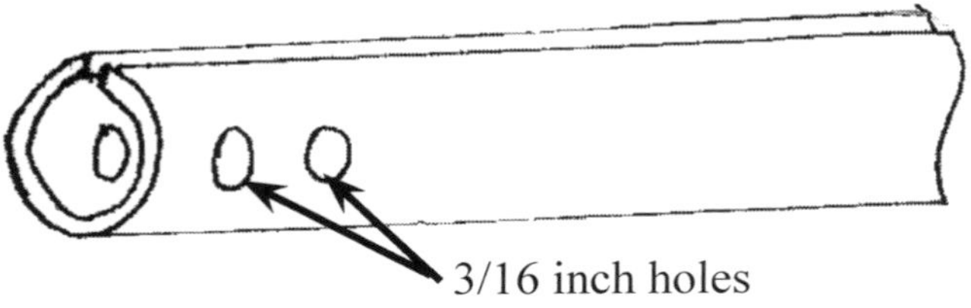

4. Cut the shoelace into 4 pieces and tie each piece to the pipe as shown.

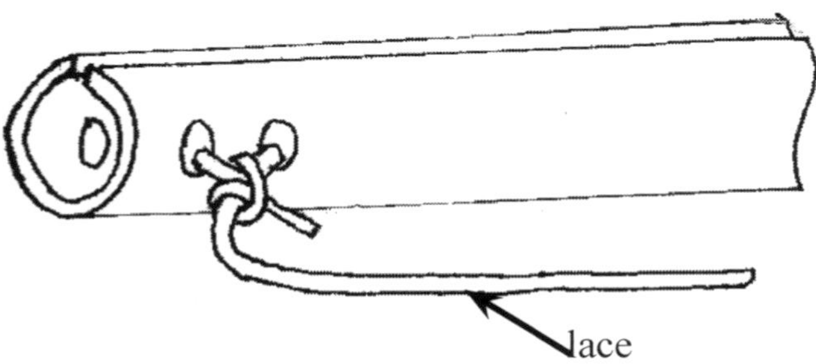

5. Use shoelace to secure the guard to the blade.

[NOTE] A piece of garden hose or other flexible tubing or pipe can be used as a guard. However, additional ties will be needed to keep the guard in place.

INNER TUBE SAW GUARD:

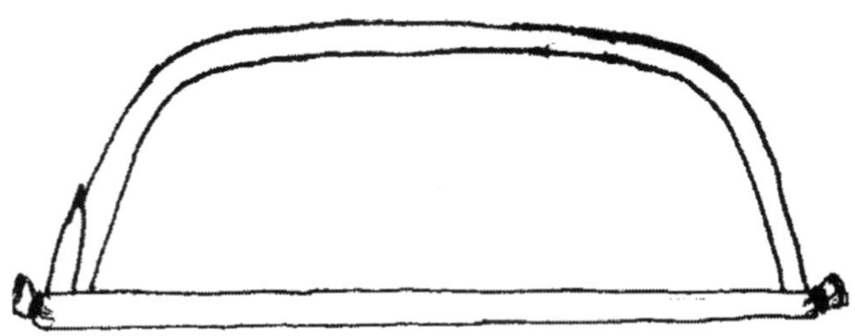

Cut a piece of bicycle inner tube to a length that is equal to the length of the saw. Slit the tube down one side. Tie off the end of the tube. Then stretch the tube over the saw blade.

[NOTES]

SPANISH WINDLASS:

A Spanish windlass is a device for moving heavy loads such as rocks and logs.

[WARNING] When setting up a Spanish Windlass, do not use nylon or other synthetic fiber rope. Synthetic rope will stretch. If you slip or let go of the poles, the energy you used to stretch the rope will be released as the rope returns to its original length. This release of energy could cause the poles of the windless to spin around causing injuries to anyone nearby. Natural fiber ropes, such as sisal, have little stretch; therefore are much safer to use.

MATERIALS:

1 — 8 foot * 3 inch pole
1 — 5 foot * 3 inch pole
1 — 3/4 inch * 50 foot natural fiber rope

SETUP:

STEP 1: Tie one end of the rope to the load and the other end of the rope to a secure anchor point. Leave some slack in the rope so that the windless can be rigged.

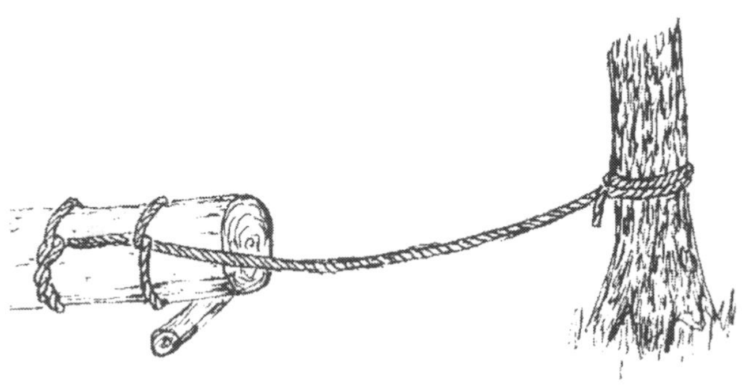

STEP 2: Follow the diagrams to set up the poles at the mid point of the rope.

STEP 3: While one person holds the upright pole, a second person rotates the longer pole around the upright so that the rope begins to wrap around the upright pole. Adjust the height of the rope so that it can be easily stepped over.

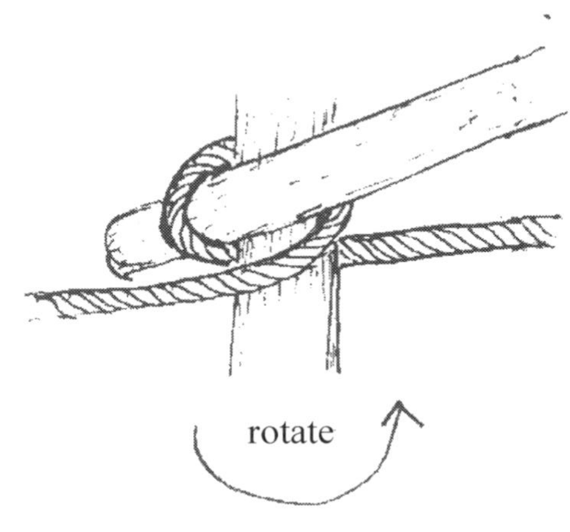

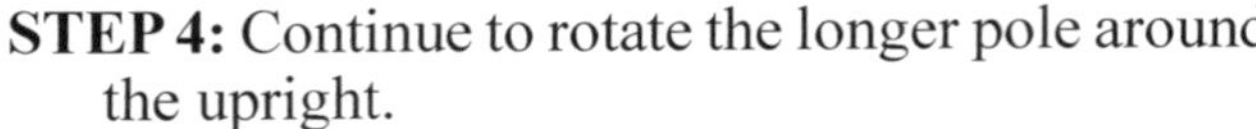

STEP 4: Continue to rotate the longer pole around the upright.

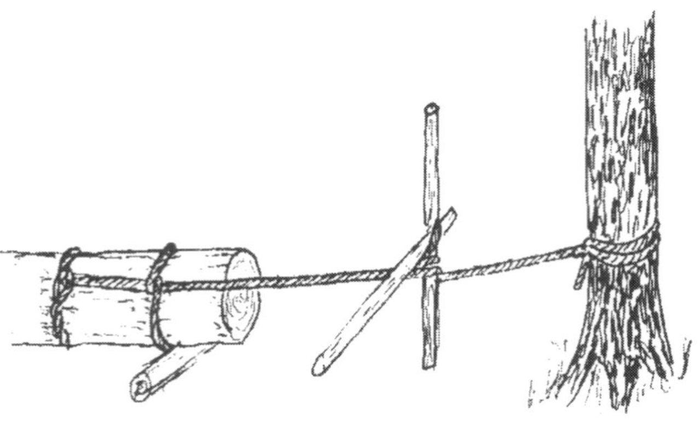

[NOTE] As the rope wraps around the upright it will be necessary to move the base of the upright to keep it vertical.

[NOTE] Be careful that the two ends of the rope are kept at the same level on the upright.

keep rope ends at same level

[NOTES]

ANCHOR POINT:

Description ---- Any point of attachment for a line that can be used to support a load.

Comments ---- Anchor points can be a natural feature such as a rock or tree or a man-made device.

STAKE ANCHOR POINTS:

The holding power of a stake depends on three things.

1. The length of the stake. The longer the stake the greater the friction between the soil and the stake.

2. The strength of the material. The stake must be able to support the load without breaking.

3. The make-up of the soil. A longer stake will be required in loose sandy soil than in more compact soil types.

Stakes For Tents and Tarps:

The most commonly used stake anchor point is the "tent peg". The size of a tent peg depends on the size of the tent or tarp that is being set up.

A tent peg should be driven straight into the ground and the angle between the ground and the guy line to the tent or tarp should be 45° or less. Driving the stake straight into the ground or even slightly inclined toward the guy line minimizes the tendency of the stake to be pulled upward through the soil. As the angle between the ground and the guy line increases, the holding ability of the stake depends more on the friction between the stake and the soil than on the resistance to being dragged through the soil.

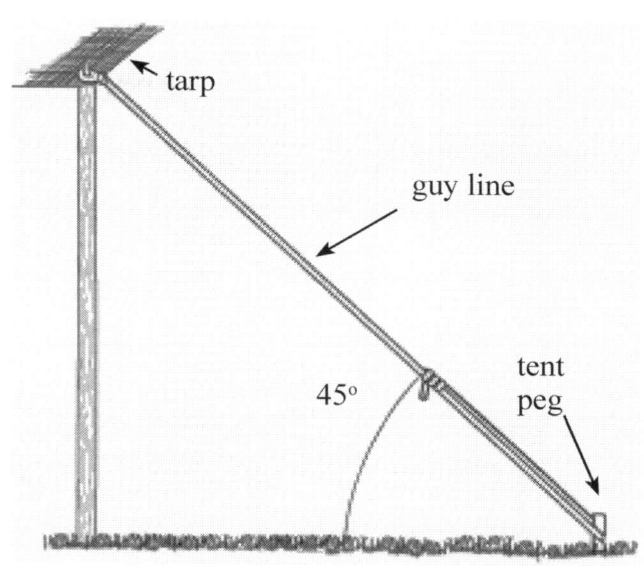

Stakes For Supporting Heavy Loads:

There are some general rules to follow when setting up and using an anchor point.

The angle between the ground and the line attached to the anchor point, in most cases, should not exceed 25°. The length of the line between the anchor point and the load should be about two times longer than the height at which the line is attached to the load (2:1).

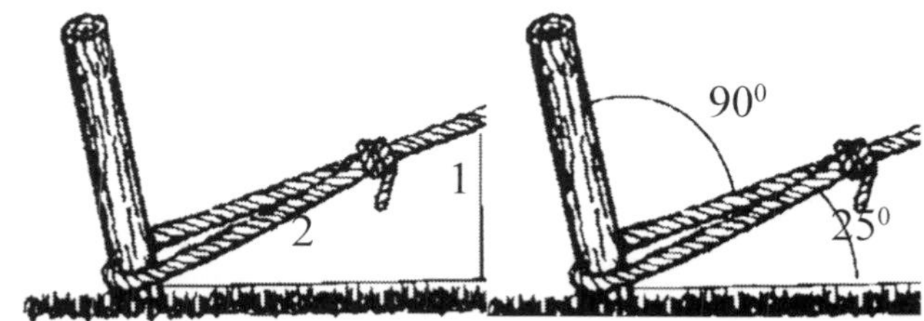

When a heavy load is placed on a stake anchor point, the direction of the force of the load should be as close to 90° to the stake as possible.

As the angle between the line and the ground increases, the upward force on the anchor point increases. This decreases the holding power of the anchor point. Larger stakes and multiple stake setups are needed.

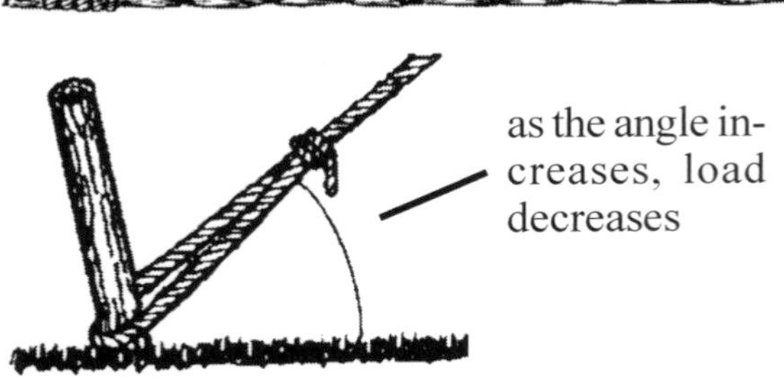

Stake Setups:

A single stake anchor point made with a stake 4 to 5 feet long, 3 inches in diameter, and driven 3 feet into firm soil will hold about 700 pounds.

A 2-1 stake anchor point made with stakes 4 to 5 feet long, 3 inches in diameter, and driven 3 feet into firm soil will support a load of about 1 ton.

A 3-2-1 stake anchor point made with stakes 4 to 5 feet long, 3 inches in diameter, and driven 3 feet into firm soil will support a load of about 2 tons.

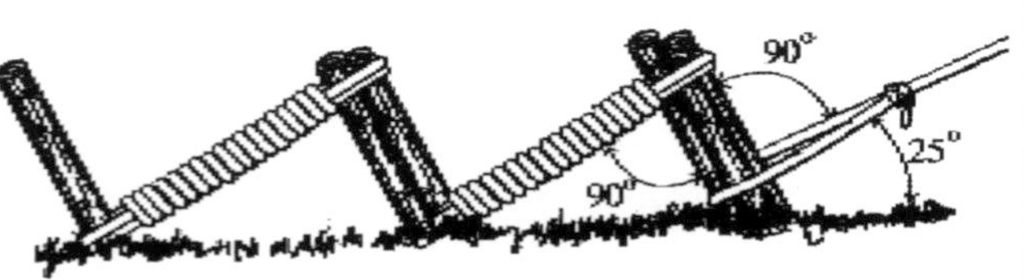

To ensure maximum holding power of a multiple stake anchor point, the angle between the load line and the ground should be less than 25^0 and the angle between the lines and the stakes should be 90^0. Also, the rope used to bind the stakes together should be pulled tight so that there is little or no movement of the stakes when the load is applied to the anchor point.

If multiple guy lines are attached to an anchor point (or if the load on an anchor point can shift from side to side, so that it is not always in line with the stake setup) a triangular arrangement of stakes can be used to stabilize the anchor point.

Stake and Log:

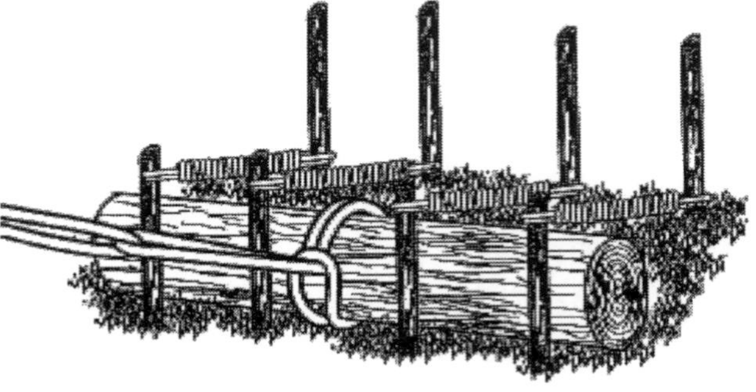

A stake and log anchor point made with stakes 4 to 5 feet long, 3 inches in diameter, and driven 3 feet into firm soil will support a load of about 1 ton for each pair of stakes. The log must be placed perpendicular to the load with an equal number of stakes on each side of the guy line. Also, the log must bear evenly on all the leading stakes and must rest on the ground.

DEAD MAN ANCHOR POINT:

A dead man anchor point is made by burying a log or some other bulky object in the ground and attaching a line to it. A dead man anchor point makes a good permanent anchor point.

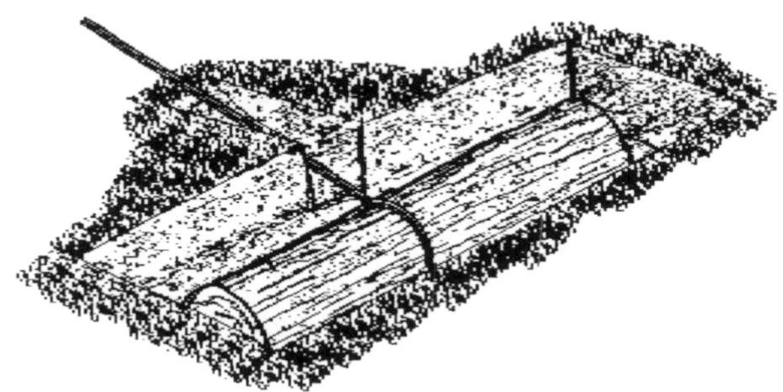

GROMMET: GUY LINE ATTACHMENT

The use of a Grommet, tied off with a Clove Hitch, provides a secure, non shifting means of attaching a guy line to an anchor point. (See section on GROMMET).

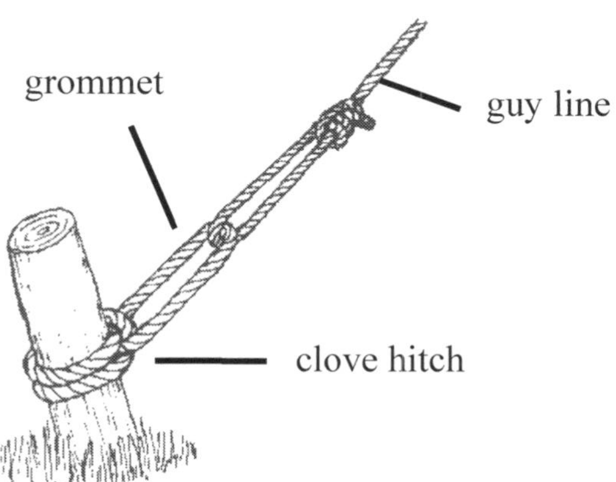

SAFETY:

SAFETY is an important consideration. Since there is always the possibility of an anchor point failing when it is being used to support a heavy load, a safety observer should be assigned to watch each anchor point and an overall safety officer should be assigned to watch the entire operation. Also, the work should be done in small predetermined steps.

[NOTES]

TARP/DINING FLY:

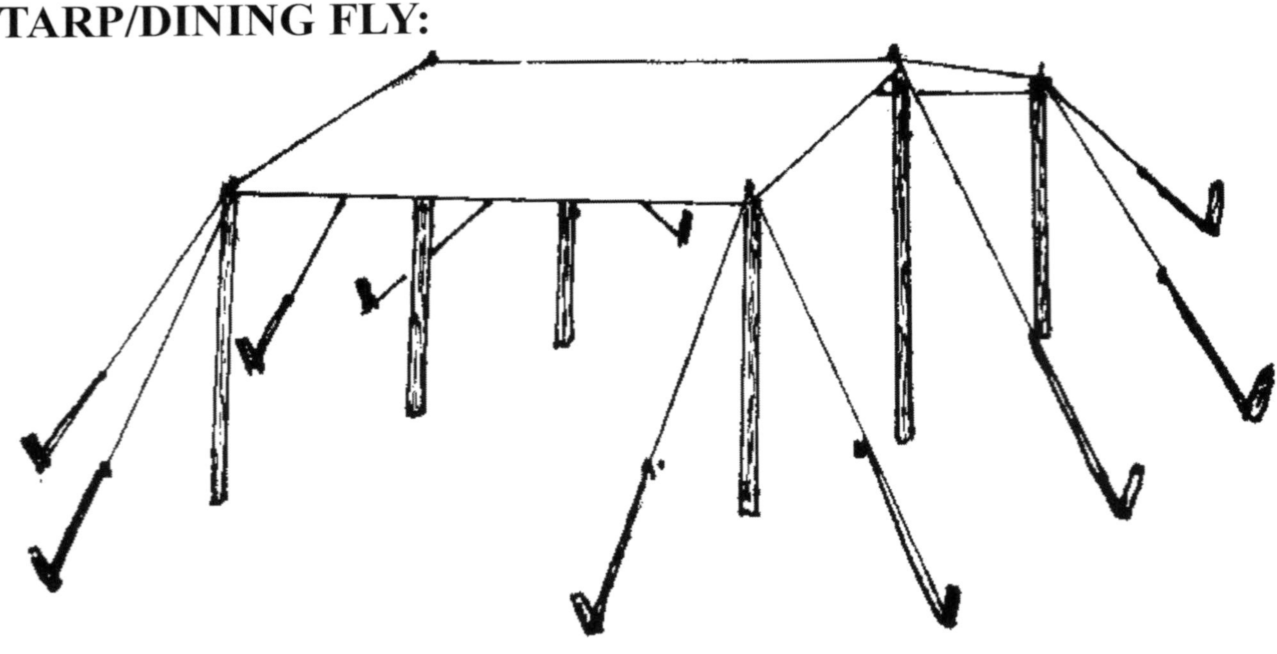

To set up a tarp as a dining fly that will be stable in a reasonable amount of wind, it is necessary to stretch the tarp equally in all directions. Wind will cause any loose edge or ripple to "pop" or forcefully flap back and forth. Each time the tarp pops, a jolting force is transferred through the guy lines to the anchor points of the tarp. The repeating jolts on the guy lines will loosen the stakes and eventually pull them out of the ground.

When two guy lines are attached to each corner of the tarp, the tension along each edge of the tarp can be adjusted so that the tarp is stretched flat. A tarp that is set up with a single guy line on each corner will seldom stay up even in a light wind. When a single guy line is used on each corner, the force is divided between the two edges. Because the force along the two edges is never equal, and is constantly changing depending on the direction and force of the wind, these uneven forces soon loosen and pull the stakes (causing the tarp to fall down).

SETTING UP A TARP:

STEP 1:. Unfold and lay out the tarp on the place it is to be set up.

STEP 2: Position the anchor points so that they are one pole's length away and slightly to the outside of a line extending from the edge of the tarp.

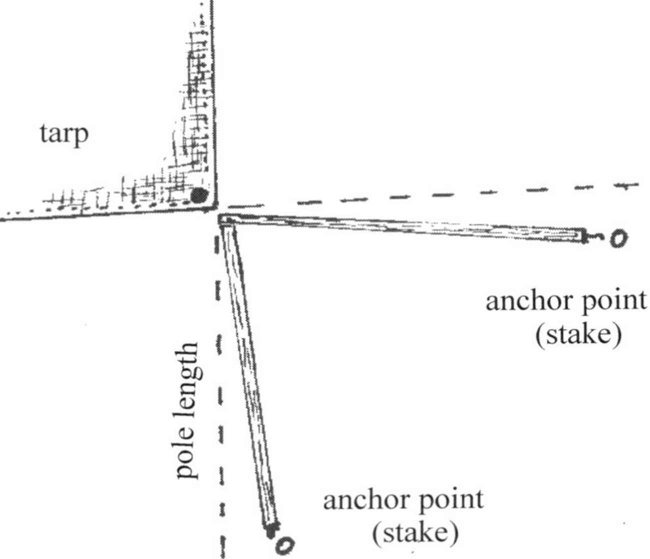

STEP 3: Place the butt of each pole where it will be resting on the ground when the tarp is set up.

STEP 4: Use the toe of your foot to mark where the butt of the pole will rest, pick up the pole, the guy lines, and the corner of the tarp. Place the corner grommet of the tarp over the pin on the top of the pole. Next, place the loops at the ends of the guy lines over the pin. Then rest the butt of the pole back at its correct location. At this stage the pole should be leaning toward the center of the tarp.

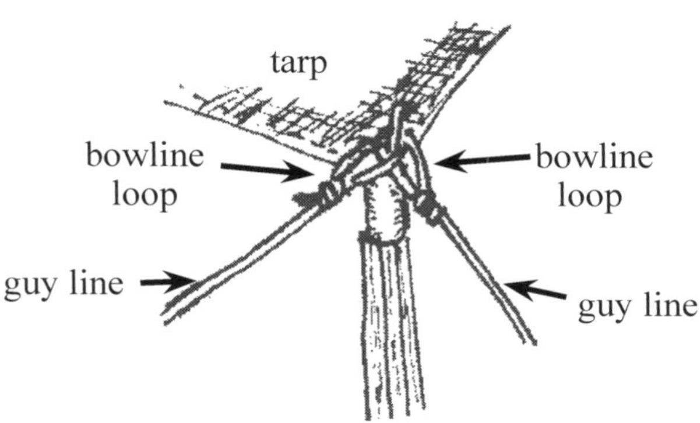

[NOTE] If you have enough help, you can set up all four corners at the same time. However, if you are working by yourself, the second pole you set up should be diagonally across from the first one.

STEP 5: Adjust the tension on the guy lines so that the corner poles are upright and the edges of the tarp are tight and square.

STEP 6: Set up any additional poles and adjust their guy lines.

[NOTES]

FLAG LANYARD:

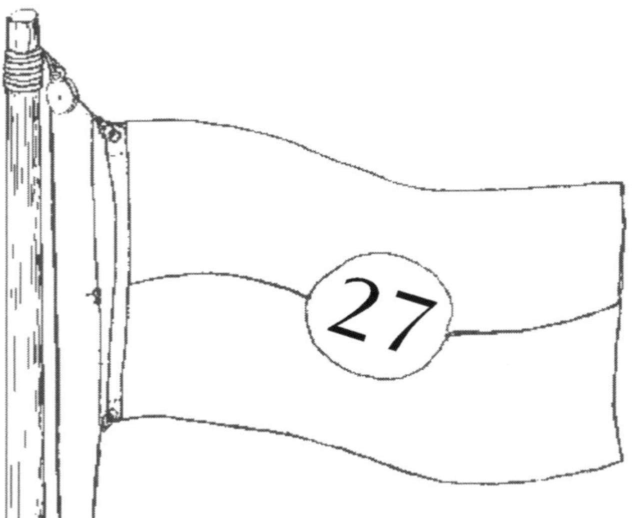

Rigging a flag lanyard so that the flag can be raised, displayed, and lowered properly is not difficult, but there are a few tricks that you may wish to try.

The lanyard is attached to the top of the pole with a pulley block and secured at the bottom of the pole with a cleat. (See Rigging a Pulley Block, Belaying to a Cleat, and Making a Cleat).

Length of Lanyard:

The length of rope that is to be used for the lanyard should be twice the distance from the pulley block to the cleat plus about 6 feet.

Attaching the Lanyard to the Flagpole:

Before the flagpole is set up, reeve the rope through the pulley block and join the ends with a Sheet Bend.

Attaching the Flag to the Lanyard:

The flag can be attached to the lanyard with snaps or toggles.

Rigging Snaps:

The snaps can be attached with Lark's Head Knots so that the snaps are on either side of the Sheet Bend used to join the two ends of the rope.

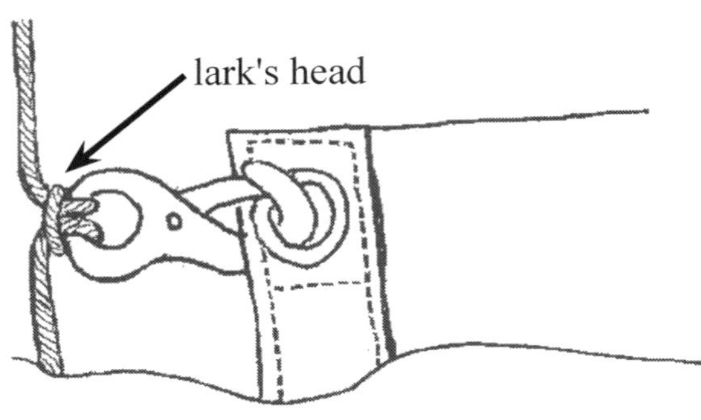

Lark's Head:

(Step 1)

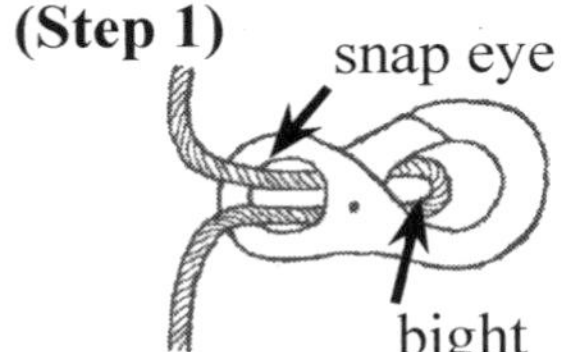

Reeve a bight of the lanyard through the eye of the snap.

(Step 2)

Enlarge the eye of the bight.

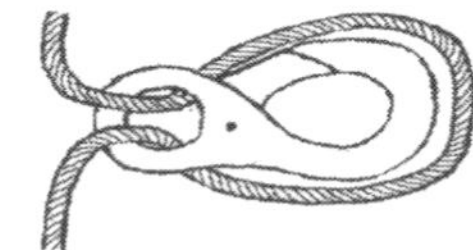

(Step 3)

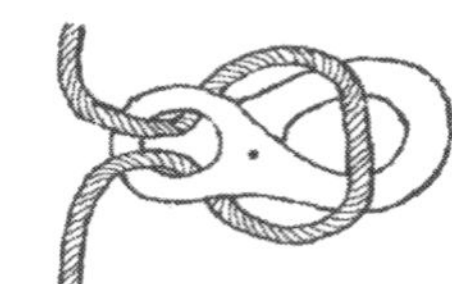

Reeve the snap through the eye of the bight.

(Step 4)

Fold the bight completely over on itself.

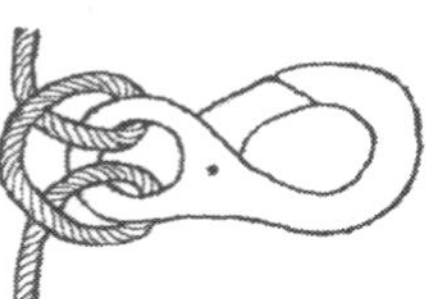

(Step 5)

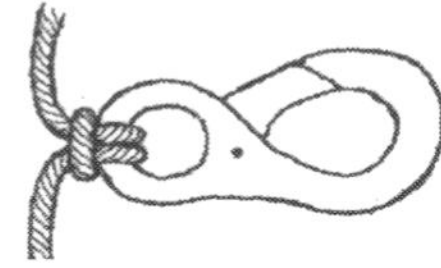

Pull tight.

Rigging Snaps: (Alternate Method)

Instead of attaching the snaps with Lark's Head Knots so that the snaps are on either side of the Sheet Bend used to join the two ends of the rope, join the two ends of the rope by tying them off to the top snap with Two Half Hitches.

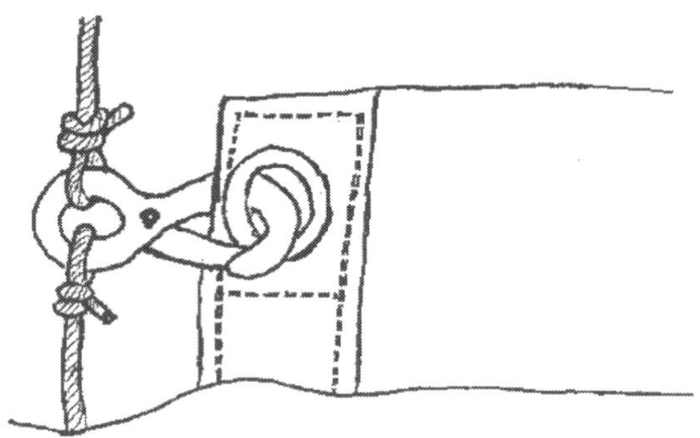

Distance Between Snaps:

Adjust the distance between the snaps so that when the flag is attached to the lanyard the spine of the flag is pulled tight. Pulling the spine of the flag tight will cause the flag to fly flatter and not "pop" and "snap" as much.

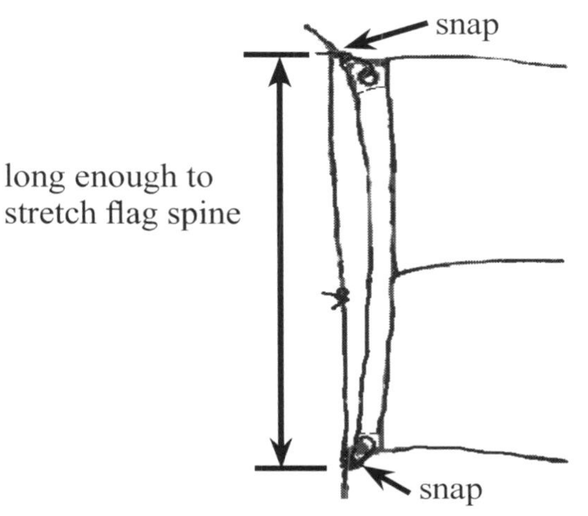

Rigging Toggles:

STEP 1: Make two toggles. Carve a 1/4 inch deep groove around the center of a 3 inch long by 3/4 inch diameter stick. The groove must be wide enough for the rope to fit snugly.

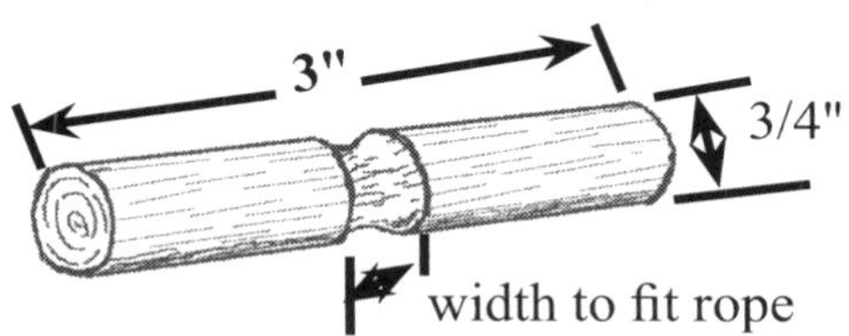

STEP 2: Tie or splice a short piece of rope around the toggle.

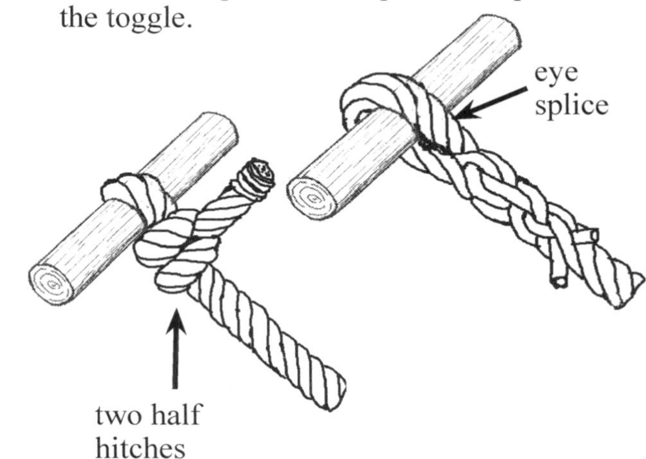

STEP 3: Attach the toggle ropes to the flag grommets with a Bowline or an Eye Splice.

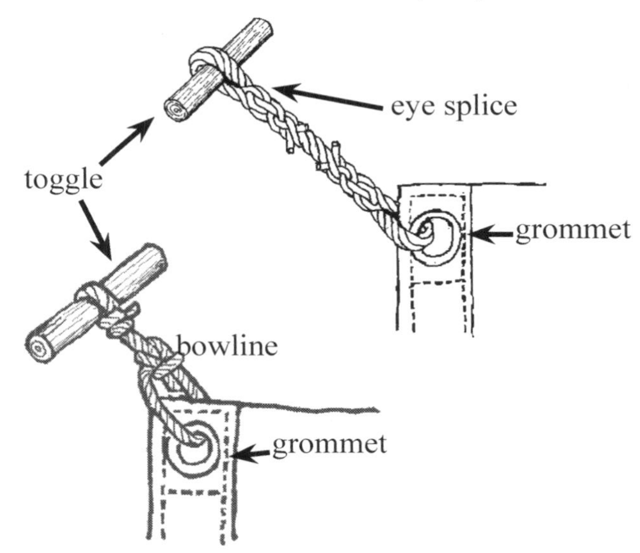

STEP 4: On either side of the Sheet Bend that is used to join the two ends of the lanyard together, tie a Figure-Eight On a Bight Knot to form loops that the toggle can be attached to. (The distance between the eyes of the two Figure-Eight On a Bight Knots should be slightly greater than the distance between the two toggles when the spine of the flag is stretched tight.

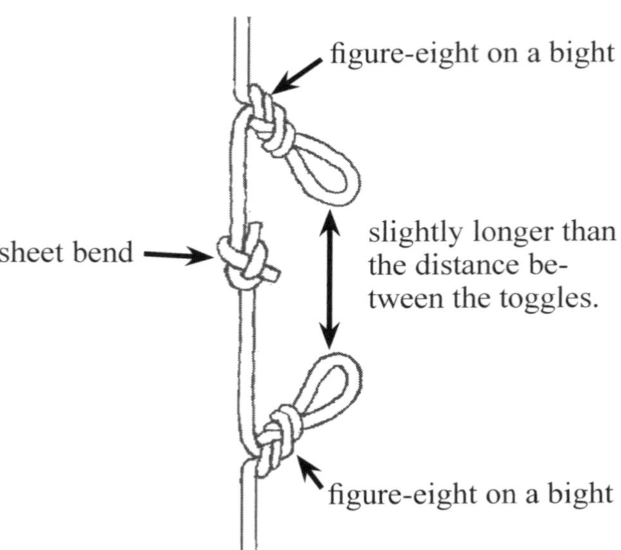

STEP 5: Attach the flag to the lanyard by hooking the toggles through the eyes of the Figure-Eight On a Bight Knots.

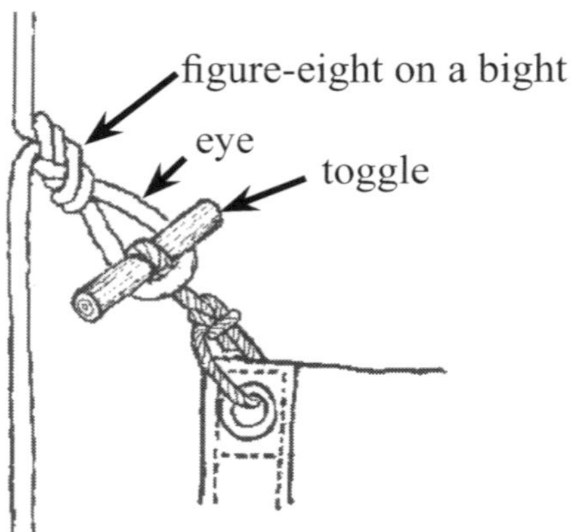

[NOTES]

MODELS:

INTRODUCTION:

MODELS are useful as a pioneering tool. They allow you to safely test your ideas, work out designs, establish construction procedure, and serve as a hands on teaching aid.

The only difference between a full sized structure and a scale model is size. Some of the advantages of scale models are: less space is needed for construction and the storage of materials; the smaller size means you are not working with heavy timbers when you are working out new designs.

SCALES:

A scale is expressed as a ratio of the measurements used for the construction of a model to the measurements for the construction of a full sized structure.

1:12 (1 inch = 1 foot) scale is a popular scale used for making models. It is a good size for making display models and for the experienced modeler to try out new designs.

1:4 (1 inch = 4 inches) or (1 foot = 4 feet) scale is a convenient scale for teaching and is still small enough to have a large supply of materials on hand. To give an example of size ratio; a full sized pole, 20 foot long and 4 inches in diameter in a 1:4 scale would only be 5 feet long and 1 inch in diameter.

CONSTRUCTING A (1:12) Model

SUSPENDED FLAGPOLE:

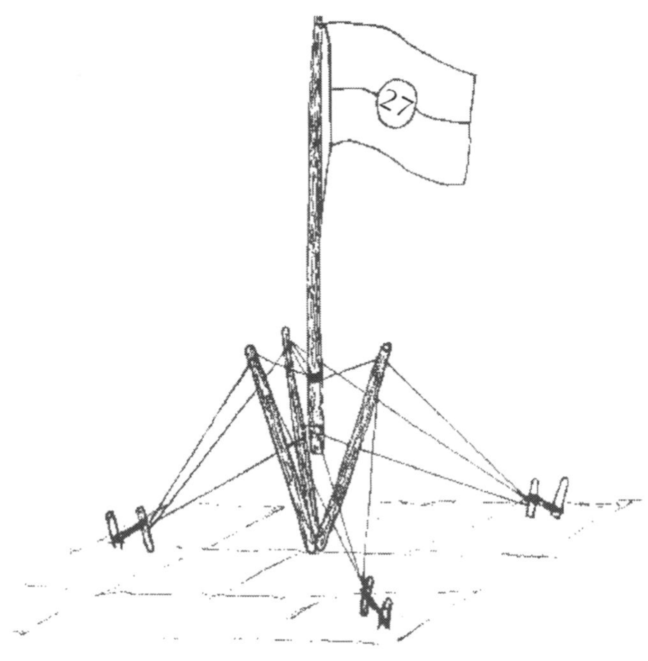

TOOLS:

pruning shears	coping saw
pocketknife	1 ft. rule
crochet hook	screwdriver

MATERIALS:

(Key: F = Full Size, S = Scale Size)

F 3 — 8 ft. * (3 in. butt) poles
S 3 — 8 in. * (1/4 in. butt) poles
F 1 — 16 ft. * (3 in. butt) pole
S 1 — 16 in. * (1/4 in. butt) pole
F 1 — 38 ft. * 1/4 in. rope
S 1 — 38 in. crochet yarn
F 1 — 8 ft. * 1/4 in. rope
S 1 — 8 in. crochet yarn
F 3 — 18 ft. * 1/2 in. ropes
S 3 — 18 in. cotton chalk lines
F 3 — 12 ft. * 1/2 in. ropes
S 3 — 12 in. cotton chalk lines
F 6 — 3 ft. * 2 in. stakes
S 6 — 3 in. * 1/8 in. stakes
F 3 — 8 ft. * 1/4 in. ropes
S 3 — 8 in. crochet yarn
S 1 — 18 in. * 18 in. * 1 in. rigid foam insulation board

S 2 — 18 in. * 1 in. * 1/4 in. wood strips
S 2 — 18 1/2 in. * 1 in. * 1/4 in. wood strips
S 8 — 1 1/4 in. wallboard screws
S —— White glue

ASSEMBLY:

While assembling the model try to think of your scale-sized pieces as though they were full-sized or that you are only 5 1/2 inches tall. Remember, the only difference between constructing the scale flagpole and the full-sized one is size and the need to construct a base for the model. To help you think this way, all measurements given for the construction of the flagpole will be full sized, except those that apply only to the model.

STEP 1: Construct the base by reinforcing the edges of the 18" * 18" block of rigid foam insulation with 1/4 in. thick wooden strips.

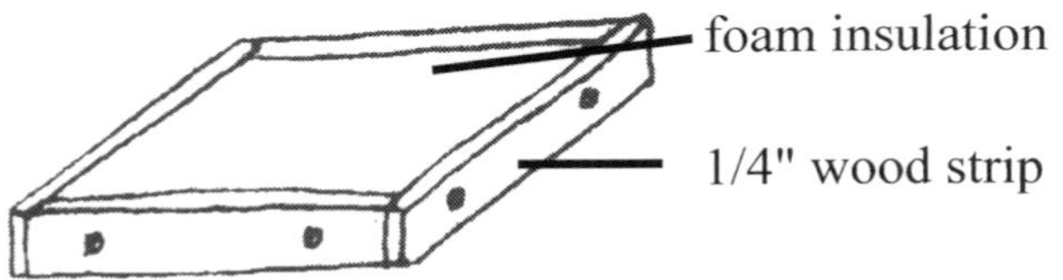

STEP 2: Lay out the anchor points. Use 2-stake, in-line anchor points located 8 feet from the center and evenly spaced around the center of the base.

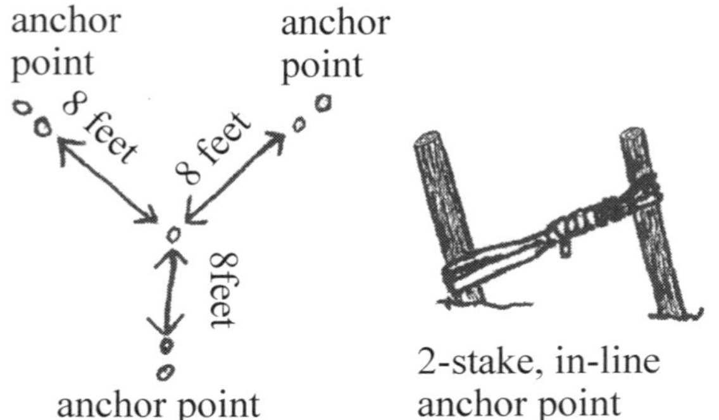

STEP 3: Make each anchor point by pushing the sharpened stakes into the foam base. Then pull the stakes out, put some glue in the holes, and push the stakes back into the holes. After the glue has dried, bind the tops of the stakes together using an 8 foot * 1/4 inch rope (see GUY LINES).

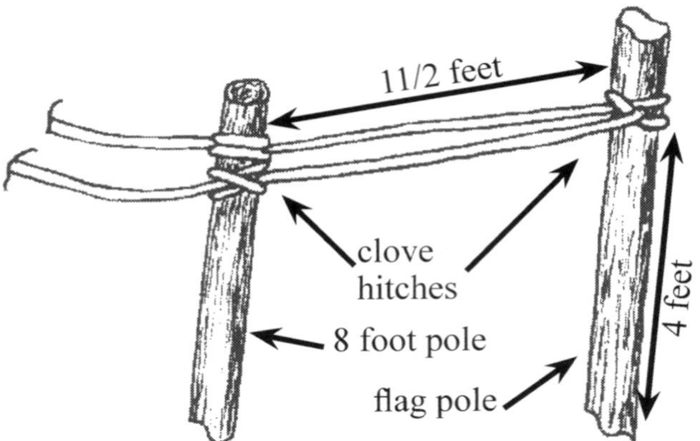

STEP 4: Prepare the flagpole by attaching the ropes to it.

4A] Use a Clove Hitch to tie the mid point of an 18 foot * 1/2 inch rope to the flagpole so that the rope is 4 feet from the bottom of the flagpole.

4B] Use Clove Hitches to tie both ends of the 18 foot * 1/2 inch rope to the top of an 8 foot pole so that the cross points of the Clove Hitches are on opposite sides of the 8 foot pole and 1 1/2 feet from the flagpole. Be careful not to cross the strands of the rope between the flagpole and the 8 foot pole.

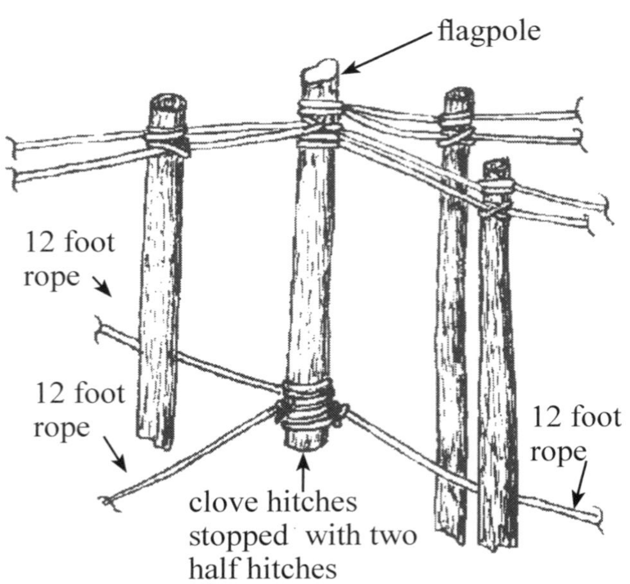

4C] Repeat steps 4A] and 4B] to tie two more 18 foot *1/2 inch ropes to the flagpole.

4D] Tie the three 12 foot * 1/2 inch ropes to the bottom of the flagpole with Clove Hitches stopped with Two Half Hitches.

4E] Attach a flag lanyard to the top of the flagpole. Use a 38 foot * 1/4 inch rope for the lanyard. (See RIGGING A FLAGPOLE)

STEP 5: Form the base by setting the butts of the 8 foot poles at the center point. Then reeve the ends of the 18 foot ropes through the anchor

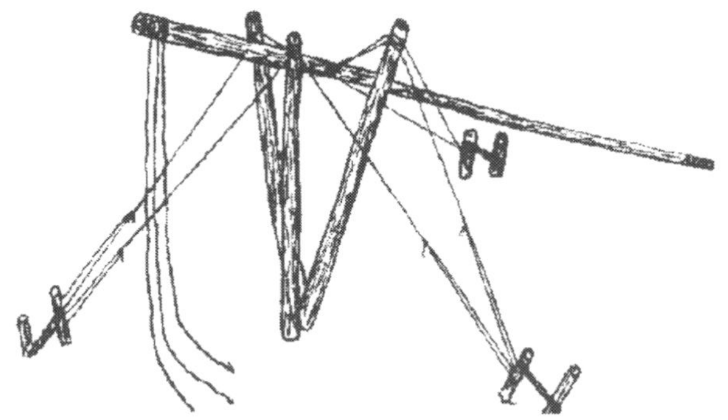

points as shown in the diagram. Tie them off with Taught Line Hitches.

STEP 6: Set the flagpole upright by pulling down on its butt. Reeve the ends of the 12 foot ropes through the anchor points and tie them off with Taught Line Hitches.

STEP 7: Tighten and adjust all guy lines so that the flagpole is centered and vertical over the base.

CONSTRUCTING A (1:4) MODEL

SUSPENDED FLAGPOLE:

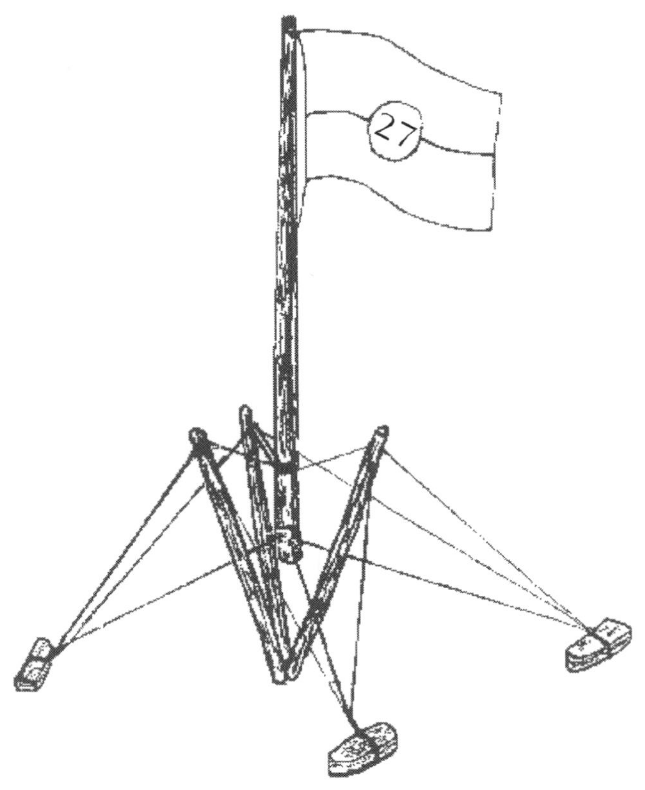

TOOLS:

rule marked for 1:4 scale
fine line marker
pruning shears
pocketknife
masking tape
coping saw
maul

MATERIALS:

(Key: F = Full Size, S = Scale Size)

F 3 — 8 ft. * (3 in. butt) poles
S 3 — 24 in. * (3/4 in. butt) poles
F 1 — 16 ft. * (3 in. butt) pole
S 1 — 48 in. * (3/4 in. butt) pole
F 1 — 38 ft. * 1/4 in. rope
S 1 — 114 in. cotton mason's twine
F 1 — 8 ft. * 1/4 in. rope
S 1 — 24 in. cotton mason's twine
F 3 — 18 ft. * 1/2 in. ropes
S 3 — 54 in. binder twine
F 3 — 12 ft. * 1/2 in. ropes

S 3 ---- 36 in. binder twine
F 6 ---- 3 ft. * 2 in. stakes
S 6 ---- 12 in. * 1/2 in. stakes
F 3 ---- 8 ft. * 1/4 in. ropes
S 3 ---- 24 in. cotton mason's twine
S 3 ---- flat rocks or sand bags

MAKING A SCALE RULE:

STEP 1: Place a strip of masking tape over the numbers on a yard stick.

STEP 2: Renumber the graduations to show the scale measurements.

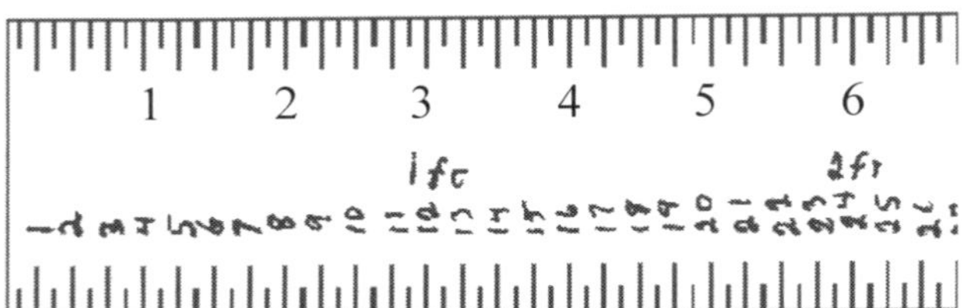

ANCHOR POINTS:

If you are setting your model up outside, you will be able to drive stakes to form anchor points. However if you are setting your model up inside, you will need to use weighted dead man anchor points.

[EXAMPLE]

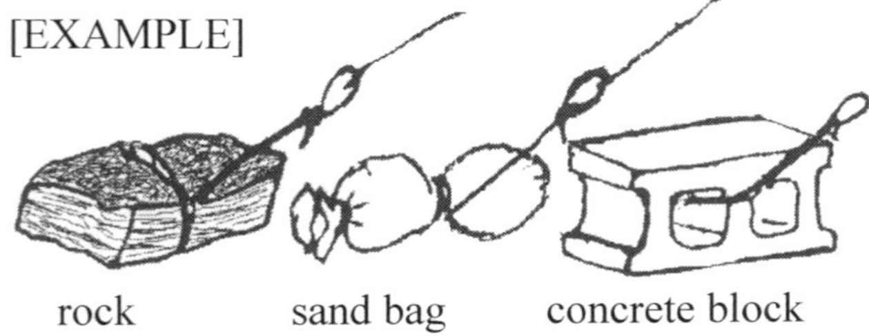

rock　　sand bag　　concrete block

These are only a few examples of weighted deadman anchor points. An anchor point can be made from any heavy object by tying a piece of twine around it.

[NOTE] To protect the floor and to help prevent the anchor points from sliding, place a rubber bath mat or a piece of rubber backed carpet under the anchor point.

CONSTRUCTION:

The construction of a (1:4) scale model differs from a full sized structure only in the size of the poles and ropes used. By using a renumbered rule to make all measurements, you can follow the directions for any structure. As an example follow the directions for the SUSPENDED FLAGPOLE.

[NOTES]

CAMP STOOL:

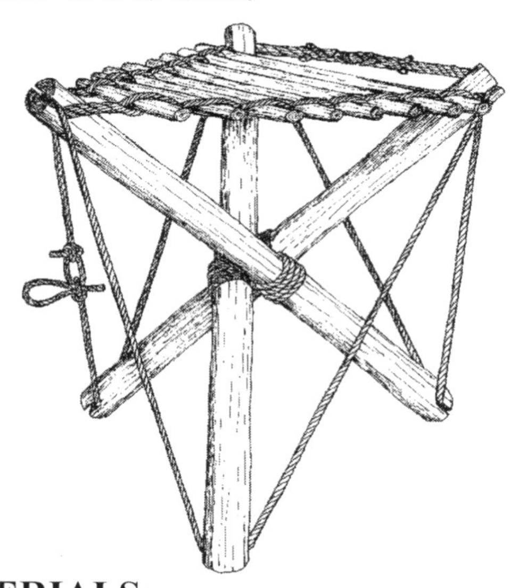

MATERIALS:

3 — 2 foot * 2 inch poles
20 — 1/2 inch diameter sticks (various lengths)
1 — 3/8 inch * 5 foot rope
1 — 1/4 inch * 12foot rope

CONSTRUCTION:

STEP 1: Cut a groove 1 inch deep and 3/8 inch wide in each end of the 2 foot poles. Be sure that the grooves are in the same direction.

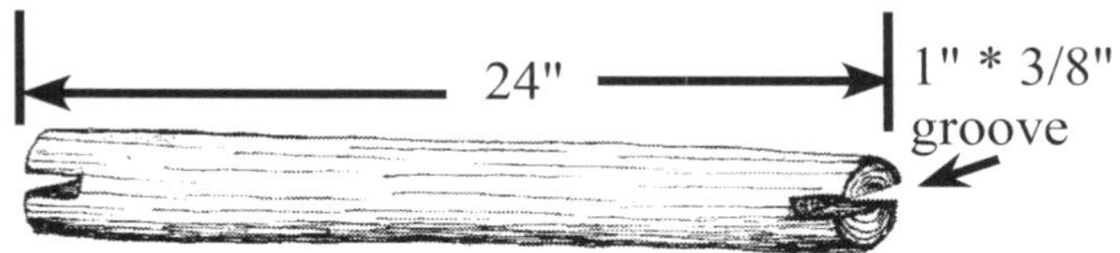

STEP 2: Lash the 2 foot poles together, at their centers, with the 1/4 inch * 12 foot rope. Use the Equal Shear Tripod Lashing shown here.

2A] Tie a Clove Hitch around one of the poles; secure the end by wrapping it around the standing end.

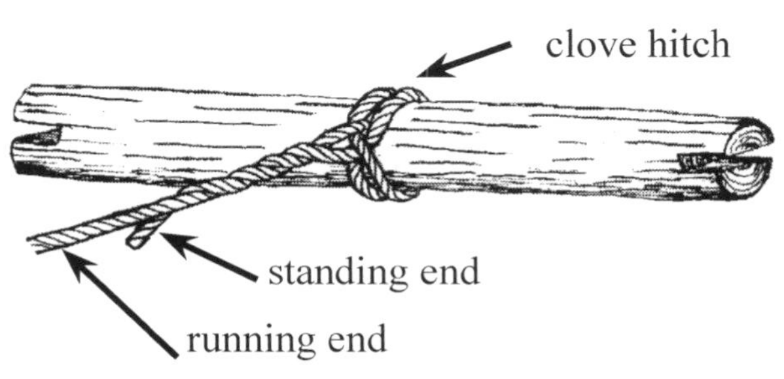

2B] Take 4 wraps around the 3 poles; follow the pattern shown for each wrap.

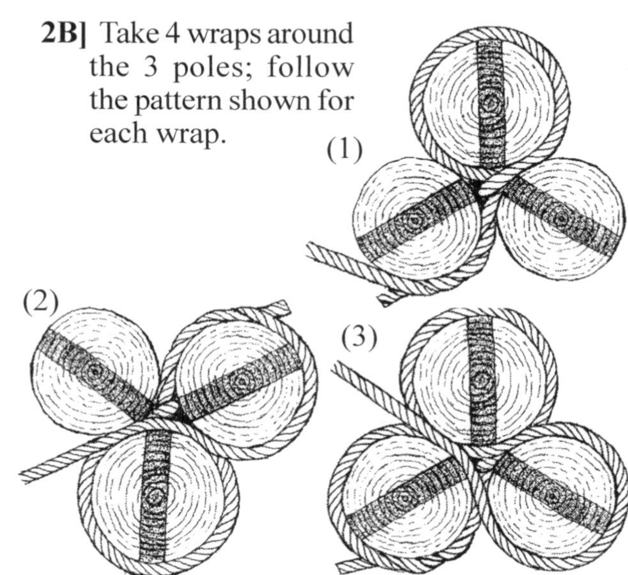

2C] Take 2 frapping turns behind each pole.

2D] End the lashing with a Clove Hitch around one of the poles.

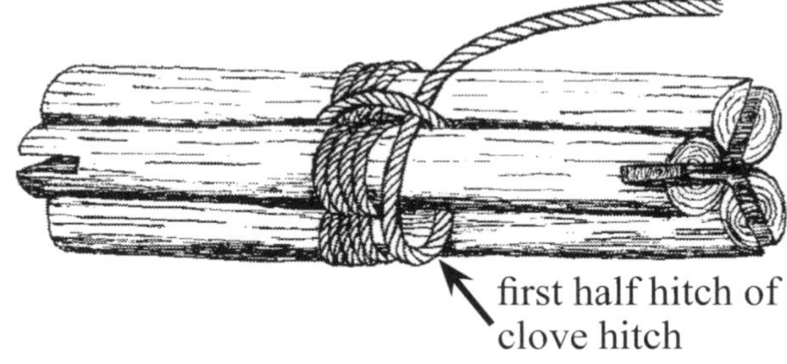

2E] Set the tripod up by rotating each leg.

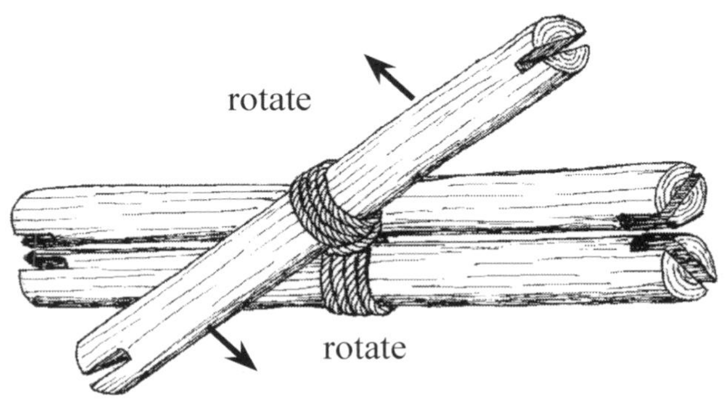

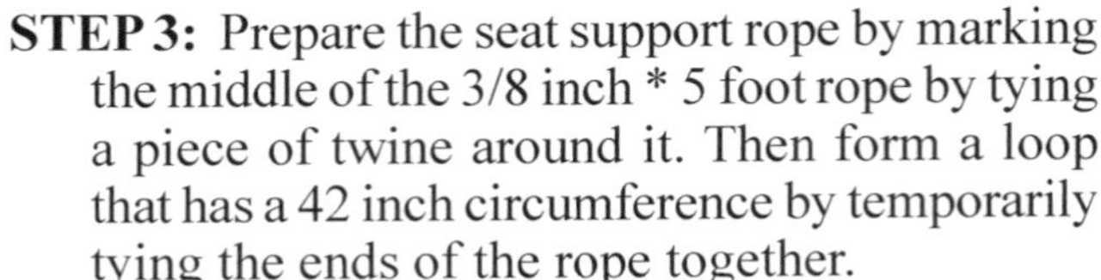

STEP 3: Prepare the seat support rope by marking the middle of the 3/8 inch * 5 foot rope by tying a piece of twine around it. Then form a loop that has a 42 inch circumference by temporarily tying the ends of the rope together.

STEP 4: Place the seat support rope in the grooves at the top of the poles so that the middle of the rope is in one of the grooves. Adjust the ends of the poles so that they are evenly spaced around the loop.

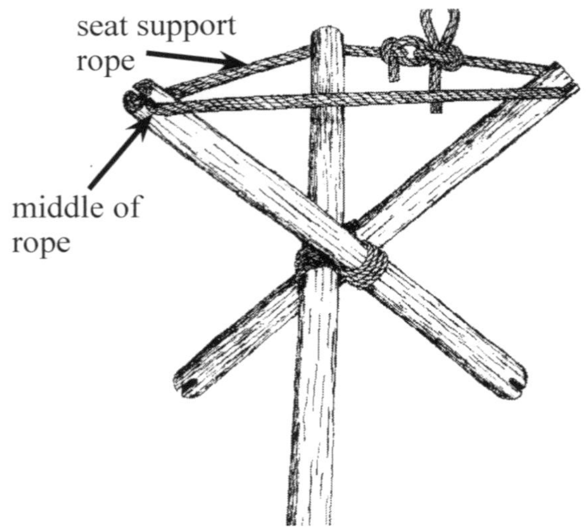

STEP 5: Add the bracing rope. Tie a Bowline into one end of the 1/4 inch * 10 foot rope. Then weave the rope back and forth between the ends of the tripod poles; follow the pattern shown in the diagram. End by tying a Slippery Half Hitch through the eye of the Bowline.

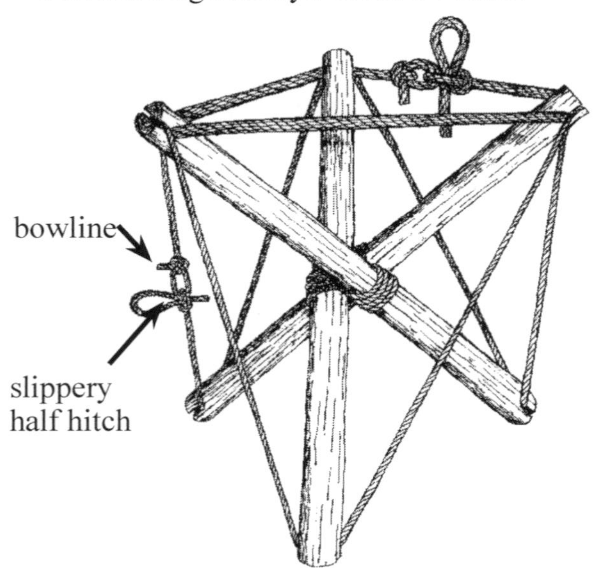

STEP 6: Assemble the seat.

6A] Lift one strand of the lay of the seat support rope on either side of the pole that is at the midpoint of the rope loop.

6B] Slide the ends of a 1/2 inch stick under the lifted strands of the seat support rope.

6C] Lift the next strand of the lay of the rope on either side of the pole that is at the midpoint of the seat support rope.

6D] Insert the next 1/2 inch stick.

[NOTE] To keep the ends of the tripod poles at an equal distance from each other as the seat is being constructed, the temporary knot that joins the two ends of the seat support rope will need to be retied several times.

6E] Continue in this manner until the seat is the desired size.

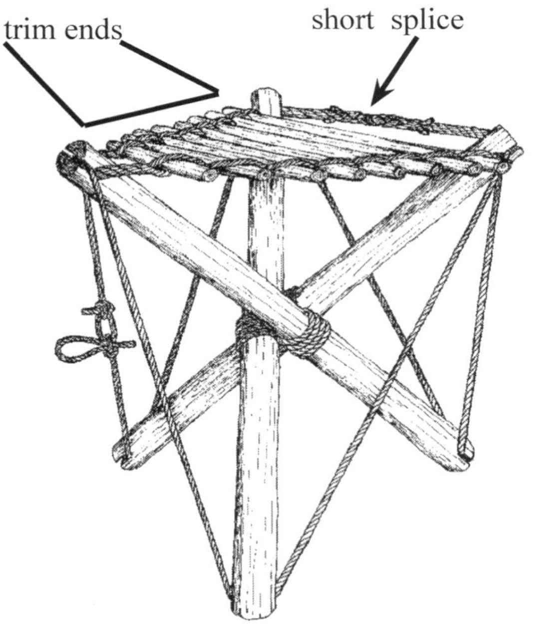

6F] Permanently join the 2 ends of the seat support rope loop with a Short Splice.

6G] Trim the ends of the 1/2 inch sticks so that they extend about 2 1/2 inches beyond the seat support rope.

[NOTE] By removing the 1/4 inch brace rope, this stool can be folded for transport and storage.

[NOTES]

LIFE BASKET:

Description ---- A body harness made by combining a Bowline On a Bight and a French Bowline.

Use ---- To lower a severely injured person when a life threatening situation exists.

Comments ---- The Life Basket is a secure harness that can be used to move an injured person who is weakened or unconscious. However; unless there is a life threatening situation such as a burning building or immediate danger of avalanche, you should wait for a trained rescue team to move the person.

If you attempt to use the Life Basket, do not allow the rope to slide through your hands as you lower the injured person. The friction caused by the sliding rope can cause severe and painful rope burns and loss of control of the rope. The rope must be let out in a hand over hand manner to ensure a safe, controlled descent.

DIRECTIONS:

STEP 1: Tie a Bowline On a Bight near the end of the rope so that one end of the rope extends about 3 feet beyond the knot.

STEP 2: Place one loop of the Bowline On a Bight around each leg.

[NOTE] The Bowline On a Bight should be large enough so that when it is in place the knot should be close to the victim's belt buckle.

STEP 3: Take a Half Hitch around the victim's chest.

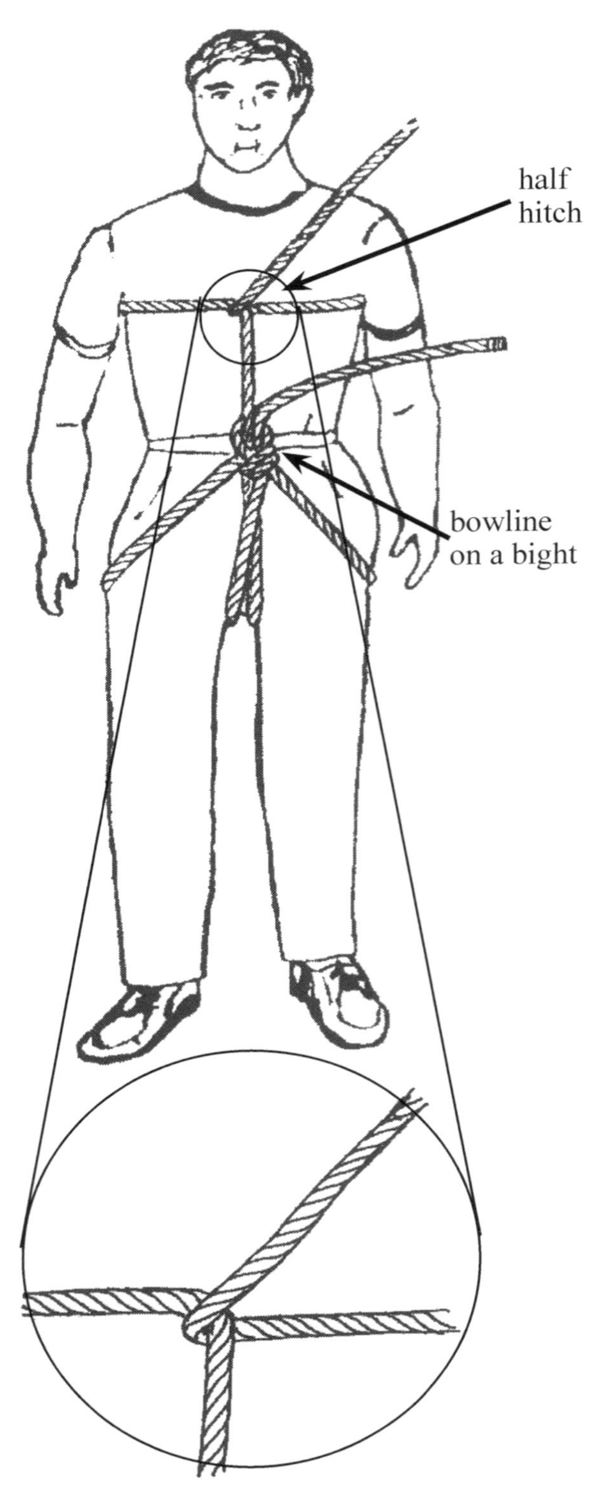

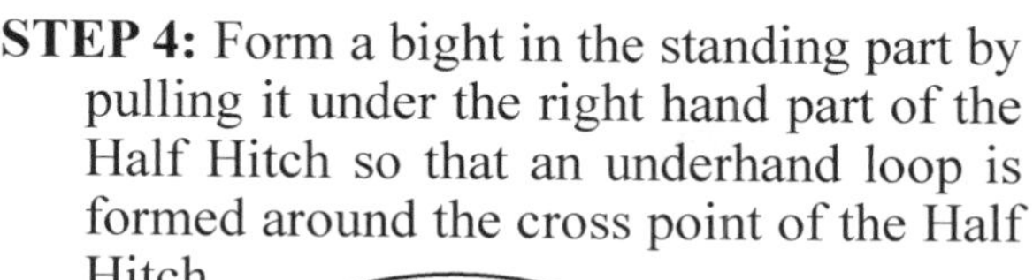

STEP 4: Form a bight in the standing part by pulling it under the right hand part of the Half Hitch so that an underhand loop is formed around the cross point of the Half Hitch.

STEP 5: Fold the bight around and reeve it through the eye of the underhand loop.

STEP 6: Reeve the running part of the rope through the bight.

STEP 7: Take the slack out of the running part of the rope and fold it over to form interlocking bights.

STEP 8: Pull on the standing part so that the bight in the running part of the rope is pulled through the eye of the underhand loop and the underhand loop flips over and tightens around the bight to form a French Bowline.

[NOTES]

GLOSSARY

Becket --- (1) A handle on a chest. (2) The eye or hook of a block strap.

Belay --- (1) To secure a rope with a figure eight turn around a cleat, a belaying pin, or bitts. (2) To hold back; to control.

Bend --- (1) A knot used to join two ropes. (2) To tie two ropes together. (3) To tie a rope to a spar or rope.

Bight --- A fold or curve in a rope.

Bitts --- A pair of posts on the deck of a ship for fastening mooring lines or cables.

Capsize --- (1) To change form under stress. (2) To upset or spill.

Chafe --- To fray or rub.

Chase --- (1) To follow. (2) To place an additional strand next to the original strand.

Clew --- The eye in the corner of some sails and at the ends of a hammock.

Cleat --- An object with horns for belaying a rope.

Deadeye --- A rounded wooden block with holes through it. Used to set up (tighten) standing rigging.

Dead man --- An anchor point that is made by burring a bulky object.

Eye --- The space enclosed by a loop.

Fid --- A tapered pin used to open the strands of a rope when working a splice.

Frapping --- A turn taken around the wrapping turns of a lashing so that the turn lies between the spars. Frappings are used to tighten the wrapping turns of a lashing.

Fray --- To unravel; to come apart.

Fused --- Melted together.

Guy --- A supporting rope used to anchor a pole or structure to the ground.

Hitch --- A knot used to tie a rope to an object.

Lash --- To bind two or more objects together.

Lay --- (1) The direction of the twist in the rope. (2) One complete turn of a strand of rope. (3) The act of twisting the strands of fiber together to make a rope.

Mesh --- (1) One of the openings between the cords that makes up a net. (2) The fabric of a net.

Overhand Loop --- A loop formed by placing the running end over the standing part.

Racking Turns --- Seizing or lashing turns taken in a figure-eight fashion.

Reeve --- To pass the end of a rope through a hole or opening.

Riding Turns --- A second layer of seizing turns taken over and parallel to the first layer of seizing turns.

Round Turn --- One complete turn.

Running End --- The end of the rope that is being used to make a knot.

Seize --- To bind or fasten together with a lashing of yarn, twine, or cord.

Service --- Cord bound around a rope to protect it from wear.

Shear legs --- Two poles lashed together so that they can partially rotate past each other.

Shears --- Shear legs.

Snug --- Compact; neat; tight.

Spar --- Any pole or timber used in the construction of a pioneering structure.

Spill --- To untie accidently.

Splice --- To secure two ropes or two parts of the same rope together by interweaving the strands of the rope.

Standing End / Standing Part --- The part of the rope around which the knot is being made.

Strand --- One part of a three strand rope.

Stop --- To seize or tie off temporarily.

Taut --- Tight.

Tuck --- To place one strand of rope under another strand of rope when making a splice.

Turn --- (1) One wrap around the standing part. (2) One time around.

Unlay --- To open or untwist the strands of a rope.

Underhand Loop --- A loop formed by placing the running end under the standing part.

Upset --- To forcefully change form.

Whip --- To bind the end of a rope to prevent fraying.

Woggal --- Neckerchief slide.

Work --- (1) The process of preforming a task. (2) The material being used. (3) To draw up and smooth out a knot or splice.

Wrapping --- A turn of rope placed around spars to lash them together.

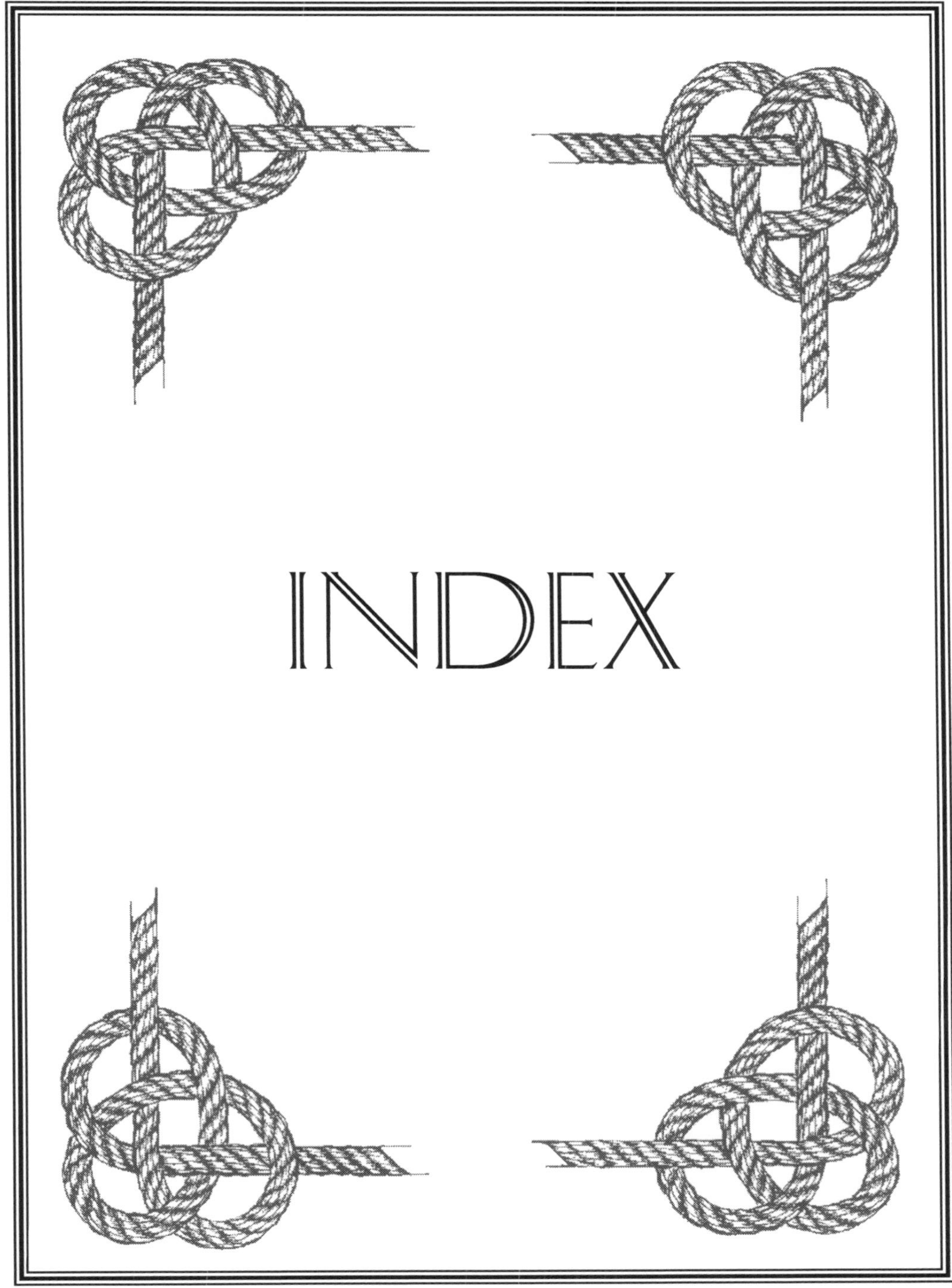

INDEX

Index

Symbols

A

ADDING A LOOP, NETTING 153
ADDING ROUND OF TUCKS 103
ADJUSTABLE JAM HITCH 66
ALPINE BUTTERFLY KNOT 46
ANCHOR BEND 69
ANCHOR HITCH 69
ANCHOR POINT 195
    DEAD MAN 197
    GROMMET 197
    SAFETY 197
    STAKE 195
    STAKE AND LOG 196
    STAKES FOR TENTS AND TARPS 195

B

BACK SPLICE 97
BAG, MESH 157
BECKET HITCH 36
BELAYING TO A CLEAT 87
BLOCK STRAP 108
BOATSWAIN'S WHISTLE KNOT 82
BOATSWAIN'S WHISTLE KNOT DOUBLING 83
BOUND WHIPPING 10
BOWKNOT
    DOUBLE 32
    HALF 32
    SINGLE 32
BOWLINE 39
    ALTERNATE METHOD 40
    FRENCH 44
    ON A BIGHT 42
    PORTUGUESE 44
BOWLINE ON A BIGHT 42
BRIDLE KNOT 85
BUTTERFLY KNOT 46

C

CAMP SAW 186
    CARE AND USE 186
    EVALUATING THE BLADE 187
    JOINING 188
    SAFETY AND USE 187
    SETTING 188
    SHARPENING 187
    TERMINOLOGY 186
CAMP STOOL 207
CANTEEN 85
CLEAT, BELAYING TO A 87
CLEAT FOR KNOTBOARD 88
CLEW, HAMMOCK 161
CLOSED FID 179
CLOVE HITCH 53
    OVER AN END 54
    STOPPED 54
CLUB MAUL 182
COCKSCOMBING 15
CONSTRICTOR KNOT 55
    METHOD # 1 55
    METHOD # 2 56
    SLIPPERY 57
COUNTRYMAN'S KNOT 71
COW HITCH 63
CROSS WHIPPING 106
CROWN KNOT 95

D

DEAD MAN ANCHOR POINT 197
DIAGONAL LASHING 125
DIAGONAL LASHING, FILIPINO 127
DIAMOND KNOT
    SINGLE-STRAND 82
    TWO STRAND 82
DIAMOND MESH NETTING 151
DINING FLY, TARP 198
DOUBLE BOWKNOT 32
DOUBLE LOOP, NETTING 154
DOUBLE SHEET BEND 36
DOUBLE SLIPPED REEF KNOT 32
DOUBLING, BOATSWAIN'S WHISTLE KNOT 83
DOVETAIL HANDLE, MAUL 184
DROPPING A LOOP, NETTING 154

E

ENDING A SPLICE 106
EQUAL SHEAR TRIPOD LASHING 207
EYE SPLICE 99
EYE SPLICE, SLIDING 105

F

FID 179
    CLOSED 179
    METAL 179
    OPEN 180
    WOODEN 179
FIGURE-EIGHT KNOT 25
FIGURE-EIGHT ON A BIGHT 26
FILIPINO DIAGONAL LASHING 127
FILLING THE KNITTING SHUTTLE 150

FISHERMAN'S BEND 69
FLAG LANYARD 200
FLOOR LASHING 145
FRENCH BOWLINE 44
FRENCH WHIPPING 13
FUSING 5

G

GAUGE, KNITTING 150
GEARED ROPE MACHINE 169
GIRTH HITCH 65
GLOSSARY 213
GRAPEVINE SERVICE 13
GROMMET 108
GROMMET GUY LINE ATTACHMENT 197

H

HALF BOWKNOT 32
HALF HITCHES. RUNNING 13
HALF HITCH ROUND LASHING 143
HALF KNOT SQUARE LASHING 121
HAMMER MAUL 183
HAMMOCK 160
HOG BACKING 15

I

INNER TUBE SAW GUARD 192
INTRODUCTION, KNOTBOARD 2
INTRODUCTION, LASHING 112
INTRODUCTION, SPLICING 94

J

JAM HITCH, ADJUSTABLE 66
JAPANESE SQUARE LASHING 116
    MARK II 116
    MARK III 116
JAR KNOT 85
JOINING, CAMP SAW 188
JUG KNOT 85
JURY MAST KNOT 89

K

KILLEG HITCH 71
KNIFE LANYARD KNOTS 82
KNITTED MESH BAG 157
KNITTING A ROW OF MESH 152
KNITTING GAUGE 150
KNITTING SHUTTLE 150
KNOTBOARD
    ADDING ROUND OF TUCKS 103
    ANCHOR HITCH 69
    BACK SPLICE 97
    BELAYING TO A CLEAT 87
    BOATSWAIN'S WHISTLE KNOT 82
    BOATSWAIN'SWHISTLE KNOT, DOUBLED 84
    BOWLINE 39
    BOWLINE ALTERNATE METHOD 41
    BOWLINE ON A BIGHT 42
    CLOVE HITCH 53
    CONSTRICTOR KNOT 55
    CROWN KNOT 95
    DIAGONAL LASHING 125
    DOUBLE SHEET BEND 36
    ENDING A SPLICE 106
    EYE SPLICE 99
    FIGURE-EIGHT 25
    FIGURE-EIGHT ON A BIGHT 26
    FILIPINO DIAGONAL LASHING 127
    FLOOR LASHING 145
    FRENCH BOWLINE 44
    GRAPEVINE SERVICE 14
    JAPANESE SQUARE LASHING 117
    JAPANESE SQUARE LASHING MARK II 118
    JUG KNOT 86
    LARK'S HEAD 63
    LINEMAN'S LOOP 46
    MARLIN SPIKE HITCH 73
    MASTHEAD KNOT (1) 89
    MASTHEAD KNOT (2) 91
    MODIFIED SQUARE LASHING 120
    MONKEY'S PAW, COIL STYLE 81
    MONKEY'S PAW,TURK'S HEAD 79
    MOORING HITCH 75
    PARTS OF A ROPE 3
    RINGBOLT HITCHING 15
    ROUND LASHING 140
    ROUND LASHING, HALF HITCH 144
    ROUND LASHING, WEST COUNTRY 142
    SEIZING 18
    SEIZING WITH RACKING TURNS 19
    SERVICE 12
    SHEAR LASHING WITH PLAIN TURNS 131
    SHEAR LASHING WITH RACKING TURNS 129
    SHEAR LASH QUICK 132
    SHEEPSHANK 48
    SHEEPSHANK, QUICK 51
    SHEET BEND 33
    SHEET BEND (SHORT END) 38
    SHORT SPLICE 101
    SQUARE KNOT 30
    SQUARE LASHING 115
    STEVEDORE KNOT 23
    STOPPER KNOT 21
    TAUT-LINE HITCH 67
    TIMBER HITCH 71
    TRANSOM KNOT 59

TRIPOD LASHING, WITH PLAIN TURN 137
TRIPOD LASHING, WITH RACKING TURN 136
TRUMPET KNOT 50
TURK'S HEAD 77
TWO HALF HITCHES 61
WATER KNOT 27
WATER KNOT METHOD 2 29
WEAVER'S KNOT 35
WHIPPING 7
WHIPPING METHOD 2 8
WHIPPING METHOD 3 9

KNOT SAFETY 2
KNOTS AND HITCHES 1

L

LADDER, MARLIN SPIKE 74
LADDER LASHING 147
LANYARD, FLAG 200
LANYARD KNOT
KNIFE 82
MARLIN SPIKE 82
PIPE 82
SAILOR'S KNIFE 82
LARK'S HEAD 63
OVER AN END 64
THROUGH A RING 64
LASHING
DIAGONAL 125
EQUAL SHEAR TRIPOD 207
FILIPINO DIAGONAL 127
FLOOR 145
HALF HITCH ROUND 143
HALF KNOT SQUARE 121
INTRODUCTION 112
JAPANESE SQUARE 116
LADDER 147
MARK III JAPANESE SQUARE 116
MARK II JAPANESE SQUARE 116
MODIFIED SQUARE 119
QUICK SHEAR 132
QUICK TRIPOD 139
ROUND 140
ROUND TRADITIONAL 140
SHEAR WITH PLAIN TURNS 130
SHEAR WITH RACKING TURNS 129
SQUARE 113
TRANSOM KNOT 59
TRIPOD 134
TRIPOD WITH PLAIN TURNS 137
TRIPOD WITH RACKING TURNS 135
WEST COUNTRY ROUND 142
LASHING, SHEAR 129
LASHINGS 111
LIFE BASKET 210
LINEMAN'S LOOP 46
LONG SPLICE 110
LOOP, LINEMAN'S 46
LUMBERMAN'S KNOT 71

M

MAGNUS HITCH 66
MARK III JAPANESE SQUARE LASHING 116
MARK II JAPANESE SQUARE LASHING 116
MARLIN SPIKE HITCH 73
MARLIN SPIKE LADDER 74
MARLIN SPIKE LANYARD KNOT 82
MASTHEAD KNOT 89
MAUL
CLUB 182
DOVETAIL HANDLE 184
HAMMER 183
ROPE WRENCH 185
MAULS 182
MESH BAG 157
METAL FIDS 179
MIDSHIPMAN'S HITCH 68
MODELS 203
ANCHOR POINTS 206
SCALE RULE 206
SCALES 203
SUSPENDED FLAG POLE 203
MODIFIED SQUARE LASHING 119
MONKEY'S PAW 79
COIL STYLE 80
TURK'S HEAD 79
MOONSHINER'S KNOT 85
MOORING HITCH 75

N

NECKERCHIEF SLIDE 77
NET MESH BAG 157
NETTING 150
ADDING A LOOP 153
DIAMOND MESH 151
DOUBLE LOOP 154
DROPPING A LOOP 154
SQUARE MESH 154
STARTING A NEW ROW 153
TOOLS 150

O

OPEN FID 180
OVERHAND KNOT 4
OVERHAND KNOT, TWO FOLD 21

P

PARTS OF A ROPE 3
PATTERN FOR CLEAT FOR KNOTBOARD 88
PIPE HITCH 62
PIPE LANYARD KNOT 82
PITCHER KNOT 89
PLASTIC PIE SAW GUARD 191
PLATTED RING 15
PORTUGESE BOWLINE 44

Q

QUICK, SHEEPSHANK 51
QUICK SHEAR LASHING 132
QUICK TRIPOD LASHING 139

R

REEF KNOT 30
REEF KNOT, SLIPPED 32
RINGBOLT HITCHING 15
RING HITCH 63
RING KNOT 27
ROLLING HITCH 66
ROPE MACHINE
  GEARED 169
  LAYING END 164
  SETTING UP 166
  SIMPLE 164
  TWISTING END 164
ROPE MAKING 163
  LAYING THE STRAND 166
  ROPE WRENCH 167
  SETTING UP 166
  TWISTING THE STRANDS 166
ROPE WRENCH 178
  MAUL 185
ROPE WRENCH, LAYING ROPE 167
ROUND LASHING 140
  HALF HITCH 143
  TRADITIONAL 140
  WEST COUNTRY 142
ROUND OF TUCKS, ADDING 103
RUNNING HALF HITCHES 13

S

SAILOR'S KNIFE LANYARD KNOT 82
SAW
  JOINING 188
  SHARPENING LARGER 190
  SHARPENING THE CUTTING TEETH 189
  SHARPENING THE RAKERS 189
SAW GUARD 191
  INNER TUBE 192
  PLASTIC PIPE 191
SAW SET 190
SAW VICE
  MAKING A 191
SCALE RULE 206
SCALES, MODELS 203
SEIZING 6,17
SEIZING WITH RACKING TURNS 19
SERVICE 12
SERVICE, GRAPEVINE 13
SERVING 6
SETTING A CAMP SAW 188
SHARPENING
  CAMP SAW 187
  LARGER SAWS 190
  SAW RAKERS 189
SHARPENING THE RAKERS 189
SHEAR LASHING 129
  QUICK 132
  WITH PLAIN TURNS 130
  WITH RACKING TURNS 129
SHEEPSHANK 48
SHEEPSHANK, QUICK 51
SHEET BEND 33
  DOUBLE 36
  ON A SHORT END 37
SHOESTRING KNOT 32
SHORT SPLICE 101
SHUTTLE, KNITTING 150
SIMPLE ROPE MACHINE 164
SINGLE-STRAND DIAMOND KNOT 82
SINGLE BOWKNOT 32
SLIDE, NECKERCHIEF 77
SLIDING EYE SPLICE 105
SLING 108
SLIP KNOT 74
SLIP NOOSE 74
SLIPPED REEF KNOT 32
SLIPPED SQUARE KNOT 32
SLIPPERY CONSTRICTOR KNOT 57
SPANISH WINDLESS 193
SPLICE
  BACK 97
  EYE 99
  SHORT 101
  SLIDING EYE 105
SPLICE, ENDING A 106
SPLICING 93
  ADDING ROUND OF TUCKS 103
SQUARE KNOT 30
  SLIPPED 32
  STOPPED 32
  UPSETTING A 31

SQUARE LASHING 113
- HALF KNOT 121
- JAPANESE 116
- MARK III JAPANESE 116
- MARK II JAPANESE 116
- MODIFIED 119

SQUARE MESH NETTING 154
STAKE ANCHOR POINTS 195
STAKE AND LOG, ANCHOR POINT 196
STAKES FOR SUPPORTING HEAVY LOADS 195
STAKES FOR TENTS AND TARPS 195
STARTING A NEW ROW, NETTING 153
STEVEDORE KNOT 23
STOPPED CLOVE HITCH 54
STOPPER KNOT 21
STRAP LOOP 108
SUSPENDED FLAG POLE 203

T

TARP, DINING FLY 198
TAUT-LINE HITCH: 66
TENT PEG 195
THREEFOLD OVERHAND KNOT 21
TIMBER HITCH 71
TOOLS 177
- NETTING 150

TRANSOM KNOT 59
TRIPOD LASHING 134
- EQUAL SHEAR 207
- QUICK 139
- WITH PLAIN TURNS 137
- WITH RACKING TURNS 135

TRUMPET KNOT 49
TUCKS, ADDING ROUND OF 103
TURK'S HEAD 77
TURK'S HEAD, MONKEY'S PAW 79
TWO FOLD OVERHAND KNOT 21
TWO HALF HITCHES 61
TWO HALF HITCHES, WITH ROUND TURN 62
TWO STRAND DIAMOND KNOT 82

U

V

W

WATER BOTTLE 85
WATER KNOT 27
WATER KNOT METHOD 2 28
WEAVER'S KNOT 33,34
WEST COUNTRY ROUND LASHING 142
WEST COUNTRY SHEAR LASHING 142
WEST COUNTRY WHIPPING 142
WHIPPING 6
- BOUND 10
- METHOD 1 6
- METHOD 2 8
- METHOD 3 10

WHIPPING, CROSS 106
WHIPPING, FRENCH 13
WINDLASS, SPANISH 193
WOGGAL 77
WOODEN FID 179

X

Y

Z